TO SEEK AMERICA

We all go forth to seek America.
And in the seeking we create her.
And in the quality of our search
shall be the nature of the America
we create.   Waldo Frank

TO SEEK

MAXINE SELLER

AMERICA

A History of Ethnic Life in the United States

Jerome S. Ozer, Publisher

Library of Congress Cataloging in Publication Data
Seller, Maxine S   1935-
To seek America.

Bibliography: p.
Includes index.
1. United States—Emigration and immigration—History.
2. Minorities—United States—History. I. Title.
JV6450.S44   301.32'4'0973   77-8248
ISBN 0-89198-117-9
ISBN 0-89198-118-7 pbk.

Manufactured in the United States of America

In memory of Annie Schwartz and Lena Wolk

Table of Contents

Preface

After four years of research and writing in the preparation of this book, I want to thank the many friends and colleagues who have contributed to its completion. I am particularly grateful to Professor Bill McNeill of Bucks County Community College, who gave me valuable insights into the sociology of minority groups, to Professor Murray Friedman of LaSalle College and the American Jewish Committee, who read the first chapter four years ago and encouraged me to continue, to Professor Warren Button of the State University of New York at Buffalo, who gave substantial advice on the colonial period and on the history of education, and to Professor John J. Appel of Michigan State University, who read the entire first draft of the manuscript and offered many useful suggestions. I am also grateful to the staff members of the libraries at the University of Pennsylvania and the State University of New York at Buffalo, who facilitated my research, and to my students at Bucks County Community College and the State University of New York at Buffalo, whose questions about ethnicity have helped shape this book. I also want to thank my publisher, Dr. Jerome S. Ozer, for suggesting that I undertake this project and for offering excellent advice on subject matter and style as well as on the technicalities of publication.

Finally, I want to acknowledge the contributions of my immediate family. My husband Bob and my sons, Michael, Douglas, and Stuart, served as an enthusiastic and discerning panel of critics for the testing of my ideas. Michael and Douglas reviewed portions of the manuscript from the student's point of view and helped with the unexciting chores of manuscript preparation. My youngest son, Stuart, showed maturity and a sense of humor in sharing his mother with a typewriter and, along with his father and brothers, helped me maintain my balance after long hours in the unreal world of the library stacks. I want to thank my sons and tell them that this book was written for them as well as my students. Most of all I want to thank Bob, whose understanding, encouragement, and support have been invaluable to me in this project as in everything else I have undertaken in the twenty-one years I have had the good fortune to be married to him.

To Seek America

CHAPTER 1

Ethnicity:

What Is It? Why Is It Important?

"Who am I?" The question is universal. We frame our own answers out of the uniqueness of our individual personalities and life experiences. But for most of us identity is more than this private sense of self. Identity has a communal, or group, dimension. Who am I? I am John or Jane Smith; but I am also a man or a woman, a member of a family, a church, a school, a business firm, a lodge, a political party, a neighborhood, a nation.

Most human beings crave the warmth and security of belonging to a group. We usually join a group because we want the comfort of feeling "at home" among others whose life styles, values, and interests are similar to our own. Some people have a strong need to define themselves as the insiders, "we," as opposed to the outsiders, "they," whose life styles, values, and interests are different. There are individuals who feel no need for identification with any group. They often discover, however, that society has made this identification for them. With or without their consent, they are classified as soldiers, taxpayers, Jews, underprivileged, or whatever other category, benevolent or malevolent, their society or its government finds useful.

Historically this human need for belonging and for classifying oneself and others has been met in many different ways. Primitive peoples usually identified themselves by membership in tribes or clans. In traditional China the extended family was the most important grouping, and in India one's fate was almost completely determined by the caste into which he or she was born. The ancient Greeks saw themselves primarily as members of the *polis*, or native city, with its own special gods and its own political and social institutions. In medieval Europe identity was based on a mixture of social and economic class; one's life style and sense of self depended upon whether one was a noble, a serf, a craftsman, or a member of a religious order.

In most cases governments recognized and reinforced these classifications by dealing with persons in terms of the groups to which they belonged. Even the relatively democratic city state of Athens denied political participation to people who were born in a different *polis*. In feudal Europe there were separate legal systems, even separate courts, for nobles, clergy, and commoners—a system which lasted in Western Europe until the French Revolution of 1789 and lingered on in Eastern Europe decades later.

In the United States we pride ourselves upon a tradition of dealing with persons as individuals, regardless of their group affiliations. Immigrants often came here to escape the rigid demands of class, sect, even family in the "old country," and to a large extent they were successful in doing so. The American Constitution recognized no collective orders or "estates," no classes, and after the abolition of slavery, no castes. The distinction or grouping which has survived the longest has been that of sex, and even this categorization seems to be fading. With few exceptions the law in the United States deals with each person as a discrete individual, standing alone.

Yet most Americans, like most other people, have felt the need to define themselves in terms of groups. As the French observer Alexis de Tocqueville pointed out over a century ago—and as any observer of contemporary American life can confirm—Americans are joiners. We join civic associations, fraternal orders, benevolent societies, political parties, bowling leagues, and labor unions. We come together in a host of changing organizations to pursue our passions for everything from bird watching to weight watching. While each of these voluntary associations has its own purpose and program, all share a common function; all bring like people together, creating, at least for the moment, a community of interest and a sense of belonging.

Yet when an individual asks himself, "who am I?" he or she is not likely to answer "an Elk," "a Rotarian," or "a member of the Garden Club." For most of us such voluntary associations are too limited in scope, too impersonal, and too transient to satisfy the human need for group identity. To satisfy so deep a need a grouping must be lasting, it must impinge upon many areas of a person's life (from infancy through adulthood), and it must provide a broad pool of people from whom one can choose a variety of associates. The ethnic community is such a grouping. Perhaps this is why throughout our history millions of Americans have responded to the question "who am I?" with an ethnic answer. I am a Polish-American. I am an Italian-American. I am a

Chinese-American. I am a Chicano. I am Puerto Rican. I am a Jew. I am black.

Ethnic identity may extend an entire life span and be passed down to the fourth generation or beyond. Americans who identify strongly as members of an ethnic community may live their entire lives in ethnic neighborhoods, attend ethnic schools, socialize in ethnic lodges, worship in ethnic churches, read ethnic newspapers, enjoy ethnic music and drama, earn their living in ethnic businesses, be ill in ethnic hospitals, and be buried in ethnic cemeteries. They may choose their friends, their doctors, their lawyers, their employees, their employers, and of course, their spouses from within the ethnic group. For most people such a totally enclosed ethnic life would no longer seem desirable, or even possible. Yet, as this book will show, many richly satisfying lives have been spent within the geographic and cultural confines of ethnic communities of the past. Equally important, ethnicity, recognized or unrecognized, remains a major factor in the lives of millions of Americans today.

What Is An Ethnic Community?

Ethnic communities in the United States are groups of people tied together by common national origin, common language, common religion, and perhaps common physical characteristics (such as skin coloring)—although not every community finds these factors equally important, or even necessary at all. Some ethnic communities are obviously based upon common national origin. Thus, Swedish-Americans are Americans whose families came originally from Sweden. Often, however, language has been more important than political geography in defining an American ethnic group. Sharing a common language led German-speaking immigrants from Bavaria, Hanover, and Westphalia to think of themselves collectively as German-Americans long before the separate political states from which they came were unified into modern Germany.

A common religion has been as important as a common national origin or language in defining ethnic loyalties in the United States. For the American Irish, for example, allegiance to the Roman Catholic Church has been as binding a cement as common origin on the Emerald Isle. Jewish families from Holland, England, Spain, South America, Germany, and many East European countries have been united by religion into what is in effect a single ethnic community. Religion can divide, however, as well as unite. The nineteenth century Irish-American and German-American communities subdivided into Protestant and Catholic segments, clearly defined and, in the case of the Irish, hostile to one another.

The idea of race as a distinctive set of biological characteristics has no scientific meaning. Still, as Chinese-Americans and Japanese-Americans, American Indians, Mexican-Americans, and blacks are acutely aware, many "white" Americans define these ethnic groups in terms of widely varying and overlapping physical characteristics such as the color of the skin, the texture of the hair, and the shape of the eyes. Because of their recognizable physical characteristics third generation American citizens whose ancestors had immigrated from Japan found themselves impounded as dangerous aliens after the bombing of Pearl Harbor.

While "race" used by hostile outsiders is a dangerous concept, a sense of biological kinship (vague and subjective as it may be) has been a unifying element within certain ethnic groups. Thus, Mexican-Americans proudly assert membership in *la raza* (the race), and blacks proudly claim that "black is beautiful." Yet many Mexican-Americans see *la raza* as a cultural, not a biological association. Similarly, many blacks find their identity more a matter of "soul" than of body.

The definition of ethnicity in the United States, then, is complex and varied. Still, significant generalizations can be made. First of all, the members of an ethnic group share the consciousness of a common historical past. For black Americans their shared historical experiences are mainly those of the New World, because slaveholders forcibly obliterated much (though not all) of the African heritage. For groups like Italian-Americans or Polish-Americans, who came to America more recently and who still maintain ties with relatives who stayed behind, there are vivid memories of shared experiences both in the old country and the new. In the case of American Jews, shared memories of the group's common historical past go back thousands of years and encompass every continent on the earth. However far back it extends and however accurately—or inaccurately—it is remembered, this sense of a common past helps to determine the life styles and values of the ethnic group in America today.

Second, the members of a given ethnic group do in fact share common life styles and common values. There are distinctive ethnic patterns in such important matters as child-rearing, marital relationships, career choices, political affiliations, and of course what goes on the table for dinner. Even in the fourth generation, the Irish "overchoose" careers in law and politics, the Germans in engineering, and the Jews in medicine. Italian-Americans remain close to their brothers and sisters in adult life, while Jewish-Americans are more likely to be close to their parents. Irish-Americans accept pain stoically; Italian-Americans are more likely to complain. Of course not every member of an ethnic group will conform to all—or any—of these ethnic patterns, but the patterns do exist. This is why many people feel more comfortable with a clergyman, a physician, a political leader, and a wife or husband from within their own ethnic group.

Third, an ethnic community has aspirations for a common future, and these aspirations are focused upon the education of the young. A significant number of those who share memories of a common past and who participate in the common ethnic life style of the present are determined to pass on those memories and that life style (and the values they embody) to the succeeding generations. From the colonial era to the present, ethnic leaders have been convinced that education is crucial to the survival of the group and to the perpetuation of the values it holds dear. It is not surprising, then, that ethnic communities invest great emotional and financial resources in the education of their children. Some ethnic groups have built their own schools either to supplement or to replace totally the educational system of the Anglo-Saxon majority. Others have sought, through "community control" or political pressure, to make the public schools more supportive of their distinctive heritages. Whatever institutions they use, all ethnic educators have wrestled with the same problem—how to instill in the young a lasting loyalty to a minority culture while the majority culture with its powerful appeal impinges on every side.

If ethnic communities have been eager to use schools to perpetuate their distinctive heritages, the Anglo-Saxon majority has been equally eager to use the schools to enforce "Americanization." From Benjamin Franklin's time to the present, educators and political leaders (and more recently, sociologists and psychologists) have seen schools as places where minority group children would be taught the language, habits, and ideas considered appropriate by the majority. Generations of social reformers have counted upon the schools to save ethnic children—and with them American society—from poverty, crime, radicalism, sexual promiscuity, and other evil traits attributed to the unpopular minority communities of their day. That such utopian dreams went unrealized is not surprising. Nor is it surprising, given the conflicting hopes, fears, and expectations of majority and minority communities, that American schools have historically been on the front line of the many battles fought among ethnic communities and between ethnic minorities and the Anglo-Saxon Protestant majority.

Finally, ethnic communities in the United States have been and still are social, economic, and political interest groups. Because members of ethnic communities share a common history and often a common religious outlook, they may take a common position on an issue such as prayer in the public schools. Because they often cluster in the same socioeconomic level, sharing the same kinds of jobs and neighborhoods, they may take a common position on property taxes, labor unions, affirmative action quotas, or busing. Emotional and family ties to ethnic communities overseas may result in a common stand on a foreign policy issue. Even the almost assimilated may find themselves stirred to action when a sudden controversy—an outbreak of war in the Middle East, or a new abortion law—lays bare an ethnic nerve. As the older generations pass away, common interests may increasingly replace common memories as the cement that binds together American ethnic communities.

Origins of Ethnic Communities

One of the most heterogeneous nations on earth, the United States contains ethnic communities varying widely in numbers and historical background. Some were already well established when they were incorporated into the United States by conquest or by purchase. A vigorous Dutch community became part of the original thirteen colonies when the British seized New Amsterdam from Holland in 1664. The French and Creole communities of New Orleans became American ethnic groups with the Louisiana Purchase of 1803. A large Spanish-speaking minority entered our population when we annexed the Southwest, the fruits of military victory in the Mexican War.

Most ethnic communities, however, were the result of people leaving their original homelands to come to our shores. All Americans are immigrants or the descendants of immigrants. Even the American Indians, our oldest ethnic group, came originally from Asia in wave after wave of prehistoric immigration. No other country has attracted so many settlers of such diverse backgrounds.

The coming of large numbers of Europeans began in the seventeenth century as part of a world-wide migration of peoples. For reasons still not completely understood, the number of people on the earth increased fourfold between 1650 and 1950. In Europe the increase in population generally preceded the ability of agriculture and industry to feed and employ it. These "excess" Europeans abandoned their overcrowded homelands for the emptier areas of Africa, Australia, and North and South America. Of the more than seventy million people who left Europe after 1600, two thirds came to the United States. Here they were joined voluntarily by thousands of Asians and involuntarily by millions of Africans.

The immigration rate has varied with what historians have called the "push" of unfavorable conditions abroad and the "pull" of favorable conditions in the United States. Calamities such as the Irish potato famine of the 1840's and Russian pogroms (massacres) of Jews at the end of the nineteenth century sent immigrants flocking to the United States with little regard for the American business cycle. But usually the attraction of favorable economic prospects here exerted a greater influence upon immigration than problems overseas. Immigration has always increased in times of prosperity and decreased in times of recession.

Sometimes an individual man or woman came alone, worked, and sent for the rest of the family as soon as savings permitted. The younger and stronger members of a family, those at the peak of their earning power, immigrated first; and their labor in America supported aged parents overseas and financed the immigration of brothers, sisters, wives and children. Often husband, wife, and children came together, taking their chances, for better or worse, as a family unit. In still other cases an entire village or parish came, transplanting a whole community all at once. This kind of group immigration was often found among members of communitarian religious sects such as the Pennsylvania Germans.

Whether they came as individuals, families, or larger groups, immigrants quickly sought out others who spoke their language. Often a friend or a relative from their native village helped them to find jobs and places to live. People of similar national and linguistic backgrounds clustered together to relieve their loneliness and to help one another. Gradually these clusters of people formed institutions—churches, schools, banks, newspapers—to fulfill their needs and express their way of life.

The ethnic community—or ghetto—was the result not only of the internal needs of the ethnic group itself, but also of the external pressure of the outsider. Other Americans were often hostile to the newcomers. All ethnic minorities faced, to one degree or another, discrimination in housing, jobs, and social relationships. The prejudices of the outside world reinforced ethnic loyalty and helped perpetuate the ethnic community.

Just as all Americans were, at one time or another, immigrants, so all Americans were, at one time or another, members of ethnic communities. The white, Protestant, English-speaking immigrants, like the Polish, the Irish, and the Japanese, preferred to settle among people of similar background, married mainly within their own group, and set up institutions to perpetuate their particular life style. The neat, white Congregational churches built by New England Puritans were in reality as "ethnic" as the tiny synagogues built centuries later by East European Jews in New York City. Irish Catholic immigrants knew before the Civil War what blacks, Puerto Ricans, and Mexican-Americans have discovered in recent years—that the little red school house of the white Protestant majority is as committed to a particular pattern of behavior and system of values as is the more obviously ethnic parochial school in the Greek, Italian, or Jewish neighborhood.

The ethnicity of English-speaking immigrants has generally been unrecognized. Originally English, Scottish, Scotch-Irish, and Welsh immigrants were distinct from each other. But political, denominational, and other differences among these groups were quickly overshadowed by the fact that they all spoke English, the language that was politically and commercially dominant in the British colonies. Gradually historians came to view the English-speaking ethnic communities as one group and to identify that group with the nation. Thus English-speaking Americans became "real" Americans while others were defined as outsiders, or "ethnics."

Nineteenth century American historians—many of whom were of New England background—saw American history as a white, Protestant, Anglo-Saxon pageant, and enshrined this interpretation of the American past in their writings. Even today there is a strong tendency to view the group that produced George Washington, Thomas Jefferson, and Daniel Webster as the "real" Americans and to relegate the story of other kinds of Americans to the footnotes, the supplementary reading list, or at best, a special chapter on the "contributions" of minority groups.

Ethnicity–A "Neglected Dimension"

Why has ethnicity been, in the words of the historian Rudolph Vecoli, a "neglected dimension" in American history? The ethnocentricity of the traditional Anglo-Saxon historian is a part, but only one part, of the answer. Also at fault was the new generation of early twentieth century historians, many of whom were from non-English ethnic backgrounds. These historians felt until quite recently that it was not academically respectable to investigate the history of their own ethnic communities. They did not want to jeopardize their academic careers with charges of parochialism.

If the ethnocentricity and timidity of historians has hindered our appreciation of the ethnic factor in our history, the popular idea of the American "Melting Pot" has hindered it even more. Nineteenth century Americans believed that the free American environment, with its republican institutions, changed whoever came here into a totally new person. Even the early generation of historians who wrote about immigration, men like Carl Wittke, Theodore Blegen, and Marcus Lee Hansen, were convinced, as Hansen put it, that "it is the ultimate fate of every national group to be amalgamated into the composite American race." Until very recently scholars and most other Americans as well shared the assumption that the ethnic characteristics so apparent in new immigrants disappeared in a generation or two. The ethnic community was of interest only as a temporary way station for the individual along the rapid and inevitable road to "Americanization."

Since the 1960's such a view has become untenable. As the decade opened, Nathan Glazer and Daniel Moynihan suggested that "the point about the melting pot is that it did not happen." Ethnic identity not only survived, it seemed to be growing stronger. Black Americans were the pacesetters. The civil rights campaigns of the 1950's and 1960's were supplemented by a new emphasis upon black ethnicity. Black cultural centers were established and Black Studies programs emerged at major universities. Other ethnic groups followed the pattern set out by blacks. Mexican-Americans and Puerto Ricans demanded—and began to get—bilingual programs in the public schools. Despite some ambivalence toward blacks, white European ethnics followed their example and began to organize to call attention to their many social and economic problems. Responding to the demands of the ethnic constituencies, Congress passed the Ethnic Studies Heritage Act of 1971 to improve the opportunity of students in elementary and secondary schools to study cultural heritages of all the various ethnic groups.

Increasing self-consciousness and activism on the part of ethnic minorities forced scholars to rethink their earlier positions on the American melting pot. Massive European immigration was cut off by 1924, Oriental immigration decades earlier, and the importation of blacks as slaves much earlier still. Yet recognizable Irish, Italian, Chinese, black, and other ethnic communities remain throughout our country. In the 1970's the melting pot was being replaced by the idea of cultural pluralism as the key to an understanding of American society.

Why Ethnic History?

The ethnic activism of recent years has stimulated a new interest in ethnic history, but there are many other, equally valid reasons for taking a long overdue look at the ethnic experience in the United States. In the first place, America cannot be understood without it. At the time of the American Revolution over half our population was non-English in origin, and in 1920 one out of every five Americans was an immigrant or the child of an immigrant. Clearly any version of American history that excludes so many millions of people is not really American history at all. The continuing influx of Europeans, Africans, and Asians had an enormous impact upon the development of American institutions and culture. But even those groups that remained most aloof from the mainstream of American life, groups like the German religious sects, are worthy of study because their experience, too, is part of the total American experience.

Ethnic history has much valuable light to shed upon the gap—often tragically wide—between ideals and realities in American life. Traditionally we have pointed with pride to statements of our democratic principles, such as the Declaration of Independence, the Bill of Rights, and the Fourteenth Amendment. Ethnic history forces us to face our failures to live up to these ideals—black slavery, the ubiquitous "No Irish Need Apply" signs of the nineteenth century, police brutality against Slavs, Italians, and Jews in early twentieth century cities, and the imprisonment of Japanese-Americans during World War II. The struggle to earn a living and hold a family together in a hostile and depressing environment has loomed larger in the lives of millions of Americans than more traditional "textbook" issues such as the raising or lowering of the tariff and the constitutionality of the National Bank. A study of prejudice and discrimination against ethnic minorities is more than an exercise in moral indignation, however. It is an attempt to understand the social and personal pressures that increase friction between majority and minority groups and, hopefully, to identify the conditions that make better relationships possible.

The widely publicized "urban crisis" of the 1960's focused attention upon American cities and the problems of the people who live in them. How do we maintain the vitality of aging neighborhoods and cope with the turmoil of shifting populations? How do we curb the destructive activities of gangs? Because most American cities are patchwork quilts of ethnic populations, ethnic history may prove helpful in our search for the answers.

Ethnic history is of special interest to the contemporary educator trying to develop a public school system that will be acceptable and useful to all segments of our heterogeneous population. The immigrant's child was the "disadvantaged" child of the past. How did the schools respond to the challenge of such a child? Did the American educational system offer immigrant children an open door of opportunity, a path to upward social mobility? Or, as revisionist historians of education have suggested, did the schools program these children for manual labor, so that they would not compete with the children of the "advantaged" for the choicest positions in our society?

Ethnic ghettos are not new to our cities; nor are confrontations between ethnic groups. Local police shot striking Slavic mine workers in Pennsylvania, angry mobs lynched Italian-born murder suspects in New Orleans, and Lincoln used Union troops fresh from the battlefield of Gettysburg to restore peace to the Irish neighborhoods of New York City during the draft riots of 1863. The social problems and the violent confrontations of our urban, ethnic past may provide useful perspectives on the problems of megalopolis today.

If ethnic life in America has been difficult, even violent, it has also been warm, intimate, and intensely human. As our mid-twentieth century institutions became ever larger and more impersonal, many people feel increasingly cut off from meaningful contact with others. In the 1960's and 1970's interest in communal living and "encounter" groups demonstrated a hunger for the warmth and intimacy that, according to our writers, comedians, and grandparents, existed in their traditional ethnic communities. Undoubtedly some people found the intensity of family ties and group loyalties in their ethnic communities stifling; yet many look back upon these very qualities with longing and nostalgia. If ethnic communities have provided an acceptable alternative to loneliness and alienation for at least some Americans, they are worthy of serious attention by all.

Finally, ethnic history has relevance for Americans today because it is the story of people reacting to rapid and radical change. All non-English immigrants faced the shock of encountering the Anglo-Saxon society of majority America which differed in many ways from what they had known in their former homes. Early immigrants left age-old patterns of village life to make new beginnings in wild, untouched frontiers. Most traumatic of all was the adjustment of the late nineteenth century or early twentieth century peasants. Born and reared in the traditional, cooperative rural villages of Southern or Eastern Europe, they plunged abruptly into the rapidly changing, competitive, highly individualistic society of urban, industrial America. For such people the voyage across the ocean was a voyage across the centuries. The tremendous differences between immigrant parents and their American born children created a "generation gap" of unprecedented dimensions.

Anthropologist Margaret Mead has suggested that all Americans born before the end of World War II are immigrants, newcomers to a totally different America from the one in which they were born and reared. Alvin Toffler, in his 1970 best seller *Future Shock,* goes even further. He finds the rate of change in our society so greatly accelerated over anything man has known in the past that our main problem in the last three decades of the twentieth century will be learning to cope with rapid change. The experience of ethnic Americans in our past, people whose lives were often consumed by their efforts, successful and unsuccessful, to cope with change may well have new meaning for us now.

There are many compelling reasons, then, for a new interest in ethnic history—an interest which has led to the writing of this book. Hundreds of scholars are investigating the ethnic experience in America, and an ever expanding bibliography of titles appears each year dealing with individual ethnic groups, prominent ethnic personalities past and present, and the meaning of ethnicity itself. This relatively short volume does not attempt to reproduce such a vast and ever increasing quantity of information. Rather it is meant as an introduction to the field. It will delineate the main outlines of ethnic history, point out the significances of ethnicity in American life, past and present, and summarize some of the results of recent research.

Because of the vast scope of the subject, I have felt it necessary to place certain limits upon the material dealt with in this study. Although white, Protestant Americans of English background are as much an ethnic group as any other, I have included them only insofar as they have interacted with "minority" ethnic groups. The fact that they have been the numerical majority and the dominant political and cultural group makes their story different. Moreover, since the history of English America has come down to us as traditional "American" history, most readers will already be familiar with it.

Two other large ethnic groups whose experience will not be covered in this book are blacks and American Indians. Because blacks were subjected to slavery and unparalleled discrimination, and because American Indians were a "native" dispossessed population rather than immigrants, the experiences of these groups are unique. The story of blacks and American Indians constitute broad fields of scholarship in their own right, and the reader should consult the bibliography for suggestions about where to begin investigating them.

The ethnic communities which this study will focus upon are those of the immigrants from Europe (including Scotland and Ireland, but not England), the Spanish-speaking ethnic communities from Mexico and Puerto Rico, and the Chinese, Japanese, and Filipino communities. Despite the many differences among these groups, they have basic similarities that make it possible to treat them in a single volume. Most of the individuals in these groups came to America voluntarily. They came for very similar reasons and shared similar problems and experiences after their arrival.

The material available on even these groups is so vast that I have set up certain additional limitations—arbitrary, but, I hope, useful. Each ethnic group has produced its leaders, its famous sons and daughters of whom it is justly proud. I have chosen to focus attention not on these leaders (who by the nature of their leadership are exceptions) but rather on the experiences of the great numbers of ordinary ethnic Americans.

There are so many different ethnic communities that it will be impossible to deal individually with every one. The book is arranged chronologically, with most of the material about any one particular group given in the chapter dealing with the period in which most members of the group arrived. For example, although Italians and Jews were in America during the colonial period, most of them came in the late nineteenth and early twentieth centuries. Therefore, most of the material about them will appear in the chapters dealing with the late nineteenth and early twentieth centuries.

Ethnic history is difficult to write not only because there are so many different ethnic groups, but because there are wide variations within each group. Ethnic groups are divided by economic class, geographic distribution, political affiliation, and in many other ways. Any attempt to write their history must use generalizations. Therefore, the reader should remember that what was true for most Swedish-Americans, Japanese-Americans, or Puerto Ricans was not true of every individual within the group.

In conclusion, this book will attempt to introduce the reader to the story of ethnicity in America and to ask, if not to answer, the important questions ethnic history raises. It will deal with the traditional subjects of immigration history. Who came to America, and why did they come? How did immigrants react to America, and how did America react to immigrants? It will also deal with the creation and survival of the ethnic communities. How were their institutions established, and what functions did those institutions perform? Why did some ethnic communities disappear rapidly, while others survived generation after generation?

The book will also attempt to shed light on some less traditional but equally important questions. What was life like for the woman and the child as well as for the man within the ethnic community? What impact did ethnic Americans have upon the educational system of the United States, and what impact did the educational system have upon them? What factors have most influenced the upward mobility of minority individuals and minority communities? What circumstances have aggravated—or alleviated—tensions between ethnic communities? Finally, what role does ethnicity play in American life today?

CHAPTER 2

Beginnings:
Ethnic Communities in
the English Colonies

As every American school child "knows," our nation began with thirteen English colonies inhabited by Englishmen with names like Washington, Adams, Jefferson, and Lee. The story is more complicated, however. Long before the arrival of the English, the Spanish and French successfully planted settlements in Florida, the Southwest, and the Mississippi Valley—settlements that would eventually be incorporated into the United States. Nor were the so-called "English" colonies along the Atlantic seacoast exclusively English. Polish, German, and Italian craftsmen plied their trades in early Jamestown, the first permanent English settlement. When William Penn established his Quaker refuge in Pennsylvania in 1681, the area was inhabited by a Swedish settlement almost fifty years old. A large colonial population of American Indians, blacks, Swedes, Finns, Germans, French, Irish, Scotch, Poles, Italians, Welsh, Flemings, Jews, and others forshadowed the variety of humanity that would populate the United States in centuries to come.

Non-English immigrants faced many of the same problems in colonial America that immigrants have faced ever since. How much of their former life style could they maintain in the new American environment? How could they best adjust to changing conditions? As permanent residents of a predominantly English culture, should they try to maintain their traditional non-English language and life style? Should they pass this language and life style down to their children? If so, how?

There were so many ethnic communities in colonial America with such widely varying experiences that it is impractical to attempt a detailed account of each. Rather, this chapter will examine the experience of four representative groups—the Swedes, the Dutch, the Germans, and the Scotch-Irish. The Swedes and Dutch were relatively small groups. Arriving in the seventeenth century, they established colonies of their own which passed into the political control of the English several decades later.

Originally the majority in their respective areas, the Swedes and the Dutch gradually became minorities in an increasingly English society. Their responses to this situation differed, however. The Swedes assimilated so rapidly that a recognizable Swedish-speaking ethnic community had virtually disappeared by the time of the American Revolution. The Dutch maintained their language and life style generations longer. At the time of the American Revolution it was difficult to assemble an English speaking jury in Albany, New York. In the closing years of the nineteenth century many elderly people in rural New Jersey still spoke Dutch.

The Germans and the Scotch-Irish were the largest colonial ethnic communities. Both arrived mainly in the eighteenth century; and both come as unpopular minorities to pre-existing, predominantly English colonies. In other respects, their experiences were very different. Though they spoke English, the Scotch-Irish were a distinctive—and unpopular—group when they arrived. Yet they merged very quickly into mainstream America. The colonial Germans, on the other hand, survived as an ethnic community well into the nineteenth century. Thousands of their descendants, members of religious sects, retain a German dialect and a pre-industrial life style today.

Peopling the Colonies

"Emigration is a form of suicide because it separates the person from all that life gives except the material wants of simple animal existence," wrote a nineteenth century American journalist. Leaving family, friends, home, church, everything dear and familiar for an unknown future in America was a drastic step in the nineteenth century, but it was more drastic still in the seventeenth. Less was known about the New World, and one's future there, even one's survival, was uncertain. It is not surprising that the seventeenth century trading companies promoting New Sweden and New Netherland had trouble finding colonists.

New Sweden began as a Swedish trading post at the site of the future city of Wilmington, Delaware, and spread along the Delaware River valley into what would later be the states of Delaware, New Jersey, and Pennsylvania. Half the colonists were soldiers, sent by the

Swedish government; the other half included farmers, craftsmen, and a minister. Though the Swedish government was willing to send anyone who would go, including debtors, poachers, and other "undesirables," the colony numbered only a few hundred families when William Penn arrived fifty years later. Scattered thinly over a relatively wide area, the Swedes were absorbed in a few generations by the English newcomers who settled among them.

Both New Sweden and New Netherland had trouble attracting settlers because company policies made it difficult for persons of humble origin to become landowners. The Dutch colony soon became more populous than its Swedish counterpart, however, because it offered more varied economic opportunities. In addition to agriculture, settlers could also engage in commerce, using New Amsterdam (later New York City), the best natural harbor on the coast. The company's policy toward outsiders in New Amsterdam was a liberal one for the time. Settlers speaking at least eighteen different languages, Catholics and Jews as well as Protestants, came to this Dutch city.

New Amsterdam absorbed the energies of all comers—women as well as men. Women managed taverns, kept shops, and served on juries. As fur traders Dutch women made trips into the wilderness to negotiate with Indian suppliers. A particularly enterprising Dutch woman was Maria Provoost, who sold thirty pounds worth of merchandise in her store the day after delivering a baby daughter. Only two people in New Amsterdam had fancy coaches—the governor and Maria Provoost!

The coming of the Swedes and Dutch was primarily a response to the economic opportunities in America. The coming of the Germans and Scotch-Irish was due to a greater extent to harsh conditions in their homelands. The Germans, the largest non-English speaking community in the English colonies, came from a variety of German-speaking provinces, including parts of Switzerland. But most came from the Rhineland, a rich and strategically located area repeatedly devastated by war. The Thirty Years War, the Wars of Louis XIV, the War of the Spanish Succession, the War of the Austrian Succession—one followed so closely upon the heels of another that despondent German farmers refused to plant the crops experience had taught them they would be unlikely to reap. Even in peace time, poverty, high taxes, and oppressive rulers made life unbearable. In this atmosphere of despair dissenting religious sects proliferated, while alarmed officials tried in vain to suppress them with the most savage persecutions. Such were the conditions that led normally home-loving Germans to set out for America during the seventeenth century.

Even more numerous were the Scotch-Irish, immigrants who came in such numbers that a contemporary complained, "it looks as if Ireland is to send all its inhabitants hither." In a sense, the Scotch-Irish who came to America were double immigrants. Lured by the British government's promise of land at cheap rentals in northern Ireland (Ulster), their families had left the bleak, impoverished hills of Scotland in the seventeenth century. In Roman Catholic Ireland they maintained their Presbyterian faith and kept intact their religious and family ties to Scotland.

Thousands of these Scots in Ireland, or Scotch-Irish as they came to be called, moved to America in the eighteenth century. Like other Irish, they were subject to discriminatory British commercial regulations. Moreover, as staunch Presbyterians in an area where the official religion was the Church of England, they were considered religious dissenters and thus forbidden to vote, hold office, and maintain their own schools. But their most serious problem, the one that led most directly to emigration, was the sudden increase in the rents they paid for their farms. Originally attracted to Ulster by the low rentals, the Scotch-Irish found their first leases expiring and their absentee landlords doubling and tripling the rates.

Both German and Scotch-Irish immigration began slowly in the seventeenth century and increased in the eighteenth as conditions in the homelands grew worse. Immigration promoters, known as "newlanders," encouraged the flow with propaganda, often in the form of forged immigrant letters, praising the New World where "the maid had become a lady, the peasant a noble, the son of the artisan, a baron. . . ." A pamphlet published in 1734 described South Carolina as a utopia where the wolves were small and tame and the bison put their heads in the windows waiting for the hunters to shoot them. Exaggerated claims led to equally exaggerated counterclaims. The town council of Bern, Switzerland, hoping to keep its inhabitants at home, warned that America was a land without schoolmasters, blacksmiths, sickles, or spades, a land where crops were ruined by game and seed was unavailable.

Many prospective immigrants discounted the claims of both sets of propagandists. They were influenced, however, by authentic letters from fellow countrymen already in America who urged friends and relatives to follow. German immigrants wrote of the abundance of game and the fertility of the soil. Robert Parks, a Scotch-Irish immigrant, assured his sister in Ireland that America was "the best country for working folk and tradesmen of any in the world . . . a man will sooner earn a suit of clothes here than in Ireland, by reason of Workmen's labor being so dear."

We do not know whether Robert Parks' sister came, but so many others did that Scotch-Irish Ulster was stricken with "America fever."

In 1728 the Archbishop of Ireland complained that "the whole North is in a ferment at present; and people every day (are) engaging one another to go. . . . The humor has spread like a contagious disease. . . ." Although frightened authorities arrested ship captains on any possible pretext and confiscated the baggage of would-be emigrants, the America fever could not be stopped. In the half century before the American Revolution over a quarter of a million Scotch-Irish came to America, bringing with them a deep hatred for English authority.

From Europe to America

Never again would opportunity be so abundant; but, never again would it be so dangerous and so difficult to seize that opportunity. European families piled their belongings on carts or carried them on their backs as they trudged from farm to seaport. Unscrupulous agents often swindled them of what little money they had even before the voyage began. Families exhausted their resources waiting for a ship to sail. Once the ship did sail, its captain might deposit the passengers many miles from their original destination. Such passengers were more fortunate, however, than a group of Swedes recruited by the trading company in the seventeenth century and then left behind in Europe because the ship could not accomodate them.

> Here was seen such a lamentation and weeping, for the unfortunate ones have sold all they possessed, yea done away with home and ground for half of the value, journeyed such a long way at their own expense, and are now compelled to take up the beggar's staff, the one going here, the others there.

The mortality rate aboard ship was high. In 1745, for example, a ship left Germany with four hundred passengers and arrived in America with only fifty. Such a crossing was not unusual. Hunger as well as disease made long voyages lethal. Starvation led a shipload of Scotch-Irish immigrants to the verge of cannibalism. Their provisions gone, they had just picked Samuel Fisher, an elder of Londonderry parish, for the slaughter when a ship was sighted bringing help.

A German organist, Gottlieb Mittelberger, left a vivid description of his voyage to Pennsylvania, a description he hoped would discourage others from undertaking the trip. According to Mittelberger, the drinking water aboard the immigrant ship was "black, thick with dirt, and full of worms," and the ship's biscuit, was riddled with "red worms and spiders' nests." Inedible food was only the beginning, however. Mittelberger continued:

> During the journey the ship is full of pitiful signs of distress, smells, fumes, horrors, vomiting, various kinds of sea sickness, fever, dysentery,

headache, heat, constipation, boils, scurvy, cancer, mouthrot. . . . Add to all that shortage of food, hunger, thirst, frost, heat, dampness, fear, misery, vexation . . . there are so many lice, especially on the sick people, that they have to be scraped off the bodies. All this misery reaches its climax when, in addition to everything else, one must also suffer through two or three days and nights of storm, with everyone convinced that the ship with all aboard is bound to sink. . . .

Misery and malice are readily associated, so that people begin to cheat and steal from one another. And then one always blames the other for having undertaken the voyage. . . .

One can scarcely conceive what happens at sea to women in childbirth and to their innocent offspring. Very few escape with their lives, and mother and child, as soon as they have died, are thrown into the water. . . .

Children between the ages of one and seven seldom survive the sea voyage. . . .

Swedish and Dutch immigrants were transported to America by the trading companies that recruited them. The Germans and Scotch-Irish had to finance their own immigration. Lacking the necessary cash, many came as indentured servants. This meant that they sold their labor in America for a period of years to whoever would pay the ship captain the price of their passage. Young healthy adults, who had no trouble finding employers in labor-starved America, usually bound themselves for three to six years. Children aged five to ten served until they were twenty-one. Husbands were often separated from wives and children from parents. The work was hard, especially for the elderly, and discipline could be harsh. Runaways were commonly punished with a lengthened term of service.

Purchase by a kind master was no permanent assurance of good treatment, as indentured servants, like slaves, could be resold. Colonial newspapers frequently carried advertisements such as the following: August 24, 1766. "A German female servant is for sale. She has five years to serve," or February 10, 1754, "Rosina Dorothy Kost, nee Kaufmann, born in Waldenberg . . . desires to let her brother-in-law, one Spohr of Conestoga know through the medium of this paper of her sale at public auction."

Though Europeans denounced the indenture traffic as the "German slave trade," indenture was different from slavery. Indentured servants worked a limited span of years, were given some money or supplies on release, and were not subject to the social and racial stigma that plagued free blacks. Indeed, some Germans who could have paid their own passage chose indenture so as to save their own money and to have time to learn the new language before venturing out on their own.

There were relatively few runaways among German servants,

probably because of the language problem, but the Scotch-Irish were considered less reliable. Colonial papers frequently carried advertisements for the return of Scotch-Irish runaways. One master ran the following poetic announcement which embodies many of the negative stereotypes commonly associated with servants, Scotch-Irish or otherwise:

> Last Wednesday noon at break of day
> From Philadelphia ran away
> An Irishman named John McKeohn
> To fraud and imposition prone;
> About five feet five inches high
> Can curse and swear as well as lie . . .
> . . . take the rogue from stem to stern
> the hypocrite you'll soon discern
> and find tho' his deportment's civil
> A saint without, within a devil.
> Whoever secures said John McKeohn
> Provided I can get my own
> Shall have from me in cash paid down
> Five dollar bills; and half a crown.

Continuity–and Change

Life was difficult for the newcomers, whether they were indentured servants or whether they were fortunate enough to acquire their own land or independent employment from the beginning. Many Germans started out in lean-tos or caves, surviving the first months on game and wild fruits. By the mid-18th century, the established German community was organizing societies to aid its impoverished new immigrants, but this aid was inadequate to meet the enormous needs.

Cultural shock was often as great a problem as poverty, especially for the Germans. Accustomed to the rigid social stratification of the German states, conservative immigrants sometimes found American egalitarianism more upsetting than liberating. Because labor hungry employers did not require references, Mittelberger concluded that Pennsylvania was an ideal country for criminals. He was appalled that learned people working as indentured servants were treated "just as if they were common wage-laborers . . . beaten like cattle until they have learned hard labor." He was also appalled at the English (American) attitude toward their women who, according to his view, lived in pampered, luxurious idleness. Doubtless many immigrants agreed with Mittelberger that America was a land of "outrageous . . . rudeness" and "excessive freedom."

Cultural shock, like poverty, was usually a temporary problem. Some solved it by embracing as rapidly and completely as possible the life they found around them. One German Lutheran pastor, for example, sent his son to England for an education and had him ordained as a minister in the Church of England. Even more complete was the adjustment of a Moravian missionary, Christian Ferdinand Post. Post married an Indian woman and spent the rest of his days living like an Indian along the western frontier.

Most ethnic immigrants responded to cultural shock by recreating in the new environment as much as possible of their former life. Immigrants built farms and homes like the ones they had left in Europe. The Swedes burned trees to clear their land and used the ashes for fertilizer, a Scandinavian custom that proved equally useful along the Delaware. Accustomed to forest life, the Swedes and Finns built homes of logs plastered with clay, like the ones they had known at home—thus introducing the log cabin that would become the symbol of frontier America. The Dutch, on the other hand, reproduced the steep roofed lumber homes they had owned in the Netherlands. The interior of a typical New Amsterdam house had divided "Dutch" doors, built-in cupboards, and large, blue, tiled fireplaces customary in old Amsterdam. Traditional Dutch windmills appeared on the American landscape.

Ethnic immigrants sought out land similar to what they had known in their homelands. Germans settled in heavily wooded areas, where they raised livestock, flax, grain, and vegetables as they had in Germany. Unlike many other colonial farmers, Germans characteristically cleared their land completely, fenced in their livestock, and were careful (as in their impoverished homeland) to make the best possible use of all their resources. Though wood was plentiful, they preferred the more efficient iron stove to the American style open fire for heating and cooking. German farms were noted for their green fields, sleek livestock, and ample, well-built barns.

The Scotch-Irish, too, chose land similar to what they had known before—usually river bottom land, not as heavily wooded as that of the Germans. While German settlement was concentrated in the middle colonies, Pennsylvania in particular, the Scotch-Irish scattered more evenly from New England to Georgia. They flocked to the frontier where land was cheapest. Unable to purchase farms, some simply squatted on whatever land was available. In Pennsylvania Scotch-Irish immigrants settled "in an audacious and disorderly way" on tracts set aside for the Penns themselves, justifying their action on the grounds that "it was against the laws of God and nature that so much land should be idle while so many Christians wanted it to labor on it to raise their bread."

The Scotch-Irish found the American frontier not too different from what they had known in Ulster. In America, as in northern

Ireland, the Scotch-Irish built new farms in an unfamiliar and sometimes hostile environment. The Scotch-Irish frontiersman chopping down trees to form a little clearing for his cabin and planting corn among the stumps became the stereotype of the typical American pioneer.

All colonial families were relatively self-sufficient, but the frontier Scotch-Irish were more self-sufficient than most. The household grew its own food, manufactured its own clothing and tanned its own leather—just as it had in Ireland. Diversions were simple and often crude; they included heavy drinking, fighting, and gander pulling (players trying to pull the head off a live greased fowl while they gallop past on horseback). The reputation the Scotch-Irish enjoyed for being boisterous and unruly originated in Ulster but was reinforced in colonial America.

In many ways ethnic immigrants reproduced their European life styles in America. But they also adapted that way of life to the new environment. Dutch farmers, for example, had been accustomed to village life in Europe, but in America they soon learned to spread out in the ample countryside. Indian culture had an enormous impact on farming methods. Ethnic Americans acquired a taste for such American Indian foods as corn and squash. Dutch women learned to make Indian-style bark cradles for their babies.

Ethnic Institutions—The Family

Three important institutions limited change and preserved European traditions: the ethnic family, the ethnic church, and the ethnic school. The more effectively these institutions perpetuated Old World traditions, the longer the community preserved its distinctive cultural identity. The first stronghold of ethnicity was, of course, the family itself. Where no other institutions existed—no churches, no schools, no organized group life at all—parents taught their children to read in the mother tongue and to worship in the traditional way. Special foods, courting customs, funeral practices, holiday celebrations—all these strengthened ethnic identity within the family. Even with little or no outside reinforcement, the family could preserve the ethnic identity of its members at least for a generation or two.

Many factors influenced how well families succeeded in passing down their ethnic traditions from generation to generation. Density of settlement made a big difference. Swedish families were so thinly scattered over the Delaware Valley that they were soon outnumbered by the English who settled among them. When the English first arrived, they adopted pidgin Swedish. The existence of this Anglicized "Swedish" made it easier for second and third generation Swedes to shift from the language of their parents to that of the increasingly English society around them.

German families were so heavily concentrated in certain areas of Pennsylvania, Maryland, and Virginia that it was difficult for English newcomers to settle among them—even if they had wanted to do so. Many Germans lived near the frontier, where there was little contact with the English-speaking world. Transportation difficulties reinforced their isolation. Until 1733, there was no road between Philadelphia and the nearby German community of Lancaster. Where Germans shared the frontier with the Scotch-Irish, mutual hostility kept the two groups apart, socially as well as geographically.

The German family had a distinctive life style that differed in many ways from that of its Scotch-Irish or English neighbors. German families were large, even in a day of large families, and were unusually frugal and hard-working. As Mittelberger suggests, German women worked harder than their English counterparts. In addition to rearing large families and caring for the livestock and garden, they shared the field work of ploughing and harvesting with their husbands—a practice that was usual only among the most impoverished English-Americans. The German woman was expected to be more docile and submissive to her husband's authority than the "pampered" English woman who, according to the misinformed but opinionated Mittelberger, had received her great privileges from Queen Elizabeth. A news item from a 1775 German paper suggests that at least one German woman was far from docile. When the sheriff offered to pay someone to whip a farmer convicted of petty theft, his wife volunteered for the job. She whipped her husband soundly, adding an extra blow for the time he had boxed her ears, and walked away four dollars richer!

Such a case was, of course, exceptional. German family life was usually warm and close. Quilting bees, sleigh rides, barn raisings, and other celebrations provided a rich social life within the German community and often within the large family unit itself, making it unnecessary for the young to look elsewhere for amusement. Family and community ties were strong and lasting. Children typically settled on farms adjoining those of their parents, thus perpetuating the influence of the older generations upon the young and thereby strengthening ethnic as well as family ties. When overpopulation in a given area made it necessary for Germans to move, they usually migrated in groups, often taking their minister with them.

Family and community life was not as close and therefore not as effective in reinforcing ethnic identity among the Scotch-Irish immigrants. Unlike the more settled Germans, many Scotch-Irish families moved to a new farm every few years. As a result, friends and relatives were frequently separated. Unlike their German counterparts, Scotch-Irish young people often left the vicinity of the family farm to set up a homestead for themselves many miles away. Thus ties between the generations were severed, a pattern which made it difficult to transmit ethnic traditions. Finally, when they moved, the Scotch-Irish typically moved as isolated family units rather than in groups, thus making assimilation more likely.

The isolation and crudeness of Scotch-Irish frontier life was well known. What is less well known is that many Scotch-Irish, particularly the "better" sort, considered such conditions an undesirable makeshift. Their goal in America, as in Ulster, was to replace frontier isolation with a more settled village life, complete with church and school and court of law. Actually, the turbulent, rough frontier life style associated with the Scotch-Irish in colonial America was as much a function of economic circumstance as of ethnic origin. By moving up economically and settling down geographically, the English-speaking Scotch-Irish, unlike the Germans, could leave their ethnic stereotypes behind. Such upwardly mobile, settled, Scotch-Irish families rapidly blended into the English community, while frontier families disappeared—literally and ethnically—into the wilderness.

The Ethnic Church

Next to the family, the church was the most important ethnic institution in colonial America. Religion played a major role in the decision of many Europeans to come to America. Some groups were fleeing from religious persecution, others were looking for an ideal place to establish a particular kind of religious community, and still others considered the new world a fertile field for missionary effort.

Colonial America was still close chronologically and psychologically, to the Reformation and the religious warfare that followed it in Europe. In the seventeenth century, religious loyalties were intense, and religion played a major role in everyday life. Swedish and Dutch trading companies carefully provided for the establishment of their national churches in their colonies. Similarly, eighteenth century Germans and Scotch-Irish brought their accustomed churches with them when they immigrated.

Religion reinforced ethnicity in many ways. Ministers born and educated in Europe preached, prayed, and taught the catechism in their native language. Prayerbooks, hymnals, and catechisms encouraged literacy in the mother tongues. In areas with large ethnic populations, ethnic churches served as community centers. Where ethnic populations were sparse, itinerant ministers helped isolated families keep in touch with one another and with the homeland.

Ethnic churches were not transplanted to the United States without problems, however. Many groups found it difficult to raise money to build and maintain churches—a responsibility often assumed by the government in Europe. There was a shortage of ministers as well as money. With no mechanism for ordination in America, ministers had to be persuaded to immigrate from Europe. In no denomination were there enough ministers.

Church discipline as well as church personnel came from overseas—another source of difficulty. As early as 1737 Dutch ministers petitioned for a governing body of their own in America, but permission was not granted until 1771. With the passing of time, American born members of ethnic churches resented being dependent upon clergy and clerical governing bodies that were too far away to respond quickly to their needs.

The most serious problem in the long run, however, was that foreign-language churches were forced to operate in an increasingly English environment. Ethnic colonists often had the double expense of supporting the established church, the Church of England in New York and Virginia, for example, as well as their own churches. More important than expense was the growing language problem. By the early eighteenth century, American-born Swedes wanted services in English. By the end of the century young people in the German and Dutch communities were making similar demands.

Ethnic communities met these problems with varying degrees of success. In the early seventeenth century, the Swedish colony in the Delaware Valley was supplied with ministers from Sweden, but after the English took control these aging pastors were not replaced. From 1648 to 1697, Swedish America was without effective leadership, secular or religious. In 1697 King Charles XI, responding to a colonial petition, sent three new ministers to Swedish America, but their struggle to save the tiny community from assimilating was unsuccessful. As English colonists joined Swedish parishes, the original Swedish churches were gradually Anglicized. In 1741 the old Swedish church at Penns Neck, New Jersey, voted to conduct its services in English and to change its doctrinal affiliation to the Church of England. In 1789 Archbishop Uno von Troil bade the American Swedish churches farewell in the name of King Gustavus III of Sweden; all church ties with the Swedish homeland were broken.

The Dutch Reformed Church was more successful than the Swedish both in maintaining its own ethnicity and in reinforcing the ethnicity of its community. Churches in New Netherlands served a variety of functions that gave them great importance to their communities. In the early years they were forts for protection against Indian attacks. They were also community centers and distribution outlets for public information. New laws were posted at the churches, as were notices of everything from political meetings to lost swine.

Charity for the sick, the old, and the poor was handled through the Dutch church. Money was collected at services in velvet bags, decorated with bells. When a Long Island minister attempted to substitute the mundane collection plate, irate congregants walked out. Often old people turned over all their assets to the church, which then paid a reputable family to board them for life and provide an elaborate funeral for them when they died.

Unlike its Swedish counterpart, the Dutch church was not disrupted by the transition to English rule. Dutch churches continued their active involvement in the life of the eighteenth century community, including the education of the children. Equally important, they solved the problems of leadership and governance. In 1766 members of the Dutch Reformed clergy established Queens College (later Rutgers) in New Jersey to educate a proper American ministry. Five years later they won permission from church authorities in the Netherlands to have a governing body of their own in America. In the nineteenth century English gradually replaced Dutch as the language of worship and other institutions took over many of the educational, social, and charitable functions the church had performed; but the church itself survived and was reinforced as new Dutch immigrants arrived in the succeeding centuries.

No ethnic community was more deeply religious than the colonial Germans. A small but significant minority, perhaps ten per cent, belonged to distinctive sects for whom religion was an all encompassing way of life. Sectarians immigrated in groups, bringing their ministers with them. Unlike Dutch and Swedish churches, the German sects had never enjoyed government support. As dissenters in Europe, they were accustomed to building and maintaining their own churches and appreciated the freedom from government harassment they found in the New World.

Years of persecution in Europe helped these sects develop such strong bonds of mutual support and group loyalty that they were highly successful in transplanting their religion-centered ways of life to America. The Seventh Day Baptists of Ephrata, Pennsylvania, lived celibate, cloistered lives of worship and study and created some of the earliest and most beautiful American church music. The Moravians established missions for the Indians, conducted schools, and expressed opposition to slavery. The Dunkers were probably the first Americans to preach and practice total abstinence from alcoholic beverages.

Of course the sectarians, like other immigrants, found it hard to resist the new environment altogether. A visitor to a vegetarian Dunker community in Virginia was surprised to find its members eating meat. The leader of the sect blamed the lapse upon a shortage of grain and roots. According to the visitor, however, "the plenty and deliciousness of the Venison and Turkeys has contributed not a little to this. . . ."

Lutherans and Calvinists—Germans who did not belong to the

nonconformist sects—had more difficulty then the sectarians in establishing and maintaining their churches. They missed the financial support they had enjoyed from their governments in Europe. Funds were scarce, and qualified ministers scarcer still. Poorly educated German immigrants sometimes fell under the influence of charlatans like John Martin, the spell caster, or Daniel Weisiger, an unscrupulous Pennsylvania fund raiser.

Eventually the Lutheran Church in Germany sent Reverend Henry Muhlenberg to America and the German Reformed (Calvinist) Church sent Reverend Michael Schlatter. Both men were talented, sincere, and generally successful in establishing ordered German worship in America. The prestige of their positions as well as their personal qualities made them influential leaders in the German community. These and other ministers from Germany renewed old links with the homeland, as did the continuation of sermons, prayers, and hymns in the native language.

Germans, more than either the Swedes or the Dutch, associated valid worship with the mother tongue and found it hard to conceive of one without the other. The struggle for the introduction of English into the German churches did not begin until well after the American Revolution and, unlike the parallel struggle among the Swedes and Dutch, did not result in a clear cut victory for the use of English. Lutheran and German Reformed congregations were torn by bitter conflict between pro-English and pro-German factions as the eighteenth century drew to a close. The Lutheran Ministerium of Pennsylvania, in the interests of peace, finally recommended that congregations divided on the language issue should split into two separate groups. Congregations did split, amidst court battles, riots, and even bloodshed as property and people were reapportioned.

"God is my witness," wrote the Lutheran minister Reverend Muhlenberg, "I worked against the English as long as I could. . . ." Eventually Muhlenberg and most other Lutheran and German Reformed ministers gave in to the demand for English, though German still survived in many rural churches. Among the sectarian Germans, sentiment for the preservation of the German language was even stronger. Many of the Dunkers and Mennonites successfully resisted the incursion of English, not only in their churches, but in their schools and in their daily lives as well.

The Scotch-Irish did not have an ethnic language, but they did have an ethnic church, the Presbyterian Church. They had succeeded in transplanting their church from Scotland to Ireland in the seventeenth century, but the move to America was more difficult. Here the scarcity of ministers, the scattered locations of their congregants, and the opposition of the Anglican Church in royal colonies such as New York made them much less successful. Moreover, in America, religious ties with other Presbyterians blurred ethnic boundaries; Presbyterians from Scotland and England cooperated with the Scotch-Irish in establishing the first American Presbytery in Philadelphia in 1692. Under this organizational structure, both Scotch-Irish and Scotch ministers were licensed and sent out to establish Presbyterian churches in the colonies.

Some of the early Scotch-Irish ministers were remarkably energetic and versatile, traveling hundreds of miles and preaching dozens of sermons every month. John Steels of Mercersburg, Pennsylvania, fortified his frontier church, led the local settlers in wars against the Indians, and arbitrated disputes over land on which his congregants had "squatted." Another interesting frontier minister was Charles Beatty, a one-time peddler, classical scholar, and, in 1755, chaplain to Benjamin Franklin's Pennsylvania militia. When Beatty complained that the Pennsylvania militiamen were not attending his services, the always practical Franklin made a suggestion:

> It is perhaps below the dignity of your profession to act as a steward of the rum; but if you were only to distribute it out after prayers, you would have them all about you.

Reverend Beatty liked the idea. According to Franklin, he became so efficient and generous in his new post of dispenser of the rum that "never were prayers more generally and punctually attended."

Despite its early ethnic flavor, the Presbyterian church was unable to provide an institutional framework strong enough to preserve Scotch-Irish ethnic identity. Possibly because of the high standards of classical scholarship demanded of its clergy, the church could never train enough ministers to serve its scattered constituency. Unhampered by language difficulties, the Scotch-Irish immigrants joined whatever existing church seemed most convenient. In remote frontier areas many lost contact with organized religion altogether. Under such circumstances, the church could not play the unifying, community building role among the Scotch-Irish that it had among the Germans and the Dutch.

Education and Assimilation

Recent minorities are acutely aware of the importance of education in preserving their ethnic identity. Colonial immigrants did not have this awareness—at least not at first. Like other colonial Americans, they considered education important, but for reasons that had nothing to do with ethnicity. Children were to be educated so that they could understand "the fundamental principles of the true Christian religion and salvation." Reading was a tool for learning the catechism, the prayers, and the hymns. Education, colonial ethnic parents hoped, would remove their children from occasions for sin and inculcate desirable habits of industry, modesty, thrift, and propriety. Literacy and some knowledge of basic arithmetic was considered useful for the sons of farmers, craftsmen, and merchants (though not nearly so useful for their daughters). Finally, living in a continent they perceived as savage, ethnic Americans considered education a bulwark to protect the young from being seduced into a life of barbarism. It was only after a generation or two in America that some, the Germans in particular, began to see education as a means of preserving the Old World tradition—ethnicity—and passing it on to succeeding generations.

There was no free public school system in colonial America. Parents educated their children at home or sent them to one of a variety of private schools ranging from the local "dame" school to the expensive Latin boarding school many miles away. In theory, ethnic Americans had a similar range of choices; in practice, their choices were narrowed by their distinctive languages and religious beliefs. Ethnic communities, therefore, set up schools of their own—or at least tried to do so.

If ethnic Americans shared the general American view that education, at least on the elementary level, was valuable, they also shared the difficulties of providing even that level of education to their children. Teachers, like ministers, were not attracted to the New World; there was always a shortage. Nor was the work of the teacher highly respected. Teaching was not even considered a full-time occupation; there were usually other duties. A Dutch schoolmaster in Long Island, for example, was expected to clean the church, ring the assembly bell, read psalms, furnish bread and wine for communion, serve as a messenger, and, when there was a death in the community, give out funeral invitations, dig the grave, and toll the bell. As might be expected, such a position did not always attract outstanding candidates. The first New Amsterdam schoolmaster, for example, had many brushes with the law, including a court conviction for "an attempt forcibly to violate Harch Sybalteen's wife in her own house."

Because of distance, lack of transportation, and the need for their labor on the farm and in the household ethnic children, like other colonial children, were irregular in their school attendance. Schools were only open a few months each year, and children attended three or four seasons at most, if they attended at all. Books were scarce, even in English; books in Swedish, Dutch, and German were scarcer still. Conscientious schoolmasters were hampered by lack of supplies of all kinds. "I am engaged in keeping school, with twenty-five children in it; but have no papers nor pens for the use of the children, nor slates and pencils," complained an early Dutch schoolmaster in New Amstel, Delaware.

When New Sweden and New Netherland were founded, the company instructed their respective governors to make provisions for the education of the colony's children. In both cases, the instruction tied education closely to religion. The Swedish authorities notified Governor Johan Printz that "all persons, especially the young, (should) be well instructed in the articles of their Christian faith." The Dutch West India Company gave teachers in its colonies, including New Netherlands, a broader charge:

> He (the teacher) is to instruct the youth in reading, writing, cyphering, and arithmetic, with all zeal and diligence; he is also to implant the fundamental principles of the true Christian religion and salvation, by means of catechizing; he is to teach them the customary prayers, and also accustom them to pray; he is to give heed to their manners and bring these as far as possible to modesty and propriety.

Under Governor Johan Printz (1642-1653) Swedish education made a promising beginning. Early ministers acted as both teacher and preacher. In 1654 the governor, Johan Rising, began plans for the construction of a school house. The colony fell to the Dutch in 1655 and to the English a few years later, and the proposed school was never built. In the second half of the seventeenth century the formal education of the young was neglected.

With few new immigrants arriving from Sweden, it was vital to the colony's survival that the ethnic tradition be passed intact to American-born children. This the 18th century Swedes were unable to do. The older generation made a valiant effort at least to preserve Swedish literacy, according to a letter written by the newly arrived Reverend Erik Bjork in 1697:

> . . . Not without wonder I can tell to the praise of this people that when there were scarcely three Swedish books here, they were nevertheless so anxious about their children that although they borrowed them (the books) from one another, all can nevertheless read a book fairly well . . .

The same colonists who petitioned the Swedish crown for ministers also asked for schoolbooks. The books arrived in 1697 and were distributed "according to the number of grownups and youths in the houses and their ability to read, in such a way that whoever would make the best use of this or that (book) received it."

Despite the arrival of the Swedish books in 1697 and despite the arrival of a dozen Swedish born and educated schoolteachers during the decades that followed, Swedish education did not take root in eighteenth century America. Swedish born ministers and teachers established a system of Swedish parochial schools, but they lacked community support. Provost Acrelius, one of the new ministers, tried to improve the schools, chided the young for staying away from them and from Swedish religious services, and made every effort to convince the adult parishioners of the importance of maintaining the mother tongue. But he was a leader without a following. As the Swedish colony became a smaller and smaller minority its people became increasingly Anglicized. Peter Kalm, a Finnish traveler, described the assimilation of the Swedish community as he observed it between 1748 and 1750:

> We had a Swedish guide along who was probably born of Swedish parents, was married to a Swedish woman, but who could not, himself, speak Swedish. There are many such here of both sexes; for since English is the principal language in the land all people gradually get to speak that, and they become ashamed to talk in their own tongue because they fear they may not in such a case be real English . . . Many Swedish women are married to Englishmen, and although they can speak Swedish very well it is impossible to make them do so, and when they are spoken to in Swedish, they always answer in English. The same condition obtains among the men . . . .

The assimilation of the colonial Swedes, like that of later Swedes and of most immigrant communities, was not the result of any visible coercion on the part of the English majority. No one was forced to give up Swedish and adopt English. But ethnic settlers received a message, unspoken but clear, that English was the language of "real" Americans. In the sparsely populated, scattered Swedish community neither family nor church nor school proved strong enough to resist this message.

Unlike the Swedes, the Dutch, with one of the best developed school systems in seventeenth century Europe, were successful in establishing ethnic schools in colonial America. Secular schoolmasters were licensed to teach in New Amsterdam as early as 1637. By mid century the Dutch had reading schools in half a dozen villages. There was a Latin grammar school for education beyond the elementary level in New Amsterdam in 1652. Though attendance was far from universal, especially in rural areas, a significant portion of the children (girls as well as boys) had some schooling, especially in the commercial community of New Amsterdam.

The earliest Dutch teachers were employees of the Dutch West India Company, chosen by the company and by officials of the Dutch Reformed Church in Amsterdam. Their pay was far from generous; at least one schoolmaster supplemented his salary by taking in washing. When the British took over the colony in 1664, they made no attempt to impose English schooling on the Dutch community. An English schoolmaster was licensed in Albany by the new British governor in 1664, but he provided little competition for his already well established Dutch counterparts.

Dutch schools were instrumental in preserving the ethnicity of the Dutch community of New York. Generation after generation, Dutch schoolmasters taught Dutch children in the language of their parents and grandparents. In the patriotic fervor that followed the American Revolution, many of the Dutch schools began a gradual transition to English as the language of instruction. This was especially true in New York City and other urban areas.

Even after English became the language of instruction, Dutch schools continued to survive as parochial schools. Since education for most New Yorkers, ethnic and otherwise, was organized along denominational lines until the coming of the public schools, such an arrangement was not considered unusual. Though the ethnic tongue was not used, Dutch Reformed parochial schools preserved a sense of social solidarity among the descendants of the colonial Dutch.

The early German sectarian communities were outstanding in their educational achievements. Germans established an excellent Quaker school in Germantown, Pennsylvania in 1701 and even ventured into the area of adult education. Their first schoolmaster, Francis Daniel Pastorius, a lawyer and a classical scholar, was well versed in natural science, philosophy, and at least eight different languages. Christopher Dock, a Mennonite schoolmaster, wrote what was probably the first book in the colonies on the management of schools. His system, innovative for its time, recommended the use of love and positive motivation in education rather than the more conventional reliance on the fear of physical punishment.

Even more innovative were the schools of the Moravians. They pioneered in opening cheerful nursery schools "to employ the little ones with short, easy lessons, and to awaken their faculties," and established excellent boarding schools for older children, some of which successfully combined vocational with academic training. While their educational system was originally intended for their own community, it attracted outsiders as well. In the early nineteenth century, the wealthiest planters of North Carolina educated their daughters in the Moravian academy at Salem. Colonial Moravian schools enrolled Germans of many religious denominations, girls as well as boys, Indians and mulattos as well as whites.

The Lutheran and Reformed (or Calvinist) German majority, who arrived in massive numbers in the eighteenth century, had more difficulty establishing schools. Poverty, geographic isolation, and a scarcity of teachers handicapped their efforts. When they could, they built schools, usually next door to their churches. Often they were unable to build either. Where schools established by the sectarian communities existed, the newer immigrants used them. Otherwise they educated their children at home. On the whole, the children of the impoverished eighteenth century German immigrants were about as well educated as other colonial Americans of comparable socioeconomic status. "There is scarcely an instance of a German of either sex in Pennsylvania that cannot read," wrote Dr. Benjamin Rush in 1789; "but many of the wives and daughters of the German fathers cannot write."

The early Germans, like other colonists, saw education as a means of teaching their children reading, religion, and manners. In the mid-eighteenth century, however, they were suddenly made acutely aware of the role education could play in the preservation—or destruction—of ethnicity. At that time an English charitable society tried to use free schools as a means of assimilating German children to the English language and life style. The German population rejected these schools indignantly and redoubled their efforts to build a school system of their own. The English charity school plan is important because it was the first—but by no means the last—attempt of the American majority to use schooling to impose cultural change on the children of an unpopular minority.

Ironically, the plan was set in motion by a Pennsylvania German minister, Reverend Michael Schlatter, who wrote the Calvinist synod in Amsterdam for funds to establish schools for the rapidly increasing numbers of Germans in Pennsylvania. Schlatter's letter, translated into English, came to the attention of the British Society for the Propagation of the Gospel in Foreign Parts. An American educator, Dr. William Smith, confirmed the "melancholy situation," of the Pennsylvania Germans for the Society adding grossly exaggerated warnings of "the approaching prospect of darkness and idolatry among them." The result was the organization of a missionary society in England and Pennsylvania to save the Germans for Protestant Christianity by establishing charity schools for their children.

Christianity was in no danger among the pious Germans, as Dr. Smith and other American supporters of the plan undoubtedly knew. Dr. Smith's correspondence suggests other motives for this educational venture:

> Without education it is impossible to preserve a free government in any country, or to preserve the spirit of commerce. Should these emigrants degenerate into a state little better than that of wood-born savages, what use could they make of English privileges?

> But further, education, besides being necessary to support the spirit of

liberty and commerce, is the only means of incorporating these foreigners with ourselves, in the rising generation . . . .

By a common education of English and German youth at the same schools, acquaintance and connections will be formed and deeply impressed upon them in their cheerful and open moments. The English language and a conformity of manners will be acquired . . . When once a few intermarriages are made between the chief families of the different nations . . . no arts of our enemies will be able to divide them in their affection; and all the narrow distinctions of extractions, etc., will be forgot . . . .

Dr. Smith, Benjamin Franklin, and other supporters of the charity school plan had concerns about the large German population, a third of the total of Pennsylvania, similar to the concerns subsequent generations have had about immigrant groups of their day. They were afraid that masses of impoverished Germans would perpetuate a low standard of living by accepting wages no respectable English worker could compete with. They were afraid that unassimilated Germans, ignorant of English tradition, would undermine their system of government. Finally, they were afraid that Germans would be disloyal in case of war with the French or the Indians.

Though the schools were designed to teach reading, writing, arithmetic, and religion, they had a "hidden curriculum"—Anglicization. According to one plan, German school boys would win impressive prizes by delivering orations in English or reading English authors with "nearest to the right pronunciation." The directors planned to educate girls in reading and sewing because "as mothers have the principal direction in bringing up their young children, it will be of little use that the father can talk English if the mother can speak nothing but Dutch [*Deutsch,* or German] to them. In that case the children will speak the mother tongue." Elementary education was to be free, but there would be a charge for all the more advanced subjects "to prevent the vulgar from spending more time upon them than is necessary." Clearly the main purpose of the charity schools was make the German children into good Englishmen, not good scholars.

The Germans themselves were given little to say about the schools being established supposedly for their benefit. Only one member of the board of directors was German. Teachers educated in Germany were not to be hired "for though they understand both languages, we could not be sure of their principles." The German community of Easton was not asked to help in the establishment of their school. Indeed, the Englishman in charge of this school considered the local German residents "so perverse and quarrelsome in all their affairs that I am sometimes ready to query with myself whether it be men or brutes that these most generous benefactors are about to civilize."

It is not surprising that the English charity school project and the persons connected with it aroused the hostility of the community they were trying to educate. Christopher Sauer, the leading German newspaper editor of the colonies, became the spokesman for German opposition to the controversial schools. Sauer denounced the entire scheme as "having only a political purpose and tendency." He questioned the religious motives of the educators, reminding them that "wicked men may preach in English as well as in German." Above all, he resented the suggestion that the German community would be disloyal in case of war with France, a suggestion that events would soon prove unwarranted.

About a dozen of these charity schools were built in the late 1750's and early 1760's. At their peak they enrolled about seven hundred students, not all of whom were German. By 1763 the schools were no longer in operation. They were discontinued because of Indian problems on the frontier, administrative difficulties, and, most important of all, the opposition of the community for whom they were intended.

The German community, having learned that schools could be used to destroy their children's ethnic heritage, now made a conscious decision to use schools to preserve that heritage. German leaders in Pennsylvania, Maryland, and Virginia worked with renewed zeal to build elementary schools of their own. Increased prosperity as well as increased determination made their efforts successful. The resulting schools taught generations of German-American children to read, write, sing, and pray in the tradition of their ancestors.

German elementary schools were successful because, unlike their Swedish counterparts, they were supported by large geographically concentrated German-speaking populations and by a flourishing German-language church. Equally important, they were supported by an influential and long-lived German press. Over two hundred publications, many of them religious or educational, were issued by the German press in America before 1755. German children had German primers from which to learn their alphabet. Between 1732 and 1800 there were thirty-eight German newspapers in Pennsylvania alone. German publications circulated in all thirteen colonies, creating a sense of unity and common interest throughout German-America. Children who learned to read in a German language school found German literacy important throughout their lives. Thus, home, church, press, and school worked together to preserve the ethnicity of the colonial German community.

In the rural communities of Pennsylvania, Maryland, and Virginia, German schools, and with them the German language, survived into the second half of the nineteenth century. Among the stricter sectarian

Germans, they still survive. A price was paid, however. Part of the price was the lack of opportunity for higher education.

A more serious price was that of social and cultural isolation. German-speaking Americans were cut off from the English intellectual heritage. At the same time, the eighteenth century rural German dialect preserved in their spoken language was also inadequate for the transmission of the German intellectual heritage. Nor was it adequate, as time passed, to meet the day-to-day needs of communication in an industrializing United States. A German vocabulary limited mainly to household, agricultural, and religious words isolated those who spoke it from the mainstream of modern life, both German and American. Some Germans tried to solve the problem by adding English words to the original German. The result was Pennsylvania Dutch, a new German-American dialect that developed a small literature of its own. The new dialect made daily life easier, but it did not alleviate the cultural or social isolation of its users.

For the stricter sectarians, however, isolation was not a problem. It was a goal. "To counteract the injurious influence of the time and to throw a safeguard about the children, the determined step was taken to have them taught in the German language only," explained a Mennonite bishop. A religious, German-language education for their children was a critical part of the sectarian's decision to reject the secular, industrial world for a simpler more spiritual life. In line with this decision, the stricter Mennonites have rejected all education beyond elementary school for the majority of their children—a decision bringing them into direct conflict with twentieth century compulsory education laws. But the Supreme Court upheld their view in 1972.

> We must not forget that in the Middle Ages important values of the civilization were preserved by members of religious orders who isolated themselves from all worldly influences against great obstacles. There can be no assumption that today's majority is 'right' and that the Amish and others like them are 'wrong.' A way of life that is odd or erratic but interferes with no rights or interests of others is not to be condemned because it is different.

Unlike most colonial ethnics, the Scotch-Irish took an early interest in higher education. Their Calvinist religion had developed a strongly disciplined intellectual tradition. Scotch-Irish ministers were scholars themselves and established schools to train their successors. The earliest was the Log College at Neshaminy, Pennsylvania, a crude cabin in which William Tennent, a graduate of the University of Edinburgh, educated his own sons and other future ministers in Latin, Greek, and Hebrew. Scotch-Irish ministers gave religious instruction to the elders of their congregations who, in turn, transmitted a sophisticated understanding of Calvinist theology to the average layman. The church that asked its clergy and elders to be well-grounded in ancient history, philosophy, and languages had a Scotch-Irish flavor, but the classical education it fostered did not. Thus while the Scotch-Irish established many schools, from one-room log huts to Princeton University, their schools did not reinforce a distinctive Scotch-Irish ethnicity.

Conclusion: On the Eve of the Revolution

Historians of the various ethnic communities have chronicled the "contributions" to colonial America made by individuals of their respective groups. There were many such individuals, of course, ranging from little known musicians, craftsmen, and physicians to better known figures such as Peter Zenger, the German-American journalist who helped to establish the principle of freedom of the press and Paul Revere, of French Huguenot origins. The idea that ethnic colonists made "contributions" to American life is misleading, however, because it implies that ethnic colonists were somehow separate from and outside colonial American life. Actually they were an integral part of every aspect of that life. In the cities and on the farms, along the seaboard or on the frontier, in schools, churches, and synagogues, in agriculture, commerce, or the beginnings of industry, ethnic Americans, along with their English-American counterparts, were building a new society.

By the outbreak of the Revolution, many ethnic individuals and communities, such as the Swedes and the Scotch-Irish, had become indistinguishable in language and life style from the dominant English majority. Others—including some Jews, some French Huguenots, many Dutch, and many more Germans, had not. Many factors influenced the survival of colonial ethnic groups as recognizable social and cultural entities—numbers, density of settlement, patterns of family life, degree of difference from the majority community, and strength of ethnic institutions such as the church, the school, and the press.

An additional variable, intangible but important, was the degree of commitment each group had to the perpetuation of its ethnicity. The Scotch-Irish appeared to have little. They did not experience the anguish of loss of a cherished mother tongue, for example, and their desire to seek new economic opportunities on the frontier was often stronger than their desire to build the settled group life that perpetuates ethnicity. The Germans, on the other hand, were determined to maintain their "German-ness," probably because it was closely linked to deeply felt values of religious faith and family life.

Even among the Germans, however, colonial ethnicity was cultural, not political. The German states had not yet been unified into a single nation, and German immigrants took little interest in the political affairs of the provinces that had been their homelands. "Our fathers lived under an Arbitrary Prince in Germany, a European Egypt," stated a German petition, "from whence they ventured to an American Canaan." The German-speaking residents of this new Canaan had strong attachments to the German language, religion, and life style, but none at all to the political interests of their "European Egypt."

Finally, the fate of colonial ethnic communities was influenced by the life around them. Even the most isolated communities felt the impact of the majority English society and of British political control. We have focused on the internal development of ethnic communities. But the development of ethnic communities was never purely an internal matter, as the episode of the English charity schools for German children suggests. The outside world did intrude. In the next chapter we will explore the interaction between colonial ethnic communities and the outside world.

CHAPTER 3

Interaction:
The Ethnics and the English to 1800

While ethnic minorities were adjusting to life in English America, the English-speaking majority was adjusting to them. They wondered whether they should keep the "aliens" out altogether, accept them with reservations, or actively recruit them? Should the British authorities grant the outsiders civil and economic rights? If so, to what extent, and how soon?

The English colonists and their governments faced these questions throughout the seventeenth and eighteenth centuries. Their answers varied from colony to colony and from year to year, depending upon circumstances and the persons involved. By the end of the colonial period definite attitudes and policies had emerged. Despite many prejudices against those who were different, the English community in America eventually decided, largely for economic reasons, that ethnic minorities should be accepted and even actively recruited. After the Revolution, the new United States government continued this hospitable policy for at least a century.

Prejudice and Discrimination

Europeans of the seventeenth and eighteenth centuries were far from tolerant. Commercial and political rivalries in Europe created animosity among the English, the French, the Spanish, and the Dutch in the New World as well as the Old. Religious hatreds stemming from the Protestant Reformation and the religious wars that followed were fresh and very bitter. Moreover, in an era of primitive transportation and communication, many people were hostile to anyone farther away than the neighboring village!

These fears and hates and suspicions came over as invisible baggage when European colonists began to settle the New World. The first impulse of the founders of each colonial empire was to keep the dangerous outsider away. The Spanish, for example, their own homeland only recently unified under the banner of militant Roman Catholicism, were most intent upon enforcing religious unity. The Inquisition followed the Spanish empire builders as far north as Mexico, effectively preventing settlement by Protestants. Spanish Jews fled to British possessions or practiced their religion underground. As late as the 1830's "Anglos" from the United States could become property owners in California or Texas only if they converted to Roman Catholicism.

The seventeenth century English, like the Spanish, tried to exclude religious nonconformists. The predominantly Puritan New England colonies outlawed Quakers, who were whipped and banished when they ventured within reach. Practically every English colony had laws to discourage the immigration of Catholics. Special duties on the importation of Irish servants, prohibition of public Catholic worship, and double taxation on the property of Catholic landowners are examples of such legislation. Jews seemed less threatening than Catholics, perhaps because there were so few of them. Moreover, English colonists associated Catholicism with France and Spain, their rivals for trade and territory in the New World. Still, Jews were also subject to political restrictions; indeed, Jews did not get full civil rights in North Carolina and New Hampshire until after the Civil War.

The restrictions on Quakers, Catholics, and Jews were religious in motivation, but ethnic prejudices were also evident in the English colonies. Ethnic prejudice clearly influenced the experiences of the French Huguenots, Protestant refugees from Louis XIV's France. When the British authorities gave these industrious people permission to settle in Virginia, the English colonists demanded that they be sent away. In the reputedly tolerant colony of Rhode Island, angry mobs attacked and destroyed a French Huguenot settlement forcing the inhabitants to flee to Boston. As these French Huguenots discovered, English colonists hated Frenchmen, Catholic and Protestant.

Economic factors also influenced English feeling and policy toward outsiders. In the early years, each colony lived at a near subsistence level. Any extra expense was to be avoided. Thus the authorities of Massachusetts objected to the landing of a group of Scotch-Irish in the early eighteenth century because of a shortage of provisions in the colony. The Pennsylvania colonial assembly was reluctant to appropriate funds for a "pesthouse" for sick immigrants, most of whom were German, because of the added tax burden. An English Calvinist mob destroyed a Scotch-Irish Calvinist church in Massachusetts to avoid paying taxes for the support of another church in their town!

Ethnic stereotypes were common among the English colonists. According to the *Pennsylvania Gazette* in 1729, "poverty, wretchedness, misery, and want are almost universal" among the Scotch-Irish. Worse yet, the Scotch-Irish were considered disorderly, intemperate, and ungovernable—"a pernicious and pugnacious people." The Germans, largely because of the language barrier, were considered stupid and uncultured. George Washington expressed the ethnocentricity of many English settlers when he said of the Germans in 1748, "I really think they seem to be as ignorant a set of people as the Indians. They would never speak English, but when spoken to they speak all Dutch."

Many English worried about the large concentrations of Germans. "May they not in time throw off their obedience to the British crown?" asked Benjamin Franklin, suggesting as a solution that they be scattered among the English and given English schoolmasters. The widespread prejudice against Germans was fed by two fears (neither grounded in reality)—that Germans would be disloyal in time of war with France, and that German culture would inundate and destroy "English culture."

Despite these fears and prejudices, the English attitude toward ethnic minorities grew increasingly liberal as the seventeenth century passed into the eighteenth. If fear and prejudice tended toward exclusionist policies in the colonies, economic needs pushed in the opposite direction. In an era of increasingly fierce international rivalry, European rulers were eager to use every possible source of wealth to finance their armies and navies. Colonies were a source of enormous wealth, but only if there was enough manpower to develop this wealth. The English colonies could be valuable to the mother country as suppliers of tobacco, sugar, indigo, rice, timber, and naval stores only if an adequate labor supply could be obtained.

It was so difficult to get this badly needed labor that the British government sent over tens of thousands of prisoners, people convicted of anything from vagrancy or debt to armed robbery or murder. Understandably, the overpopulated British Isles were glad to see such people go. Understandably, too, the American colonists were unhappy to see them arrive. "Our Mother (Great Britain) knows what is best for us," sarcastically noted the *Pennsylvania Gazette* in 1751. "What is a little House-breaking, Shop-lifting, or Highway-robbing; what is a son now and then corrupted and hanged, a Daughter debauched and Pox'd, a wife stabbed, a Husband's throat cut, or a child's brains beat out with an Axe, compared with this Improvement and Well peopling of the Colonies!"

Given the severity of the labor shortage, the ethnicity of a prospective immigrant seemed insignificant as long as that immigrant could work. William Penn actively recruited settlers from Germany in the late seventeenth century, and Queen Anne financed the immigration of thousands of Germans from the Rhineland in the early eighteenth century. Colonial landowners sometimes sent agents to Europe to recruit whatever labor they could, and ship captains filled their vessels with kidnapped victims when willing immigrants were not available. By 1660 Negro slavery had become institutionalized throughout the English colonies, but even the ever increasing importation of Africans failed to meet the insatiable demand for labor.

By 1700 the predominantly English settlers of the middle and southern colonies recognized the economic value of attracting non-English settlers. Within a few decades the less hospitable settlers of New England, outdistanced by the more rapid growth of the other colonies, did likewise.

Debates in the eighteenth century Pennsylvania legislature provide an excellent example of the conflicting and gradually liberalizing attitude of the English population toward non-English immigrants. Time and again legislation was proposed to cut off German immigration altogether. This restrictive legislation was always defeated, however, on the basis of the economic self-interest of the colony itself. In 1738 the lieutenant governor reminded the legislators that

> The present flourishing condition of it (Pennsylvania) is in a great measure owing to the industry of those people (the Germans); and should any discouragement direct them from coming hither, it may well be apprehended that the value of your lands will fall and your advance to wealth be much slower.

Ethnic immigrants did provide badly needed labor and, by their presence, did raise the value of the lands owned by the older, established colonists. Also, by settling along the frontier, they shielded the East from Indian attack. Thus, there were many reasons to encourage their coming. Recognizing this, the Pennsylvania legislators abandoned their policy of trying to restrict immigration and began to pass legislation to help immigrants. In 1742 the colony bought a 342 acre site for a "pesthouse" for the care of sick immigrants. Pressured by the *Deutsche Gesellschaft fur Pennsylvanien*, a German-American charitable society, Pennsylvania passed additional laws for the benefit of immigrants. Ship captains were directed to provide medical care, sanitary quarters, and a minimum of space for each passenger, "no more than two passengers in one bed unless parents want children with them." Immigrants were not to be separated from their baggage, an entire shipload was not to be held responsible for the profits of the captain, and, in case of disputes, new immigrants were to have the right to appeal to Pennsylvania courts.

Colony after colony passed similar regulations to protect non-English immigrants and to lure them not only from Europe, but also from their sister colonies. Pennsylvania and Maryland offered the inducement of religious toleration. Many colonies offered tax benefits, even bounties. The most powerful attraction of all, of course, was the offer of cheap land. Ownership of land in colonial America ensured economic independence. It was also the key to social respectability and, if the holding was large enough, to political enfranchisement. Property owners, whatever language they spoke, were eligible to vote. Easy access to land attracted new settlers of every ethnic background.

Laws of naturalization—or denization, as it was called at the time—varied from colony to colony, but the tendency was to make them increasingly liberal. A period of residence in the colony, from a few months to a few years, and an oath of allegiance to the English crown were all that was required. Often groups of non-English immigrants were given papers of denization, even before they embarked for the colonies. They were citizens upon their arrival. The ease with which they could become naturalized undoubtedly attracted many non-English settlers to the English colonies.

Population increase meant growth and prosperity. British authorities had recognized this even earlier than the colonists by encouraging settlement by ethnic minorities in the seventeenth and early eighteenth centuries, often in the face of local prejudice and opposition. The Stamp Act crisis and other acts of colonial insubordination in the mid-eighteenth century caused the British authorities to reverse their position. After 1764 royal governors were instructed to grant no new lands to settlers, to prevent settlers from buying Indian lands, and to refuse permission for all land surveying. All naturalization of aliens was forbidden. In 1774 Parliament stated that "the great increase of people in said colonies has an immediate tendency to produce independency," and levied a tax of fifty pounds on each person leaving England or Ireland for America. Parliament was afraid that the colonies, growing more populous and prosperous all the time, would be increasingly hard to control.

This last minute effort on the part of Great Britain to slow down the peopling of the colonies was too late. The vast migration of Germans had already taken place. The Scotch-Irish had already come, bringing with them their anti-British bias which, as Parliament recognized, did indeed contribute to the growth of the independence movement in the colonies.

By 1775 immigration had become one of the many issues over which the colonies and the mother country disagreed. Britain hoped to limit immigration and curtail westward expansion, both to make the colonies more easily governable and to avoid trouble with the Indians west of the Alleghenies. But by now immigration was so strongly identified in the colonists' mind with continued growth and prosperity that any effort to obstruct it was intolerable. Indeed, the new British policy was denounced by Jefferson in the Declaration of Independence as one of the reasons for dissolving the political bond with King George III.

The variety of languages, religions, and nationalities present in colonial America has had an enormous impact upon our subsequent history. The only possible way in which English, Dutch, Swiss, Germans, Swedes, Finns, Poles, Italians, Jews, Welsh, Irish, Scotch-Irish, and others belonging to an even longer list of churches and sects could survive in the same land was by developing a policy of "live and let live." There was prejudice, and political and economic advancement often depended upon a mastery of the English language and conformity to English ways. Still, the labor shortage of the colonies coupled with the great diversity of the population made a degree of tolerance a practical necessity. This tolerance was not extended to nonwhites—Indians and blacks were not embraced by it. Still, limited as it was, it was the beginning of an ideal powerful enough to make at least some Americans of every generation uncomfortable in its breach.

Common Experiences: The Great Awakening

Throughout the eighteenth century a series of common experiences drew many members of minority communities into increasing interaction with English America. The first of these experiences was the Great Awakening. The Great Awakening was a wave of emotional religious revivalism that swept through the English colonies in the first half of the eighteenth century.

The Great Awakening brought emotion and drama to American religion which had become too dry and intellectualized for many Americans. It offered the hope of heaven for all, not just for the chosen few who, according to orthodox Calvinist doctrine, were predestined for salvation. Traditional ministers were shocked by its methods and its content. By the 1740's the Great Awakening had caused many conflicts between its opponents, who were called the Old Light clergy, and its advocates, the New Light clergy.

As the Great Awakening reached out to people on the frontier and in the towns and villages throughout the colonies, the New Light preachers attracted many ethnic Americans. Some were convinced by these dramatic new ministers to abandon their ethnic religious affiliations—if, indeed, they had any—in favor of English-speaking evangelistic denominations such as the Baptists, the Methodists, and the New Light Presbyterians. Henry Crum, a German-American, left us a description of his conversion at a Methodist camp meeting:

> I prayed in Dutch (*Deutsch*, or German). I am Dutch and must get converted in Dutch . . . . These are all English people, and they get

converted in English. I prayed and prayed in Dutch, but could not get the blessing. At last I felt willing to get converted in English, as the Lord pleased. Then the blessing came, and I got converted in English.

Crum became a Methodist minister and spent many months traveling along the frontier to bring the message of salvation to others. Because frontier life was lonely, revivals attracted Americans of every ethnic background, people in search of human sociability as well as divine forgiveness. Crum's experience was not unique. Other ethnic Americans too moved into the majority community through the gates of the English churches, because, like Crum, they were influenced by the traveling evangelists of the Great Awakening.

Common Experiences: Politics

Politics was even more influential than religion in bringing eighteenth century ethnic Americans into the current of English American life. Prominent Dutch families who had been influential in the government of New Netherland continued to play an important role in the public life of New York. Jews were few in number and in many colonies were barred from holding office; hence they were not important politically. By the mid-eighteenth century, French Huguenots, Welsh, Swedes, and other Protestant ethnic groups who were well assimilated in other ways were also well assimilated politically. Individuals of French Huguenot background in particular played important roles in colonial political life.

The colonial Germans had a tradition of noninvolvement in public affairs. Many of the sectarian communities regarded all governments as instruments of the devil, institutions with which good Christians should have nothing to do. Bad experiences with government in the homeland had influenced many of their countrymen to adopt a similar attitude. The Germans of Pennsylvania were so hostile to participation in government that they were often fined in order to force them to serve as magistrates in their own communities. By the eighteenth century, however, even the Germans had begun to move in the direction of greater involvement in the public life of the colonies.

There were concrete reasons for this increasing involvement. German colonists, especially those on the frontier, found that they had needs which only government could satisfy—a new bridge, a new road, a fort for better protection, a court to enforce justice. Ethnic Americans joined their English neighbors to petition for these and similar improvements. Soon a sprinkling of ethnics, including the initially reluctant Germans, were seeking and holding local political positions. In sparsely populated areas of eighteenth century Virginia, German-speaking Lutherans served as officers of the parishes that constituted the units of local government.

Leaders emerged within the ethnic communities to help mold the political opinions and actions of their groups. Such a leader was Christopher Sauer, the German editor previously mentioned as the leader of opposition to the English charity schools. Sauer used his newspaper and his considerable personal influence to promote a political alliance between the Germans and the Quakers in Pennsylvania, an alliance which voted against the plans of the English proprietary government. In 1754 this alliance defeated Benjamin Franklin's famous Albany Plan for a unified colonial defense against the French and their Indian allies. Sauer convinced the frugal, peace-loving German farmers that the Albany Plan would crush them with taxes and make soldiers of their sons. German participation in politics remained slight as late as the middle of the eighteenth century, but, as the episode of the Albany Plan indicates, Germans could be stirred to political action when they believed their own interests to be at stake.

Unhampered by language barriers and by either fear of or deference to the existing authorities, the Scotch-Irish had a far greater impact on colonial politics. From their arrival, they plunged into public life to agitate two major issues—the question of military action against the Indians along the frontier and the relationship of the undeveloped West to the more established East.

It is surprising that the Scotch-Irish, with their insatiable land hunger and their tradition of frequent moves, did not come into conflict with the Indian population sooner. The absence of a large Indian population near the Virginia frontier and the tradition of fair dealings with the Indians followed by the Quakers and the Germans of Pennsylvania postponed the conflict in these areas. Eventually, however, the expansion of white settlement made the Indians realize that their way of life was endangered. They determined to resist.

By midcentury relations between Indians and whites along the Pennsylvania and Virginia frontier had degenerated into a series of raids and counterraids, atrocities and counteratrocities. The pacifistic German settlers often returned eastward rather than fight, but the Scotch-Irish remained to do battle. In their zeal they sometimes made no distinction between peaceful Indians and hostile ones, and they did not hesitate to move into the lands vacated by the Indians they had killed. From the vantage point of the twentieth century, the Scotch-Irish appear clearly as the aggressors, as it was they who were displacing the native inhabitants. Even their contemporaries condemned their brutality and their insensitivity to the rights of the Indians. As the historian James Leyburn pointed out, however, the Scotch-Irish pioneer had made a home in what, to him, had been wilderness and empty land, and "he had no intention of retiring supinely from what he had created with his own toil."

The Scotch-Irish population of Pennsylvania agitated constantly for military action against the Indians. They were instrumental in pressuring the governor and the council to declare war against them in 1754. Even after the French and Indian War, the pressure was maintained. In 1763 a group of five hundred frontiersmen, mostly Scotch-Irish, went to Philadelphia to demand continued protection from the Indians.

The Scotch-Irish who went to Philadelphia in 1763 had other grievances as well. They saw the failure of the colonial government to protect them from the Indians as part of the larger problem of western lack of influence in the eastern-dominated political structure. The Scotch-Irish of western Pennsylvania were angered by the unequal representation in the colonial government that made their interests secondary to those of the Philadelphia merchant gentry.

A similar situation existed in North and South Carolina, where the English tidewater planters looked down upon the Scotch-Irish frontier farmers. The Scotch-Irish of North Carolina protested against the abuse of eastern government power—disproportionate taxes, dishonest judges and lawyers, lack of paper currency, quitrents, abuse of land laws, and religious intolerance. The Regulators, as these protesters were called, caused so much disorder that Governor Tryon sent troops to defeat them in a pitched battle in 1771. Five Regulator leaders were hanged, and hundreds fled to new settlements in what would later be Tennessee. The remaining North Carolina Regulators were pardoned after taking a special oath of loyalty to the Crown.

In South Carolina the eastern authorities showed their indifference to the needs of the Scotch-Irish and other frontier people by refusing to provide them with courts, judges, or any local government whatsoever. In the resulting legal vacuum, gangs of outlaws terrorized the countryside. After petitioning in vain for help from the East, the Regulators formed vigilante groups that killed suspected outlaw leaders and burned their homes. In South Carolina the Regulators were more successful than they had been in North Carolina. In 1772 the Assembly finally agreed to bring local government with the long desired law courts to the troubled areas.

The French and Indian War

The French and Indian War drew ethnic Americans into the life of the general community from New England to Georgia. The war, which had long been brewing, was the great watershed for ethnic, particularly German, participation in American civic and political life. The Scotch-Irish, as has already been noted, were in favor of the war even before it began, as a move against the Indians. The Germans, on the other hand, were indifferent or even opposed. The pacifist sects refused to become involved in violence on religious grounds. Having always gotten along well with the Indians themselves, the Germans considered talk of Indian warfare an exaggeration. Indeed British authorities in the early stages of the war suspected the frontier Germans of being secretly allied with France because of their unusually peaceful relations with the Indians. The staunchly Protestant Moravians were suspected of being French Jesuit spies because of their robes, their crucifixes, and their concern with missions to the red men. The German community repeatedly voted against military appropriations.

When war came, Benjamin Franklin threatened and bribed indifferent German farmers into driving the supply wagons for General Braddock's disastrous march against Fort Duquesne in the summer of 1755. When Braddock's defeat seemed imminent, the German drivers headed their wagons for home as fast as they could. Later, much to Franklin's disgust, they not only demanded payment for their services but even pressed claims for damage to their crops caused by the fleeing British soldiers!

Braddock's defeat at Fort Duquesne in 1755 opened the entire frontier from New York to the Carolinas to a devastating series of Indian attacks. The Scotch-Irish and the Germans, living as they did in the western regions, bore the brunt of these attacks. The frontier settlements were devastated. Thousands fled their homes. Hundreds were killed or taken captive. Even the resolutely pacifistic Moravians were not spared; their missionary settlement at Gnadenhutten was attacked and destroyed.

Now for the first time the frontier Germans joined the Scotch-Irish and the English authorities in large-scale efforts to defend their homes. The Pennsylvania German press and clergy urged German-speaking communities from Massachusetts to Georgia to join the common cause. Many knew from their own tragic experience or that of relatives or friends how necessary such action was. Germans and other ethnic Americans flocked to the militia of every colony. The pacifistic sectarians supplied food and money and cared for the wounded. By the end of the war, German participation was active enough to assure even Benjamin Franklin, formerly their severest critic, of their loyalty and patriotism.

The impact of the French and Indian War upon the German community was enormous. For many German-Americans the war was their first close and sustained contact with their non-German countrymen. After the war the use of the English language, English dress, even English manners noticeably increased in areas of German settlement. Participation in colonial politics increased too. For the first time, Germans began to protest the necessity of paying taxes to support the established Anglican church in Virginia. When Indian problems reappeared with Pontiac's Rebellion many Germans joined the Scotch-Irish "Paxton Boys" march on Philadelphia to demand—and to get—better protection.

The French and Indian War created new traditions and new memories to bind ethnic Americans more closely to their new environment. After the war settlers taken captive by the Indians began to drift home. Their harrowing tales of life behind the enemy lines were told and retold around firesides for many years to come. A historian of the German community of Virginia suggests the cultural significance of these stories:

> Thus people who had come to Virginia from far-off lands, after enduring the pains and suffering the destructions, became attached to the soil they had chosen. The legends of the Black Forest and the Alps faded out of their memory. The tales of death on the New River and in Narrow Passage Creek now were their own legends in which the names of heroes and victims had a familiar ring.

The Revolution

The most far-reaching experience which the eighteenth century ethnic communities shared with their fellow Americans was, of course, the American Revolution. In the decade following the French and Indian War the increasing tension between the colonies and Great Britain was felt even in the most isolated ethnic enclaves. After the fighting began ethnic Americans, like other Americans, were forced to take sides. Some ethnic historians have emphasized the patriots within their respective groups, creating the false impression that each ethnic community was practically unanimous in its support of American independence. Actually ethnic Americans, like other Americans, were reluctant to sever their ties with Great Britain, ties which had been beneficial in many ways.

Each ethnic group produced its Tories as well as its Whigs. Many Scots fled to Canada, preferring the known prosperity of trade within the British Empire to an unknown economic future outside it. German sectarians had a double reason to hesitate before embracing the rebel cause; as pacifists they dreaded the bloodshed that revolution would bring, and as unpopular minorities they appreciated the tolerance and protection they had known under British authority. Would a new regime treat them as well?

Even the Scotch-Irish, who had ample cause to hate the British, were not unanimous in their support of independence. The upcountry Regulators of North Carolina had only recently sworn an oath of allegiance to the Crown, an oath which some were reluctant to break so soon. More important, the Scotch-Irish farmers of the Carolina Regulation were in no hurry to support the revolutionary cause of the tidewater planters who, to their way of thinking, were a closer and thus more dangerous foe than the British.

Even allowing for these exceptions, ethnic Americans supported the Revolution as enthusiastically as most other Americans. About a third of all colonial Americans were Whigs, another third were Tories, and the final third were ill-informed, indifferent, or undecided. Tory sentiment was strongest among office holders and others whose jobs depended upon British authority, and among the clergy and devout members of the Church of England. Few ethnic Americans were to be found in these categories. Having already rejected their original mother country in the act of immigration, ethnic Americans probably found it less difficult than their English countrymen to sever their ties with the Crown and the British Empire.

"Call this war by whatever name you may," wrote a Hessian captain in 1778, "only call it not an American rebellion; it is nothing more or less than a Scotch-Irish Presbyterian Rebellion." Many contemporary observers agreed that the Scotch-Irish were an important factor in the revolutionary equation. Horace Walpole is supposed to have remarked in Parliament, "There is no use crying about it. Cousin America has run off with a Presbyterian parson, and that is the end of it."

Undoubtedly many of the Scotch-Irish did seize the occasion to settle old scores with England. Some historians have claimed that Presbyterianism itself contained the ideals of self-government and resistance to authority. But the Scotch-Irish, like other Americans who supported the Revolution, were probably responding to immediate political and economic grievances rather than to elements within their national or religious background. Whatever the reason, the Scotch-Irish of Pennsylvania and Virginia were virtually unanimous in their support of the Revolution. Scotch-Irish soldiers constituted a large proportion of the Continental army, remaining loyally at Washington's side without pay during the gloomy winter at Valley Forge.

With a few exceptions, the Germans were also committed to the revolutionary cause. Franklin testified to an English investigating committee that the Pennsylvania Germans were even more strongly opposed to the Stamp Act than were their non-German neighbors. In 1772 leaders of the German community organized the "Patriotic Society of the City and County of Philadelphia" to prepare for the struggle ahead. A German Correspondence Committee set up in Pennsylvania in 1774 sent out a flood of letters and pamphlets to the German communities of other colonies, urging them to stand firm against the British. The same German farmers who could scarcely be persuaded to sell supplies to the British troops at the outbreak of the French and Indian War now filled their Conestoga wagons to overflowing with food for Boston when the Intolerable Acts closed the

Boston harbor. Throughout the war, the rich German farms of Pennsylvania and the Shenandoah Valley were the breadbasket of the colonial army.

Among the Germans as among the Scotch-Irish, religious leaders helped rally their congregations to the war effort. Reverend Peter Muhlenberg gave his last sermon in January 1776 and then, dramatically revealing a military uniform beneath his clerical garb, led the mustering of three hundred troops just outside the church. Despite their initial hesitation, most of the German sectarians eventually joined the Lutherans and Reformed in support of independence. Mennonites, Dunkers, Schwenkers, and Moravians furnished supplies and cared for the sick and wounded. The Moravians of North Carolina voted to pay triple taxes in lieu of military service. Most sectarian communities clung to their pacifism, however, causing serious conflicts for eager young patriots. Young men who enlisted were expelled from their church communities, a shattering experience for them, their families, and indeed, for the close-knit communities themselves.

The wartime emergency drew even the more isolated elements of the colonial population out of their accustomed orbits and threw them into the life of the wider community. Ethnic Americans served on a variety of local committees of safety and correspondence and participated in local political conventions. Even when these patriotic groups were organized within the ethnic community, their members soon found themselves cooperating or even merging with similar nonethnic organizations. Individual ethnic communities often recruited their own regiments and companies and served under their own officers. The fortunes of war soon mixed them with other ethnic groups and with their fellow Americans of English background. Differences within the colonial forces seemed less significant than the fact that they were united against a common enemy. Common hardships, common dangers, and a common victory did much to break down old barriers and suspicions and to hasten the acculturation of the minorities.

After the successful conclusion of the war a wave of patriotic pride swept over the new nation. Former Tories, who had not already fled to Canada or England left the country, were discreetly silent, or suddenly discovered that they had been in favor of independence all the time. Patriotic painters, sculptors, and writers glorified the new national heroes. The Fourth of July became the national holiday, and George Washington was canonized by his biographers and by a grateful people as the national saint. Noah Webster produced a new American spelling book to legitimize American spelling habits. Even language had to declare its independence of Old World ties.

Ethnic Americans joined their neighbors in celebrating the new national spirit and breaking their Old World ties. Old World mother tongues were the most obvious casualties. Languages already well on their way to extinction before the Revolution now vanished altogether. The use of Dutch and German in the cities declined sharply and even in rural areas began to give way to English. The German press reflected the trend. Before the Revolution New York, Philadelphia, and Baltimore had each supported two or three German newspapers, but in 1815 these cities could not boast of even one among them. The German language and German schools survived mainly in the small towns and rural communities of Pennsylvania and Virginia.

Ethnic Americans declared their religious as well as their linguistic independence from Europe. The gradual replacement of the ethnic language by English in the church services was given a definite boost by the patriotic fervor of the post Revolutionary years. In all ethnic churches local governing bodies were substituted for authority from across the sea. The Dutch Reformed churches now insisted that ministers ordained in Europe be approved by the new American governing bodies before being allowed to preach in American pulpits. Even the conservative German Lutheran Ministerium of Pennsylvania demanded a three year probationary period in America for German ministers from overseas.

Before the Revolution some ethnic Americans had begun to object to paying taxes for the support of the established church, usually the Church of England. Now, after fighting a war in which the slogan "no taxation without representation" figured prominently, they objected even more strongly. Ethnic minorities in Virginia joined the Baptists to campaign for complete separation of church and state. Jefferson and Madison spearheaded the successful drive and in so doing won the lasting support of many ethnic Americans in Virginia and elsewhere. Similarly, Benjamin Franklin won the gratitude of the sectarian Germans, his old enemies, when in 1785 he led the successful effort to eliminate the "Test Act" requiring certain religious oaths as prerequisites for the holding of office in Pennsylvania.

The loosening of religious restrictions after the Revolution made it easier for ethnic Americans to aspire to political careers. The military and political experience gained during the revolutionary period encouraged at least a few to move from leadership in their local communities to political activity on the national level. Michael Hillegas, a Pennsylvania German leader who served as treasurer for the Continental Congress, was elected to the United States Congress in 1789. A French Huguenot, James Bowdoin, president of the Massachusetts Constitutional Convention during the Revolution became governor of Massachusetts in the postwar years.

Ethnic communities as a whole maintained a much higher level of interest in politics than they had before the Revolution. Recognizing this, office seekers made special efforts to win the ethnic vote. One politician in Virginia even learned German to ingratiate himself with the German-American voters, most of whom were quite fluent in English. Robert Morris, Benjamin Rush, Benjamin Franklin, and other Pennsylvania politicians rallied German support for a revision of the Articles of Confederation by backing the establishment of the German-sponsored Franklin College. Franklin College itself was a testimonial to the growing political consciousness of the German community. In addition to training American born ministers, it had the specific mission of instructing German youth "in such languages and sciences as to qualify them in the future to fill public offices in the Republic."

The American Revolution also speeded up the acculturation of ethnic Americans by encouraging the breakup of ethnic enclaves. Mennonites and Dunkers left Pennsylvania for Virginia and elsewhere after the war, partly because of the pressure of natural population growth, and partly because their pacifism had made them unpopular among their militantly patriotic neighbors. Western lands given to American soldiers in lieu of cash stimulated many ethnic families to leave their old communities. Some headed for the frontier, away from their countrymen, where it was easier for them to become assimilated.

Immigration and the New Republic

An important factor in the increasing Americanization of ethnic communities was the slowing down of immigration between 1776 and 1815. The Old World languages and traditions were no longer reinforced by new arrivals from Europe. The unsettled conditions of the United States during and after the American Revolution, followed by the disruptive events of the French Revolution and the Napoleonic Wars, cut European immigration to a small fraction of what it had been earlier. Americans still wanted Europeans to come because labor was still in great demand. But immigration dwindled because European countries wanted to keep skilled laborers and young men of military age at home. In 1788 Britain forbade the emigration of artisans from Ireland as well as England, and in 1803 Britain sharply curtailed the number of passengers an immigrant ship could carry—two actions which effectively killed the trade in indentured servants from the British Isles.

After the Napoleonic Wars the German indentured servant trade revived, but only briefly. An epidemic aboard an overcrowded ship resulted in the restrictive Congressional Passenger Act of 1819. Although the Passenger Act was an attempt to protect the health and safety of the immigrants rather than to prevent their coming, its effect, like that of the earlier British laws, was to make traffic in indentured servants unprofitable.

Despite the political turmoil in Europe and America and the gradual disappearance of the indenture trade, there were significant, though numerically small, additions to the ethnic communities between 1776 and 1820. Thousands of German mercenaries, mainly Hessians, had been hired by the British during the Revolution. Christopher Ludwig, the Pennsylvanian German patriot who baked bread for Washington's army, suggested that captured Hessians be taken to Philadelphia, "Show them our beautiful German churches, let them taste our roast beef and homes. . . . You will see how many will come over to us." Ludwig conducted a group of captured Hessians on a personal tour of Lancaster county, and his tactic was amazingly successful. Many Hessians did come over to the American cause, and at least five thousand stayed after the war, settling permanently among the German communities of Pennsylvania and Virginia.

A second immigrant group, smaller but economically more significant, were the skilled artisans from Scotland, Ireland, and England who left for America regardless of governmental regulations aimed at preventing their emigration. Hoping to establish manufacturing in the United States, Secretary of the Treasury Alexander Hamilton launched a deliberate effort to attract such men. Even Washington participated until 1791, when he decided that "it would not carry an aspect favorable to the dignity of the United States for the President in clandestine manner to entice the subjects of another nation to violate its laws." Much of the technology of the fledgling New England mills came to America with these illegal immigrants from the British Isles, immigrants who blended almost immediately into the native-born population.

Some immigrants came as refugees from political and social upheavals. About twenty-five thousand French-speaking immigrants came to the United States during the 1790's. Exiles from all parts of the political spectrum fled their homeland during the French Revolution. The largest number of French-speaking immigrants, however, came from the French islands in the Caribbean rather than from France. Slave uprisings there caused an exodus of virtually the entire white population. American public opinion was warmly sympathetic to these refugees, perhaps a reflection of insecurity about America's slave population. Private individuals launched fund-raising campaigns for these Caribbean French, and in 1794 Congress appropriated $15,000 for their relief.

Some of the French refugees moved to New Orleans and St. Louis, where they became valuable additions to the older French communities already there. (They became part of the United States with the Louisiana Purchase of 1803.) Most, however, settled in the eastern seaboard cities of Charleston, Baltimore, Philadelphia, and New York. A general enthusiasm for French culture swept across the United States in the 1780's and 1790's, largely because of the friendship and invaluable aid the French government had provided during the American Revolution. Taking advantage of this enthusiasm, French immigrants became teachers of etiquette and dancing, fencing masters, wigmakers, and managers of elegant restaurants and boarding houses.

The most aristocratic "émigrés" produced a lively though short-lived adaptation of French court life—a miniature Versailles—in Philadelphia. Louis Philippe, later to become king of France, held court on Fifth Street. He was attended, among others, by the wily diplomat Talleyrand and the great epicure Brillat-Savarin, who did what he could to improve the quality of American cuisine. The French impact was as brief as it was colorful. When the conservative Directory came into power in France in 1798, many of the political refugees returned to their native land. Those who remained were rapidly assimilated.

Like the French, the Irish who came at the end of the eighteenth century were political refugees. In 1798 a major rebellion against British rule broke out in Ireland. The rebellion failed, and thousands of disappointed Irish patriots came to the United States. Rufus King, the American minister in London, protested that the United States wanted no more "wild Irish," a protest that, published in the Irish-American press, may have cost him the governorship of New York in 1816. Despite the opposition of King the "wild Irish" continued to come. By 1815 there were Irish fraternal lodges and Irish newspapers in all the major cities.

The first official policy of the United States on the naturalization of foreigners was generous: citizenship, with voting rights, could be obtained after only two years in the country. But as French and Irish immigrants began to cluster in urban communities, and to become increasingly vocal in the press and in the political arena, native-born leaders became apprehensive. In 1795 Congress revised the naturalization laws, lengthening the period of residency to five years.

A few years later President John Adams' administration introduced a bill to increase the residency requirement for citizenship from five to fourteen years. Although this bill was not passed, Congress did pass the Alien and Sedition Acts of 1798. The Alien Act, which was never used, gave the President the power to deport "dangerous" aliens at his discretion. The Sedition Act provided for the fining and imprisonment of persons criticizing the government. Among those arrested under its provisions were two foreign-born newspaper editors, William Duane of the Philadelphia *Aurora* and John Daly Burk, of the New York *Time Piece*.

The new Irish and French immigrants had become pawns in the political battle between the two American political parties—the Federalists, whose leader was President John Adams, and their Republican opponents, whose leader, Thomas Jefferson, was gaining adherents among the small farmers and the Irish and French. The Federalists were frightened by what they considered to be the excesses of the French Revolution, a revolution with which Jefferson and his followers sympathized. The Federalists were even more frightened by the prospect of losing office. Legislative measures against the foreign-born were a symptom of political panic on the part of the faltering Federalists, an attempt to silence the pro-Jefferson French and Irish.

The Alien and Sedition Acts may have temporarily stifled some attacks on the Federalist administration. In the long run, however, they rallied the new ethnic communities, and most other Americans, to the Jeffersonian cause. The French and Irish vote in New York City carried the state for Jefferson in the closely contested election of 1800. The episode is significant because it was the first, but not the last, case in which the foreign-born would become victims of domestic controversy.

American policy toward non-English immigrants at the opening of the nineteenth century was ambivalent. The Alien and Sedition Acts were repealed, and immigrants were welcomed as needed additions to the labor force, but there remained an undercurrent of fear and suspicion. Immigrants were welcomed, but with the tacit understanding that they would quickly become assimilated to a culturally Anglo-Saxon America. "They must cast off the European skin," said John Quincy Adams, "never to resume it. They must look forward to their posterity rather than backward to their ancestors; they must be sure that whatever their own feelings may be, those of their children will cling to the prejudices of this country."

The opening decades of the nineteenth century mark a watershed in the history of American ethnic communities. The era of the mass importation of indentured servants was over, and by 1820 the old colonial communities appeared to have taken John Quincy Adams' advice. The Dutch and large numbers of Germans were on their way to assimilation, as were the more recently arrived French and Irish. By 1820 the population of the United States was closer to Anglo-Saxon culture than it had ever been before, or would ever be again.

Within a single generation, however, this relative homogeneity would disappear. A new ethnic migration, more massive than any experienced in the colonial or early national era, would set out for the shores of the young republic. The lives of these immigrants would become enmeshed with the westward expansion, urbanization, and industrialization that changed the face of the country in the nineteenth century.

CHAPTER 4

New Frontiers:
Rural and Urban America

At the opening of the nineteenth century the United States was a quiet, slow-moving land not much different from the world the colonists had lived in for a hundred and fifty years. Forests still covered most of the land, minerals lay unmined beneath the earth, and two-thirds of the population clustered within fifty miles of the Atlantic Ocean. Most Americans were farmers. They tilled their acres with a technology similar to that of medieval Europe and lived in farmhouses that, according to the historian Henry Adams, were "hardly so well built, so spacious, or so warm as that of a well to do contemporary of Charlemagne." Yet within the span of one lifetime all this would change beyond recognition. By 1880 this quiet agrarian nation of modest size became an industrial giant, sprawling from coast to coast.

Change was rapid and all-encompassing. Between 1800 and 1880 the American population of five million exploded into fifty million. It spread so rapidly across the land that by 1890 the federal government announced that the frontier was no more. Cities increased tenfold in number, the population of many doubling every decade. The railroad, the telegraph, and the telephone brought New York City closer to Los Angeles in 1880 than it had been to Richmond in 1800. New technology revolutionized traditional farming and handicraft activities, abruptly quickening the pace of daily life for everyone. By 1880 Carnegie and Rockefeller had launched their careers, the United States was the world's largest producer of iron and steel, and the sky over Pittsburgh was black with smoke.

In each of these momentous changes—the settlement of the West, the rise of cities, the building of the transportation network, and the industrial revolution—ethnic Americans played a vital role. This chapter will explore that role. Like others, ethnic Americans were profoundly influenced by the changes they helped to create and were often the victims as well as the beneficiaries of their country's growth. This, too, will be explored. Finally, we will explore the problems of the ethnic newcomer trying to adjust to the new United States at a time when even the native-born were dizzied by the rapid changes in their nation and their lives.

Immigration Again

The resumption of large-scale, non-English immigration in the early nineteenth century was in itself a momentous new development on the American scene. Between 1815 and 1860 about five million immigrants came to the United States, a number equal to the entire population of the nation in 1790. By the eve of the Civil War, about thirteen per cent of the entire population was foreign born, a proportion never exceeded in the century that followed. In major cities as much as half of the population was composed of the foreign born and of their children.

The largest single source of this massive immigration was Ireland, which sent over two million people in the decades before the Civil War and continued to send sizable numbers well into the twentieth century. The second largest contingent, both before and after the Civil War, came from Germany, with smaller but significant groups coming from the Scandinavian countries, Holland, Switzerland, China, Scotland, and Wales.

This great new wave of ethnic Americans came as a surprise to a nation which, for about two generations, had experienced only a trickle of immigration. The ethnic communities of the mid-nineteenth century seemed, to the generation that greeted them, an entirely new phenomenon. The Irish and some of the Germans practiced what to many Americans seemed an alien religion, Catholicism. The brogue spoken by the Irish seemed almost as foreign as the unfamiliar languages of the Germans, Norwegians, Swedes, and Chinese.

The immigrants saw themselves as a new phenomenon, with little relation to anything or anyone in the American past. Norwegian immigrants had never heard of Leif Ericson, the Norwegian discoverer of America. Few nineteenth century Swedish immigrants knew of the existence of the earlier Swedish colony on the Delaware. To many nineteenth century German immigrants the remnants of the colonial German communities seemed quaint and old-fashioned.

Europeans in Motion

Why did millions of Irish, Germans, Scandinavians, Chinese, and others flock to our cities and scatter across our land in the decades just preceding and following the Civil War? The first Norwegians were Quakers who settled on farmland near Rochester, New York, to escape religious harassment in their homeland. Religious persecution was a factor in the immigration of thousands of Jews from Germany and thousands more Protestants from Germany and the Scandinavian countries. Political motives were also a factor. A few thousand disappointed political liberals left the German states after the failure of the Revolution of 1848; and these "forty-eighters," an unusually articulate and active group, had an impact in the United States far out of proportion to their numbers.

But the overwhelming majority of mid nineteenth century immigrants, like their colonial predecessors, did not come in search of the ballot or the Bill of Rights. They came in search of a better livelihood. Economic forces rather than political or religious repression set them in motion. The first of these economic forces was a rapid rise in population. Between 1750 and 1850 the population of Europe rose from 140 million to 260 million, and by the outbreak of World War I it approached 400 million. Even with the relief afforded by emigration, there were three persons in Europe in 1915 for every one that had been there in 1750.

Some scholars attribute the rise in population to a dramatic decline in infant mortality and that, in turn, to improvements in sanitation and public health. Others cite the sudden spread of the potato as the basic food crop. Easily cultivated, the potato provided a higher caloric yield per acre than traditional grain foods. A recent scholar has suggested still another explanation—a rise in freely chosen as opposed to arranged marriages, with a corresponding rise in sexual activity and births.

While the cause of the population rise remains unresolved, its results are clear—too many people trying to live off too little land. Where formerly one son survived to inherit the family farm, now there were two or three. The pressure of growing population on a limited land supply drove up the price of vacant land. It became increasingly difficult to buy farms for the younger sons (after the eldest inherited his father's) and to provide adequate dowries for the daughters. Farmers tried to provide for larger numbers of children by dividing their land among several sons instead of passing it intact to the eldest. This only increased the pressure on the next generation which had more mouths to feed on a smaller amount of land.

The situation was most critical in Ireland where the population, supported by the cultivation of the potato, increased sixty per cent between 1780 and 1840. "Every (potato) patch produces a new family," wrote an observer in 1822, "every member of a family, a new patch. . . . Hence a country covered with beggars . . . a complete pauper warren."

A member of the British Parliament further described the deteriorating conditions in Ireland:

> It is impossible for the able-bodied, in general, to provide against sickness . . . or against old age, or the destitution of their widows or orphans. . . . A great portion of them are insufficiently provided at any time with the commonest necessities of life. Their habitations are wretched hovels; several of a family sleep together upon straw or the bare ground. . . . Their food commonly consists of dry potatoes; and with these they are at times so scantily supplied as to be obliged to stint themselves to one spare meal in the day.

The failure of the potato crop in Ireland and parts of Germany increased the stream of emigration from these countries to a torrent by mid century. During the Great Potato Famine (1845 to 1851) a million Irish starved to death and a million more emigrated to England or to the United States. They took with them the memories of eating nettles, wild mustard seeds, and dogs, and of laying their dead in false bottomed, hinged coffins "to provide for more than one burial and yet preserve the decencies." Irish-Americans could not forgive the lack of assistance from the mother country, England, during the devastating famine. Some survivors had difficulty forgiving their own relatives for going so passively to paupers' graves. "They died like whipped curs awhinnin' under the lash—whimpering from the ditches and the bogs. Holy Mary—Mother of God—pray for us starvin' sinners now an' at the hour of our horrible death—Amen."

Other pressures compounded the basic problem of overpopulation. A rapid expansion of the population of cities in Western Europe increased the demand for agricultural products, encouraging landlords to evict their tenant farmers and consolidate their holdings for more efficient large-scale production. Reverend Michael Collins, reporting to a Parliamentary investigating committee in 1826, described the result of this policy in Ireland:

> As the leases fall in, they (the landlords) get rid of the surplus population by turning them out entirely from their lands. Those poor people, not getting employment, either erect temporary habitations like sheds on the highway, or they come into towns . . . perhaps four or five families will live in a garret or small hovel, huddled together there, without clothes or bedding, or food, living upon the chance of employment. . . . The men could get no employment, the women and children had no resource but to go to beg. . . .

Independent peasant farmers, as well as tenants, were hurt by economic change. The enclosure of the old common lands by landlords took away from these farmers important sources of firewood and grazing land. Moreover, as the large landowner consolidated his holdings and began to use the new farm machinery, the small farmer was unable to compete. These factors, plus a series of bad harvests in the 1840's and 1850's, made it increasingly difficult for independent peasant farmers to meet their obligations to family, church, and government. In a last desperate effort to save their independence, land-owning peasants supplemented their incomes by becoming itinerant laborers, traveling hundreds of miles each season in search of work.

Increasingly European peasants looked to emigration as a solution. Some fled from actual famine, aided by charitable societies or by the local gentry, who found it cheaper to finance their way to the next parish or the nearest seaport than to support them in the poorhouse. The majority did not wait until destitution left them no choice. Seeing that the future held nothing for them or their children, peasant families took the momentous step of selling land their families had lived on for centuries. As the farmers left, so too did the tailors, coopers, innkeepers, and other craftsmen and tradesmen whose livelihood depended upon them.

Many went to the nearest city to swell the growing ranks of urban industrial workers. Others set out to build a new life elsewhere. Emigrants from the British Isles sought refuge in Canada, Australia, and South Africa. Germans went to Brazil and Argentina. Chinese spread throughout southeast Asia, Hawaii, and Latin America. No destination beckoned so invitingly, however, as the United States, "the glorious country, the mountain of gold."

Despite economic pressures common to all, individuals decided to emigrate for immediate and personal reasons. Many fled oppressively rigid social structures. Young people left parental homes that denied them independence or the mate of their choice. Sometimes a jail sentence, an illegitimate child, or similar scandal made life in the old village unbearable. Young men left to avoid serving in the army. Some people went in search of adventure and excitement. Others were simply swept along by the outbreak of "America fever" that crossed their land, emptying entire villages as it passed.

Most of the emigrants were young, between the ages of fifteen and thirty-five, and the majority were male. Chinese emigration was almost entirely male, as strong tradition dictated that Chinese women remain at home to care for their husband's parents. Germans and Scandinavians usually came as family groups. Among the Irish and Scandinavians, single girls frequently came first, taking service in American homes to earn passage money for the rest of the family.

Except during the years of the potato famine, paupers were few among the immigrants to the United States, and criminals were fewer still. Those who traveled with the aid of charitable societies had to convince their benefactors of their good character and willingness to work. The Chinese were popularly believed to be "coolies," unskilled laborers imported under contract to mining or agricultural corporations. This was not the case, however. Those who came to the United States were usually free agricultural peasants fleeing areas devastated by the Taiping Rebellion. "Young, thrifty, and industrious . . . they possessed unusual independence of character," wrote Mary Coolidge, an early historian of the Chinese in the United States. As for the European immigrant, a German official echoed the observations of many:

> Those who are emigrating are the tillers in the fields and vineyards, men who are necessarily the largest contributors to our agricultural welfare, and who have generally some mechanical skill as well. They compose the element we can least afford to lose.

The most eloquent tribute to the value of the emigrants was their governments' efforts to keep them at home. An imperial decree banned emigration from China. Clergymen in the Scandinavian countries preached of the dangers to body and soul inherent in desertion of the fatherland. Many of the German states outlawed emigration.

All efforts to stop the stream of emigrants were futile, however. The Chinese bribed the local officials, who eased their conscience with the knowledge that remittances from California were enriching their provinces. The Scandinavian clergy eventually resigned themselves to the departure of their congregants, some even choosing to follow. Emigrants from the German states stole across the borders, embarking at seaports in Belgium, Holland, or France.

Folk songs of the era give insight into the mixed feelings of the emigrants. Songs from Norway complain bitterly of the hardships of life in the Old World: "Farewell, Norway, now I must leave thee. . . . All too sparing wert thou in providing food for the throng of thy laborers," said one. "Norway is a poor and wretched land . . . and now I am going to America. Here I have to save and suffer want; in America everyone can make a living. . . . Farewell," said another.

However difficult life in the old country had been, few could leave home and family and friends without the deepest of sorrow. This too was expressed in songs:

> Farewell, now, o Valley of Seljork; farewell to church and woods and home. Farewell to parson and parish clerk, to kith and kin, and the lovely gardens of home. Would to God this were undone! For the old home lies there grieving. . . .

The following song, taken from a popular Norwegian play, expresses the special sorrow of a woman looking for the last time at the home to which she had come as a bride:

> Farewell my old spinning wheel. How I shall miss you; the thought of leaving you breaks the heart in my breast.
>
> No more in the evening shall we sit by the fireside, old friend of mine, and gossip together.
>
> Ah, all that I see has its roots in my heart. And now they are torn out, do you wonder it bleeds?

The Magnetism of the United States

If "surplus" Europeans and Chinese were pushed out of their homes by economic and personal problems, many forces pulled them toward the United States. Still close to their own revolutionary origins, Americans enjoyed having their land play the role of the refuge of the oppressed. More important, the growing nation recognized its great need for labor. Special interests actively encouraged immigrants and tried to direct them to specific destinations.

Among the people in the United States who recognized the economic value of immigrants and made every effort to attract them were the ship owners. American ship owners sent bulky cargoes of raw materials to Europe, but the return cargoes of finished goods were less bulky. Immigrants filled the half-empty vessels coming from Europe to America, thus increasing the shipper's profit. Immigrant fares were an important source of income for ship owners in the Pacific as well as the Atlantic. Chinese embarking for San Francisco in 1852 alone paid a million and a half dollars in fares; and as many returned home within a few years, the profit was doubled. American ship owners found it profitable to open offices and keep agents overseas in the areas where emigration was common.

Railroad companies as well as shippers encouraged immigration. Immigrants were needed to perform the arduous labor of laying the track, work considered undesirable by most native-born Americans. Equally important, immigrants were good customers for the land the government had granted to the railroads. Having purchased railroad land, the immigrants would settle along the railroad and use it continuously to bring in supplies and to market their crops. Such an immigrant family could be counted on to provide two to three hundred dollars worth of business for the railroad every year.

Little wonder, then, that railroads competed fiercely with one another to attract immigrants. Some maintained agents who traveled to European countries to recruit new settlers. In American ports the agents of the various railroads provided food and other services for the new arrivals, hoping to win their confidence and their business. Railroad companies prepared handbooks in Swedish, Norwegian, German, Dutch, and Polish and offered special travel rates to attract immigrants to their areas.

The states were as zealous in their efforts as the ship companies and railroads. New population was an asset that increased their representation in Congress, swelled their tax receipts, brought in new skills, and increased the value of their land. As early as 1852 Wisconsin had a Commissioner of Emigration, assisted by German and Norwegian speaking deputies. Other states, particularly in the West and in the South, followed.

The states distributed thousands of pamphlets in many languages. They helped immigrants arriving in the eastern seaports by providing interpreters, food, shelter, and protection from the swindlers who were always at hand to prey upon the inexperienced newcomers. Not content with touting the advantages of their own states, "boosters" portrayed rival states in as bad a light as possible. Thus an enthusiastic Kansan warned newcomers to avoid Minnesota, "a land of ice and snow and perpetual winter where, if the poor immigrant did not starve to death, he would surely perish with cold."

Undoubtedly immigrants were intrigued by attractive leaflets and brightly-colored posters and by the blandishments of the various commercial and political agents. What really attracted them, however, was the economic opportunity America presented. In the first half of the nineteenth century the United States acquired the vast and fertile Mississippi Valley, Texas, Oregon, and the Southwest including California. Immigrants were attracted by this seemingly inexhaustible supply of cheap, fertile land. Immigrants were also attracted by the mineral wealth, especially the gold in California, and by wages that were many times what they could earn at home. Their knowledge of American business conditions was amazingly accurate. When jobs were scarce and wages low, as during the panics of 1837 and 1857, immigration slowed abruptly. When business recovered, immigration resumed its normal rate.

Obviously a great deal of information was flowing from ethnic Americans already in the United States to would-be immigrants. Some of it came from guidebooks written by travelers, ministers, journalists, and early settlers. These guidebooks set to rest many rumors (some Europeans feared that if they came to America they would be sold into slavery or eaten by wild animals) and gave details on practical concerns such as the price of land, the cost of salt, wages in different areas, and health hazards. Most guidebooks warned that immigration was for the young and strong and advised people to shun the eastern cities in favor of the Mississippi Valley, where wages were high and land was plentiful and easily cleared.

Another source of information was the successful immigrant, returned to visit relatives or perhaps marry a childhood sweetheart. As in the colonial period, immigration was considered a final parting; indeed, the Irish held wakes for friends and relatives going to America. Still, a few did return. People came from miles away to talk with such distinguished travelers, who often went back to the United States with friends and relatives in tow.

More important still was the flood of "America letters" written by immigrants already in America to the family and friends at home. Such letters were passed from hand to hand, read aloud in the village church, published in the local press, even printed and distributed as handbills. The letters told of the difficulties of the journey, of loneliness, of hard work, of monetary losses through fraud and natural disaster, and of the death of beloved members of the family, especially children. But the feeling in most of them was one of optimism, of promise fulfilled or soon to be fulfilled, of a land where life was better:

> Now for the first time am I able to breath freely. . . . No one is persecuted here because of his religious faith . . . everyone secures without hindrance the fruits of his own labor. . . . Norway can no more be compared with America than a desolate waste with a garden in full bloom.

> The hired man, maid, and governess eat at the husbandman's table. . . . On the street the maid is dressed exactly like the housewife.

> We are free to move at any time and to any place without a certificate from the employer or from the pastor.

> I am well pleased with my decision to come to this place. I believe I have achieved that which I desired: a higher welfare for all my children.

Moving West

Immigrants went immediately to the areas where opportunities could be found. Welsh miners went to the coal and iron centers of Pennsylvania where their specialized skills were needed. Scottish weavers settled in the textile producing areas of New England. Chinese headed for the farms and mines of California. Successful immigrants of every ethnic group served as a magnet attracting friends and relatives to their area of settlement, thus creating new ethnic communities.

A sprinkling of the Irish went as far west as San Francisco, where they were among the earliest and most prominent English-speaking settlers. Most of the immigrants who joined the westward movement, however, were Scandinavians and Germans. As in the colonial years, immigrants chose frontier areas that resembled as closely as possible the terrain of their native country. Scandinavians settled in the northern part of the Mississippi Valley, from Iowa to Minnesota, where the cold climate, lakes, and forests reminded them of home. Interestingly, they tended to occupy the same latitudinal positions relative to one another in America as they had in Europe, immigrants from Iceland settling furthest north, Danes furthest south, and Swedes and Norwegians in between.

A few Germans went to the edges of the frontier, like John Sutter, on whose land gold was first discovered in California. But most of the Germans who went west settled in Missouri, Wisconsin, Illinois, Indiana, and Texas, where they usually bought improved land, wooded and well watered. Wisconsin was highly favored because the traditional German crops of oats and hops could be grown there and because Milwaukee boasted a Roman Catholic bishop of German origin.

Ethnic Americans who settled the interior and western farmlands in the mid nineteenth century shared the hardships of their Anglo-Saxon neighbors, plus a few more distinctly their own. Like other frontier Americans, they suffered from lack of medical care. Because many immigrants were debilitated from the long ocean and overland journey, the bad housing, poor water, and inadequate sanitation of the new settlements were even more devastating to them than to the native born. Cholera, typhoid, pneumonia, and malaria were so common that immigrants declared the American air unwholesome and doubted that American food could nourish them as well as the familiar grains of their homeland.

Like other frontier Americans, ethnic immigrants came into conflict with the Indians in whose territory they took up residence. A German settlement at New Ulm, Minnesota, for example, was wiped out by the Sioux, angry at the broken promises and unfulfilled treaties foisted upon them by the American government. Ethnic Americans, particularly the Irish and the Germans, served in the American army in numbers greater than their proportion in the population and thus played a major role in the bloody Indian wars of the nineteenth century. Immigrants had no particular grudge against Indians. It was simply a job, well-paid and, unlike many other jobs, available to all without discrimination. Moreover, by serving under the Stars and Stripes, the immigrant could assert that he was, after all, a "real" American.

European knowledge and experience were not always relevant to American situations. In Europe farmers tilled small plots using the methods of their ancestors, and looked to the tightly-knit community of relatives and neighbors for assistance in time of need. In America, farms were larger and more isolated, soil and weather conditions were unfamiliar, and the supportive network of friends and relatives was often not available. Individual families were thrown back on their own resources.

Sometimes ethnic farmers tried to bring their European communities with them. Mennonite communities from Germany settled in Kansas, where they worked out a profitable blending of religious conservatism and agricultural innovation. Other attempts to transplant whole communities were less successful, especially when the enterprises were directed from Europe.

One such experiment was the German colony of New Braunfels, Texas, established as a profit-making enterprise by a company of German nobles who pooled their money to buy a tract of land. The company planned to sell the land in small parcels to German colonists, provide them with free schools, churches, and medical care, and sell them supplies. A handful of colonists did purchase land and actually went to New Braunfels to live, but poor choice of location, bad management, and misuse of funds crippled the settlement from the start.

New settlers brought in as reinforcements were left stranded on the Texas coast, many miles from New Braunfels, without jobs, shelter, or transportation to the interior. Those who finally reached their destination found the original colonists demoralized by Indian attacks, poor harvests, and disease. So many had died under the hand of the company physician, a Dr. Kester, that the cemetery was called "Kester's Plantation." According to an observer, the survivors decided to enjoy what they believed would be their last days. "Resorting to a wooden booth where there was dancing every night, the hale and the sick together raved in a dizzy reel of enjoyment to the shrill music of a clarinetist, an individual who was also the professional gravedigger of the place."

New Braunfels eventually recovered and even prospered. Not so the Norwegian settlement of Oleana in western Pennsylvania. Founded by Ole Bull, an eccentric violinist, Oleana was part of a plan to establish a "New Norway" in the United States. The plan was ill-conceived and ill-executed from the beginning. Bull purchased a tract of land from an unscrupulous speculator, paying a ridiculously high price. Not only was the land inaccessible and unsuitable for farming, but the sale itself proved fraudulent, for Bull did not have clear title to the land. After months of backbreaking toil, the settlers received only half the wages they had been promised. The once hopeful residents of Oleana abandoned their colony in disgust, leaving behind a wry ballad that has become part of the folk lore of both Norway and America:

CHORUS:

I'm off to Oleana, I'm turning from my doorway
No chains for me, I'll say goodby to slavery in Norway.

They give you land for nothing in jolly Oleana
And grain comes leaping from the ground in floods of golden manna.

The grain it does the threshing, it pours into the sack, Sir
And so you take a quiet nap a stretching on your back, Sir.

The crops they are gigantic, potatoes are immense, Sir
You make a quart of whisky from each one without expense, Sir.

The salmon they are playing, and leaping in the brook, Sir
They hop into the kettle, put the cover on, and cook, Sir.

REPEAT CHORUS

The cows are most obliging, their milk they put in pails, Sir
They make your cheese and butter with a skill that never fails, Sir.

Two dollars for carousing they give each day, and more, Sir
For if you're good and lazy, they will even give you four, Sir.

I'm off to Oleana, to lead a life of pleasure,
A beggar here, a count out there, with riches in full measure.

REPEAT CHORUS

Settlers who escaped fraud and incompetence had to contend with drought, blizzards, prairie fires, snakes, and hordes of locusts that consumed the crops before they could be harvested. Loneliness was a major problem. While some settled in communities, others, especially after the opening of the prairies and the passing of the Homestead Act, found themselves miles away from their nearest neighbors. Isolation, overwork, and early and frequent childbearing, took a heavy toll. Even the landscape could take on a hostile aspect. A Norwegian-American novelist recorded the frightened reaction of a woman accustomed to the hills, forests, and seas of Norway to her first encounter with the barren, silent plains of the Dakota territory:

> This formless prairie had no heart that beat, no waves that sang, no soul that could be touched, . . . Here no warbling of birds rose on the air, no buzzing of insects sounded. . . . Had they travelled into some nameless, abandoned region . . . empty, desolate wastes of green and blue. . . . How *could* existence go on. . . . ? If life is to thrive and endure, it must at least have something to hide behind!

Immigrants often had to cope with a strange and hostile moral landscape as well as a hostile physical landscape. Customs and values long honored in the old environment seemed out of place, even counterproductive in the new. In the relatively stable society of the European farming village, the family that behaved peaceably, cooperatively, and predictably, fulfilling its traditional obligations to its own members and others, was respected by all. Such a family was likely to be successful in its undertakings.

Not so in the rapidly changing, highly individualistic United States, particularly in the frontier areas in the mid nineteenth century. In the raucous, often violent, "boom or bust" world of the American West, population spread more quickly than legal institutions could follow. Cut loose from the moorings of family, church, and community back east, many of the new westerners felt free to make their way in the world at any cost. Under such conditions, might often meant right. It was the aggressive individual, unhampered by traditional morality, who seized the best mining claim or the well-watered homestead or who succeeded in getting the new railroad, canal, or county seat in the location most favorable to his interests.

Some ethnic Americans accepted, even thrived upon, the pragmatic, rough and ready frontier morality. "Just kick the dog that bites you, that's always the easiest way, and the simplest, too," said Per Hansa, the central character in Rölvaag's novel, *Giants in the Earth*. Others could not give up the traditional values taught them in an Old World childhood. Appalled by the changes she saw taking place in her husband, Per Hansa's wife worried that the entire family would desert the Christian decencies to become savages in a new and savage land.

If immigrants were more vulnerable than the native-born to the hardships of frontier life, they were also more appreciative of its rewards. Coming from a land of tiny farms that had been cultivated century after century, they rejoiced in the size and virgin fertility of their new American holdings. Their traditionally large families, liabilities in overcrowded Europe, became assets in labor-starved America. Of course, many ethnic homesteads were not successful. Thousands returned to the East, or even to Europe, defeated by loneliness, illness, or natural disasters. Agrarian America prospered, however, in the mid nineteenth century; and as it prospered, becoming the supplier of raw materials to America's growing cities and to the outside world, ethnic farmers prospered too. In time, sod houses and log cabins were replaced by sturdy frame and brick farmhouses, with large and well stocked barns and silos. Many humble families, heir to a few rocky acres in Europe, became the proud owners of the American manors that exceeded their wildest dreams. Oleana may have collapsed in failure, but private, less pretentious utopias materialized.

Other Occupations

Not all immigrants who headed west became homesteaders. Lacking the resources, skills, or inclination to become independent farmers, many turned to other means of making their livings. Young men from Germany, Ireland, and the Scandinavian countries became the badly needed "hired hands" to help other farmers with the planting, harvesting, land clearing, draining, and whatever other work had to be done. By 1884 at least half of the agricultural workers in California were Chinese. Five million acres of farmland at the mouth of the Sacramento and San Joaquin Rivers, including much of the present site of San Francisco, were reclaimed by Chinese labor, working without benefit of mechanical aids. The victims of intense prejudice, the Chinese had little choice but to accept such undesirable work. Similarly, Irish labor reclaimed swamp land in Virginia and other parts of the South, work considered too dangerous to be given to slaves. "If a Negro dies, it is a considerable loss, you know," explained a contemporary.

Ethnic Americans provided personal and commercial services to the newly opened West, and indeed, to the entire country. Irish, German, and Scandinavian women worked in American homes, where they cooked, cleaned, nursed the sick, and reared other people's children—invaluable services in a land where labor was scarce and women scarcer still. In the Far West Chinese men performed these traditionally "female" services in mining camps, hotels, and homes. Later they put this experience to good use by opening restaurants, laundries, and other services. This made them financially independent of the oppressive white community which monopolized better sources of income for itself.

An expanding nation needed commercial as well as personal services; and ethnic Americans played a major role here too. German immigrants, many of them Jews, traveled the roads in every corner of the land, from New England to the Sante Fe, bringing pins, needles, pots, pans, tools, news, and companionship to the most isolated homestead, logging camp, and mining village. One such peddler, Levi Strauss responded to frontier needs by inventing Levi's, the sturdy denim pants that still bear his name. The successful immigrant peddler settled down to become the proprietor of the dry goods or "general" store in many a crossroads town.

The skills and labor of ethnic Americans were instrumental in the development of many frontier industries. Scandinavians were important in dairying, lumbering, the manufacture of furniture, paper, and farm equipment; the most successful purchased grain elevators or became local bankers or wholesale commodities merchants. Germans were important as mining engineers and cattlemen and helped introduce crop-related industries such as cigar-making, wine-making, and sugar refining.

Nothing changed the face of nineteenth century America as radically as the building of the transportation network. Miles of new turnpikes, canals, and most important of all, the railroads, opened the West to settlement, supplied the growing urban areas, and provided the new industrialists with the largest tariff free market in the world. This revolutionary transportation network was built largely by ethnic Americans. German-trained engineers contributed much of the technology, and foreign capital, raised by the foreign-born, was indispensable. But the greatest contribution of ethnic Americans was, of course, their labor.

The work was backbreaking—too unpleasant and too poorly paid to appeal to any but the most desperate. In the East it was done by Irish, in the South by Irish and blacks, in the Midwest by Irish and Scandinavians, and in the Far West by Chinese. Railroad companies advertised in urban newspapers or sent agents to ports where immigrants landed to recruit gangs of workmen, a system used by mining and logging companies as well. The worker was offered what appeared to be good wages, with an advance for transportation to the work site, often hundreds of miles from his home. Upon arrival he found the work harder, the wages lower, and his supplies (available only at the company commissary) costlier than he had anticipated. Already in debt for his transportation, he had little choice but to stay.

Sometimes entire families followed the progress of the railroad as laborers for—and victims of—the corporations. In 1841 Charles Dickens described the plight of a colony of Irish families building railroads in upstate New York:

> With means at hand of building decent cabins, it was wonderful to see how clumsy, rough, and wretched its hovels were. The best were poor protection from the weather; the worst let in the wind and rain through the wide breaches in the roofs of sodden grass and in the walls of mud; some had neither door nor window; some had nearly fallen down, and were imperfectly propped up by stakes and poles; all were ruinous and filthy. Hideously ugly old women and very buxom young ones, pigs, dogs, men, children, babies, pots, kettles, dunghills, vile refuse, rank straw and standing water, all wallowing together in an inseparatable heap, composed the furniture of every dark and dirty hut.

Conditions were so bad in some of these labor camps that the state governments abandoned their usual hands-off policy to pass laws against the grossest abuses. From the point of view of the Irish, however, conditions in railroad towns were no worse than they had been in the old country—indeed, they were probably better. There was at least one beneficial side effect. The railroad shantytowns helped spread the Irish population out of the overcrowded eastern cities, creating little "Paddy's Quarters" in Indiana, Ohio, Illinois, and even west of the Mississippi.

On the west coast, railroad building was done by Chinese. Driven from the newly discovered gold mines by discriminatory taxes and by physical violence, Chinese immigrants were looking for employment while the first transcontinental railroad was being built. Chinese were considered too weak and unskilled for construction work, however, until Charles Crooker, an executive of the Central Pacific, pointed out that their ancestors had built the greatest piece of masonry in the world, the Great Wall of China. This convinced the company to give them a chance.

Crooker's Pets, as the new Chinese railroad workers were called, more than lived up to his expectations. With wives, children, and elderly parents in China depending upon their remittances, the Chinese went to work with amazing zeal. They chipped away at the sheer granite cliffs of the Sierra Nevadas, working suspended from ropes when they could find no foothold, until they had carved a shelf wide enough for the laying of the track. In winter they braved blizzards and avalanches, working in tunnels burrowed under fifteen feet of snow. The spring thaw uncovered Chinese corpses, shovels and picks still clutched in their frozen hands.

The Urban Frontier

At least half of the new immigrants never got to the rural frontier, either as homesteaders, hired hands, peddlers, or railroad workers. By choice or by necessity they settled in the mushrooming towns and cities instead. San Francisco had its famous Chinatown. Milwaukee, Chicago, St. Paul, Minneapolis, Cleveland, and Cincinnati had large German and Scandinavian colonies. Many Germans settled in the older eastern urban centers of New York, Philadelphia, and Baltimore. The largest ethnic community in the eastern cities, however, was the Irish.

A rural people in the Emerald Isle, ninety per cent of the Irish settled in cities in the United States, concentrating their population in New York, Boston, and Philadelphia. Many of the Irish lacked the skills and the capital to become farmers in America. By mid century the frontier was a thousand miles or more from the port of arrival. Even if land were cheap or altogether free, impoverished immigrants could not afford the cost of transportation, seed, and equipment, nor could they maintain themselves until the first crop was harvested. Moreover for many of the Irish, the isolation of rural life in the United States had no appeal. They preferred the city, where Catholic churches were available and where they could enjoy the sociability of being among their countrymen.

As immigrants poured into an expanding urban America, so too did the native-born. The cities were magnets, luring all kinds of people with their promise of adventure, excitement, and fortunes to be made.

As centers of commerce and transportation, the cities were, indeed, filled with opportunities. Moreover, as farms began to mechanize, proportionately fewer people were needed to produce the nation's food. Thus while the western farming frontier has often been seen as a "safety valve" for the excess population of the city, the opposite was closer to the truth. From mid-century on, the growing cities provided a safety valve for the excess farm population of both Europe and the United States.

Never before or since has urban growth taken place at such a rapid rate. The old eastern cities got larger, while whole groups of new cities in the Mississippi Valley, along the Great Lakes, and on the west coast made their sudden appearance. New York City grew from 60,489 in 1800 to 202,589 in 1830, to more than a million in 1860. St. Louis doubled its population every nine years; Buffalo, every eight; Cincinnati, every seven. In the two years following the completion of the transcontinental railroad, Los Angeles increased its population five hundred per cent!

Unprecedented growth presented unprecedented problems. How could the cities provide jobs and housing for so many newcomers? What about drinking water, waste disposal, transportation, and fire protection? How could law and order be maintained when neighborhoods changed in a matter of months and when people were strangers to one another? American cities were totally unprepared to solve such problems. Many had corrupt and antiquated forms of government and were unaccustomed to providing any but the most elemental services. At mid century New York City had no public police force or fire department. Such order as there was was kept by private guards, the militia being called out in case of dire emergency. Volunteer fire companies fought with one another while buildings burned. Disease, crime, and vice were rampant in an urban society growing too fast to meet its needs.

Foresight, planning, and the judicious use of regulations and public moneys might have alleviated some of the problems. Such policies were impossible, however, given the climate of opinion in the mid nineteenth century. Political leaders, like most of their constituents, were committed to "privatism," a government hands off policy in the area of social problems. Cities provided poorhouses and public hospitals, dreary institutions shunned by all but the most desperate, and committees of benevolent women dispensed food and fuel to "deserving" widows with small children. Beyond this, little was done. Poverty and other social problems were believed to be the result of vicious and improvident personal habits which the victims could correct if only they would try.

Because so many were concentrated in the poor and working

classes, ethnic Americans suffered proportionately more than the native-born from the growing pains of the city. Immigrants were coping with many changes at once. First they were moving from the European or Asian culture of their birthplace to the predominantly English culture of the United States, a change that often involved a totally different language and life style. In addition, most were moving from a rural to an urban environment—a formidable change in itself. And finally, the city to which they were coming was in itself in a state of constant change. Under these conditions, the urban frontier, like the rural frontier, offered problems as well as opportunities.

One of the most immediate and most difficult problems was finding a decent place to live. At no time in American history has the supply of urban housing kept pace with the demand, but in the pre-Civil War years the situation was especially acute. As newcomers poured into the cities, all hoping to live near commercial areas where jobs were available, there was simply no place to house them. Dwellings built for one family were divided and subdivided as the population doubled and doubled again. Sheds, stables, and warehouses were pressed into service, as were windowless garrets and underground cellars. By 1850, 29,000 people in New York City were living underground.

Recognizing the profits to be made from the housing shortage, landlords erected rows of tenements. The tenements often used every available foot of land on the building lot leaving many of the rooms without sunlight or ventilation. Outdoor privies in the alleys over-flowed, contaminating the water supply and seeping into the buildings. Still, the hapless tenants rarely complained, fearful of being put upon a "black list" and unable in any case to find other quarters. The prudent set aside the rent money before buying lesser necessities such as food, fuel, and clothing.

The impact of the tidal wave of new population (and the inability of the city to provide for it successfully) is illustrated by the history of the fourth ward in New York City. At the turn of the century the fourth ward was an elegant neighborhood of dignified family mansions shaded by blossoming cherry trees. John Hancock, signer of the Declaration of Independence had lived here, as had President Washington at the time of his inauguration. By 1840, however, the fourth ward had become a notorious slum. In one double row of tenements, Gotham Courts, sewer rats as big as cats swarmed freely. One third of the newborn children did not survive their first few weeks of life. Outsiders foolish enough to venture into Gotham Court were beaten, robbed, or worse; a murder a night was not uncommon. Police entered in groups of six—when they entered at all.

With the building of the trolley lines, those who could afford the fares—skilled workers and the middle class—moved out of the old, inner city neighborhoods, leaving them to immigrants, blacks, and others at the bottom of the economic ladder. Like blacks, immigrants could rarely afford to move and when they could afford better housing, discrimination prevented them from obtaining it.

The housing problems of ethnic immigrants were complicated by their inexperience in urban living. The European housewife had been poor in the old country, but she was at least accustomed to an adequate supply of sunshine, fresh air, open space, and clean water. In a cramped tenement five flights above the outhouse and the polluted well, the routine tasks of caring for a household and disposing of wastes became complicated and arduous chores.

As late as 1857 New York City had only 138 miles of sewers to serve five hundred miles of streets; twenty-four million gallons of sewage accumulated in the yards, gutters, and alleys of the city every day. In such an environment, it is scarcely surprising that bad health was a major problem. Dysentery, typhoid, cholera, tuberculosis, and smallpox were part of the price ethnic Americans paid for their participation in urban growth. Eighty-four per cent of the patients admitted to New York City's Bellevue Hospital between 1849 and 1859 were foreign-born. Throughout the country the Irish appeared to have the most illness, probably because they were the most debilitated upon arrival. Because of their poverty they were the most likely to be dependent upon public treatment facilities. The Chinese appeared to be the healthiest. If this was true, it was probably related to the fastidious care they took in the preparation of their food and the boiling of their drinking water. Moreover, Chinese rarely appeared in city hospitals, preferring—perhaps wisely—to die at home or in the streets.

Once they solved their housing problem (however unsatisfactorily) immigrants turned to their most important long-range concern, earning a livelihood. Contrary to popular opinion and stereotypes, many immigrants had valuable skills. They were brewers, weavers, printers, engravers, metalworkers, writers, manufacturers of musical instruments, and professionals of various kinds. Such people had no trouble finding their places and contributing to the expanding urban economy.

Less fortunate were the displaced farmers and peasants, who had no marketable urban skills. But they had muscle and an eagerness to work—commodities still needed in the nineteenth century city. The men found jobs at the docks, in shipyards, railroad depots, stockyards, sewers, and streets. They built, dug, lifted, carried, and packed whatever needed building, digging, lifting, carrying, packing. Such jobs were seasonal, poorly paid, and short-lived. Better paid employment and job training were frequently unavailable to the immigrants who needed them most because of the prejudices of employers. Help wanted notices commonly ended with the warning that "no Irish need apply."

Women had a double employment handicap; sexual discrimination compounded the problems of ethnic discrimination. The more personable young women, especially those who spoke English, could find work as domestics in American homes, but such work was hardly desirable. Irish "girls" (aged sixteen to sixty) in Boston or Philadelphia rose before dawn to work a sixteen hour day, six days a week, for a weekly salary of a dollar and a half! Less fortunate women took in washing or sewing at home for wages competitive with those paid to the women inmates of the public almshouses. The loss of husbands through sickness, accident, or desertion left many widows to support large families with few job opportunities open to them. During the years 1845 to 1850 the Boston Society for the Prevention of Pauperism received applications for employment from 14,000 female "foreigners" as opposed to 5,034 males.

Urban families worked together at the most menial and unpleasant tasks in order to survive. Impoverished Germans in New York City became scavengers. Men, women, and children gathered discarded bones from slaughter houses and filthy rags from hospitals and gutters. In their tenement apartments they boiled the rotting flesh off the bones, washed and dried the vile-smelling rags, bagged the products, and sold them to refuse dealers for a few cents a bag.

The earliest factory jobs were filled by native-born workers. New England's textile mill owners, for example, prided themselves on their carefully chaperoned work force of Yankee farm girls. By the mid 1850's, however, the farmers' daughters were becoming disillusioned with the low wages and drudgery of mill work. Irish and French Canadian immigrants began to take their places, establishing shanty towns and Catholic churches at the edges of neat New England villages, to the horror of the native-born inhabitants. In California, Chinese moved into the cigar, textile, and shoe making industries. As industry expanded in the decades after the Civil War, ethnic Americans moved into factory jobs in increasing numbers.

Life in Europe had been hard, but there were greater opportunities for relaxation and celebration in the traditional village than in the nineteenth century industrial city. Immigrants missed the singing, public games, festivals, and street dancing of the Old World. They complained that here "a gloomy, churlish, money-worshipping spirit" had "swept nearly all the poetry out of a poor man's existence." American employers had no time for poetry.

The new capitalists considered workers a commodity, like wood or iron, to be used as impersonally and as profitably as possible. They demanded long hours of work under unhealthful conditions, for which they paid as little as they could. Workers responded with absenteeism, alcoholism, even violence. Railroad workers protested company exploitation by destroying newly-laid track and attacking railroad personnel. Irish miners in Pennsylvania, working for their old ethnic enemies, the English and the Welsh, resisted the hated bosses with the organized terrorism (including murder) of the Molly Maguires.

Despite a generally expanding economy, periodic depressions caused serious urban unemployment. The groups who suffered most were those at the bottom of the economy—Irish and blacks. Sharing the worst housing and the most limited employment opportunities, Irish and blacks were forced into cutthroat competition for the same low-paid menial jobs. Economic competition combined with racial prejudice to produce the tragic Draft Riots of 1863 in New York City. The Irish community was angry because native-born liberal crusaders appeared more concerned about the plight of the southern slave than about economic evils closer to home. They were aroused still further by the injustice of a wartime draft that exempted the rich but took the immigrant poor. Anger boiled over into senseless violence. Burning and looting, Irish mobs vented their fury on the nearest blacks, hanging and mutilating dozens of people, even setting fire to the local black orphanage. Days of violence took a heavy toll in human life and in property before Federal troops fresh from Gettysburg restored order to the battlefield of New York City.

Pauperism, Crime, and Vice

As urban America grew, so too did pauperism, crime, and vice. Ethnic Americans were part of this as of all other aspects of the country's growth. When earning a living became too difficult, some immigrants sought refuge, temporary or permanent, in hospitals and almshouses. In 1860, eighty six per cent of the inmates of New York's poor house were ethnic Americans. A majority of the inmates of nineteenth century prisons were immigrants and their children. In the East the principal offenders were Irish (hence the nickname "paddy wagon" for the police van), while in Midwestern cities Scandinavian offenders were more numerous.

Because their living quarters were cramped and gloomy, immigrants spent much of their time on the streets. Here there was plenty of opportunity for people to get into trouble. Saloons, gambling establishments, dance halls, and houses of prostitution were common in ethnic neighborhoods; one did not have to go far to practice a favorite vice. Among the Irish, reputedly heavy drinkers even before immigration, alcohol all too often provided an escape from the dismal realities of daily life. Chinese brought their favorite vice, gambling, to America with them. Indeed, gambling had a wide appeal among immigrants. Only the miracle of winning the lottery could lift the unskilled laborer in an instant to the prosperity of his dreams.

About half of the prostitutes in the Eastern cities were foreigners, or the daughters of foreigners, a figure roughly equal to their proportion in the total population, and they were patronized by the foreign born and native-born alike. Gangs had a special appeal for the young men of the nineteenth century ethnic slums. At a time when advancement seemed beyond the reach of many, the gang offered opportunities to acquire money, status, and power. For some youths the gang leader served as a substitute father, teacher, and role model. For the young ethnic, uprooted from the culture of the Old World but not yet assimilated into that of the new, the gang offered companionship and the certainty of a set of rules. Finally, in the most violent neighborhoods, the gang was a practical response to the anarchy of the streets, a necessary means of survival.

Sometimes the ethnic gang was an offshoot of a similar organization in the old country. The notorious Chinese "hatchet men," for example, were an outgrowth of a secret political organization begun in China during the Taiping Rebellion. Consisting of criminals from China as well as native-born hoodlums, the hatchet men imported prostitutes, blackmailed respectable businessmen, engaged in street fighting, and served as paid assassins in San Francisco's Chinatown. In the East, gangs of young men (and occasionally women), many of them Irish, moved about with bludgeons, brickbats, and pistols, terrifying and sometimes even killing peaceful bystanders during bloody pitched battles that lasted for days.

While immigrant pauperism and crime did exist, much of the outcry against it was based upon exaggeration and misinformation. Immigrants outnumbered the native-born in urban public institutions because they were less likely to have friends and relatives who could help them through sickness, old age, or unemployment. Prejudice on the part of law enforcement officials contributed to the high arrest rate among some ethnic groups. Most of these arrests, moreover, were for minor offenses such as drunkenness, vagrancy, and petty theft of the necessities of life—food, clothing, tools, even laundry tubs. If human life was cheap in the worst immigrant slums, it was equally cheap in the mining and ranching towns of the Anglo-Saxon frontier.

Immigrant vice, like immigrant crime, was exaggerated by many of the native-born, who projected their own moral failings upon the foreigner. Saloons, gambling establishments, and brothels, for example, were not tolerated in "respectable" neighborhoods, but they could be located with impunity in ethnic ghettos, where they were patronized by the native-born. Excessive drinking was a universal American problem (the temperance movement predated the mass Irish immigration by decades) and the gambler is a classic Anglo-Saxon American stereotype. Prostitution thrived among predominantly male immigrant societies such as the Chinese, because a shortage of women made conventional family life impossible. But the same conditions produced the same results in Anglo-Saxon male communities. There was one prostitute for every one hundred and fifty men in the native-born white community of San Diego! Local politicians encouraged urban gangs, both native-born and immigrant, finding them useful for keeping "undesirable" voters away from the polls on election day.

Dismal living conditions, ill health, poverty, alcoholism, violence, loneliness—immigrants had many obstacles to surmount in the frontiers of nineteenth century rural and urban America. Some were defeated. Immigrant aid societies had many requests from individuals for money for return tickets to Europe. Unemployed men left their families in the cities to find work elsewhere and sometimes "forgot" to return. Scattered items in the contemporary press hint at the dimensions of the tragedy. "A Jewish young woman, having a healthy child about eighteen months old, would be greatly indebted to any religious family who might adopt it," ran an advertisement in the *Occident,* a Jewish periodical. The *New York Sun* reported that "a German . . . in a fit of desperation on account of pecuniary embarrassments . . . with a hair trigger pistol terminated his existence."

The overwhelming majority of the new ethnics were not defeated, however. Somehow they maintained their mental and moral balance in the midst of a dizzying world. Whenever possible they helped one another, bringing food to a sick neighbor, finding room in a cramped tenement for still another relative or unemployed friend. Gradually they established a variety of self-help organizations in which individuals pooled their resources to insure one another against sickness, death, or unemployment. Unfortunately such societies were often short-lived, because their resources were too limited.

There were other sources of assistance. The Catholic Church provided orphanages and, eventually, schools in major cities. Ethnic Americans who had been in the country for a number of years, or a generation or two, often helped new arrivals. German physicians gave free medical care to needy German immigrants in New York, for example, and Jews in the major cities provided fuel, clothing, and food for needy Jewish newcomers. Efforts by well established ethnics to help newcomers were most effective when the resources of the established community were great and the number of newcomers not overwhelmingly large. Such efforts were more successful among Germans and Jews, therefore, than among the Irish.

Clearly the new ethnic Americans were in many ways the victims of urban growth. But they were also its beneficiaries. As the economy expanded, the lot of the ethnic immigrant improved. Few followed in the footsteps of Andrew Carnegie, the Scottish immigrant boy who became a millionaire. Success was more likely to be measured in a move from a series of temporary, menial jobs to steady semiskilled or clerical employment—if not in the first generation, then perhaps in the second. Many immigrants never moved up the American socio-economic ladder. They worked at the same unskilled jobs and lived in the same tenements year after year, saving every spare penny to support aged parents abroad or to bring their families to the United States. This, too, was a kind of success.

CHAPTER 5

An American Style Emerges: The Common Man, the Common School, the Common Culture

In the years between 1820 and 1840, only a generation or two removed from colonial status, the citizens of the young republic had to define just what it meant to be an "American." What would "good" Americans believe in, how would they live, toward what goals should they strive? During the Jacksonian era, the "age of the common man," Americans explored these and similar questions.

Ethnic Americans participated in the definition of Americanism. But certain ethnic groups encountered problems when they got in the way of the new Americanism or deviated too far from its recently established norms. In the age of the common man there were great pressures to conform. What happened to immigrants who differed from the majority in language, religion, or life style?

Democracy and Protestantism

By the time the great wave of pre-Civil War immigration was well underway, the majority society had agreed upon two distinguishing principles of national identity—republican democracy and militant Protestantism. Americans saw their country as a unique experiment, "a city upon a hill." America was to be an example to the world of the blessings of republican institutions and Protestant Christianity. Nor were Americans modest in their view of what God had in mind for them. George Bancroft, the leading historian of the Jacksonian era, and indeed the most widely-read American historian of the nineteenth century, proclaimed the American Revolution the most momentous event since the birth of Jesus. It heralded "a new and most glorious era" in which the United States would bring the salvation of true liberty to all the world. In the opening decades of the nineteenth century, most Americans shared Bancroft's sense of a great and holy mission for their new nation.

Americans admitted that their country was not perfect—yet. Democracy must be expanded, institutions improved, and morality purified if the United States was to carry out its God-given mission. Such a task was sure to be accomplished—Americans were firm believers in the inevitability of progress—if only everyone put their minds to it. By 1850 the nation would be hopelessly divided on the most basic moral and political issues, slavery and the nature of the republic itself; but in 1828 Andrew Jackson's inaugural address expressed unbounded optimism and faith in the future.

> I believe man can be elevated; man can become more and more endowed with divinity; and as he does, he becomes more God-like in his character and capable of governing himself. Let us go on elevating our people, perfecting our institutions until democracy shall reach such a point of perfection that we can acclaim with truth that the voice of the people is the voice of God.

Manifest Destiny

Inspired by a missionary zeal for the spread of its own revolutionary ideology, nineteenth century America assumed the role of the champion of revolution all over the world. When Latin American nations declared their independence from Spanish rule, the United States issued the Monroe Doctrine, warning European powers against intervention in Spain's behalf. It was the opposition of the British navy rather than American declarations that prevented the recolonization of Latin America; nevertheless, Americans felt good about championing the independence of small nations whom they saw as following in their own footsteps.

Throughout the nineteenth century the United States assumed the role of verbal champion of freedom overseas, a role encouraged, or even initiated in many cases, by the immigrant population. In 1840 immigrant Jews enlisted the support of Protestants and Catholics to protest Turkish atrocities against the Jews of Damascus. As a result the State Department joined European governments in remonstrating, with eventual success, with the Sultan of Turkey. When revolutionary leaders, such as Louis Kossuth of Hungary, came to the United States after the unsuccessful revolutions of 1848 to raise money for the liberation of their homelands, recent immigrants from these countries welcomed them, contributed to their cause, and encouraged native-born Americans to do likewise. Similarly, Irish-Americans rallied themselves and their anti-British allies among the native-born population to the financial and verbal support of Irish freedom. Thus the concern of ethnic communities for their countrymen and coreligionists overseas reinforced America's concern for the rights of peoples all over the world. This concern, praised as humanitarian and condemned as meddling, has become a lasting part of our national heritage.

During most of the nineteenth century, the young nation usually limited its commitments to the spread of democracy to pious declarations and financial and moral support. In North America, however, Americans identified the spread of democracy with the spread of their own boundaries—a project to which they were willing to commit military as well as moral support. Most Americans were eager to spread the blessings of democracy and Protestantism—and acquire valuable real estate—by expanding across the continent. If peaceful means failed, force was used for the realization of expansionist goals.

Immigrants found it easy to identify with and to encourage the expansionist policies of their nation. The Irish in particular were enthusiastic; indeed, the term "manifest destiny," the watchword of the expansionists, was invented by an Irish journalist, John O'Sullivan. Long and bitter foes of Great Britain, the Irish joined American super-patriots in agitating for the annexation of Canada, which they saw as a blow to weaken the British Empire and thus free the Irish homeland. Indeed, several filibustering expeditions were launched against Canada by Irish American radicals, but to no avail.

Although European immigrants usually favored territorial expansion, some ethnic communities were victimized by this expansion. Native Americans—Indians—were driven from their lands, their way of life destroyed, their numbers decimated, the survivors confined to barren reservations.

Others found themselves in the path of an expanding United States. A French community had existed in the Mississippi Valley since the founding of such settlements as St. Louis and New Orleans in the early seventeenth century. Though never large in number, the French, like other settlers, had brought with them their own architectural preferences, their own churches (Roman Catholic), their own parochial schools, even their own theaters. The Louisiana Purchase incorporated this French community into the United States. French influence lingered on in the social life of the city, in the laws of the state, and in the Creole language and culture of the Mississippi Delta, but after a troubled transitional period, the old French America became little more than a tourist attraction.

More tragic still was the fate of the Spanish-speaking population of the American Southwest. "The Mexican, like the poor Indian, is doomed to retire before the more enterprising Anglo-Saxon," wrote an American soldier. Texas and the southwestern part of the United States had been settled as a military and religious outpost of the Spanish Empire in Latin America, an empire which boasted rich cities and universities before the landing of the Pilgrims. Some of the earliest English speaking settlers to venture into this Spanish realm were so favorably impressed that they converted to Catholicism, married Spanish speaking women, and settled down to farming or ranching in the Latin style.

By the fourth decade of the nineteenth century, however, the situation had changed. The Spanish had lost their empire, and the Southwest was now part of the struggling new nation of Mexico. Anglo-Americans no longer respected the Spanish speaking inhabitants; after all, they argued, their government was not democratic, their religion was not Protestant, and their skin was not even the proper shade of white! More important, their lands were attractive and poorly defended.

The Mexican-American residents of what were to become the southwestern states found themselves the victims of forces they could not control. The Mexican War placed them, against their will, within the territorial limits of the United States. Then the discovery of gold and other minerals, followed by the completion of the transcontinental railroad, brought in a flood of Anglo-Americans and European immigrants. Mexican-Americans were reduced to second class citizenship in lands they had considered their own for centuries. Discriminatory taxes and violence were used to drive them out of mining and other industries. Promises to protect their property rights were not honored. Though a few of the wealthiest landowners managed to hold on to their estates and their social positions, many Mexican-American families lost their lands to drought, taxes, foreclosures, and the "sharp" dealings of the aggressive new "Anglos." By 1890 most of the Mexican-Americans had become low paid laborers for the Anglo-American miners and growers of the Southwest. Denied opportunities for employment and decent living conditions, Mexican-Americans were stereotyped by the newcomers as lazy, shiftless, backward, and immoral.

The Age of the Common Man—The Democratization of Politics

The United States justified its expansionist policies with the dubious claim that it was spreading democracy to areas that would not otherwise know its blessings. Within the United States itself the expansion of democracy was indeed a basic tenet of the new American creed. Property qualifications for suffrage were dropped, so that all white males could vote. The aristocratic caucus system of nominating national officers was replaced by popular party conventions, and birth in a log cabin became a much sought after qualification for the highest office in the land. Finally, this became the age of the new, democratic political corruption—the age of the stuffed ballot box, the "boss," and the political machine.

Ethnic Americans were an important part of the new political democracy. With the exception of the Chinese (barred "forever" from citizenship under a racist ordinance of 1790) all male immigrants were voters or potential voters. In an era of white manhood suffrage, their numbers and geographic concentration, especially in the cities, made immigrants a valuable prize to aspiring politicians. Leaders of every political party ate sauerkraut, wore the green, and proclaimed that "some of their best friends" were Irish, German, or Swedish. More to the point, they passed ordinances giving immigrants the vote in local elections even before they became naturalized citizens. Hoping to win the Norwegian vote, legislators in Minnesota established a "professorship of the Scandinavian language" at the "State University," oblivious of the fact that there was neither a "Scandinavian language," nor an institution called the "State University"!

When Germans and Scandinavians arrived in the prairie states they were not usually interested in politics. Often their main motive for taking out "first papers" for citizenship was to qualify for government land. Later western immigrants were drawn into politics almost against their will. In isolated rural areas, they were often the only settlers, so they had no choice but to take up the task of naming and organizing the new townships, laying out roads, levying taxes, establishing schools and other services, and carrying out the first elections. After this rather thorough initiation into American political processes, they went on to hold county and state offices, even governorships.

The Germans were numerous enough and well enough organized to become influential in urban as well as rural politics. Typical of the first generation of German urban politicians was Philip Dorschheimer of Buffalo, New York. Dorschheimer had emigrated from Germany at the age of nineteen and was fluent in both German and English. He is said to have taken the entire German community of Buffalo with him from the Whig party to the Free Soil Party, and, eventually, to the Republican Party, where a grateful Lincoln appointed him a federal revenue collector. An example of acculturation at work, Dorschheimer's son broke away from his father's ethnic political base, established a "respectable" career independent of his father's machine, and eventually became the Democratic vice governor of New York.

No ethnic group entered the world of expanding democracy more enthusiastically or with more far-reaching consequences than the Irish.

When Jacksonian democracy opened the political door to the common man, the urban Irish rushed in and took over. Accustomed to political controversy and secret societies in their homeland, the Irish had developed great skill in political organization. Their American experiences—the family and neighborhood loyalties and the discipline imposed by boyhood gangs—gave them a good start, as did their numerical strength in particular wards. Building on these assets, they created political machines with precinct captains, neighborhood clubhouses, and a party hierarchy culminating in the city-wide leader, or "boss." After the Civil War Irish machines frequently took over the local Democratic parties. In many cities they functioned as shadow governments, more powerful than the legal bureaucracy.

The Irish political machines handed out jobs and lucrative government contracts to friends, relatives, and loyal supporters. In an era of rapid urban growth there were many such favors to be distributed. Cities governed by machines were notoriously corrupt; in six years the Tweed gang stole over thirty million dollars from New York City. Machine politicians had no qualms about accepting "kickbacks," protecting illegal businesses, buying votes, and using local gangs to terrorize their opponents.

Although the activities of the new political machines horrified the "good government" people, from the point of view of the Irish immigrant there was much to be said in their favor. The Irish had few financial and educational resources; their political cohesiveness was their chief asset in the struggle to survive and move up in nineteenth century America. Through the machine the Irish got jobs as firemen, policemen, construction workers, and, for those with education, jobs as civil servants and teachers. The machine provided picnics and excursions for recreation, and assistance in case of sickness, unemployment, fire, or other misfortune—person-to-person help with no embarrassing investigations or red tape.

"Good government" forces denounced the machines as evil, and urged civil service examinations for the selection of public employees. The continuing war between reformers and the machine was actually a cultural conflict between differing concepts of government. The reformers considered political office an exalted public service to be rendered as impersonally and impartially as possible. According to the political mythology of the reformers, office should not be sought. Rather it should be bestowed by the public upon a reluctant benefactor who would supposedly assume it unselfishly as a public service. The Irish, however, saw politics as the legitimate competition for power and the rewards to be gained therefrom. Individuals openly sought careers in politics in the same way they sought careers in law or business and for the same mixture of selfish and unselfish motives. Little wonder, then, that despite the constant exposure of corruption and graft, Irish voters did not "throw the rascals out." The machine meant power, and Irish immigrants needed power, both for the material benefits it could bring and as a compensation for centuries of powerlessness in Ireland. The urban Irish used the new democracy for their own ends, setting a precedent that other ethnic groups would follow as soon as they could.

Immigrants as Reformers

"What is the good of having a republic unless the mass of people are better off than in a monarchy?" asked an Irish American newspaper in 1878. "Does not a real republic mean that all men have an equal chance and not millions born to suffering and poverty?" Many Americans were beginning to ask whether the American dream had dimensions beyond the bounds of traditional political activity. Was white manhood suffrage and a republican constitution enough for the Promised Land? Or should America concern itself with further reforms—economic, social, and moral, as well as political—if it was really to be the "last best hope of man"?

Yes, answered many; more reform was needed. To perfect their "city upon a hill" Americans plunged into a variety of crusades in the decades preceding the Civil War, crusades whose goals ranged from the most noble to the most preposterous. Reformers organized and flooded the land with lectures, pamphlets, and petitions urging their countrymen to abolish slavery, improve education, give equal rights to women, humanize the treatment of convicts and the insane, end war and poverty, and ban alcohol, private property, marriage, coffee, tea, tobacco, sexual intercourse, Catholicism, and white bread flour!

Most ethnic Americans were too busy trying to survive in America to become involved in reform movements which, to a great extent, were the luxury of the Protestant, native-born middle class. A surprising number of ethnic Americans did become involved, however. Economic reforms interested them most of all, because these had a clear bearing on the problems of their lives, but political and social reforms were also of interest.

With the development of the new industrial capitalism and the widening of the gap between rich and poor, socialists in Europe and the United States began to question the free enterprise system itself. The earliest socialist organizations in the United States were heavily German in leadership and membership, including brilliant idealistic "forty-eighters" like Dr. Adolph Dounai, editor of the leading Marxist journal in the United States, and Wilhelm Weitling, founder of the Central Committee of United Trades in New York in 1850.

Unable to realize their revolutionary dreams in Germany, some political refugees transferred their hopes to the United States. Taking the American Declaration of Independence at face value, a small but highly articulate clique of German-born intellectuals shocked most Americans, foreign-born and native-born, by combining socialism with other causes such as the abolition of slavery and the radical democratization of the American government. Among the changes German radicals advocated were abolition of the Presidency, direct and universal suffrage for men and women (black and white), the abolition of all legislation regarding religious practices, the abolition of private ownership of land and utilities, the eight hour working day, free legal services, public care for the aged, progressive taxation, complete equality of the sexes, and the abolition of money.

The Irish, like the Germans, produced a small but articulate number of liberals intent upon solving the problem of poverty. John Boyle O'Reilly wrote poems such as "From the Earth, a Cry" and "City Streets," in which he described the plight of the poor and denounced "charity scrimped and iced in the name of a cautious statistical Christ." Patrick Ford, a liberal journalist, took a more doctrinaire approach. Ford blamed the depression of the 1870's, which put many Irish-Americans in bread and soup lines, on what to him was the immoral taking of interest for the use of money and rent for the use of land. In the pages of the widely-circulated *Irish World* he familiarized his many readers with the ideas of Henry George and the Land Reform League of California years before publication of George's internationally famous work, *Progress and Poverty.*

When Henry George ran for mayor of New York City in 1886 on a platform of social reform, free access to land for everyone, and the "single tax" on profits from the sale or rental of land, Irish liberals paraded in the streets in his support. George's ideas on conquering poverty through land reform were more appealing to the immigrant Irish than Marxism because their own experience with poverty had been agrarian rather than industrial. The Irish immigrant could well understand a reform philosophy in which the landlord was the villain! Irish-Americans took George's ideas back to Ireland, where they influenced attempts at land reform already underway.

Irish attempts to abolish rent and open land to all who wanted it met with staunch opposition from the Catholic Church both in Ireland and in the United States. Beleaguered by revolutionaries, the Pope took a strong stand against nationalism, socialism, liberalism, indeed, practically every reform "ism" of the mid nineteenth century. With a few exceptions, American churchmen followed the lead of Rome. The Bishop of Cleveland, for example, denounced the women's branch of the Land League as "destructive of female modesty," and warned Patrick Ford that inequalities in life are good because "some men must rise, others must fall; without this there would be no motive for individual effort."

The Irish women of Cleveland continued their activities in support of the Land League, and Ford suggested that the "ironhearted" bishop must be in the service of the monopolists. Moreover, if poverty were such a good thing, "why not distribute its blessings around?" But most Irish immigrants hoped to rise within the American system rather than to change that system. Taking their cue from their religious leaders, most of the Irish, like most of the Germans and Scandinavians, were socially and politically conservative. As for the Catholic Church, Protestants who had little good to say about it in any other context praised it as "an instrument of discipline and control over 'the dangerous classes'."

Immigrants and Utopias

Seeking alternatives to an increasing competitive and materialistic society, mid nineteenth century Americans produced experiments in group living—Brook Farm, Oneida, Hopedale, Deseret, and a variety of communes, phalanxes, and other utopias. "Not a leading man but has a draft of a new community in his waist-coat pocket," said Ralph Waldo Emerson. In these communities, social experimenters hoped to solve all social, sexual, and spiritual problems as well as all economic difficulties. What the utopias achieved on a small scale would then, it was hoped, spread everywhere.

Ethnic Americans, too, built utopian communities in which they hoped to solve all the problems of humanity. Some of these communities were completely secular in origin, like Icaria, created by the French socialist and author Etienne Cabet. Religiously motivated communities were more common, however. They were also more successful, as faith provided the discipline and unity of purpose necessary for a cooperative venture.

Thousands of Swedes, Norwegians, and Danes came to the United States because of the preaching of Mormon missionaries. They joined the great Mormon social experiment of Deseret, in the territory of Utah. Other Swedish religious dissenters built a utopian community at Bishop Hill in Henry County, Illinois. Their leader, Eric Jansson, was a charismatic prophet who claimed to represent the second coming of Christ. Founded in 1846, his theocratically ruled, communistic community flourished by growing flax and manufacturing linens and carpets. By 1851 it had grown to eleven hundred, about a third of the county's total population. Jansson's death, however, followed by the economic panic of 1857, brought Bishop Hill to financial ruin.

The most enthusiastic builders of ethnic utopias in nineteenth century America were Germans. In 1814 Father George Rapp of Württemberg, convinced that the end of the world was near, emigrated to the United States with seven hundred followers to build a godly new Jerusalem. Harmony, the colony he established in Indiana, was dedicated to celibacy and to communally organized, highly regimented labor. This colony and its successor, Economy (later Ambridge) Pennsylvania, were noted for their physical prosperity and their harsh discipline. Father Rapp was said to have executed his own son for breaking the ban he had imposed upon sexual intercourse, a ban so well observed that the colony literally died of old age in the early twentieth century!

Less bizarre and more permanent were the peaceful, industrious villages of the German pietist settlement at Amana, Iowa. When the original cooperative was dissolved in 1932 (ninety years after it was founded), Amana was operating thirty different commercial enterprises, including a winery and a woolen factory. Its tranquil, noncompetitive atmosphere still survives. Unlike Amana, most nineteenth century utopias were short lived. Their presence, however brief, indicates that some Americans were rejecting the new, competitive industrial society and seeking alternative ways to live.

Most people lacked the utopian commitment to a total restructuring of society. They tended to advocate one or more particular reforms—educational reform, abolitionism, or women's rights—as the key to the perfecting of American society. Ethnic Americans were involved in these humanitarian and democratic crusades in a variety of ways. German born educators played a major role in reforming American schools, for example, from the introduction of kindergartens and physical education to the establishment of graduate level university programs.

Though few ethnic Americans were active abolitionists—with the exception of some of the German "forty-eighters"—many played an indirect role in this vital reform. Scandinavian and German farmers in the midwest were staunchly opposed to the extension of slavery into the territories. Like other western settlers, they wanted to keep the frontier a white man's land of family farms and feared the introduction of a plantation system. In the 1850's the newly organized Republican Party gained popularity among Germans and Scandinavians both because it opposed the extension of slavery and because it favored free homesteads and federal aid for improved transportation. German-born Carl Schurz became a leading figure in the Republican party and helped bring in many other German-Americans. By voting in large numbers for Lincoln in 1860, Germans and Scandinavians in the midwestern states played an indirect role in the eventual ending of slavery throughout the country, though this had not been their intention.

Similarly, ethnic Americans played a role in the movement to improve the status of women. Most ethnic women were too busy rearing large families, earning a living, or both to be much concerned with the seemingly abstract issues of sexual equality raised by Lucy Stone, Elizabeth Stanton, and other pre-Civil War feminists. Moreover, their European ethnic and religious backgrounds reinforced the conventional American view that the only proper place for a woman was in the home, subordinate to a man, whether husband, father, or son.

For many immigrant women, however, reality dictated a lifestyle that departed from the conventional feminine stereotype. Sometimes illness, accident, or desertion eliminated the protective husband. Far from the help of fathers, uncles, or other supportive males, ethnic women became the sole breadwinners, parents, and decision makers for many families in the New World. In addition, thousands of young single women came to America on their own, showing by this act alone an unusual amount of supposedly unfeminine initiative and independence.

At least one ethnic woman, Ernestine Rose, was an active feminist. Ernestine Rose was born in a Polish Jewish community and educated by her father, a rabbi. Rejecting an unwanted arranged marriage (she later arranged her own), she emigrated first to England and then to the United States. Here she became known as an active freethinker and abolitionist, as well as a feminist. Soon after her arrival she began a campaign to give the women of New York State the right to control their own property and to become the guardians of their children. The campaign opened with a petition to the state legislature:

> After a good deal of trouble I obtained five signatures . . . . Some of the ladies said the gentlemen would laugh at them; others, that they had rights enough, and the men said the women had too many rights already. . . . I continued sending petitions with increased numbers of signatures until 1848, when the legislature enacted the law which granted women the right to keep what was her own. But no sooner did it become legal than all the women said: 'Oh, that is right. We ought always to have had that.'

Ernestine Rose became a close and active colleague of Susan B. Anthony and Lucy Stone. Although English was not her native language, she became one of the most effective orators of the women's movement.

Immigrants as Objects of Reform

If economic, social, and "humanitarian" reforms appealed to at least some ethnic Americans, "moral" reforms, such as temperance, sabbatarianism, and other religiously inspired "uplift" endeavors, had virtually no appeal at all. Not only were ethnic Americans unlikely to be participants in such reforms, they were likely to become their targets.

To many Protestant, native-born Americans, the new immigrants were sinners and their lifestyles were plagues to be eliminated.

Emotional, revivalistic religion which had lain dormant since the Great Awakening of colonial times, emerged again in the early nineteenth century. A new generation of zealous evangelists led the sons of the enlightenment freethinkers in a frenzied religious revival that spread from the college campuses to the country campgrounds throughout the land. The revivalist preached a simple, emotional, and democratic message: everyone must accept Jesus Christ as personal savior, and there was no time to lose. The Second Coming was imminent. One evangelist, William Miller, even set the date: October 22, 1844.

> Soon, very soon, God will arise in His anger and the vine of the earth will be reaped. See! See! . . . the clouds have burst asunder; the heavens appear; the great white throne is in sight! . . . He comes! He comes! Behold the Savior comes!—Lift up your heads, ye saints—He comes! He comes! He comes!

In this atmosphere church membership in Protestant evangelical sects soared. A variety of church-directed reform societies arose to make America worthy of the Second Coming. These societies distributed Bibles and religious tracts, sent out speakers, established Sunday schools and built homes for the wayward. They worked diligently to make America godly by converting Catholics and Jews to Protestantism, and by outlawing liquor, Sabbath breaking, and, in some cases, slavery (which churches saw as an institution fraught with sexual temptation for both master and slave).

Many of these reforms were directed at ethnic Americans, who responded with indifference or outright hostility. Efforts to convert immigrant Catholics and Jews met with virtually no success. Efforts to "uplift" ethnic slum dwellers through neighborhood preaching missions were equally unrewarding. A more promising approach was taken by Reverend and Mrs. Lewis Pease, who established a school and an industrial workshop in their mission at Five Points, New York, to fight sin by attacking poverty. The women's home missionary society that had engaged Reverend Pease relieved him of his post, furious that he had neglected his proper duty, preaching sermons to the poor.

The most popular campaign of the new militant Protestantism was the effort to outlaw the "demon rum." While there were advocates of temperance among the Scandinavians, and at least one temperance worker in the Irish Catholic clergy, most ethnic Americans (and many of the native born, as well) considered the effort to ban alcohol as unwarranted and outrageous interference with their lives. To the German-American, beer was as wholesome a drink as water (given the polluted condition of much of the urban water supply, it may often have been more wholesome) and the beer garden was a social center for the entire family. For many Irish-Americans, whiskey made a hard life more bearable, and the corner saloon was one of the few places a man could feel at ease. In addition, Catholics and Jews used wine as part of their religious ceremonies.

Sabbatarianism, strict Puritan observance of Sunday as a day of rest and prayer, had as little appeal as temperance. The Germans and Irish were accustomed to spending their Sundays in socializing and relaxing rather than in worship and meditation. For religious Jews, who observed the Sabbath by keeping their businesses closed on Saturday, Sunday "blue laws" were an economic hardship. They reduced the working week to five instead of six days.

Influenced by pressure from Protestant church groups, townships, counties, and states proposed laws against some or all alcoholic beverages and against Sabbath violation. In many communities the laws created hardships for dissenters. In some areas, people were arrested for working on their own farms on Sunday. Sometimes the laws were defeated because of the opposition of ethnic minorities, as well as other Americans who shared their views. The question of whether the majority can impose its concepts of morality and proper behavior on minorities was raised, debated, but not resolved, and remains controversial as ever.

Frustrated by immigrant resistance to their moral reforms, militant Protestants, including many ministers, were among the leaders of a movement against the "foreigner." Immigrants were associated in the public mind with many of the problems of nineteenth century society—poverty, crime, alcoholism, political corruption. As these were primarily the problems of rapid urbanization, concern about them focused on the urban immigrants, particularly the Irish.

The Scandinavians aroused the least hostility, probably because they were Protestants and because they tended to disappear into the vast prairies of the West. Prejudice against Germans was more common. Because they clung to their native language and, like the colonial Germans, enjoyed a social life of their own, they were considered clannish. They were criticized because of their drinking habits, and the political activities of a few led to the entire group being condemned as abolitionists, socialists, and atheists.

The Chinese bore the brunt of anti-immigrant feeling on the west coast, where their distinctive life style and their economic competition to whites made them immensely unpopular. Taxed, harassed, even lynched by the white population, the Chinese were eventually excluded by law from further immigration.

In most of the rest of the country it was the Irish who occupied the least favored position. Like the Germans, the Irish were condemned as clannish and intemperate. The activities of a few Irish nationalists, as well as the general Irish practice of remitting money to relatives in the old country raised charges of dual loyalty. In a country accustomed to associating virtue with rural living, the heavily urban Irish were associated with the crime, vice, and political corruption of the cities.

Most damaging of all, the Irish were Roman Catholics. To militant, nineteenth century American Protestants, Catholicism was the grossest of superstitions, associated with tyranny, immorality, and as in the colonial era, threats from overseas. Many Americans were convinced that Catholic monarchies were plotting to undo both the American Revolution and the Protestant Reformation and were sending masses of Roman Catholic immigrants to the United States as their instruments in pursuing these sinister aims.

Nativism, and hatred of Irish Catholics in particular, was the dark side of the nineteenth century effort to define Americanism. To some, the process of defining an American nationality required the existence of outsiders against whom they could measure their own qualifications as insiders, or "real" Americans. The existence of an Irish Catholic minority provided the necessary "outsiders."

For nativists, patriotism was heightened by the perception of foreign threats. European monarchies and the Papal States fulfilled this need in the mid nineteenth century. They did, at this time, represent repressive political ideologies hostile to the American democratic philosophy. In 1828 a conservative German scholar Friedrich von Schlegel gave a series of lectures connecting monarchy and Catholicism, while denouncing democracy and Protestantism. Calling the United States the "nursery of revolution," he urged Catholic missions for this troublesome country.

A few such missions were established, but they were of little importance. Certainly the massive immigration of Irish and German Catholics had nothing to do with them. Protestant superpatriots refused to believe this, just as they refused to believe that the social problems of their society could be indigenous, rather than caused by outsiders. Looking back at an idealized past, they blamed Irish Catholic immigration for all the ills of a rapidly changing, increasingly urban society. Samuel F. Morse, inventor of the telegraph, summarized this kind of thinking in his book *Imminent Dangers to the Free Institutions of the United States through Foreign Immigration*, published in 1835.

> How is it possible that foreign turbulence imported by shiploads, that riot and ignorance in hundreds of thousands of human priest-controlled machines should suddenly be thrown into our society and not produce turbulence and excess? Can one throw mud into pure water and not disturb its clearness?

Morse's dire warnings were followed in the 1830's and 1840's by a flood of anti-Catholic literature. Salacious tales of corrupt priests and immoral nuns were relished in the homes of Protestant churchgoers all over the country, serving as a kind of pious pornography. The most famous of such works was Maria Monk's *Awful Disclosures of the Hotel Dieu Nunnery of Montreal*, supposedly an eyewitness account of sexual licentiousness within the convent. According to the book, babies born of illicit unions between nuns and priests were thrown into a pit in a tunnel between the convent and the neighboring monastery. But no such tunnel or pit existed. Moreover, Maria Monk was a delinquent girl, neither a nun nor a Catholic. Her work was exposed as a fraud, and she ended her career in prison for picking the pocket of one of her clients in a house of prostitution. Nevertheless, her book continued to be circulated, read, believed—and profitably imitated.

The Schools as Battlegrounds

Anti-Catholic books, lectures, and sermons added to the cultural and economic tensions already present between the native-born and the ethnic communities. The results were often tragic. Mobs attacked Germans in Midwestern cities and rioting between the native-born and the immigrant was a common occurrence at election time. But no area aroused more emotion-laden conflict—and more violence—than the school.

The mid nineteenth century saw the beginnings of the public school system in most of the United States. The public elementary school—or common school, as it was called at the time—stood at the center of concurrent, and often conflicting social movements. Unlike traditional European societies, which looked reverently to the past, the United States was a new society whose members concentrated their attention upon the future. Immigrants and native-born, ethnic and nonethnics alike—everyone agreed that their best efforts and sacrifices were to be directed toward building for their children. In the nineteenth century, as today, observers from overseas noted that the United States was a child-centered society. In a future-oriented, child-centered society, the school became the focus of enormous hopes and expectations, and the object of enormous emotional as well as financial investment. Because different socioeconomic classes and ethnic groups had different hopes and expectations, no "common" school could possibly satisfy them all.

Urban working people hoped that the new common schools would offer social mobility for the next generation. In colonial America craftsmen had taught remunerative skills to their sons through the apprenticeship system. By the middle of the nineteenth century, however, factory-made goods were making many of these traditional skills obsolete. Skilled workmen realized that their children needed a new kind of education, a "book-learning" education, if they were to compete successfully in the world of commerce and industry. The same Jacksonian democrats who fought against the economic "monopolies" that deprived them of equal opportunity also fought against educational monopoly for the same reason. Unable to afford the private schooling available to the rich, they demanded public education as necessary to the realization of the American dream of equal opportunity and, more specifically, socioeconomic mobility for their children.

As revisionist historians of American education have recently pointed out, not all advocates of the common school were working people motivated by the desire for economic advancement. Many of the founders of common schools saw these institutions as instruments of social control rather than as avenues of social mobility. Linking urbanization with immigration, educators hoped to use schools as means of fighting crime and "turbulence" by providing urban children with the structured environment their families could not or would not provide. "As population increases, and especially as artificial wants multiply, the temptations increase, and the guards and securities must increase also, or society will deteriorate," wrote an educational reformer.

Schools were established to take young people away from the evil influences of the street—and of the slum home—and teach them "control," "self-discipline," "earnestness," and "restraint." Education was seen as a bulwark not only against crime, but also against sexual licentiousness (the "passions" of which middle class educators were so much afraid) and against labor disturbances, unions, and strikes. Diligence, docility, punctuality, cleanliness, and industriousness were the "hidden curriculum" of the new schools. These schools were designed to instill a Protestant, even Puritan, middle-class morality and life style in the children of the urban, often the immigrant, poor.

The founders of the common schools had patriotic as well as moral goals. Education was seen as the handmaiden of democracy. The electorate must be educated if it was to make wise decisions. Patriotic education it was hoped, would teach children the duty of changing laws and leaders by ballot rather than by rebellion. Moreover, it was believed, education would eliminate the political corruption of the cities. Horace Mann wrote:

> If the responsibleness and value of the elective franchise were duly appreciated . . . elections would be among the most solemn and religious days in the calendar. Men would approach them, not only with preparation and solicitude, but with the sobriety and solemnity, with which descreet and religious-minded men meet the great crises of life.

Education would end the practice of the urban working class, many of them Irish and German, of making election day an occasion for drinking and brawling as well as voting.

Finally, many of the early school reformers saw the common school as the place in which to forge a common American culture. In the common school children of varying denominations would come together to hear the Bible read and to worship together "a common Father." The debate over the use of German in Pennsylvania's common schools called forth comments such as the following: " . . . we ought no longer to be divided into separate races, and by distinct languages and habits. . . ." and "I think that the whole people of the state should be amalgamated as soon as that end can possibly be accomplished."

The new public schools were seen by their founders as crucibles of a common American culture—virtuous, Protestant, republican, and Anglo-Saxon. It was important, then, that the major threats to that culture—Catholics, the urban poor, immigrants from nonrepublican lands—become part of that system. Despite various stratagems to attract them, however, these very groups did not flock to the new common schools. Impoverished parents sometimes kept their children out of school because their meager earnings were vital to the immediate survival of the family. Because school was not compulsory, many children simply refused to attend. Besides, classrooms were usually grim, joyless places, offering little that could compare with the excitement of the street.

Parents and children resented the condescending attitude of school authorities who considered them inferior and tainted and who viewed their lives as devoid of beauty, culture, or virtue. Nor did immigrant parents share the optimism of the native-born working class that schools were in fact certain avenues to social mobility. Assessing their situation realistically, they saw that their children were unlikely to remain long enough to reap the much touted social and economic benefits, if indeed such benefits existed. Of what value was schooling in a society where "no Irish need apply"?

Finally, many immigrants resisted the public schools because they did not want their children absorbed in the Protestant Anglo-Saxon culture represented by the common school. To avoid this, Norwegians, Swedes, and Germans—Protestant and Catholic alike—set up schools in which their native language, religion, and historical traditions were preserved. The largest group to resist the common schools for religious and cultural reasons, were the Irish Catholics. Their resistance, which seemed especially sinister, led to bitter controversy and violence.

The earliest Catholic schools in the East were often private convent schools, patronized by the daughters of wealthy families, Protestant as well as Catholic. Such a school was the Ursuline convent in suburban Boston, forty of whose sixty pupils were the daughters of wealthy Unitarians. The failure of a rival Protestant school, the violently anti-Catholic sermons of ministers like Lyman Beecher, and recurrent friction between native-born and Irish-Catholic laborers touched off a riot in which anti-Catholic mobs burned the convent school to the ground. The nuns and their pupils barely escaped with their lives. Leaders of the mob were prosecuted, but their trial was a mockery; no one was convicted and no reparations were paid. Lyman Beecher continued to warn Protestant America in sermons and in writings of the dangers to republican institutions inherent in the sinister Catholic schools.

Private convent schools were only for the few, however. The vast majority of Catholics, especially the new immigrants, could not afford them for their children. Recognizing the need, urban parishes opened schools for the poor. These parish schools lacked the teachers, facilities, and above all the money to educate the masses of new children. For most children, the choice was between education in the new common schools or no education at all.

The choice was not an easy one. The Catholic clergy recognized the Protestant tone of the public schools, pointing out that the textbooks made derogatory references to Catholicism and that Protestant prayers, hymns, and Bible reading were part of the daily schedule. Irish priests discouraged parents from sending children to the public schools. Needless to say, this only heightened the suspicions of a Protestant population rapidly becoming committed to the public school as the cornerstone of Americanism. Could people who rejected the public schools be good Americans, it was asked?

In New York, Bishop John Hughes tried to solve the educational problems of his flock in 1840 by requesting money from the Public School Society for separate Catholic schools. He was encouraged by Governor Seward's public statement that

> The children of foreigners are too often deprived of the educational advantages of our system of public education in consequence of prejudice arising from differences of language or religion. . . . I do not hesitate, therefore, to recommend the establishment of schools in which they may be instructed by teachers speaking the same language with themselves and professing the same religion.

Seward's statement and Hughes' request touched off a storm of controversy. Catholics considered their request for part of the public school fund only fair, as their taxes contributed to that fund. Protestants worried that sectarian demands for public funding of parochial schools were unconstitutional and, worse yet, subversive of the whole idea of the "common" school. Already, other churches were requesting funds for their schools. If such requests were granted, could the public school system survive?

In New York the issue was resolved by the institution of local school districts, locally controlled. In their own neighborhoods, at least, Catholics could eliminate the most objectionable features of the Protestant public school system by secularizing the education offered and by appointing secular Catholic teachers. Bishop Hughes regarded this as a temporary makeshift, however. His goal was not secular education, but Catholic education taught by members of religious orders. With great financial sacrifice, the nineteenth century Catholic community in New York and indeed throughout the country, moved toward that goal. Meanwhile the public school system, recognizing its need to serve a heterogeneous population, became increasingly secularized.

Bishop Francis Kenrick of Philadelphia was faced with essentially the same problem as Bishop Hughes of New York. Rather than request public funds for parish schools, he asked that Catholic children be allowed to bring their own Bibles to public schools and be excused from religious instruction there. When the school board agreed, angry Protestant militants accused Catholics of trying to "kick the Bible out of the school." "Godless" schools could not be proper vehicles for real Americanism! In 1844 anti-Catholic "patriots" held a mass meeting in the Irish Catholic Kensington section. Rioting broke out. Catholic churches and schools were destroyed, several people killed, and many more wounded.

Nativism—Its Rise and Fall

The anti-Catholic violence begun during the school controversies escalated into institutionalized nativist activity. "A revolution has begun," announced a New York nativist publication, the *American Republican*. In the 1830's and 1840's nativists formed secret societies such as the Order of the Star Spangled Banner, the Order of the Sons of the Sires of '76, and the Order of United Americans, with a women's auxiliary, the United Daughters of America. Quasi-political from the beginning, these organizations united with local nativist political parties in the early 1850's to form the Native American, or Know Nothing, Party. Anti-foreign and anti-Catholic, the Know Nothings sought to deny political rights to immigrants, lengthen the naturalization period, and above all, close the doors to further immigration.

A strange collection of people took shelter within the Know Nothing Party. Native-born working men who were not rising as fast as they felt they should joined because they feared the competition of immigrant labor. Urban workers joined because they saw Catholics a threat to the existence of public schools, and hence to their children's futures. Southerners joined because they considered all foreigners abolitionists. In the North, on the other hand, abolitionists joined because they saw immigrants as stumbling blocks to their reforms, as did temperance workers and Sabbatarians. Though the party was rabidly anti-Catholic, French Catholics joined. As native-born Americans, they felt their position in the nation, and in the Church, threatened by the arrival of the Irish!

The Know Nothing Party had "as many elements of persistence as an anti-cholera or anti-potato-rot party would have," observed Horace Greeley, a contemporary editor. The party won control of the state legislatures of Rhode Island, New Hampshire, Connecticut, and Maryland in 1853 and of Kentucky, Texas, and California two years later, but its achievements were negligible. Know-Nothing legislators investigated convents and other Catholic institutions, usually as a pretext for junkets around the state at the taxpayers' expense, but did little else. In the presidential election of 1856 the party's candidate, Millard Fillmore, carried only the state of Maryland. Politically, the nativist movement was dead before the end of the decade.

It is significant that a nativist political party arose on the eve of the Civil War. Nativism was a last attempt to find an issue which would unite a divided nation by transcending increasingly bitter sectional disputes over slavery, tariffs, internal improvements, and the nature of the Union itself. These were the real issues confronting the nation in the 1850's, and a national outcry against the "foreigner" could not make them go away, any more than it could ease the stresses and strains of rapid social change.

Lack of relevance to America's real problems killed the Know Nothing Party, but other factors helped. Its following had always been a vocal but small minority. Native-born Americans opposed nativism and immigration restriction as denials of the principles of religious freedom and equal opportunity for which they believed their country stood. Many individuals, including Abraham Lincoln, rose to the defense of the newcomers.

Ethnic communities themselves fought nativism. Priests and rabbis explained their "alien" faiths in articles, lectures, and public debates with their Protestant detractors. Ethnic leaders appealed to economic expediency as well as to idealism in defense of continued immigration, pointing out fallacies in the nativist arguments and matching them statistic for statistic.

Faced with nativist attacks, German-Americans tended to withdraw into their own ethnic communities, strengthening them until they became bastions for survival. The Irish, on the other hand, took the offensive, seizing control of the machinery of urban governments whenever possible to guarantee their rights. The Plug-Uglies, Blood Tubs, Rip Raps, and other Irish gangs of New York fought nativism with their fists, defending Catholic churches from mobs and forcing Know Nothing voters away from the polls.

Irish intellectuals began the now time honored tradition in which minority groups write their own histories to prove what good Americans they are. When German, English, and American historians attributed all favorably viewed aspects of life to the inventiveness of the Teutons and Anglo-Saxons, Irish-American historians countered with the equally unrealistic "Celtic Myth." According to the Celtic myth, representative government, trial by jury, popular education, and other "American" traditions originated in Ireland. America was discovered by St. Brendan the Navigator, Columbus was rowed ashore by an Irishman, and Irish soldiers won the Revolutionary war almost singlehandedly. Native-born Americans were scarcely aware of the existence of the Celtic myth, but it boosted the confidence and self-esteem of the Irish newcomers.

The Civil War itself helped to kill the nativist movement. The great crusade to save the Union and abolish slavery swallowed up all other crusades—including the nativist movement. In the Union and in the Confederacy ethnic communities joined their neighbors in four years of tragic fighting. Most immigrants lived in the North, where they responded in large numbers to Lincoln's call for troops. However they felt about the issue of slavery—and most shared the antiblack prejudice of their society—they had suffered much to cast their lot with the United States and did not want to see it destroyed.

After the Civil War interest in nativism, like interest in many other prewar crusades, declined. Four years of bloodletting left the nation physically and emotionally exhausted. Though some individuals remained loyal to their favorite causes, the reforming zeal of the majority was spent. America entered a postwar period of materialism. Individuals devoted themselves to the pursuit of their own interests— and the main interest of almost everyone seemed to be making money. Ethnic Americans, whose main concern had, of necessity, been economic survival, fitted comfortably into this national pattern.

Contrary to the dire predictions of the nativists, ethnic Americans did adapt themselves successfully to the United States. In the postwar decades many moved up the socioeconomic ladder from poverty to solid working class, from unskilled to skilled occupations. Economic improvement brought with it changes in lifestyle, so that ethnic Americans no longer seemed threatening to the "American" way of life. While the Irish tended to advance more slowly than the Germans and Scandinavians, even they produced their millionaires. By the end of the century, this once-despised community had produced a large number of upwardly mobile "lace curtain" families whose obsession with the proprieties rivaled that of the native-born middle class.

In addition to their own hard work and determination, ethnic Americans in the middle decades of the nineteenth century had still another factor in their favor. They had arrived in a country that thought of itself as young with an unlimited potential for growth. In such a country there was ample room, geographically and psychologically for newcomers. Nativists worried that too many "outsiders" would destroy the nation, but most Americans did not agree. Firmly convinced that environment was stronger than heredity, they believed that their beneficent land, air, and institutions would make the immigrant a "new man"—an American. If, as the evangelists said, a man could be "born again," transformed from sinner to saint, then why couldn't the immigrant be transformed from foreigner to American? Despite the doubts and hesitations of some, nineteenth century America's unbounded optimism, its belief in the inevitability of progress, and its confidence in its own strength and rectitude made it secure enough to accept the new ethnic communities.

CHAPTER 6

The Urban Ghetto: Immigrants in Industrial America, 1880-1924

By 1880 the Irish, German, and Scandinavian immigrants, once so alien and even frightening, were familiar figures on the American scene, their American-born children growing to adulthood. Soon, however, native-born Americans (including, often, the children of these earlier immigrants) would express alarm about a new group of "aliens" in their midst. Another wave of immigration was entering the country, a wave which began in the 1880's and peaked in the early twentieth century. The people it brought congregated in the great metropolitan areas, creating massive ethnic ghettos whose remnants are still visible. Who were these late nineteenth and early twentieth century immigrants? Why did they come? What conditions of life and work did they find in the great cities of a nation which was rapidly becoming the industrial, financial, and military leader of the entire world?

Immigration at the Turn of the Century

Contemporary observers were struck by the rapid increase in the number of immigrants. Total immigration in the three decades preceding the Civil War had numbered five million. Between 1860 and 1890 that number doubled, and between 1890 and 1914 it tripled. Over a million newcomers entered annually in the peak years of 1905, 1906, 1907, 1910, 1913, and 1914. By 1920 almost sixty per cent of the population of cities of one hundred thousand or more inhabitants were first or second generation ethnic Americans. Over three quarters of New York City's school children had foreign born parents.

As the century neared its close, there was a steady decline in immigration from the British Isles, Germany, and the Scandinavian countries. At the same time, immigration from eastern and southern Europe increased. By 1896 Italians, East European Jews, Poles, Ukrainians, Slovaks, Bohemians, Hungarians, Greeks, Portuguese, Armenians, Syrians, and Lebanese outnumbered western European immigrants, and by 1907 they constituted over eighty per cent of the total. They were joined by smaller numbers from Asia and the Western Hemisphere—including many Japanese, French Canadians, Mexicans, West Indians.

The religious backgrounds of the newcomers varied widely. The largest single religious group was Roman Catholic, but millions were Jews or members of Greek and Russian Orthodox churches, and some were Moslems and Buddhists. The cultural baggage they brought to America was equally varied. Slavic farmers came from traditional, closely knit peasant villages similar in many ways to those from which the earlier Irish, German, and Scandinavian peasants had come. Southern Italians were also tillers of the soil, but they lived in rural towns, often miles from the fields they tilled for their absentee landlords. Jews, too, were town dwellers. Forbidden for centuries to own land, they earned a precarious living in petty commerce and in crafts such as woodworking, capmaking, and tailoring.

The peasant village was the primary social and economic institution in the life of the Slavic farmer. For the southern Italian, this function was fulfilled by the family, a tightly knit unit in which the interests of the individual were subordinated to those of the group. The Japanese left a land in which nationalism, symbolized by devotion to the Emperor, was a strong unifying element. Jews, on the other hand, were scarcely touched by the emerging nationalism of the countries within which they lived. The unifying element in their lives was their age old religious tradition, an all-encompassing way of life. Clearly the cultural backgrounds of these immigrants varied widely and were radically different from the industrialized, secular, and individualistic society to which they came.

The newcomers varied just as widely in educational background and in skills. Half of the Italians were unable to read or write, but Jews, Bohemians, and Finns had a high literacy rate. Ninety-eight per cent of the Japanese who immigrated were literate, a percentage considerably higher than that of the total American population. Most of the early twentieth century immigrants had agricultural skills. But Syrians, Lebanese, and Jews often had commercial experience, which proved invaluable in the increasingly nonagricultural American economy.

Russian Jews and Scots had the highest percentage of skilled laborers of all immigrant groups.

The late nineteenth century marked the appearance of numerous "birds of passage," immigrants who spent a few years in the United States and then returned, permanently or temporarily, to their former homes. The great steamship lines, which made travel faster, cheaper, and safer than it had ever been before, made this possible. The movement of these "birds of passage" closely followed the ups and downs of the American business cycle, with some individuals shuttling back and forth many times as though unable to decide where they really wanted to live.

For every hundred immigrants to enter the country between 1900 and 1910, thirty eight left. Most of these were young single men—Italians, Slavs, Greeks, or Japanese—who had come to earn enough money to buy land or a small business in the old country. Many reached this goal; a majority of the small landowners in some south Italian villages were returned American immigrants. Others went home without reaching their goals, victims of tuberculosis, industrial accidents, or discouragement and disillusion.

Like earlier immigrants, most came to better themselves economically. By 1880 East European peasants were feeling the same pressures of too much population on too little land that had set their West European counterparts moving a generation or two earlier. As industrialization and urbanization moved from west to east, eastern European farmers had to compete with newly-consolidated large estates in supplying food to the growing cities. They also had to compete with the grain growers of Argentina, Canada, the United States, and Australia, whose products could now be shipped everywhere on newly constructed railroads and newly opened steamship lines. The following letter was written to an emigrant aid society by a Polish peasant in the early twentieth century. It could as easily have been written by an Irish, German, or Scandinavian immigrant a generation or two earlier.

> I have a very great wish to go to America. I want to leave my native country because we are six children and we have very little land. . . . So it is difficult for us to live. Father got me married and gave me . . . 200 rubles . . . my share (of the value of the family farm) and now I am alone with my wife. . . . Wages are very small, just enough to live, so I would like to go (to America) in the name of our Lord God; perhaps I would earn more there. . . . I am a healthy boy 24 years old. I do not fear any work.

Local problems set people in motion. Sometimes new transportation facilities brought in competition that ruined the livelihood of the local merchants and craftsmen. The McKinley Tariff of 1890 ruined the Bohemian button making industry, causing many Bohemians to come to the United States. French tariffs on Italian wines and Greek currants caused the emigration of Italians and Greeks from the wine and currant producing areas.

Many individuals made the decision to emigrate because of personal difficulties, Oscar Ameringer's autobiography, *If You Don't Weaken*, is a case study of such a decision. Even as a child, Ameringer did not fit into the life of his village in the Austro-Hungarian Empire. He outraged the staunchly Catholic school authorities by writing an essay favorable to Protestantism. An impulsive teenager, he plunged into a tavern battle to defend a peasant who was being abused by the emperor's soldiers. This incident led directly to his emigration. As Ameringer explained:

> I was already the town Pariah. In the opinion of its burghers and burghesses, all but mother, I was doomed and damned. There were only two courses for young hellions like me. The gallows and hell—or America. So to America I went. There were no tears shed at my departure, save mother's and mine.

As in earlier years "America letters" played a role in recruiting immigrants. Equally important, however, was the role of the "bird of passage," the former neighbor, returned from the "Golden Land" for a visit or to stay. The "Amerikanec" was an enviable character, glorious in his store-bought blue serge suit and gold watch, generously distributing gifts to friends and relatives from a bulging, imitation leather suitcase. Children listened wide-eyed to his tales of ranches as big as their entire province, of buildings as tall as mountains, of trees a thousand years old—and made up their minds to see these wonders for themselves.

Many immigrants were never quite sure why they came. They were the new victims of the old disease, "America Fever," which spread with industrialization and economic hardship. In his autobiography, *An American in the Making*, Marcus Ravage described how an emigration epidemic hit his Rumanian village. Prices plummeted as an entire village tried to sell its possessions all at once and headed for the local train station. "America had become, as it were, the fashionable place to go," wrote Ravage. "All my relatives and all our neighbors—in fact, everybody who was anybody—had either gone or was going to New York . . . and what took place in Vaslui was only typical of what had come to be the state of affairs everywhere in Roumania."

Political and religious oppression were important motives for emigration in the late nineteenth and early twentieth centuries. In the multinational empires (the German, the Russian, the Austro-Hungarian, and the Ottoman) the numerous ethnic groups were asserting their distinctive national identities. Intellectual and political leaders of these "subject nationalities" revived traditional languages, literatures, and religions and began to work for political as well as cultural independence. The rulers responded—sometimes with concessions, usually with repression. Poles within the German Empire were forbidden to teach their native language. The Russian Empire launched a program of forcible "Russification" of many minorities. Armenians and Greeks were constantly harassed, even massacred in the Turkish Empire.

The largest oppressed minority to come to the United States were the Jews of Russia. Wracked by the political and economic crisis that was to culminate in the Russian Revolution of 1917, the tottering Tsarist Regime adopted a policy of vicious anti-Semitism in order to divert attention from its own failures. Jews were segregated into the crowded "Pale of Settlement," denied access to education and employment, and systematically reduced to poverty by special taxes, fees, and the need to pay constant bribes in order to survive. The Russian government instigated periodic massacres, or pogroms. Mary Antin described these pogroms in her autobiography *The Promised Land* as times when ignorant peasants, filled with vodka and slanderous stories, invaded the Jewish quarters:

> They attacked them (the Jews) with knives and clubs and scythes and axes, killed them or tortured them, and burned their houses. . . . Jews who escaped pogroms came to Polotzk (Mary Antin's town) with wounds on them, and horrible, horrible stories of little babies torn limb from limb before their mothers' eyes. Only to hear these things made one sob and sob and choke with pain. People who saw such things never smiled any more . . . sometimes their hair turned white in a day, and some people became insane on the spot.

Millions of East European Jews fled to the United States, where they formed a new ethnic community second in size only to that of the Italians. Their immigration peaks were linked to outbreaks of persecution rather than to the American business cycle. Entire families left and rarely went back.

Entering the Economy

If most of the problems that drove immigrants from their homes between 1880 and 1924 were not new, neither were the attractions that lured them to the United States. The expansion of our transportation and manufacturing facilities and the building of our cities continued at a dizzying pace. This remarkable economic growth created an insatiable demand for unskilled labor, a demand which, as in the earlier decades, could not have been met without immigration. By the end of the nineteenth century the labor force of the western industrialized areas of Europe no longer wanted the unskilled and poorly paid jobs America had to offer. To the agricultural laborers of southern and eastern Europe, however, such positions were attractive.

Immigrants went where the jobs were—to the cities. By the turn of the century the frontier was gone, and the grain-growing prairies and other agricultural areas had fallen upon hard times. On the other hand, the cities which had been primarily commercial centers before the Civil War were now manufacturing centers as well, with a corresponding geometric increase in job opportunities. It is not surprising, then, that over three quarters of the new immigrants settled in the cities, creating foreign colonies of unprecedented size.

Many Americans were alarmed at the enormous concentration of immigrants in the cities. Uncomfortable with its giant new metropolitan areas (by the turn of the century over half the American population was urban), America believed that immigrants would assimilate faster in the presumably more wholesome environment of the farm. Charitable societies, churches, even foreign countries from which the immigrants came tried to encourage the newcomers to spread out, to go south or west, and to work the land. Such efforts met with very limited success.

One such effort was the campaign to bring Italian farmers to the southern states to supplement (or perhaps to replace) black farm labor. Thousands went but soon complained about working conditions and prejudice. Many southern states had severe laws requiring the poor to work off their debts or go to prison—laws originally passed to keep blacks "in their place," but which now victimized Italian labor as well. In some areas Italian workers were deprived of their civil liberties, even lynched. Between 1874 and 1915 twenty five were killed in Arkansas, Louisiana, Mississippi, and North Carolina.

Italians were more fortunate than blacks, however, because they had an outside government to speak for them. The Italian government protested and tried to get written guarantees from local authorities that Italian immigrants to the South would be protected. Because of the failure of local authorities to protect Italians or even to punish offenses against them, the Italian government soon refused to issue passports to immigrants bound for the southern states. The official campaign to get Italians to "spread out" as agricultural workers in the South came to an end.

Some immigrants did settle successfully on the land. Assisted by their own philanthropies, a small number of Jews established flourishing agricultural settlements in New Jersey. Italians and Slavs came to rural areas to build railroads and sometimes stayed to farm. The most successful specialized in one or two cash crops, perhaps peaches or lettuce or onions, and sold them in the nearby urban centers. Italian families sometimes peddled their own produce in the towns, beginning a long lasting and profitable connection with the urban food distribution industry. Poles bought the cheapest, least desirable land and coaxed it into productivity. According to Polish-American historian Joseph Wytrwal, the fact that Polish immigrants had practically to create the land they farmed made it especially dear to them. "They consider it a part of themselves and they love it as much as they formerly loved their own dear Polish land."

Immigrants from northern Italy established vineyards and orchards in California in a climate very similar to what they had known in Italy. On the west coast Japanese replaced Chinese as agricultural day laborers. Despite discrimination they were often able to acquire farms of their own. Like the Poles in the East, they purchased marginal land, arid and abandoned, and coaxed it into productivity with prodigious labor.

Most of the newcomers turned their backs on agriculture. Like the Irish a few decades earlier, the south Italians considered agriculture a "cruel stepmother," synonomous with "degradation, humiliation, and virtual starvation." In Italy rich landowners, lawyers, physicians, nobles—the people who counted—lived in the cities. Little wonder, then, that in a land of urban opportunities this is where the southern Italians went.

Most immigrants could not invest the time needed to make money from farming, even if they had wanted to. They needed cash immediately—to pay debts, to provide for themselves, and to send help to the families they had left behind. Cash would buy the farm or shop in the old country that would mean comfort and security for loved ones. A job in a factory or mine, street vending, construction work—these were the best means of obtaining ready money. "Cash, mobility, and the dream of going home at the earliest opportunity dominated his thoughts," says Theodore Saloutos of the Greek immigrant. The statement is applicable to many Italians, Slavs, and others as well.

The new steamship lines channeled most of the immigration into New York City, where Ellis Island became an assembly line for processing new arrivals. Many Poles and other Slavs moved inland to Buffalo, Pittsburgh, Detroit, Cleveland, and Chicago. The coal mines and iron and steel works of Pennsylvania and Ohio attracted Poles, Lithuanians, Ukrainians, south Slavs, and Italians. Working from bases in the northeast, Armenians, Lebanese, and Syrians peddled dry goods and notions from coast to coast.

Most ethnic groups, including the two largest, the Italians and the Jews, concentrated in the industrial Northeast—urban New England, New York, Pennsylvania, and New Jersey—where job opportunities were plentiful and varied. The Italians and Slavs did the pick and shovel work earlier done by the Irish. French Canadians and immigrants from the Middle East worked in New England's textile mills. Skilled in the needle trades before their arrival, Jews created and dominated the ready-to-wear garment industry of New York City. Jews, Italians, Bohemians, Hungarians, along with the Germans and Irish, made the clothing, costume jewelry, artificial flowers, suspenders, shoes, lamps, soap, cigars, candy, and an incredible variety of other items, large and small, that were produced in the dark workshops of the eastern cities.

Women worked as hard as men. Middle Eastern women helped their husbands peddle or managed small shops, as did women of virtually every ethnic group. Slovak and Bohemian women did domestic work, a highly undesirable job which other immigrant women considered "too heavy." Women did kitchen work and cleaning in hotels, restaurants, and office buildings. Jewish women were most commonly found in the clothing "sweatshops." Immigrant women of virtually every group worked in foundries, canneries, twine mills, tobacco factories, stockyards, and commercial laundries. Those who stayed at home often ran rooming houses for new arrivals. By cooking, cleaning, and washing for ten or more boarders, such women often earned as much or more than their husbands.

Sometimes immigrants came to live with friends or relatives, who took them to their own employers to find a job. But many were alone, penniless, unable to speak English, and therefore unable to get a job without outside help. Such people turned to the padrones or to the employment agencies, both of which provided needed services—at a price.

The padrone was a private labor broker of the same ethnic background as the group he served—Italian, Greek, Bulgarian, Turkish, or Mexican. He was a middleman who recruited laborers, sometimes in Europe, more often in ethnic neighborhoods in American cities, and delivered them, for a very high commission, to American employers who needed their services. Workers from the Northeast were sent as far south as Florida and as far west as Nebraska. Workers from midwestern cities were sent to New England or even to California. Gangs of immigrant labor organized by padrones worked on railroads, in mines, and on temporary construction sites. They harvested timber, farm products, and ice.

Some padrones stayed at the job with the laborers, acting as interpreters and as mediators between them and the English-speaking bosses or foremen. Often padrones provided lodging for their clients as well as the ethnic food they enjoyed and would not otherwise be able to obtain.

Because he spoke their language and provided services not otherwise available to the "green" immigrant, the padrone was able to compete successfully with private, government, and charitable employment agencies, despite the exorbitant fees charged by the more unscrupulous. In 1900 padrones controlled over half of the Italian laborers in New York City. The padrone system was most pervasive in the early years, when most immigrants were inexperienced. Greater sophistication on the part of the workers, the beginnings of unionization, and the labor shortage caused by World War I finally broke the power of the padrones.

Private employment agencies competed with the padrones. They recruited unskilled labor for seasonal or temporary employment in rural areas, or for construction, wrecking, or other unskilled jobs in the cities. Like the padrones, they sent large gangs of workers hundreds of miles for employment and were, if anything, more exploitive and less responsible than the padrones. Fees were erratic, but always high. "We charge all we can get," admitted one agency.

Agencies specializing in immigrant labor rarely investigated prospective employers and were often parties to deceit. Young girls were sent, under false pretenses, to work at "sporting houses" and similar institutions. Workers traveled many miles to misrepresented, even nonexistent jobs and were often stranded far from home. A young Slavic workman was sent from Chicago to Wyoming in midwinter for a nonexistent job. Penniless, he walked miles in deep snow to reach home, where his foot was amputated because of frostbite. Two Hungarian immigrants from Chicago were stranded in Arkansas by a disreputable agency. When they tried to board a freight train to get home, the local police shot them.

The Urban Ghetto

Immigrants from southern and eastern Europe concentrated in the largest American cities produced something new—the twentieth century urban ghetto. These were enclaves of ethnic Americans—little Italys, Polonias, little Syrias, "Jewtowns," and other foreign quarters— in the heart of the sprawling American metropolises. Each ghetto had its own distinctive national flavor, its own churches, its own games and amusements, its own newspapers, and its own "green ones," new arrivals in beards, kerchiefs, and other distinctive dress. "You could always tell which state you were in," reminisced journalist Mike Royko, "by the odors of the food stores and the open kitchen windows, the sound of the foreign or familiar language, and by whether a stranger hit you in the head with a rock."

Before the Civil War, the Irish had often settled in shantytowns on the outskirts of the growing cities, as well as in the cities themselves. By

1900, however, the outskirts were too far away from the industrial centers to attract immigrant settlement. The growing "streetcar suburbs" that surrounded the cities housed the middle class and the skilled workers. They were financially out of the immigrant's reach. New ethnic Americans crowded into the old housing near the commerical and industrial centers so that the various breadwinners in the family could be within walking distance of a variety of possible jobs.

Large ethnic ghettos developed for a number of reasons. Sometimes an ethnic group was heavily concentrated in one industry—Jews in the garment factories of New York, or Poles and Lithuanians in the stockyards of Chicago. Naturally the neighborhood nearest the job housed a heavy concentration of that particular ethnic group. There were other factors as well. Once a neighborhood had a large number of one ethnic group, it developed ethnic institutions to serve them—stores specializing in favored ethnic foods, churches similar to those they had known in the old country, parochial schools teaching the traditional language and history. The existence of these institutions attracted an even heavier concentration of this ethnic group into the neighborhood.

Prejudice played an important role in the creation and perpetuation of the ethnic ghetto. People who wanted to move elsewhere often found that they could not buy or rent housing at any price. An Italian-American minister and social worker, Constantine Panunzio, tells how the Italian vice consul, "a man of fine and keen intelligence, tall and pleasing in appearance, and a gentleman in every sense of the word," was unable to find decent housing in a major American city. Even the chairman of a Protestant Americanization committee turned him down because "the neighbors would object to having an Italian (pronouncing the "I" long) next door to them."

"Majority" Americans regarded the mushrooming ethnic ghettos with a mixture of fascination and horror. To some, they were quaint, romantic places where one went "slumming" to watch Sicilian church processions, Syrian ritual sword dances, and other "exotic" celebrations. Robert Woods, organizer of the National Foundation of Settlements, loved to wander through the Italian quarter of Boston, where "the lightheartedness of the Italians and their keen love of pleasure makes an atmosphere so full of gayety that a spectator . . . is led to overlook the many discomforts. . . ." In the Jewish quarter, Woods admired the fine old brass candlesticks and leather bound parchment books in the shop windows. He also admired the Jewish children, "all great lovers of music . . . who dance as if by instinct"—a stereotype usually reserved for blacks!

William Dean Howells, the best known novelist of the day, took a romantic view of New York's Jewish quarter:

> Everywhere I saw splendid types of that old Hebrew world which had
> the sense if not the knowledge of God when all the rest of us were sunk in
> heathen darkness. There were women with oval faces and olive tints, and
> clear dark eyes, relucent as evening pools, and men with long beards of
> jetty black or silvery white, and the noble profiles of their race. I said to
> myself that it was among such throngs that Christ walked, it was among
> such people that he chose his disciples and his friends. . . .

Other American intellectuals, equally attracted by the color and
vitality of the immigrant quarters, described them more realistically. In
his famous novel, *The Jungle* Upton Sinclair wrote about the grinding
poverty of Chicago's Slavs, who worked knee deep in blood and entrails
in the grotesque demiworld of the stockyards. A group of urban artists,
derisively termed the "Ash Can" school, found the ghettos excellent
material for their socially conscious paintings. The Danish born writer
and photographer Jacob Riis stirred the conscience of the comfortable
with his photographs of ghetto life and his widely acclaimed exposé of
immigrant (and native) urban poverty, *How the Other Half Lives*.

> Cherry Street. Be a little careful, please! The hall is dark and you might
> stumble over the children. . . . Not that it would hurt them; kicks and
> cuffs are their daily diet. . . . The sinks are in the hallway, that all tenants
> may have access—and all be poisoned alike by their summer stenches.
> Hear the pumps squeak! It is the lullaby of tenement house babes. In
> summer, when a thousand thirsty throats pant for a cooling drink in this
> block, it is worked in vain. But the saloon whose open door you passed in
> the hall, is always there. . . . Listen! That short hacking cough, that tiny,
> helpless wail—what do they mean? . . . a sadly familiar story—The child is
> dying with measles. With half a chance it might have lived; but it had
> none. That dark bedroom killed it.

If intellectuals saw the ghettos as exotic, romantic, or tragic, most
other people saw them as filthy and dangerous. To many, the ghettos
were alien cesspools of alcoholism, crime, and vice. What was the early
twentieth century ethnic ghetto really like? Obviously the answer
would vary from ghetto to ghetto, from city to city, and from decade to
decade. Some generalizations can, nevertheless, be made.

Ethnic ghettos were ugly. Immigrant quarters in mill and mining
towns consisted of grim and grimy rows of ramshackle frame houses
along trash-littered, muddy streets. Smoke, soot, and other industrial
wastes made urban ghettos in industrial cities as unwholesome as they
were ugly. Industrial Pittsburgh, as journalist Lincoln Steffens put it,
"looked like hell, literally."

Ethnic quarters in late nineteenth century New York City were
characterized by tightly packed rows of tenements as much as seven
stories high in which only one room in four received direct air or light

from outside. These were damp, foul smelling, rickety structures, lacking indoor plumbing or water supply, and, in the words of a little girl who lived in one, "so dark it seemed as if there weren't no sky." Ventilation was so bad that four hundred and twenty tenement dwellers died from intense and continuous heat in August of 1896.

As in the pre-Civil War era, housing was bad because the supply fell far short of the demand. Inadequate buildings quickly and cheaply constructed to meet temporary needs were pressed into service as permanent dwelling places, always for more families than they had been intended. Ghetto housing was bad; but because of the great demand, it was not cheap. Many immigrant families could not afford the rent—hence the widespread practice of taking in boarders. About half of all Hungarian households included boarders; among Lithuanians the number reached seventy per cent.

In the typical ethnic ghetto every building was crowded. People slept on fire escapes, on the roof, in stair wells, and within the apartments on rows of mattresses spread edge to edge across the floor. In mining and mill areas people slept as they worked—in a day shift and a night shift—so that each bed did double duty. In no place on the face of the earth was humanity packed as closely as the Lower East Side on New York City, where three thousand shared a single city block.

There were health problems in the ghettos, but surprisingly little correlation between population density and death rates. Death rates were high among the Italian born, perhaps because of dietary deficiencies or the difficulties of adjusting to the damp cold winters. Death rates in the Irish ghettos, where many of the residents were second generation, were even higher. Perhaps the more vigorous members of this group had moved elsewhere, leaving the older, more infirm behind. In the more densely populated Jewish neighborhoods, however, death rates were among the lowest in the city. The Jewish population was young and many Jews had already made their adjustment to urban life in Europe. Also, Jews had the advantage of many hygienic practices built into their religious ritual.

Generally, environmental factors had a greater impact upon immigrant health than ethnic background. Tuberculosis and other respiratory ills were common among all immigrants who worked at dust producing occupations, the manufacture of cigars, for example, and the packing of soap. Many immigrants were forced to live in housing sites that were unsuitable for human habitation—badly drained, swampy areas, or polluted areas bordering stockyards, slaughterhouses, steel mills, and similar industries. Such sites proved lethal to their inhabitants, regardless of ethnic background. Conversely, improvements in the water supply, sanitation, and drainage resulted in improved health, regardless of the population density or the supposed "slovenly" habits of the inhabitants. As New York City's ghettos increased in population density, sanitation and services were improved and death rates declined. Although the ghettos of Philadelphia and St. Louis were less crowded, structural defects and bad sanitation kept death rates there considerably higher.

" . . . the popular belief that the foreign born are filling the prisons has little foundation in fact . . ." reported the United States Census on Prisoners and Juvenile Delinquents in Institutions in 1904. In survey after survey, the foreign born were shown to have lower arrest and conviction rates than the native born (and more recently arrived groups such as Jews and Italians had lower rates than groups that had been in the country longer). Nevertheless, the stereotype of the immigrant as a criminal persisted.

One reason for the persistent identification of the foreign born with crime, vice, and drink was the large number of saloons, brothels, and gambling houses located in their neighborhoods. As in the pre-Civil War period, such institutions were concentrated in ethnic neighborhoods because it was politically inexpedient to license them in "better" neighborhoods. "Tourists" from other parts of the city used the ghettos as convenient places to indulge in their favorite socially unacceptable behavior. Of 3,124 persons arrested for drunkenness in 1901 in the predominantly Jewish and Italian North End of Boston, for example, only 450 were residents of the area. Of these, only five or six were Italian and none was Jewish!

Crime and vice did, of course, exist among immigrants. While Italian and Jewish culture never condoned excessive use of alcohol, Irish and Slavic immigrants came from cultures that were more permissive in this area. For them, alcoholism was more likely to become a problem. Violence, promiscuity, desertion of families occurred among all ethnic groups.

Though the crime rate was low among the foreign born, it was high among their American-born children. Fleeing their cramped tenement apartments and their "old fashioned" parents, young people took to the streets, forming gangs and getting into trouble. Arrests for juvenile delinquency were alarmingly high in every ethnic group. A sympathetic social worker, Grace Abbott, pointed out that many ethnic youths were brought to court for offenses which, had they been committed by old-stock Americans in "better" neighborhoods, would have been dismissed as mischievous pranks. Off to a bad start, a small percentage of these children moved on to more serious offenses and even organized crime.

There were many misunderstandings between the newer ethnic communities and the police, most of whom were native-born or Irish-American. Called to quell disturbances in ethnic ghettos, bigoted policemen sometimes clubbed rioters and bystanders alike. The behavior of the New York police during a disturbance at Rabbi Jacob Joseph's funeral in 1902 was so outrageous that Mayor Seth Low appointed a committee "to investigate the incident and its wider implications of police inefficiency and brutality—particularly toward the Jews of the East Side."

The problems of the police were complicated by the fact that many immigrants, accustomed in Europe to regard every official as an enemy, gave them little cooperation. Language difficulties, too, created problems. Unable to understand policemen's instructions, immigrants sometimes seemed defiant when they were actually bewildered. A Slavic boy in Chicago was shot and killed by a policeman for disobeying a command that he had not even understood. When an immigrant woman in Chicago begged a policeman to protect her children from her abusive husband, the policeman, unable to understand her, jailed her overnight as an alcoholic. Such incidents did not endear the police to the ethnic community!

Older stock Americans feared that the inhabitants of the ethnic ghettos would never shed their "alien" ways and become part of American life. Such fears were based on misconceptions about the nature of the ghetto. First, ethnic ghettos were not homogeneous. Especially in the early years, predominantly Italian, Jewish, or Slavic neighborhoods rarely had more than half of their population composed of the dominant group. Italian produce peddlers served New York's Jewish ghetto, Jewish tailors served Italian neighborhoods, and Irish brogues could be heard in Boston's "little Syria." Throughout the southern and eastern European ghettos there were pockets of Germans, Scandinavians, and old-stock Americans who would not or could not move away and who mingled with the newer arrivals in the streets, the schools, the stores, and the settlement houses.

The Industrial Ghetto—a World of Change

Contrary to uninformed public opinion, ghettos were not stagnant pools of immobilized humanity. They were in a constant state of flux. Within any given year one third to one half of the families moved—by choice or because the landlord evicted them—sometimes to a house in the same block, sometimes to a different neighborhood, sometimes to a different city. Sometimes the entire ethnic composition of a neighborhood changed within a few years. Boston's "little Syria," which became Boston's Chinatown, had been Irish earlier.

From the moment they arrived in the ethnic ghettos, immigrants were caught up in many changes. Most of these immigrants were moving from agricultural to industrial work, from rural to urban living, from cooperative to competitive societies. The cultural shock was great and was made greater still by changes in language, religion, and life style.

Language was one of the first and most obvious changes. Their inability to speak English kept many skilled workers from getting jobs appropriate to their abilities. Immigrants stayed up late to memorize long lists of the English words needed for work or for personal convenience, spelling them phonetically in any alphabet they knew. Within a few days, a Slovenian or Croatian immigrant could ride a "subvej" (subway) to work, and buy a "lonc" (lunch) consisting of a "senvic" (sandwich) and "ajs krim" (ice cream). More important, he could ask his "bas" (boss) for his "paycheki" (paycheck).

Religion, like language, called for major adjustments. Many Syrians, Armenians, Serbians, and Japanese found no American churches with which they could identify. Roman Catholics from southern and eastern Europe often found Irish Catholic churches inhospitable, too far away from their neighborhoods, or too unfamiliar in ritual and tradition. Probably no group suffered so sharp a break in religious continuity as Orthodox Jews. In Eastern Europe they had lived in an isolated, all-Jewish world where dress, food, hygiene, marriage, indeed every detail of life, was prescribed by religious law and tradition. In America, even in the Jewish ghetto, that world was gone.

Some immigrants, Poles, Ukrainians, and other Slavs in particular, struggled to maintain as much of their old religion as possible. Others, like the main character in Abraham Cahan's novel, *The Rise of David Levinsky*, made compromises. Often they discovered, like David Levinsky, that "if you attempt to bend your religion to the spirit of your new surroundings, it breaks. It falls to pieces. The very clothes I wore, and the very food I ate had a fatal effect on my religious habits. . . ."

Sometimes change was motivated by the immigrant's desire to avoid embarrassment. People shaved off their beards and altered their style of dress rather than suffer the scorn or the pity of those less "green" than themselves. Sometimes change was dictated by the demands of American institutions. Hours for rising, eating, and going to bed were set, not by the sun and the farm routine as at home, but by the demands of the foreman of the mine, the mill, or the sweatshop. Chinese families altered centuries-old patterns of meal times to fit the schedules of the American public schools their children attended.

Perhaps the most radical change for the new immigrant was the change in the pace of everyday life. To the former inhabitant of a slow moving traditional village, the urban ghettos of New York, Chicago, Boston, and Detroit must have seemed like life run at double or triple speed. Many immigrants noted a change in the "feel" of life—an emotional as well as a physical quickening. David Levinsky describes his reaction to New York's lower East Side:

. . . The scurry and hustle of the people were not merely overwhelmingly greater, both in volume and intensity, than in my native town. It was of another sort. The swing and step of the pedestrians, the voices and manner of the street peddlers, and a hundred and one other things seemed to testify to far more self-confidence and energy, to larger ambitions and wider scopes, than did the appearance of the crowds in my birthplace.

Work

Work loomed large in industrial America at the turn of the century, and it loomed larger still in the ethnic ghetto. "Work! Serve! Or America beautiful will eat you and spit your bones into the earth's hole," shouts the foreman to an Italian construction crew in Pietro Di Donato's novel *Christ in Concrete*. A guidebook for immigrant Jews gave similar advice: "Forget your past, your customs, and your ideals . . . do not take a moment's rest. Run, do, work. . . ."

Ethnic Americans were fortunate that the period 1880 to 1924, with the exception of a depression in the mid 1890's, was one of prosperity. Still, the wages paid for unskilled and semiskilled labor in a country run largely by and for business interests provided such a marginal livelihood that women, children, the aged, and even the sick, were often forced into the labor market. The Massachusetts Bureau of Statistics estimated that a family of five needed $754 a year to live. Yet the average annual wage of the male South Italian was $368, the Pole $365, and the Syrian $321. Women earned about half as much, even when performing essentially the same jobs. At a time when the New York Bureau of Labor considered ten dollars a week inadequate for a working man with a family, working women received as little as three dollars a week. A married woman might use this to supplement her husband's earnings, but widows and single women with dependents could not live on it. Some turned to prostitution to escape starvation or the poorhouse.

Because of language problems and the prejudice of prospective employers, skilled workers often faced years of unskilled work. A skilled metalworker in Chicago committed suicide because he could not satisfy his strong craving to practice his art. Professional people such as lawyers, teachers, and writers, whose skills depended on language, were often unable to pursue the occupations for which they were trained. Sometimes their own communities no longer wanted their skills. Talmudic scholars, honored in Europe, were ignored in the Jewish quarter of New York. The suffering of such people, through poverty and loss of self-esteem, was enormous.

The typical working day in immigrant industries was twelve to sixteen hours, under conditions that were dangerous, even lethal. Soap powder, lacquer, and tobacco dust in unventilated workshops caused tuberculosis and other respiratory illnesses. "I never knew anyone who worked in a laundry long," said an immigrant woman, "the work is too hard and you simply can't stand the heat." Loss of limbs, eyesight, or life was common among the men and women who labored in laundries, foundries, factories, and mines.

Employers blamed the high accident rate entirely upon the carelessness of the workers. Crystal Eastman's carefully researched study *Work Accidents and the Law* (1910) indicated, however, that employers were more likely to be at fault. Although the injured workers were often young, new to the job and to the country, ill, or overtired, most accidents were caused by equipment malfunction, careless inspection of working areas, and the overzealousness of supervisors. Despite their responsibility for most accidents, employers rarely did more than contribute to medical or funeral expenses, after which the disabled workers or their dependents were left to fend for themselves.

Much late nineteenth and early twentieth century manufacturing was done in the home, where families huddled far into the night rolling tobacco into cigars, stitching garments, or twisting wires and papers into artificial flowers. In January 1907, *Cosmopolitan Magazine* estimated that over sixty thousand children worked in the garment industry of New York City alone.

> Nearly any hour on the East Side of New York City you can see them—pallid boy or spindling girl—their faces dulled, their backs bent under a heavy load of garments. . . . Once at home with the sewing, the little worker sits close to the inadequate window, struggling with the snarls of the thread. . . . Even if by happy chance the small worker goes to school, the sewing which he puts down at the last moment in morning waits for his return . . . (by) the sacrifice of all that should make childhood radiant, a child may add to the family purse from 50 cents to $1.50 a week. . . .
>
> Besides work at sewing, there is another industry for little girls in the grim tenements. The mother must be busy at her sewing or, perhaps she is away from dark to dark at office cleaning. A little daughter must therefore assume the work and care of the family . . . washing, scrubbing, cooking. . . .

After 1900 work in the factory increasingly replaced work in the home. Here, as in home labor, the system of paying for work by the piece led to enormous pressure and great abuse. Seeking to maximize profits by keeping labor costs down, employers and contractors frequently lowered the amount paid for each finished piece, thus forcing the employee to work faster and faster in order to receive the same meager wage. Each of the many thousands of mills and shops had its own horrors, but the most highly publicized industrial disaster was the Triangle Shirtwaist factory fire of 1911. The fire began on the eighth floor of a ten story building and spread rapidly, fed by the lacy fabrics and bolts of silk. Locked doors (so the workers could not leave early) and inadequate fire escapes compounded the tragedy. *The New York World* estimated the dead at 154:

> Screaming men and women and boys and girls crowded out on the many window ledges and threw themselves into the streets far below. They jumped with their clothing ablaze. The hair of some of the girls streamed up aflame as they leaped. Thud after thud sounded on the pavements . . . on both the Greene Street and Washington Place sides of the building there grew mounds of the dead and dying. And the worst horror of all was that in this heap of the dead now and then there stirred a limb or sounded a moan. When Fire Chief Croker could make his way into these three floors he found sights that utterly staggered him . . . bodies burned to bare bones . . . skeletons bending over sewing machines.

The Worker's Response

Individuals responded to the pressures and horrors of industrial life in ways that ranged from passive resistance and sporadic violence to trade unionism and the adoption of revolutionary philosophies. Accustomed to working at their own pace with time off for holidays of many kinds and breaks for refreshment and rest, immigrant workers from rural backgrounds sometimes refused to conform to the rigid and grueling time demands of the modern factory. With legislative prodding, employers eventually reduced the length of the working day and added vacations and "coffee breaks," thus institutionalizing the more humane (as well as more efficient) schedules their employees seemed determined to follow anyway. Meanwhile, many employers hoped that education would improve the work habits of their immigrant laborers. With this in mind, the International Harvester Corporation issued pamphlets teaching English and industrial discipline simultaneously. Lesson one reads:

> I hear the whistle. I must hurry.
> I hear the five minute whistle.
> It is time to go into the shop.
>
> The starting whistle blows.
> I eat my lunch.
> It is forbidden to eat until then.
>
> I work until the whistle blows to quit.
> I leave my place nice and clean.

Desperate immigrants sometimes turned to violence to express their frustration. Weavers, miners, and other workers stoned factories and burned equipment to protest their employers' use of the police against them. Italian railroad construction gangs tore up track to punish dishonest contractors. Jewish women in New York City paraded through the streets carrying chunks of meat on pointed sticks to protest the rising cost of kosher meat. One observer described how religious rituals were incorporated into labor battles. During a strike of Slavic steel workers in Hammond, Indiana, "The lights of the hall were extinguished. A candle stuck into a bottle was placed on a platform. One by one the men came and kissed the ivory image on the cross, kneeling before it. They swore not to scab."

The relationship between southern and eastern European immigrants and the rising union movement was complex. Employers skillfully exploited and even created hostilities between ethnic groups to prevent them from organizing. Newly-arrived Italians and Slavs were often used as strikebreakers, especially when the work force was predominantly Irish or native-born. Hoping to return to Europe as soon as they had saved enough money, many Italian and Slavic newcomers avoided unions fearing the loss of income during strikes or lockouts would delay their return. As their stay in America lengthened and showed signs of becoming permanent, these workers became more receptive to the long-range economic benefits offered by unions. On the eve of World War I one of the most important unions, the United Mine Workers, was composed largely of immigrants.

Religious tradition as well as previous experience with factory jobs in Europe predisposed Jewish immigrants to take the lead in unionizing New York's predominantly Jewish garment industry. "Ours is a just cause," said a striking vestmaker in 1898. "Saith the Law of Moses: 'Thou shalt not withold anything from thy neighbor nor rob him! . . .' So you see that our bosses who rob us . . . commit a sin." Tragedies such as the Triangle Shirtwaist fire led to massive demonstrations which engaged the sympathy of many middle class Americans.

A small percentage of immigrants turned from capitalism altogether to espouse one of many varieties of socialism or anarchism. While a minority of these believed that the destruction of the oppressive capitalist order required violence, most looked for peaceful change by means of the democratic process. Indeed, in the pre-World War I years socialism was in vogue throughout the nation, as muckraking journalists and other reformers exposed the abuses of the capitalist economy. In 1912 three quarters of a million Americans, native born and foreign born, voted the Socialist ticket.

Most ethnics, like most other Americans, were not involved in socialism, unionization, rioting, or even "passive" resistance to the new industrial order. Their goal was not to change American capitalism but to succeed in it. Their greatest fear was neither injury nor death, but unemployment, which would mean hunger and homelessness for their families. Work brought danger and grinding fatigue, but it also brought satisfaction and the hope of a better future. "Blessings to thee, O Jesus," says an Italian bricklayer in Pietro Di Donato's novel *Christ in Concrete.* "I have fought wind and cold. Hand to hand I have locked dumb stones in place and the great building rises. I have earned a bit of bread for me and mine."

The vast immigrant ghettos of the early twentieth century embraced all the evils characteristic of modern urban slums—dirt, disease, overcrowding, crime, vice, gang wars—but hope was more common than despair. Most immigrants earned more here, even in the worst jobs, than they could have earned at home. Poverty, after all, is relative. Immigrants evicted from tenement apartments in the United States piled store-bought chairs and couches on the sidewalk—possessions which in the old country would have marked their owners as wealthy indeed. "In Italy we were poor, always on the verge of starvation," explained an Italian immigrant. "We were not poor in America; we just had a little less than the others. In America no one starved, though a family earned no more than five or six dollars a week. . . ."

It was the age of the Horatio Alger story, the American rags-to-riches myth. Newcomers soon discarded naive ideas that the streets of America were paved with gold, and they had probably never heard of Horatio Alger. Still, most of them set to work with optimism and purposefulness. The Jewish family sewed pants sixteen hours a day in an airless tenement; but, they had escaped pogroms. With luck and perseverance they might see their children through high school, or even college. The Italian "shovel man," descending for the first time into the coal mines of Pennsylvania or the subways of New York, was already dreaming of the house and garden he would eventually buy with his carefully hoarded savings. In America he might attain the enviable status of landlord—a status beyond his wildest dreams in Calabria or Sicily.

CHAPTER 7

Progressive America:
Home, School, and Neighborhood

In America anything was possible—but nothing was easy! If some immigrants saw their dreams come to fruition, others met only with frustration and defeat. Every individual had his or her private difficulties, but certain kinds of problems were almost universal. Most immigrants had difficulties with language, religion, housing, and especially with earning a living. They were also confronted with the problem of interpersonal relations, for America had an impact upon the immigrant family. It affected the relationship between husband and wife and between parents and children.

Immigration and Family Life

For many immigrants, their journey to America meant the end of all normal family life. These were the people who came alone, leaving parents, spouses, children, brothers, sisters, and all other relatives behind. Men who came alone often worked in gangs, living in the crudest, cheapest dormitory arrangements. Saving every penny either to bring their families here or to return home themselves, they were often unwilling to spend the money or the time to establish churches, clubs, or other institutions. Such men led a lonely and drab existence, scarcely relieved by an occasional drinking or gambling spree.

Though the majority of immigrants who came alone were men, many women were in a similar situation. Between 1912 and 1917 half a million single women under the age of thirty came to the United States. Most of these were very young. Of 120,000 Polish women, 84,000 were under twenty-one. While a man without his family usually lived and worked with other men from the same background, the woman often found employment as a household servant, where she rarely met anyone who spoke her language."I so lonesome, I cries all the time," said a Polish housemaid.

Loneliness was often intensified by guilt at having left elderly parents at home and anguish at not being able to send them the help they expected. ". . . says our Lord Jesus and the Holiest Mother Virgin Mary, do not abandon thy parents. . . ." a Polish immigrant wrote his parents in 1914. "I wear this in my heart and I remember. . . . Only dear parents, you demand too much . . . my work does not suffice for this." Immigrants did the best they could, often at great sacrifice to themselves, to satisfy the financial needs of those left behind; millions of dollars went from America to overseas relatives every year. But there were always letters asking for more.

Often young children were left with relatives in the old country while their parents came to America to earn money. The Yiddish poet M. Teitsch captures the yearning of immigrants who could not see their babies grow into toddlers, their sons and daughters enter young adulthood.

> There's a town in Lithuania on the shores of the Wilna—
> Whichever way my eyes look, that town meets my gaze.
>
> There's an alley there, and close by, a little house—
> Me thinks I would give away half my years for that little house.
>
> And a child lives in the little house, whom I love as my life—
> All my years I would give away for this child.

Husbands who came to America alone to earn passage for their wives often found the months of separation lengthening into years. Eagerly awaited letters sometimes brought more grief than comfort. Wives left behind complained that the work was too hard to do alone, that the hired hands were unruly and unreliable, and that the children were disobedient without their father to oversee them. "The wheelbarrow of life is too heavy for my shoulders . . . take me there, where you are. . . . Otherwise I shall perish," wrote a Polish woman.

Not all marriages were happy ones, and the desire to escape contributed to some men's decisions to emigrate. Such men were not in a hurry to send for their wives, especially if they had already found a desirable American substitute. "Klastor took his wife five weeks ago, Mania Pawlowska is going away presently. Only for me there is no place!" complains a suspicious wife. Sometimes the woman postponed joining her husband on one pretext or another, either from fear of the unknown land, or because she, too, had found someone else.

Husbands in America were often frantic with jealousy, justified or unjustified. Many an Italian husband refused to consummate a marriage that took place immediately before his departure; if his wife were unfaithful while he was gone, at least he would know about it!

In some cases love and trust survived the years of separation only to evaporate when the couple was reunited. "Once between us the Atlantic, yet I felt your hand in mine," wrote Israel Zangwill. "Now I feel your hand in mine, yet between us the Atlantic." After years of separation the Americanized husband might find his immigrant wife too drab and old fashioned. The newly arrived wife might be shocked to find that her husband had abandoned the traditional religion or life style. Such problems could put a strain on even the best marriages, and lead to separation or divorce.

In the old country—Europe, the Middle East, or Japan—a network of relatives and neighbors was always available to see that husband and wife fulfilled their obligations to each other and that children were respectful and obedient to their parents. In the United States, however, this network was absent, and such interference would not have been tolerated had it been available. The nuclear family— husband, wife, and children—were on their own. The result could be a new closeness, or, in times of stress, a rapid disintegration.

In a traditional European village each partner in the marriage had a socially recognized status, derived from the known qualities of their families going back for many generations. In the United States, no one knew or cared how prominent the husband's family had been or how large the wife's dowry. Status in the American community was more likely to depend upon how much money the couple could make. Visible signs of success—store-bought clothing and furniture, a larger apartment, ultimately a house, could become more important to the ethnic American family in the United States than they had been in the old country. Moreover, material success would justify the sacrifices and hardships of immigration.

The desire to succeed produced many conflicts, particularly in the husband. Now his status in the eyes of his family as well as his neighbors often depended on his ability to make money. Failure could lead to loss of self-respect so severe that the defeated man turned to the anesthetic of alcohol or deserted his family altogether.

The pressure on the male immigrant was intensified by the fact that behavior he had been brought up to accept as appropriate and effective did not bring the same satisfactory results in America as it had in Europe. Indeed, in this strange country success and status often came to those who would have scarcely been tolerated in the old country. An Italian immigrant complained that in Boston "it was the misfits of Italian society who were 'i prominenti' and held dominance;

. . . those who could 'bluff it through' . . . the unscrupulous politician . . . the quack . . . the shyster lawyer. . . ." Many new immigrants faced the same problem their predecessors had faced—the conflict between traditional rural values and the fiercely individualistic, competitive behavior apparently demanded by the new environment. Now that the United States was more heavily industrialized and more completely urbanized, the conflict was even more acute.

The Immigrant Woman

Women faced their own special problems of adjustment to the new environment, not the least of which was overwork. The grandmother or maiden aunt who had shared the burdens of housework and child care in the old country was no longer part of the household in America; the ethnic wife had to manage these things herself, often in addition to working for wages. Immigrant women often worked night shifts in the mills or cleaned office buildings at night so that they could care for children, household, and boarders during the day. Such a regime left little time for rest, recreation, or education.

Housework and child care were more burdensome in America because of the vastly different life style. In the old country a tiny hut with an earthen floor needed little care, and children could play safely in the fields under the watchful eyes of their parents. An American tenement, however, required endless scrubbing, and there was no place but the dangerous streets for young children to play.

In an agrarian economy, five and six year olds could be put to work at tasks that contributed to the family's welfare. In America there was little a young child could do to be useful, and after the turn of the century older children were kept in school by law until their early teens, or even later. Under such circumstances, the large family that religious and cultural tradition, as well as economic reality, defined as a blessing in the old country now became a source of endless anxiety. Even childbirth itself was newly complicated. The trained midwives immigrant women had used in the Old World were not generally available here, and many women were unwilling to use a male physician, even if they could afford the fee.

But there were advantages as well as disadvantages for the immigrant woman. The United States was far from egalitarian in its attitude toward women. Still, immigration often improved the position of the ethnic woman within her nuclear family. Economic and social conditions in the United States sometimes gave her more freedom of action than she had had in the old country. The most extreme example of such a change is that of women within the Arabic speaking immigrant community. In the Middle East women were carefully secluded from public life and rarely seen by any men but their own husbands or fathers on whom they were economically totally dependent. Functioning almost as servants, they exerted little independent influence even in the rearing of their children.

In the United States, many Arabic men were surprised to discover that their economic success—the reason for immigration in the first place—was dependent upon their wives. Men who sold dry goods from door to door, a common occupation for Arabic immigrants, found their wives welcomed into American homes from which they were turned away. Many wives began to peddle with their husbands, learned English, and eventually became equal partners in prosperous family businesses. Some went on to become leaders in their communities. Lebanese-born Mrs. Mantura Frangiea, of Springfield, Massachusetts, for example, a partner in her husband's wholesale dry goods business, became the advocate for the local Arabic community and was well known and respected as such by the politicians, judges, lawyers, social workers, and police.

Changes in the economic area brought other changes as well. The Mediterranean tradition of men socializing with other men in coffee houses while their wives stayed at home gave way rapidly to the American pattern of husbands and wives going out together. Similarly, the traditional pattern by which the Middle Eastern man assumed responsibility for school-aged children, disciplining them, supervising their recreation, even buying their clothes rapidly disappeared. In the United States, teachers, nurses, doctors, and school counselors consulted the woman, not the man, on matters concerning the children. The Arabic woman, like many other immigrant women, assumed increasing importance as the director of her children's social and academic lives.

Sometimes immigration speeded up changes that were already underway, as in the case of Jewish women. Though never secluded like Arabic women, Jewish women from Eastern Europe were expected to devote themselves entirely to home and family. Education was valued for men, but a third of the women who immigrated were illiterate. Even the most traditional Jewish woman, however, was often familiar with the world of the marketplace. Many a pious wife kept shop or did other paid work so that her husband could devote all his time to religious study.

During the era of mass immigration, the roles of Jewish women in Europe were already changing. Young women were beginning to participate in new secular movements such as socialism and Zionism, both of which included a strong commitment to the equality of women among their other ideological goals. Though Russian universities discriminated against Jews, a few women of unusual ability and determination were able to acquire a secular, even a professional education. These "new" Jewish women brought their nontraditional life styles to America with them.

A popular journalist, Hutchins Hapgood, described the "new" Jewish women of New York City in 1902:

> They have lost faith completely in the Orthodox religion . . . read Tolstoy, Turgenev, and Chekov, and often put into practice the most radical theories of the new woman, particularly those which say that women should be economically independent of man. There are successful female dentists, physicians, writers, and even lawyers by the score in East Broadway who have attained financial independence through industry and intelligence. . . . They are ambitious . . . and often direct the careers of their husbands. . . . There is more than one case on record where a girl has compelled her recalcitrant lover to learn law, medicine, or dentistry, or submit to being jilted by her. . . .

Many of the "new" Jewish women became effective champions of causes such as trade unionism, woman's suffrage, and birth control. Their influence combined with the impact of the new environment, produced changes in traditional Jewish family life. Jewish women began to limit the size of their families, to enroll in night school in massive numbers, and to see that their daughters as well as their sons got higher education whenever possible.

"The man who does not beat his wife is not a man," says a South Slavic proverb. In Servia or Croatia it was not unusual to see women pulling plows while their husbands walked unencumbered beside them. In Southern Italy, women were subject to the authority of their fathers, brothers, husbands, male cousins, even teen-aged sons.

Slavic and Italian women did not gain the relative freedom of action achieved by Arabic and Jewish women in America. The subordination of women was an important part of the distinctive, centuries old South Italian family system, a system so strong and so functional that it survived immigration virtually intact. Because this system demanded close supervision and protection of women, South Italian women were more likely than other women to work within the home or, if employed outside, to work among people from the same Old World village or even the same family. Such women had fewer opportunities than their counterparts in other ethnic communities to achieve economic and social independence. Moreover, Italian and Slavic women were less likely than Jewish women to have abandoned religious orthodoxy, either before or after immigration. Traditional religion continued to play and enormous role in their lives. Thus the social philosophy of Roman Catholicism reinforced long established patterns of female subordination in the Italian and Slavic communities.

Even for the traditional Slavic and Italian women, America opened up new possibilities. Wife beating declined when women discovered that abusive husbands could be reported to the police! Ukrainian men complained American laws were made for women. Many Slavic and Italian women became active within their ethnic communities. Antonietta Pisanelli Alessandro, a South Italian wife and mother, founded Italian theaters in New York and San Francisco. Bohemian-born Josephine Humpel Zeman edited a nationally circulated Bohemian feminist newspaper. Polish, Lithuanian, Ukrainian, Slovakian, and other women developed national organizations that published newspapers and magazines and pursued educational and charitable work within the ethnic community. Members of religious orders established and ran much needed schools, hospitals, and orphanages. Nor were the activities of such women limited to their own communities. In Chicago, Slavic women helped organize a Woman's Civic League to register voters and campaign against a corrupt city administration. Women in other cities engaged in similar activities.

In most ethnic families the traditional authority of the male survived, in form if not in fact. It was not unknown for a woman to attribute important decisions she had made to her husband. Although he was often belittled in the outside world, the immigrant male had the satisfaction of being looked up to as the head of the household. Still, enough change had taken place that when immigrant families considered returning to Europe, it was the woman who most often did not want to go. Life was better for her in America.

The Immigrant Child

Children, like adults, had special problems adjusting to the new American environment. While adults might mingle primarily with those from within their own ethnic community, children were often forced into a school situation in which they were conspicuously "different." Eager to be accepted by their teachers and their peers, young people found minority status a devastating experience, as these childhood recollections of schooldays reveal:

> I was nervous from nine o'clock until three. . . . I never spoke right, I did not walk right, my tie was atrocious, my mother did not take good care of me, and so it went. . . .

> In elementary school I was often ridiculed for the clothes I wore until I began to believe myself that the dresses of other girls in school were by all means more proper than mine.

> My mother gave me each day an Italian sandwich, that is, half a loaf of French bread filled with fried peppers and onions. . . . Such a sandwich

would certainly ruin my reputation; I could not take it to school. . . . My god, what a problem it was to dispose of it. . . .

Timid and ill at ease in an "American" school, many ethnic children felt better in schools where their own group predominated. Undoubtedly this was one reason for the popularity of the parish parochial school. As immigration increased and ethnic ghettos grew, however, even public schools often acquired a predominantly ethnic population. "It made me feel at home. What a difference!" said an Italian boy after transferring from an Anglo-Saxon to a predominantly Italian school. "Even the cop in front of the school was an Italian." Segregated ghetto schools were often crowded, dark, and understaffed. There were other disadvantages to schools where most students were very poor. In the case of the Italian child quoted above, the new all Italian peer group reinforced his parents' view that earning was more important than learning. The boy lost interest in school work and dropped out at the age of thirteen because "everyone around me spoke of nothing but making dough."

Eager to "Americanize" their students, teachers often spoke disparagingly of the Old World language and traditions of their students. Children were torn between the old and the new. Some resolved the problem of conflict between the ethnic culture of their home and the American ways of the public school by dividing their lives into two separate compartments. Though dutiful and respectful within the home, they did not introduce their American school friends to their parents, thus avoiding exposure of their foreignness. Nor did they take their parents to functions at school; "that was our life, exclusively ours."

Other children devoted themselves with amazing patience and sensitivity to building bridges between the New World and the Old. Such children brought their parents proudly to their teachers, carefully translating what each said to the other to show them both in the best possible light. These children gave their teachers insight into their parents' lives, while introducing their parents to the mysteries of America. They were pioneers in breaking down parental resistance to American social customs, such as dating, and thus eased the path for younger brothers and sisters. Indeed, the oldest children were often surrogate parents to younger siblings, pleading their causes with the immigrant parents, helping them with their problems, even sacrificing their own higher education so that brothers and sisters could stay in school.

The realities of life in a new culture gave the child, like the woman, greater independence and status within the family. Children born in America or brought here at an early age learned English more rapidly than their parents, understood more of American life because of their American schooling, and could often earn money in their teens because of the job opportunities available in the American city. These new facts of life meant a reversal of the traditional family roles in which children were dependent upon adults for sustenance and for wisdom to cope with life. Now it was often the parents who were dependent upon the children—upon their earnings, and upon their ability to deal in English with teachers, social workers, doctors, and landlords.

Parents were proud of their children's achievements and appreciated their help, but many had mixed feelings. They worried that their Americanized children would lose respect for them and their way of life. Sometimes their fears were justified. Many Americanized children rejected their parents as totally old fashioned, rebelling against their authority, and against all other authorities as well. From among such children came the juvenile delinquents of the ethnic ghettos—and as police records indicate, there were many of these. Some parents were so painfully aware of their own "foreignness" that they accepted their children's version of what "everybody" did in America without question and did not attempt to control their children's behavior as they would have done in Europe. Other parents, equally unfamiliar with American life, reacted in the opposite way, imposing such severe restrictions that their children were driven into rebellion.

Journalist Lincoln Steffens described the extremes to which cultural and generational conflict could go and the anguish it could cause. He writes of the conflict between traditional Orthodox Jewish fathers, "parents out of the Middle Ages, sometimes out of the Old Testament days" and their sullen, rebellious sons, "the children of the streets of New York today":

> We would pass a synagogue where a score or more of boys were sitting hatless [traditional Jewish males keep their heads covered] in their old clothes, smoking cigarettes on the steps outside; and their fathers, all dressed in black, with their high hats, uncut beards, and temple curls, were going into the synagogue, tearing their hair and rending their garments [in mourning]. They wept tears, real tears. It was a revolution. Their sons were rebels against the law of Moses; they were lost souls, lost to God, the family, and to Israel of old.
>
> . . . If there were a fight—and sometimes the fathers did lay hands on their sons, and the tough boys did biff their fathers in the eye . . . the police would rush in and club now the boys, now the parents . . . bloodily and in vain. . . . I used to feel that the blood did not hurt, but the tears did . . . the old Jews were doomed and knew it. Two, three thousand years of continuous devotion, courage, and suffering for a cause lost in a generation.

Similar conflicts were acted out between the parents and children of virtually every ethnic group. The underlying problem was the children's desire to be "more American even than the Americans," as one school principal put it, and the parents' fear of indiscriminate change and of the consequent rejection of their values and way of life. In his study *Democracy and Assimilation*, Julius Drachsler summarized their fears:

> It is not merely the natural desire of parents to retain influence over the child. . . . It is a vague uneasiness that a delicate network of precious traditions is being ruthlessly torn asunder, that a whole world of ideals is crashing into ruins; and amidst this desolation, the father and mother picture themselves wandering about lonely in vain search of their lost children. . . .

Success and Failure–Two Case Histories

The crowded, unhealthful environment, the long, tedious hours of work, changes within the family relationships, conflicts between new ways and old—these problems touched the lives of all. Some families were unable to cope. Their unhappy stories can be found in the files of the newly organized urban charities. Many aspects of the social pathology of the ghetto are apparent in the story of the Judziewicz family, which came to the attention of the United Charities of Chicago in September, 1909. Mr. and Mrs. Judziewicz had immigrated from Poland in 1896. Mr. Judziewicz was unable to hold a steady job. He deserted his wife frequently, returning to live with her for brief periods, until she finally procured a divorce. At thirty, Mrs. Judziewicz was left with tuberculosis and five children under the age of eight. The youngest was a sickly infant, fathered by a boarder. The terse records of the social worker describe the situation shortly after the birth of the baby.

> *September 19, 1910.* Landlord in office to ask rent. . . . Says woman is a very untidy housekeeper and children do a great deal of damage about the premise.

> *September 21, 1910.* Woman in office asking help with funeral expenses as baby died 6:30 a.m. Her brother will buy [cemetery] lot. . . . The woman . . . says church will not help. Two teachers gave $5.00 and some friends $2.00. She had gone from house to house begging. . . . [the apartment] was extremely dirty and children playing in the room where the corpse was lying. Woman seemed utterly indifferent perhaps because she was so tired . . .

The future seemed bleak for the Judziewicz family. But for every family that fell apart under the stress of ghetto life, others, like that of

Mary and Martin Grubinsky, showed amazing strength and resource-fulness. According to Katherine Anthony, author of a study of working women in 1914, the Grubinskys immigrated from a remote corner of rural Hungary, stopping first in a Hungarian city for a few years before moving to New York. Perhaps this two-step immigration eased the shock of change for the Grubinskys and contributed to their ability to cope with urban America.

In New York the couple devoted themselves to one another and to the rearing of their eight children, four born in Hungary and four born in the United States. At the time Katherine Anthony described the family, Mr. Grubinsky had been working in the same furniture factory for seven years. He never missed a day and often took extra work home to finish on Sundays or in the evenings. He spent his free time doing things for his wife and children and entertaining his friends from the neighborhood. As for Mrs. Grubinsky:

> She helps her husband with the chair caning, makes the children's clothes, mends for her own family and also for hire, cooks, washes, irons, scrubs, tends her window boxes, minds the children of a neighbor who is doing a day's work, fetches ice from the brewery where it is thrown away, forages for kindling around warehouses, runs to school when the teacher summons her. . . . In her home nothing is wasted, nothing lost. Even the feathers from a Thanksgiving turkey were made into cushions and dust brushes.

Unlike the Judziewicz family, the Grubinskys have health, energy, a strong family commitment, and realistic plans for the future:

> . . . when Mary Grubinsky's parents die, she will have a small remittance from Hungary. Then, too, the children will be working and Mrs. Grubinsky will be able to go out [to work] more days. . . . When they get together $600 they will move to a little place on the other side of the Hudson. . . . It is a sustaining hope equally for the husband and the wife, and unites them through every other difference.

Outside Help

Immigrants struggling to cope with the changes in their lives in the early twentieth century ghettos had to depend primarily upon themselves, their own immediate families, and their ethnic com-munities (see Chapter Nine). But there was also help from the larger American community. Much of this help was motivated by the Progressive Movement, a broadly based attempt to improve American life. Progressives wanted to make the nation more efficient, more democratic, and more humane—goals which could be mutually contradictory. Progressive reformers tried to curb the excesses of the giant corporations, provide a better life for farmers and workers, and bring honesty, efficiency, and expertise to government, to industry, and to education.

Comprehensive national programs for economic relief did not exist until the Great Depression of the 1930's. The late nineteenth and early twentieth century did, however, see an increased understanding of the plight of the poor, an understanding that proved helpful to the immigrant. "Progressive" clergymen and social workers began to perceive that poverty might be caused by bad environment, poor health, or other unavoidable circumstances, rather than the innate depravity of the poor.

"... The man who cannot live on bread and water is not fit to live at all," proclaimed the traditional Reverend Lyman Beecher, who undoubtedly ate very well on his own salary of $20,000 a year. But other theologians, such as Washington Gladden, Walter Rauschenbusch, and Charles Sheldon disagreed, urging instead that Jesus' concern for the poor be translated into Christian efforts to solve the social problems of the day.

Influenced by this new "Social Gospel," the major Protestant denominations formed welfare organizations to work for such goals as the elimination of factory hazards to life and health, reduction of hours "to the lowest practical point, with work for all," and "a living wage in every industry," goals of obvious value to the immigrant poor. Instead of abandoning inner city parishes to follow congregants to the suburbs, some of the wealthier "Social Gospel" congregations maintained branches in the old neighborhoods to serve the new urban population. These "institutional churches" established soup kitchens, nurseries, libraries, gymnasiums, clubs, clinics, employment bureaus, and many kinds of classes. Church related organizations also planned programs of "outreach." The YMCA and YWCA offered recreation, education, and other services. The Salvation Army operated a comprehensive welfare program including emergency food and shelter, public nursing services, and special "rescue missions" for alcoholics, unwed mothers, prostitutes, and ex-convicts.

Several factors limited the effectiveness of these church-related programs. First, Protestant leaders often planned their programs without consulting the immigrant communities they sought to serve. Second, the tendency to use social welfare programs as missionary efforts to win converts for Protestant churches alienated the potential beneficiaries who were usually Catholics and Jews. Finally, many of the "helping" persons saw as their major goal the Americanization of their immigrant clients who must be persuaded to give up their ethnic language and habits both for their own benefit and for that of majority

America. "Business pleads for it, patriotism demands it, and social considerations require it," said one clergyman. However, even children resented help that was based on social manipulation and the belittling of their religious and cultural traditions. When the notice of the death of a prominent churchman was posted on a public bulletin board in a Jewish part of New York, "every boy of twelve or fourteen who stopped to read the notice deliberately spat upon it in the coolest and most matter-of-fact manner."

More acceptable to many of the new immigrant communities were the facilities provided by the better settlement houses. Many settlement houses were secular institutions. Jane Addams, a founder of the settlement house movement, understood that one could be as valuable a human being in a shawl as in a hat and that there was no danger to American life in the use of black bread instead of white! "Our aim is to work *with* the people rather than to work *for* the people," said James B. Reynold, head of the University Settlement on the Lower East Side of New York. Inspired by European examples and by the leadership of Jane Addams of Hull-House in Chicago, social workers, teachers, college students, and people of all ages who wanted to be "where idealism ran high" moved into large old homes, settlements, in the ethnic ghettos.

Responding to the needs and interests of the people among whom they lived, the settlement house personnel offered a variety of activities, such as social clubs for all ages, counseling services, employment agencies, and emergency relief. They offered classes in Shakespeare and Goethe as well as basic English, violin and ballet as well as sewing and woodworking. One of the strong points of the better settlement houses was their willingness to recognize the skills and the cultural heritages of the ethnic peoples they served. When the women who conducted cooking classes in a Milwaukee settlement published their still famous *Settlement Cook Book* as a fundraising project for the settlement, they included the treasured family recipes of the German, Bohemian, Jewish, and other immigrant women of their neighborhood. Hull-House in Chicago developed an industrial arts exhibit where residents of the neighborhood displayed their skills in weaving, spinning, woodcarving, and other traditional handicrafts. Evening entertainment at Hull-House featured ethnic costumes, dance, and song. Such programs gave American born children a new appreciation of their "foreign" parents and enhanced the self esteem of all who took part.

Many settlement houses worked closely with the public schools, suggesting programs, even sharing facilities. In Buffalo, for example, the kindergarten of Public School 41 met at Zion House, a Jewish settlement. Creative settlement workers in Boston, New York, and elsewhere used dramatics to teach immigrant children English and to help them "work through" their problems of adjusting to American life. This innovation led to the creation of some of the earliest children's theaters and was rapidly picked up by the public and parochial schools.

Responding to the needs of working mothers, settlement houses pioneered in quality comprehensive day care for young children. The goal of many settlement day care centers was to provide a complete program—education and medical and dental care for the child, educational and social services for the child's family, and special training for the teachers and other staff. By 1916, 695 settlement day care centers were in operation. Like many other Progressive reforms the day care movement declined in the conservative atmosphere of the 1920's. Ironically, the success of another reform, widow's pensions, helped kill the day care movement. As state legislatures enacted laws giving widows pensions to remain at home with their children, the day care clientele became stigmatized as the "undeserving" poor. There was a subsequent decline in the quality and the use of the day care centers.

Middle class women, including many second and third generation immigrants, staffed a variety of agencies that offered assistance to the population of the ethnic ghettos. Consumers Leagues worked to improve health and safety conditions in sweatshops and factories. The Women's Trade Union League assisted garment workers of New York in their attempts to unionize for better pay and working conditions. The Immigrant Protection League of Chicago helped immigrants reach their American destinations safely, protected them from fraud, and assisted them in their dealings with immigration officials, police, banks, and employers. Large cities established public charities, staffed by men and women social workers, new professionals to meet the emergency economic needs of the poor. These public charities were supplemented by ethnic or religious charities, often staffed by second generation Americans eager to help their more recently arrived countrymen.

Though good work was done by the settlement houses and by the various public and private charitable agencies, their resources were never adequate to their task. Only a small percentage, perhaps no more than five per cent, of the ghetto population were touched by their services. Moreover, like their religious counterparts, the secular agencies often approached their clients in a patronizing way, motivated more by a desire, conscious or unconscious, to preserve the "American" way of life than by a desire to help individuals solve their problems.

Too often aid was given grudgingly, with excessive investigation and red tape, and condescension. The immigrant paid a high price in self-respect for such assistance. An immigrant writer, Anzia Yezierska, left us vignettes of ghetto "caretakers" at their worst. The social worker: "By pictures and lectures she shows us how poor people should live without meat, without butter, without milk, and without eggs . . . why can't you yet learn us how to eat without eating?" The charity clinic: " . . . how that doctor looked on us, just because we were poor. . . . He only used the ends from his fingertips to examine us with. From the way he was afraid to touch us or come near us, he made us feel like we had some catching sickness that he was trying not to get on him." The unsympathetic school teacher: "She never perceived that I had a soul. . . . She could see nothing in people like me, except the stains on the outside." The truant officer: "What learning can come into a child's head when the stomach is empty."

Books, Schools, and "Progressive" Education

The two governmental agencies that did most to help the immigrant in the early twentieth century were the public libraries and the public schools, both of which expanded enormously during the Progressive era. The impact of the newly opened libraries can scarcely be overestimated.

> You can imagine my happy surprise when I found that here in this wonderful country are established free libraries, [wrote an immigrant] with thousands of books in many languages and everybody may take home a book or two. . . . With reverence I stepped into the Aguilar Library . . . and with a throbbing heart I told the girl what book I wanted and when I had the book in my hand, I pressed it to my heart and wanted to kiss it, but I was ashamed to do it.

Sympathetic librarians made their institutions community centers for classes, parties, meetings, and a variety of other activities. They befriended the local children, helping them select reading material for school and for leisure. Such librarians received smudged, misspelled thank you letters such as the following, quoted in the New York *Evening Post* of 1903: "My dear Miss Cheerin. Only God knows how much I love you. I send you as many kisses as there are pennies in the world." Perhaps the best thanks for Miss Cheerin and others like her was the knowledge that some people they helped, young adults as well as children, went on to higher education, pursuing careers in teaching, medicine, and other professions.

Ethnic newcomers were fortunate that they arrived at a time when public education in the United States was expanding. When the Irish and German immigrants arrived before the Civil War, public schools were just beginning and education was not compulsory. By the early twentieth century public school systems were well established everywhere and in most states education was compulsory at least to the age of fourteen. Educational reformers, the most famous of whom was John Dewey, were rethinking the entire purpose and process of education for a new urban and industrial society.

Reform was undoubtedly needed. The huge influx of new students, from rural America and from overseas, augmented pre-existing problems and created new ones. Overcrowding was so severe that classes were held in basements, attics, cloakrooms, corridors, and hastily built annexes. Buildings were old, dark, poorly ventilated and badly heated. Many teachers had less than a high school education themselves. Despite new pedagogical theories, memorization and rigid discipline were common. A journalist observing New York City schools a few years before World War I noted one in which "I did not once hear any child express a thought in his own words."

Progressive educational reformers spoke hopefully of changing all this—of creating self-governing, self-disciplined schools where "the teacher will float on the interest which the pupils manifest." The new educators urged classroom teachers to use "projects," dramatizations, and other innovative methods, to encourage students to express and pursue their own interests, and to create a democratic community in the classroom. Recognizing that many children, including many immigrant children, were not doing well in the traditional academic curriculum, educators urged that the curriculum be changed to meet what they saw as the needs of the "non-academic" child. Music, art, and physical and vocational education were to be stressed. Children were to be given the option of taking commercial or industrial rather than academic courses at the high school level, or even earlier. Teachers and counselors (a new educational professional) guided students into choices they considered appropriate for their socioeconomic background, assisted after World War I by a battery of newly developed, culturally biased psychological tests. In sum, the school was to concern itself with the social, physical, and vocational as well as with the mental development of the child.

Much of this program was constructed with the immigrant child in mind. In major cities two-thirds to three-quarters of the public school population was composed of immigrants or the children of immigrants. In the early twentieth century, as in the days before the Civil War, educators saw the public school as the answer to the social problems of rapidly growing polyglot cities. What Diane Ravitch found true of the situation in New York City was equally true in cities throughout the nation:

In the early twentieth century the public school was transformed into a vast, underfinanced, bureaucratic social work agency, expected to take on single-handedly the responsibilities which had formerly been discharged by the family, community, and employer . . . the idea took hold that the public school was uniquely responsible for the Americanization and assimilation of the largest foreign immigration in the nation's history.

Though Progressive educational reform varied from one city to another, and indeed, from one classroom to another, certain general changes were widespread. New school buildings were constructed, some with showers, swimming pools, and laboratory or "shop" facilities for instruction in home economics and industrial arts. (Unfortunately, the urban population grew faster than the new facilities, so that overcrowding remained a problem.) Commercial and industrial curricula were offered and vocational guidance was introduced. Physical education was emphasized. Free physical examinations and medical and dental care were made available. Special classes catered to the needs of children with physical or mental handicaps. Hot lunches were provided for the undernourished. Playgrounds were built for school and neighborhood use. School buildings were opened to the community for evening activities. Kindergartens and summer schools were opened. Night schools taught English and citizenship to adults. In California visiting "home" teachers took education to immigrant women in the neighborhoods.

Critics of immigration pointed out that the children of Southern Italian, Slavic, and other immigrant communities lagged behind the children of the American born in school achievement and were more likely to be truant. Many factors influenced the school performance of ethnic children. Contemporary studies indicated that children from communities that had been in the United States longer, such as Germans and Scandinavians, performed better than those who had arrived more recently, such as Poles and Italians. Critics considered this evidence that the "new" immigration was inferior to the "old." What the studies really showed was that when groups had had time to become familiar with American language and culture and to move from poverty to a more acceptable living standard, the school performance of their children improved. Cultural background as well as economic status and length of time in America influenced school performance. Finns, Japanese, Jews, and other recently arrived immigrant groups from urban backgrounds or from cultures where schooling was widespread and learning highly valued performed better even than earlier, rural, English-speaking groups such as the Irish. Indeed, they often outperformed the native-born children of old American stock.

There were many causes for the "retardation" of some groups of immigrant children. Even those born in the United States were often handicapped by unfamiliarity with the language and with the middle class Anglo-Saxon cultural atmosphere of the public school. School districts were gerrymandered to keep immigrant children segregated, and more money was likely to be spent in "American" districts. Schools in immigrant ghettos were old, overcrowded, and lacking in facilities. In some ethnic neighborhoods the population turnover was so great that children rarely stayed in the same school more than a year or two. Immigrant parents were unable to help children with their school-work. Lack of proper clothing, illness, the need to earn money or to take care of younger brothers and sisters kept some children at home. Finally, some children were too tired and too hungry to pay attention to their teachers.

Cultural factors played an important role in determining how children of a particular ethnic group would react to the American public school. In the parts of Poland controlled by Russia and Germany schooling was either forbidden or used as a vehicle to force Russian and German culture on Polish speaking populations. Peasant children who went to school usually attended only for a few years to gain basic literacy along with a little Polish history, folklore, and catechism. They were not expected to go further, nor did their early education prepare them to do so. The pattern survived in the United States. Polish children attended elementary school, achieving about at the same level as most other children for the first four or five years. Then, as they approached the age of twelve, they were likely to fall behind and they rarely went to high school. As in Poland, they were expected to start work in early adolescence. It must be remembered, however, that fewer than ten per cent of all American children went through high school in the early twentieth century. The pattern within the Polish community was similar to that of the American urban working class in general.

In poverty stricken southern Italy it was essential for children to perform meaningful tasks such as tending animals, building fences, and helping with housework by the time they were six or seven and to make adult contributions to the family livelihood by the time they were twelve. Southern Italian parents found it hard to accept American laws that kept "big" boys and girls in school to the age of fourteen or longer when the family needed their earnings. Dutiful children sometimes dropped out of school before the legal age to go to work. Such behavior was labeled "bad" by school authorities who could not understand why the parents insisted that the truant was a "good" boy or girl!

Differences in educational philosophy caused further problems. To the Southern Italian peasant, education was a process by which children learned to respect and obey their elders, to perform their traditional family roles (the roles of males and females were sharply differentiated), and to do economically useful work. They had little sympathy for "progressive" American schools that stressed individualism and self-expression, permitted boys and girls to mingle freely and do many of the same things, and taught "useless" subjects such as drawing and physical education. In Southern Italy secondary schooling was a serious affair, leading to lucrative and prestigious occupations such as law, medicine, and the priesthood. Not so in the United States wrote an irate Italian parent!

> It is very, very bad that the little children are taught in school to do nothing else but play ball. But I cannot understand how it is possible for a high school to do the same thing. . . . When my boy went to high school, I was pleased that one in our family may become a learned man. But I was disappointed. . . . How can he learn when they compel him to play more than to study? I remember they called me to school to explain why my son does not want to attend his playing lessons! I did not go, because I brought up my boy well. I did not teach him to play. . . . This play business is the ruination of the family.

The complaints of this South Italian parent are ironic because physical education was added to the curriculum at least partly as a response to what educators mistakenly saw as the nonacademic interests, or low aspiration level, of immigrant children. Vocational education was added for a similar reason. In the early twentieth century, however, most vocations could be learned more effectively on the job than in school, especially with the added inducement of a paycheck. The automatic counseling of immigrant children into vocational rather than academic programs by guidance personnel with preconceived ideas of what was appropriate for such children was resented by many immigrant parents. Having come to America to improve the prospects for their families, they had higher aspirations for their children. The immigrant population of New York City indignantly rejected the "Gary Plan," a progressive reform in which children would spend half of their school day on the playground, in the shops, and in other nonacademic pursuits.

Because of language problems, immigrant children were often placed in classes with children many years their juniors, or with children who were mentally retarded. Inappropriate materials were another handicap to the education of the immigrant child. School books inherited from America's agrarian past pictured little blond Johnny skipping down the flower lined country lane to his slender, carefree mother—a world so far removed from that of the ghetto child as to be almost beyond belief. Many teachers were sympathetic and understanding; but others could be callous, even cruel. Well meaning teachers were sometimes so eager to instill love for America that they presented children a picture of their new country that was romanticized beyond recognition and that denied the reality of the child's own experience:

> The virtues of honesty and American courtesy which he (the teacher) recited so dutifully were forgotten by me as soon as I realized that my existence depended upon my own ability to get things by hook or by crook. . . . The teacher talked about civic beauty . . . the only civic beauty that appealed to me was the East River where . . . I could take a swim in summer. The teacher spoke of the officer at the street crossing as a "gentleman of peace." I realized soon that he was nothing but a big fat Irish bastard. . . .

Similar problems faced the tens of thousands of men and women, already overburdened with work and family obligations, who nevertheless found time to attend the "lighted schoolrooms" of the public night schools. Steel workers in Cleveland read juvenile stories about flowers and birds ("I am a yellow bird. I can fly.") and recited sentimental poems such as, "Oh baby, dear baby, Whatever you do, You are king of the home and we all bend to you." Students in English classes were forced to differentiate between the past, past perfect, and pluperfect tenses. Candidates for citizenship studied manuals that told them the dimensions of the Senate chambers and informed them that in 1916 the Bureau of Fisheries produced 4,800,000,000 fish and fish eggs! English speaking teachers often were unable to communicate with their students. Adult students in Passaic, New Jersey, and in many other cities as well, expressed a desire for teachers of their own nationality. "Then we will not get discouraged."

Undoubtedly preconceived ideas about the intellectual capacities, proper social stations, and interests of immigrants, as well as simple thoughtlessness, contributed to the inappropriate content and methods of immigrant education. Immigrant women were burdened with sexual as well as ethnic stereotypes. Though a million and a quarter foreign born women worked outside the home in a typical year, and though ethnic women like ethnic men had a wide range of interests, from art and music to politics, materials developed for the education of immigrant women were of the "I cook. I wash. I mop. I sweep." variety. A model English lesson on how to seek employment shows quite clearly what occupation was considered appropriate for ethnic women:

> First pupil   — I want to work.
> Second pupil— What can you do?
> First pupil   — I can wash and iron.
> Second pupil— What else?
> First pupil   — I can wash windows and clean house.

Americanization—getting immigrants to adopt not only American loyalties, but also American food, dress, and life style—was an important part of education for children and adults. Immigrants who understood no English were drilled in the recitation of patriotic songs and poems. Los Angeles "home" teachers were instructed to maintain a model cottage and to give model tea parties and dinners so that foreign-born women would learn the American life style. "I am happy. I have money. I go to the store," said the Los Angeles English instruction manual, giving the immigrant woman training in her role as an American consumer as well as in English vocabulary!

Despite these difficulties, free public education had much to offer immigrants, and they flocked to take advantage of it. The desire for social mobility was the main reason for immigration in the first place, and most immigrants, even "birds of passage" soon realized that "to learn to speak and read English was to make their investment of time, expense, and money gilt-edged." Immigrant adults attended night schools at great personal sacrifice, petitioning the local authorities to establish them where they did not already exist. Parents of every ethnic group made enormous efforts to educate their children, sometimes leaving areas where jobs were better to move to cities where kindergartens and other special facilities were available. Among many groups the public school teacher was as revered as a priest or a rabbi. Recognizing the value of education in America, immigrant fathers wrote letters home insisting their children be sent to school in the old country even before immigration. Illiteracy was common among older immigrants, but the literacy rate among their American born children was higher than that of the old stock American population.

The public schools have received credit for the education and Americanization of the early twentieth century immigrants. Immigrants did become educated and Americanized, and public schools did contribute. They were able to do so because what they offered, the chance to become literate in English, supported the social and economic aspirations of the immigrant. But it must be remembered that public schools were only one of many institutions that helped immigrants adjust to the United States—and not necessarily the most important one. The job, the union, the political machine, the ethnic school, the ethnic press, indeed the ethnic community itself—these too, played significant roles in Americanizing and educating the immigrant.

The Immigrant and the Progressive

The relationship between the immigrant and the Progressive movement is a complex one. Progressive reformers were often middle class Anglo-Saxons who had their first experiences working with the immigrant poor through the institutional churches, settlement houses, and immigrant assistance leagues. Some social workers and reformers who began in those areas went on to become involved in political action. Recognizing the needs of the urban poor and the evils of unrestrained capitalism, they began to campaign for housing laws, factory inspection, child labor laws, compulsory education laws, workmen's compensation, widow's pensions, the ten (then the eight) hour day, and similar measures. Immigrants joined the Progressives in working for such changes.

Progressivism was an "umbrella" term which sheltered many different kinds of reforms, not all of which were supported by ethnic Americans. Many Progressives were intensely interested in the prohibition of alcoholic beverages, a reform which, then as in the pre-Civil War years, had little appeal to the ethnic voter. Even less appealing was the idea endorsed by some of the Progressives that the way to solve the social problems of the city was to cut off further immigration, especially immigration of "inferior" southern and eastern Europeans and Asians. Racism, directed at both immigrants and blacks, was a part of the "best" reform thinking of the day. Woodrow Wilson, a "Progressive" president, segregated all government agencies in Washington, D.C.!

Ethnic Americans were not usually sympathetic to Progressive appeals for political reform in the interests of efficiency or honesty. Political bosses opposed by good government reformers were often useful to the new ethnics, as they had been to the Irish, for reasons already discussed. They provided jobs and helped the party faithful in time of trouble. But when political bosses resisted factory inspection, sanitation improvements, or other "bread-and-butter" issues, immigrants joined with middle class reformers to unseat them. Unhampered by the old American tradition of hostility to active government, immigrants joined the wing of the Progressive movement that favored strong government action to limit the traditional freedom of landlords and business men to run their affairs as they saw fit. In states such as Massachusetts and New York, ethnic Americans were vital to the success of many economic and social reforms. Though most of the Progressive leadership was Anglo-Saxon, ethnic politicians like Robert Wagner and Fiorello LaGuardia began their careers as Progressive reformers.

Historians continue to debate the effectiveness of Progressivism and to question its motivation. From ethnic America's point of view Progressivism was a beginning, but only that. Parks, schools, and other facilities were built, but never enough to meet the need. Charities operated, but with limited effectiveness. Industrial states established health and safety regulations, forbade child labor, and extended compulsory education, but these laws were poorly enforced. Civil service and other "structural" reforms put many areas of government in the hands of trained experts, but in doing so they decreased the patronage power of the local ethnic politician. The substitution of "at-large" city wide elections for ward elections made it more difficult for ethnic communities to achieve any political representation at all.

Progressivism, then, was not the solution to ethnic America's problems. In the Progressive era, as in earlier years, ethnic Americans were essentially on their own. Success or failure depended less upon outside aid than upon the individual's own skills, health, determination, and luck. The most important source of help and support for virtually every ethnic American was the ethnic community itself.

CHAPTER 8

Building a Community:
Ethnic Institutions, 1820-1924

Even when outside help was not available, nineteenth and early twentieth century ethnic Americans did not face their problems alone. They joined together to share their experiences and their resources. Through this sharing, they created their own greatest asset, their "secret weapon" for entry into American life—the ethnic community. Arising from efforts to ease the shock of immigration for new arrivals, ethnic communities survived to meet the needs of subsequent generations and to become permanent features of the American social landscape.

An ethnic community was more than a ghetto, a geographic area in which a particular group was heavily concentrated. An ethnic community, like any other community, was a group of people who knew and cared about one another, enjoyed a common life, and shared common problems and concerns. The individuals in such a community related to one another in a variety of structured, or institutionalized, ways—some informal like the corner grocery or saloon, others formal, like the church, the school, or the fraternal lodge. Ethnic communities consisted of a network of such institutions, some as local as the nearby street corner, others as extensive as a national press.

The Neighborhood vs. the Community

The first step—but only the first—in the establishment of ethnic communities was the establishment of ethnic neighborhoods. Critics saw "foreign quarters"—little Italys, little Syrias, Polonias, Chinatowns, and the like—as evidence of the immigrants' clannishness and unwillingness to recognize that they were now living in the United States. This view was based on a lack of understanding of the nature and function of the ethnic neighborhood. Ethnic neighborhoods, like ethnic communities, were not "un-American." Rather they were the first step toward Americanization. Many immigrants arrived with little or no money, no job, no knowledge of English, in a land far different culturally and economically from the one they had left. The ethnic neighborhood met their immediate needs. Here they found information in their own language, familiar food, and lodging they could afford among people with whom they felt at ease. Here they got help in finding work, usually among coworkers who spoke their language and could help them learn the new occupation. Equally important, here they found the sympathy and friendship of others who shared their values and life experiences. These factors helped ease the cultural shock of immigration and made new beginnings possible.

In some cases ethnic neighborhoods were synonymous with ethnic communities—in small German, Scandinavian, or Dutch settlements in the Midwest, for example. Not every ethnic neighborhood grew into a true community, however. A community implies a degree of permanence and the institutionalization of interaction between its inhabitants. Sometimes immigrant neighborhoods were populated by members of so many different ethnic groups that no single group was numerous enough to establish its own institutions. Sometimes the inhabitants of an ethnic neighborhood did not remain there long enough to build a community. Immigrant enclaves at the edges of commercial or industrial areas were especially short-lived; as the cities grew, this property was quickly turned to more profitable commercial uses.

If some ethnic neighborhoods could not support even one ethnic community, others, Boston's South End, for example, and New York's Lower East Side, supported more than one. Several ethnic communities could coexist in the same immigrant neighborhood because an ethnic community was a network of interpersonal and institutional relationships, not a geographic location. By the beginning of the twentieth century, southern and eastern European immigrant groups had created communities that operated on a local, state, and national scale; northern and western European groups had created similar communities decades earlier.

To native-stock Americans the ethnic community, with its foreign language shops, churches, organizations, and publications seemed transported from an alien culture; but to the newly arrived immigrant it was an introduction to America. The familiar ethnic tongue spoken there was liberally seasoned with "Americanisms." "I was ten or twelve years old before I found out that such words as *pa tikkele* (particular), *staebel* (stable), and *fens* (fence) were not Norse but mutilated English words," wrote a Norwegian-American in 1900. The familiar tongue was used to express unfamiliar American ideas. Italian immigrants looked forward to the day they could purchase a *carro* (an automobile). Jewish immigrants found the new Yiddish vocabulary of their community a quick introductory course in American life: *blufferke* (hypocrite), *allrightnick* (an upstart), *next-doorige* (neighbor), and *consumptionick* (victim of tuberculosis).

What was true of language was equally true of virtually every institution within the ethnic community. Even the most familiar institutions, such as churches, were not the same; and new institutions existed that had no counterpart in the old country at all. The ethnic community was more American than foreign. Created on American soil to deal with American problems, the ethnic community was a halfway house between the old and the new. The familiarity of some aspects of life—language, food, religion—gave the immigrant the time, energy, and emotional security to concentrate on the many other things that were totally new. For some, the ethnic community was a temporary stop on the way to total assimilation into the life of the larger American community. For others, it became a permanent resting place.

Informal Institutions–Information and Companionship

In the European peasant community there were long established traditions about what should be done, by whom, and how. In America, on the other hand, obtaining work, keeping house, and rearing children raised troublesome new questions. In the European community there were well established places for people to get together to exchange ideas and information—the village tavern, the well or stream, or the job itself. In America, substitutes for these places had to be created. Informal institutions arose to meet the simple need for places to come together, share experiences, exchange information, and enjoy one another's company.

Even the earliest, most transient ethnic neighborhoods had at least a few of these "informal" community institutions. The first might be a boarding house where newcomers roomed with those who had been in America a little longer. Immigrants who ran such boarding houses often found that income from providing food, drink, and sociability to fellow immigrants exceeded their income from factory or mine and thus expanded into the operation of commercial taverns or saloons.

In Irish, Polish, and other Slavic neighborhoods, the corner saloon was often the first important ethnic institution—the place where men came to meet their friends and talk of the old country, of jobs, of women, and the like. Among Syrian, Greek, and Armenian men, coffee houses played a similar role. Among German-Americans, the beer garden was a social and recreational center for the women and children as well as the men. In 1914 Mrs. Fernande Richter, a German-American from St. Louis, warned a Congressional committee that for Germans Prohibition—not alcohol—was a danger to family life!

In like manner, the local grocery store, the butcher shop, the bakery, even the dry goods store could serve as a social center where neighbors exchanged ideas and information. Indulging in gossip along with their shopping, people learned who among them was in trouble and thus were able to give help in the event of sickness, unemployment, or other catastrophe. Hearing how other people handled problems helped the listeners to solve their own. Even the good fortune of others was useful. Parents who bragged about the achievements of their children provided a "grapevine" of information about the opportunities available to the young.

The leaders of these informal institutions often became the leaders of their ethnic communities. In a Ukrainian neighborhood, for example, the owner of the tavern was often the most prosperous and influential man, the man who took the lead in building the first church and calling in the first priest. Other successful businessmen and sometimes businesswomen—undertakers, barbers, steamship agents, the owners of restaurants, physicians, and lawyers—played a similar role in other communities.

Young people as well as adults had their centers of information and recreation. The local poolroom, dance hall, or even a particular front stoop provided the recognized setting for such interaction. Among the boys, a special street corner might be the jealously guarded headquarters of an ethnic gang in which the strongest, shrewdest, or most charismatic boy instructed his fellows in the arts of urban survival. Though members of such groups sometimes got into trouble, often their activities were only mischievous, and the relationships they established survived a lifetime. Leaders trained in these neighborhood street corner gangs often graduated into careers of politics and community service or organized crime.

The home itself functioned as an informal community institution. People of all ages gathered in one another's kitchens to eat, to talk, to share—and by sharing to minimize hardships and maximize pleasures. Special celebrations like the wedding described in Di Donato's novel of Italians in New York, *Christ in Concrete,* became ritual events for the entire community. Traditional foods and familiar faces evoked common memories of the Old World, creating warmth and comfort in the New:

Annunziata and Cola passed the platters of antipasta as the paesanos found their seats. Bitter green Sicilian olives, sweet Spanish olives, whitings, and squid pickled in saffron, Genoese salami . . . pickled eggplants . . . soup with eggs, fennel, artichoke roots, grated parmesan and noodles that melted on the lips . . . boiled fat eels garnished with garlic and parsley . . . thick red wine. . . . The stuffing of the roast was rich with nuts, chopped squab, figs, cheese, eggs, and peppers, and hands that shoved it between wide lips were soaked in its flavors.

Ah, brother and sister, this is the life—cuddlingly arranged close to the flesh and smell and joy of them who are your own people. . . . I would this night last forever and more!

Five hours had they been at table, and now they sat back and in the strong tobacco clouds that nearly obscured the gaslight they talked of other days.

Remember the orange groves. . . .

The Campobasso where grazed the sheep of Don Pepe. . . .

And the Basilica of Saint Michael on All Soul's Day.

They reconstructed the beautiful terrain of Abruzzi and tenderly restored their youths and the times of Fiesta and Carnival.

The Lodge

As ethnic neighborhoods grew toward becoming ethnic communities, informal gathering places like the tavern, the shop, and the home were supplemented by more structured social organizations. The most common was the lodge, established by immigrants from the same county, parish, or district. As Italian immigrants often settled in the same blocks, even the same buildings, with their old neighbors from Calabria, Naples, or elsewhere, such organizations were natural in their communities. Eventually these local lodges were federated into a national network, the Sons of Italy. Similarly the Chinese of San Francisco formed the famous Six Companies, based upon the districts from which their members had emigrated. Japanese-Americans organized themselves into Kenjin-kai, again based upon common geographic origin. Jews from particular East European towns organized lodges known as landsmanschaften. Norwegians and others formed similar groupings.

The lodges usually began as social centers to supplement the cramped tenements, places to meet old friends, sing old songs, celebrate old holidays, and simply reminisce. They helped ease the shock and the loneliness of immigration for the newcomer. Though they were based upon common birthplace in the old country and their members spoke the same language, ethnic lodges were American in organization. They were voluntary associations with democratically elected officers and all the other trappings familiar to native-born "joiners" but perhaps unknown in the peasant village from which its members came. Their leaders were often men who had been of little consequence before immigration but who, because of luck or ability, had become influential in America.

Through the lodges, immigrants took on new tasks and learned to handle old tasks in new, American ways. Social life in the old country had taken care of itself. In America it was carefully fostered by the lodges which organized countless picnics, dances, parades, conventions, and other festivities for that purpose. Sometimes these activities were for men only, while branches, or even separate organizations, provided similar activities for women and children. Often the whole family participated together. As local lodges united into citywide, statewide, even national federations, the summer picnics, the New Year's Day parade, or the annual convention might involve thousands of people. Planning, publicizing, and handling the financial arrangements for such massive undertakings plunged many ethnic Americans into contacts with the general American community and its ways which they might not have known before.

Through the lodges, ethnic Americans took initiatives that would have been the responsibility of government officials in the old country. Lodges sponsored cultural programs and religious processions and established churches, synagogues, and schools. The Chinese Six Companies collected debts owed to Chinese immigrants by others within the community. The Japanese Kenjin-kai campaigned against gambling and other vices and served as an unofficial branch of the Japanese government, registering Japanese citizens at birth and doing other semiofficial business. Virtually every ethnic lodge became involved in economic self-help, acting as an informal employment bureau, lending small sums to help members buy farms or businesses, giving scholarships to deserving young people, and conducting insurance plans to cover funeral expenses, sickness, unemployment, and other needs.

Economic Self-Help

A variety of special institutions, some under the auspices of lodges, some independent, grew up to meet the very serious economic problems of the immigrants. Like the lodges, these organizations were essentially American solutions to American problems. In the old country close relatives or neighbors helped a family in need, and orphans and old people lived with the nearest kin. In an agrarian economy this system worked fairly well; there was always room for one or two more on the farm and always work they could do to help earn their keep. If the next of kin tried to shirk their duties to the unfortunate, the entire village would exert pressure to insure that responsibilities were met.

In the United States, as in Europe, tragedy was close at hand. Unemployment, illness or death of the breadwinner, a disabling accident, even another unplanned baby—such events could prove catastrophic when subsistence was precarious. But in America a family might be far from any relatives. When they were present, relatives were often unable to find room for the unfortunates in already crowded city apartments where they would take up space and contribute little. Nor was the old village social pressure available to force people to shoulder such obligations. New solutions had to be found.

When disaster struck, immigrants turned to neighbors who spoke their language. A collection might be taken up in the saloon, the bakery, the tenement house, or the lodge. Soon the idea arose that if everyone paid a small amount at regular intervals into a common fund, money would be on hand for emergencies. Thus arose the countless mutual benefit societies that provided funeral expenses, unemployment and sickness insurance, and even capital loans and college scholarships to large numbers of ethnic Americans. Most families were covered by one or more of these associations which existed in some form in every ethnic community.

From small beginnings, ethnic mutual aid societies sometimes grew into prosperous banks, building and loan associations, and insurance companies—a process which brought members of ethnic communities into the mainstream of American business life. The first Hungarian benefit society was formed by a group of miners pooling their resources to save a sick colleague from being evicted on a stormy night for nonpayment of rent. It began with a capital of $17.25. By 1945, the association had 364 chapters and assets of seven and a half million dollars.

An even greater success story is that of the Ukrainian National Association, which began as a mutual aid society in Shamokin, Pennsylvania in 1893. Founded by four clergymen, the association charged its members 50 cents a month for seven years in return for a small death benefit. Mutual benefit associations have become the most important institutions in the Ukrainian community. In the 1930's they insured over 137,000 Ukrainian-Americans, and had capital assets of close to twenty million dollars. In addition to their insurance activities, Ukrainian mutual benefit societies aided the poor, awarded scholarships, sent relief funds to the Ukraine, and held local and national meetings that were major events in the community.

Mutual aid societies were only one of many ethnic institutions that addressed themselves to economic problems. Because American banks were often reluctant to lend money to immigrants (who did not feel at home in these austere institutions anyhow), ethnic banks arose in every immigrant neighborhood. They provided badly needed services such as transmitting money overseas and making small loans. Japanese, West Indians, Chinese, and others with some commercial experience had informal "pools" for raising capital for prospective small businesses. Chinese trade guilds helped their members deal with American employers, provided aid to the unemployed, and, in the case of the laundries, divided the business territory among the competing firms to prevent cutthroat competition. Japanese farmers' societies disseminated information on improved farming methods and helped their members buy land, obtain supplies, and market their products. The activities of these and similar organizations in other communities were invaluable in helping newcomers secure a living.

Labor unions often functioned as ethnic organizations. In large cities unions were sometimes composed almost entirely of one ethnic group. There were Polish and Ukrainian unions near the Chicago stockyards, and Jewish unions in New York City's garment district. Though ethnically "segregated," these unions had an Americanizing effect. They taught their members about the American economy and about American politics. They encouraged their members to learn English, to become citizens, and to vote. Many sponsored classes, athletic events, parties, even theatrical activities for their members. The International Ladies Garment Workers Union owned a vacation resort and sent promising young workers to special labor colleges. Ethnic unions were often members of ethnic federations, such as the Hebrew Trade Unions of New York, but they were also integrated into the general American union structure through their craft affiliations. Unions dominated by a particular ethnic group were a bridge over which many workers passed into a fuller participation in American life.

Equally valuable as Americanizing agents were the ethnically mixed unions found in small mining or mill towns or in ethnically mixed urban neighborhoods. A study of Nanticoke, Pennsylvania during World War I noted a well integrated multiethnic population of 25,000 consisting of old stock Americans, second generation Welsh, Irish, and Germans, and immigrant Poles, Slovaks, and Lithuanians. The businessmen and their employees represented all of these ethnic groups. The tax collector was a Pole, the president of the Board of Health a Welshman, one of the appraisers a Slovak. Even "Quality Hill" had its foreign born residents. English was spoken everywhere. The cooperation among the various ethnic groups evident in all aspects of the town's life was the result of ties built up through the one organization common to all and central to the life of the entire town—the United Mine Workers local.

A similar role was played by the longshoreman's union in an ethnically mixed neighborhood in New York City. According to a union official, himself of Irish parentage:

> We understand one another, whatever the nationality. . . . Our meetingplace is open all the time and the men come here at any time when waiting for work. They read and discuss everything. . . . I know many a boy who has learned English because he had something to say at our meetings and he wanted everybody to understand him. . . . I have taken many a fellow up to naturalization court myself, and helped to put him through.

Though unions existed in Europe, the minority of immigrants who became union members did so for the first time in the United States. Because immigrants of every ethnic group were overwhelmingly working class, union membership was a unifying rather than a divisive force within each ethnic community. It was equally important as a force uniting the working classes of different communities and drawing them into a common American cause. The 1912 textile strike in Lawrence, Massachusetts, is an excellent example. Strike meetings were held at the Portuguese Center, the Franco-Belgian cooperative, and the Syrian Church. Issues were discussed in French, German, Italian, Polish, and Yiddish before Local 20 voted to begin the strike. Even though the strikers relief committees were organized along ethnic lines, all worked together in a common effort.

While most immigrants acquired their unionism in the United States, ethnic Americans brought another economic self-help institution—the cooperative—with them from abroad. More popular in Europe than in the United States, the cooperative movement was brought here mainly by Finns, although Russians, Lithuanians, Ukrainians, Poles, Italians, and other groups were also involved. Like unions, cooperatives were often located in ethnic neighborhoods. In 1920 the Finnish community of Fitchburg, Massachusetts, operated three successful cooperatives, a large grocery store, a boardinghouse-restaurant, and an apartment house. By purchasing shares, members of the cooperatives participated in the planning and management of these enterprises and shared the profits in the form of dividends. Meanwhile, outsiders as well as Finns enjoyed excellent products and services at the cheapest possible prices.

The Finnish Woman's Cooperative Home was begun in 1910 by a group of Finnish domestic servants in New York City who were looking for a place to spend their days off. They pooled their money to rent a few rooms for common use. The cooperative grew until its members, many of them young women still in their teens, owned and operated a commodious four story building with sleeping accomodations for forty, social lounges, club rooms, a library, a public dining room, and an employment bureau. The cooperative sponsored classes, provided music and other cultural programs, and held parties for the single young women of the Finnish community. The women who managed the cooperative learned a great deal about business, about America, and about their own capabilities.

Not all ethnic Americans were in a position to help themselves, either through mutual aid societies, unions, or cooperatives. Charities were needed for the sick, the disabled, the widow, the orphan, the aged. Through their lodges, churches, or independent organizations, ethnic communities made efforts to take care of the less fortunate among their numbers. Lack of resources and lack of experience in voluntary charitable organization limited the effectiveness of the efforts of some groups, the Irish, for example, and the southern Italians. Other groups, the Germans, the Japanese, the Chinese, the Syrians, the Lebanese, and the Jews were highly effective. Educated in the belief that charity is the obligation of every just person, Jews were particularly successful in this area. Accustomed to providing for their own poor in the hostile environments of Christian Europe, they built orphanages, old people's homes, hospitals, and other charitable institutions in the United States. The Jewish community pioneered new programs in social services, such as putting children in foster homes rather than orphanages whenever possible and devised fund raising techniques, such as the federation of charities idea, which were widely copied by other ethnic groups and by the larger American community.

Religious Institutions

Religious belief was part of the cultural baggage of every immigrant group; and every ethnic community reproduced, as far as possible, the religious institutions of its homeland. Catholic immigrants heard Mass in the United States just as they had in French Canada, Poland, or Austria. Jews sanctified the name of God in New York and San Francisco with the same prayers they had used in Russia and Rumania. Even Bohemian "freethinkers" established temples and Sunday schools to perpetuate their philosophy in the New World.

Religious belief did not survive immigration unchanged. In many cases an individual's religious faith and practice was weakened, even lost. Paradoxically, institutionalized religion, the church itself, was often strengthened. Visitors from Europe were often surprised to find that the institutionalized church had an influence far greater in the United States than in the old country. Pre-Civil War Irish immigrants, for example, grew up in Ireland where priests and nuns were in short supply, two thirds of the population never attended Mass, and "the ignorance of the people in matters of Religion is frightful." Yet the Irish became the staunchest and most devout supporters of the Catholic Church in the United States.

During the mid-nineteenth century, the Irish underwent what historian Emmet Larkin called a "devotional revolution." In their homeland pressures from their English rulers were causing them to lose their Gaelic language and culture. They became ardent Catholics because the Church provided them "a substitute symbolic language . . . a new cultural heritage with which they could identify and be identified and through which they could identify with one another." In like manner the Irish immigrants to the United States, finding other aspects of their Gaelic culture fast disappearing, made Roman Catholicism the touchstone of ethnic as well as religious identity.

Among other immigrant groups too the church increased in importance. It came to be not one ethnic institution among many, as in the old country, but the main bearer of ethnicity. The Polish Catholic parish became the American counterpart of the Old World communal village, for example; and the Greek Orthodox Church became the matrix of virtually all Greek ethnic life in the United States. To many immigrants the ethnicity of their church—its identification with their homeland and traditional culture and language—became more important than its religious content. This explains some of the difficulties immigrants faced in trying to transplant their old religious institutions to the New World. They were not just transplanting religion, they were transplanting ethnicity as well.

And there were difficulties. In theory the Roman Catholic Church was a universal Church, with services in a universal language, Latin. An immigrant from any European parish should have had no trouble fitting into any American parish. In practice this was not the case. Social and ethnic differences drove coreligionists apart. French and English stock Catholics were not enthusiastic about the waves of impoverished Irish Catholics who came in the mid-nineteenth century. The Irish, in turn, literally relegated the Italians and Poles to the church basement when they arrived, considering them scarcely human, much less Catholic. Nor were Catholics unique in this reaction. German Jews, settled and acculturated, were embarrassed by the arrival of impoverished, Orthodox Jews from Eastern Europe.

Part of the problem was the natural social snobbery shown by the newly respectable second or third generation toward their counterparts just off the boat. The newcomer presented a threat to a status won only recently and with much hard work! Other factors were also involved. The American Catholic Church experienced a struggle for leadership, a struggle won so decisively by the Irish that even in the mid-twentieth century Polish and Italian Catholics remain numerically underrepresented in the American hierarchy and are resentful of this situation.

There were ritual as well as social differences between ethnic coreligionists. East European Jews complained that the services of German Jews were cold and unfeeling, while German Jews considered the emotionalism of the newcomers undignified and improper. To Sicilian Catholics, the Catholicism of the Irish-dominated American church seemed puritanical, materialistic, and overly subservient to Rome. To the Irish, Italian Catholicism, with its devotion to local patron saints, its love of processions and pageantry, and its anticlerical tendencies seemed immoral and superstitious to the point of paganism.

In mixed parishes, Catholics fought over everything from the nationality of the priest to the name of the church. Ethnic groups that hated one another for political reasons in Europe could scarcely be expected to cooperate amicably in the same parishes in the United States. When Hungarians and Slavs, for example, or Poles and Ukrainians found themselves in the same parishes, Christian forbearance was rare. When a Ukrainian community in Pennsylvania left a Polish parish to establish its own church, the Polish priest urged his congregation to pray for its failure!

Such disputes led to the Cahenslyite movement, an attempt to divide the American Catholic Church, including its hierarchy, along ethnic lines. An enthusiastic Polish Cahenslyite took his case for a separate Polish church directly to President Grover Cleveland rather than the Pope. Perplexed, Cleveland referred the complaint to the Irish Cardinal Gibbons, who dismissed the Polish priest as "something of a crab." The Papacy, too, dismissed the idea of separate ethnic branches, considering it destructive of the unity of the American church. Undaunted, Polish dissidents seceded to form the still active Polish National Church. French Canadians fought the Irish dominated church fiercely, but in vain. Small groups of Italians, Czechs, and others turned to Protestantism. But most Catholic immigrants remained within the Church, establishing their own ethnic flavor in any parish in which they attained numerical dominance.

Ethnic churches in the United States were social centers as well as places of worship. This was especially important in rural areas, where the immigrant generation had few other outlets. Novelist O. E. Rölvaag described the reaction of a group of frontier Norwegians to the coming of the first minister, a reaction clearly more social than religious.

> It was so fun and jolly . . . the gathering together; now there would be some excitement in the settlement. . . . One was thinking about the congregation they would organize, another about the cemetery . . . men

would be needed to manage these activities . . . they would of course start a ladies aid, now that they had a minister; and that would be great fun, with meetings and cakes and coffee and sewing and all. . . .

In cities as well as rural areas, the church served as a social center for the ethnic community. A large urban parish included literally dozens of committees, religious fraternities, social clubs, and similar activities for men, women, children, and a new category scarcely recognized in the Old World, the teen-agers, or "youth."

While Christian and Jewish houses of worship had always recognized a "fellowship" function even in the Old World, the idea of the church as social center was new to Oriental religions. In Asia, Buddhism, Confucianism, and Shinto centered in home ceremonials and sacrifices at shrines; congregational worship was practically unknown. In the New World, however, Oriental immigrants either joined American missionary churches in their neighborhoods or established American style temples of their own—complete with women's committees and "youth" activities. Soon Oriental-American children were attending Sunday schools and singing, to the tune familiar to generations of American Sunday school children, "Buddha loves me, this I know. . . ."

With the church and synagogue changing from a place of worship to a community center also, the role of the priest, minister, and rabbi also changed. Religious leaders became administrators as well as spiritual leaders and took on additional responsibilities as fund raisers, educators, and social directors. Some clergymen established newspapers, insurance companies, even housing projects. Clergymen became counselors, helping their congregants adjust to America. At the same time, they became spokesmen for their community on the greater American scene, and were recognized as such by outside authorities. Thus when the participation of ethnic communities was needed in a charity drive, Fourth of July celebration, or other civic occasion, contact was made through the ethnic religious leader. As a result, one criteria in the selection of an ethnic clergyman was whether he would make a "good appearance."

Laymen also assumed new roles in America. In the early days of an ethnic community, religious services were often held in farmhouses, tenements, and storefronts. Laymen organized and conducted the services themselves, performing tasks reserved for officials and trained clergymen in the homeland. "We conducted our religious meetings in our own democratic way," said a Norwegian immigrant. "We prayed, exhorted, and sang among ourselves, and even baptized our babies ourselves."

In many European countries religion was supported by the

government. In the United States the lay community struggled, often for years, to build a house of worship and pay the salary of a minister when he was finally summoned. It is not surprising that laymen, accustomed in the early years to much independence, balked at relinquishing that independence to the clergy. There was constant bickering and factionalism in most of the Protestant denominations. The Catholic Church was shaken in the mid-nineteenth century by the controversy over control of church property—whether it should continue in the hands of lay trustees, as had become the custom in the United States, or whether it should be given to the hierarchy. The hierarchy was victorious, largely because it was supported by the increasingly numerous and influential Irish immigrants. Nevertheless, in most ethnic churches the move to America expanded the power of the laity.

When religious denominations moved to the United States, they often changed in content as well as in form. Protestant denominations moved away from their emphasis upon sin, judgment, and eternal damnation to a more optimistic emphasis upon salvation for all from a loving God—an evolution similar to that undergone by American Puritanism much earlier. Catholicism, too became more worldly, more optimistic, more "American," so much so that Pope Leo XIII warned American Catholics against overemphasis of the "active" virtues at the expense of traditional humility, charity, and obedience.

Similarly, age-old principles of Oriental religions were altered by the American environment. Filial piety, the absolute devotion and self-sacrifice of the young for the sake of their parents, was given a surprising redefinition by a Japanese bishop: "Parents may feel lonesome in some way or other and they will need your consolation," he told a group of young Japanese-Americans. "Tell them that good parents must think more of the future of their children than their own. To give in this life is to receive in another."

Beliefs and practices in Judaism changed as much as in any other faith. Reform Judaism, a movement to modernize traditional religion in the light of nineteenth century secular rationalism, came to America with mid-century German immigrants (although it had appeared independently in Charleston as early as 1825) and was successful almost immediately. Congregations split, factions took each other to court, and at least one rabbi was locked out of his synagogue as the battle between Orthodoxy and Reform raged. When the smoke cleared, the more radical reformers had abandoned the age-old authority of Jewish law, had dropped the Hebrew language from worship services altogether, had changed the traditional Sabbath from Saturday to Sunday, and were proclaiming the United States the new Jerusalem. The influx of East European Jews around the turn of the century led to a revival of Orthodoxy and to the growth of Conservative or Historical Judaism, a creative compromise that proved increasingly attractive to the second and third generations.

Ethnic churches were loved by their immigrant congregants because they preserved some of the ethnic feeling of the old country—the native language, the favorite saints, the special holidays. Church leadership was more deeply committed to preserving the religion, however, than the ethnicity. Thus when it became obvious that the traditional language was alienating the younger generation, many clergymen switched partly or completely to English over the vociferous objections of older congregants.

Recognizing that their denominations would survive in the United States only if they identified with the new land, ethnic churches soon began holding special services for American national holidays, participating in civic events and charity drives, and encouraging their congregants to do likewise. Thus even the most conservative churches became agents for change in the lives of their ethnic constituents, and that change was in the direction of greater involvement in American life. Many clergymen became skilled and trusted counselors for immigrants seeking help with problems of Americanization. Congregants who hesitated to use the settlement houses, night schools, and other public agencies took advantage of parallel services within their reassuringly familiar ethnic churches. Some immigrants accepted English lessons for themselves and mixed dances for their teen-agers only when these events were sponsored by their church. Thus the changing ethnic churches became effective agents of Americanization even though they maintained much of the Old World tradition—or perhaps *because* they did so.

The Ethnic School

Ethnic schools were an essential part of the life of most ethnic communities, especially Roman Catholic communities. Though the official goal of a parochial school education for every Catholic child was never realized, the nineteenth century Irish Catholic immigrant community built an extensive parochial school system at great financial sacrifice. German Catholics also built parochial schools in the nineteenth century, though they were perhaps less intensely committed to their use than the Irish. Twentieth century Catholic immigrants were more divided in their views. First generation Italian Catholics preferred public education for their children, because there was no tradition of church supported education in Southern Italy. Polish and other Slavic immigrants, on the other hand, were accustomed to church involvement in education in their homelands and were therefore more ardent in their support of parochial schools in the United States.

Parochial schools reflected the ethnicity of the sponsoring parishes. In Polish, Ukrainian, French-Canadian, and other parish schools, teachers from the mother country struggled valiantly to give their American born students a grasp of the language, traditions, songs, heroes, and holidays cherished by their parents. Many of these schools were bilingual, teaching religion and other ethnic subjects in the traditional language and "American" subjects such as American history, geography, and bookkeeping in English.

Parents, clergy, and community leaders spent untold money and emotional energy in building and maintaining parochial schools. To the devout, the parochial school was a religious necessity; the public schools were considered hotbeds of atheism. But most parents sent their children to parish schools for reasons that had more to do with culture, or ethnicity, than with faith. Parents and community leaders hoped that ethnic parochial schools would insure their children's loyalty to their ethnic heritage and the ethnic community and would encourage social relationships, including marriages, within that community. Finally, many parents disapproved of what they considered to be the lax discipline of the public school. Nuns, they believed, could be trusted more than public school teachers to teach their children proper manners and respect for their elders.

Catholics were not the only sponsors of ethnic education. Scandinavian and German Lutherans also built parochial schools. Of the 370 parish day schools in South Dakota in 1900, 213 used German or one of the Scandinavian languages for instruction. Norwegian and Swedish children who did not attend parochial schools during the school year often attended ethnic schools sponsored by their churches during the summer months. Chinese, Japanese, Greek, and Jewish parents supplemented their children's public school education with ethnic and religious schooling in the afternoons, or evenings, or on weekends. Here children studied the language, literature, philosophy, and religion of their ancestors.

A small percentage of ethnic schools were completely secular. Finnish socialists and Bohemian "freethinkers" conducted weekend schools to transmit their economic ideology as well as their national language and history to their children. Jewish groups such as the Workmen's Circle conducted secular Jewish schools. While synagogue schools concentrated upon the teaching of Hebrew, the traditional language of prayer, secular Jewish schools taught the East European vernacular, Yiddish, and its literature.

Stormy debates raged within ethnic communities and between ethnics and older stock Americans about the desirability and effectiveness of ethnic schools. Parochial schools, which enrolled as many as half of the eligible ethnic children in urban areas, undoubtedly relieved the pressure on the overcrowded public schools. Like the public schools, they ranged in quality from very good to very poor. Chronically short of money, ethnic schools, even more frequently than public schools, had poorly trained teachers and inadequate facilities. In parochial schools sixty or eighty children might be assigned to an enthusiastic but insufficiently trained teen-aged nun who had not yet finished her own high school education. Afternoon and weekend schools were conducted in makeshift quarters—the back of a store, or the basement of a church or synagogue—and were taught by anyone who could be persuaded to take a job with such meager financial and emotional rewards. Tired children rebelled at attending these unattractive and seemingly superfluous schools after a full day at the public school, and exasperated parents bribed, cajoled, and forced them to attend.

Contrary to the suspicions of their critics, ethnic schools transmitted a great love of the United States to their young pupils. Parochial schools taught American history and geography with great enthusiasm and held elaborate pageants to celebrate national holidays. Members of religious orders whose English was poor brought in special American born teachers to give the children a good English background and sent children to the public schools for high school or for vocational courses when this education was not available in the parochial system. The English part of the curriculum was the most successful part taught in the parochial schools, because parents and children both saw its relevance to American life. Bilingual education of the parochial school was especially valuable to the child who had just immigrated or who had had little or no opportunity to learn English. These children were frequently able to transfer to the public school system at their appropriate grade level after a few years of parochial school education.

The ethnic curriculum of both day and supplementary schools was less successful. Children who did not speak the mother tongue from birth rarely acquired more than a smattering of it—and in homes where it was no longer spoken, even this smattering was soon lost. Some of the children who attended these schools retained little of the ethnic history, literature, and language that was so laboriously taught them. What many did learn, however, was that their collective past extended beyond the squalid tenements to the glories of ancient civilizations and the achievements of great scholars, artists, and kings. Scorned by many of their Anglo-Saxon contemporaries, shabbily dressed immigrant children must have suspected that, like their illustrious ancestors, they too could achieve.

There were other benefits from ethnic education. The ability of ethnic teachers to maintain discipline and to communicate effectively with parents may have resulted in more years of education for at least some ethnic children. Good ethnic schools gave the American born generation a better understanding of their foreign born parents. By keeping lines of communication open, they enabled children to provide useful American information to their parents and parents to provide guidance and security to their children. Finally, loyalty to the local ethnic school was an important factor in building the cohesiveness of the ethnic community, both in the immigrant generation and in the generations that followed.

Cultural Institutions, Adult Education, and Athletics

Opportunities to enjoy their native culture, long established in the homeland, had to be created from scratch in the New World. Immigrants formed special associations—or used the auspices of lodges or churches—to bring artists, singers, actors, musicians, theatrical companies, and opera from the homeland. Culture was something one did as well as watched, however. From their earliest years in the United States ethnic Americans joined together to create their own folk dancing groups, musical ensembles, and drama companies which performed for the general American public as well as for the ethnic community itself.

The more highly educated ethnic Americans formed intellectual groups of various kinds. Bohemians, Germans, and Jews read and discussed classics and modern books. Arabic speaking intellectuals formed the Golden Link, a literary society, in 1918. Ethnic intellectuals did not always confine their activities to their own circles. The Hungarian Free Lyceum offered lectures to Hungarians and to the general public in Magyar (Hungarian) and in English. Topics included "Modern Hungarian Poets," "The Americanization of Hungarians," "The Discovery of America and Colonial History," "The American Revolution and the Civil War," "Industrial Hazards," and "The Influence of the Press." As the topics suggest, the Lyceum hoped to teach about the Hungarian heritage and also the United States.

Unlike the bilingual Hungarian Free Lyceum, the Polish University of Chicago held its sessions in the ethnic language only. It was begun by Polish socialists whose main aim was to educate the Polish working class, and its approach to learning was broadly humanistic. The scope of the Polish University's activities and their value to Polish immigrants and to the United States are suggested in this description by one of the University's moving spirits:

. . . we took up questions about the beginning of things . . . the creation of the world, the theory of evolution, primitive man, the development of language. . . . Almost all of our members could understand and speak ordinary English, but many others who attended the lectures could not. But obviously the use of Polish was necessary if such subjects, which are hard enough to grasp anyway and which involve many scientific terms and fine shades of meaning, were to be got across to our audiences.

. . . Gradually . . . we came to subjects connected with America and civil problems. But here we do more than have lectures. We go and see for ourselves how civic agencies work. At different times we have visited most of the public departments and institutions of this city. . . .

We hold our meetings at the public park center in the neighborhood . . . over a thousand people came to the last lecture. . . . We haven't preached "Americanization" . . . but practically all our members are citizens who take an active interest in civic affairs, and if what America wants is people who can think and act for themselves, then we're *doing* Americanization.

Athletic societies played a major role in the life of the American ethnic community. Groups such as the German *Turnverein*, the Scandinavian *Turners*, the Bohemian *Sokol*, and the Polish *Falcons* began with gymnastics and other kinds of physical training and branched out to include music, drama, and social and educational activities for the entire family. In Europe, these societies were often involved in politics; the Bohemian *Sokols* drilled their members for action against the Austrian rulers and the Polish *Falcons* did likewise against the Russians. In the United States such organizations took on an American patriotic flavor. They urged, even required, their members to learn English and become citizens, and encouraged them to serve in the American armed forces.

Of course, the young people played the traditional American team sports of baseball and football, often on ethnically mixed teams in their schools or neighborhoods. (A good ethnic athlete had access to American social circles, regardless of how hard the native born found his name to pronounce.) Adults came together to enjoy the sports of their homelands—wrestling, swimming, rowing, fencing, shooting, and gymnastics. Societies formed within an ethnic community for this purpose were soon in touch with one another and with their American counterparts. In 1920 the Amateur Athletic Union of New York included immigrant athletic societies representing Scandinavians, Jews, Hungarians, Finns, Bohemians, Scotch, Irish, Greeks, and Germans, who competed on even terms with a variety of native American teams. Similar arrangements existed throughout the nation. Athletic teans, like so many other ethnic institutions, functioned both to solidify the ethnic community itself and to bring that community in closer touch with the outside world.

Nationalist Societies

Many ethnic Americans maintained ties to their homelands, sending aid in time of war, famine, or other catastrophe. Ethnic communities institutionalized these ties in the form of nationalist societies. These societies encouraged interest in the traditional language, history, and culture of the homeland, defended its reputation (and at the same time, their own) and raised money for educational and charitable projects. Many of the nationalist societies worked to liberate the homeland from foreign domination. American Poles worked for the restoration of the Polish national state that had lost its independence in the late eighteenth century. The Irish and the south Slavs sought the establishment of free nations for peoples that had been ruled by outsiders for many centuries. Jews sought a Jewish state in Palestine after a lapse of almost two thousand years.

Nationalist societies might appear at first glance to be the ethnic institutions most foreign to American life, but such was not the case. Though intellectuals wrote and agitated for nationalist causes in nineteenth century Europe, most immigrants were simple people who acquired their ethnic nationalism after they arrived in the United States. Among rural Europeans, which included most of the immigrants, loyalties were parochial. "I never realized I was an Albanian," said one immigrant, "until my brother came from America in 1919. He belonged to an Albanian society over here." Immigrants from the Ukraine called themselves "Little Russians" or "Ruthenians" until World War I, when the most Americanized among them began to use the term "Ukrainian." Even the strong tradition of nationalism in Poland rarely reached the peasants until after they had emigrated. Polish nationalism in the homeland was strongest among the educated and well-to-do. "The lord was a Pole, he (the common man) was a peasant."

National consciousness in ethnic communities sprang largely from the American environment. Here for the first time some immigrants met a wide enough variety of people to be aware of the similarities and differences among them. Because there might be only a few people from a particular town or parish in an American city, ethnic colonies expanded to include countrymen who would have been considered "foreigners" at home.

American education gave many immigrants their introduction to the history and national aspirations of their homelands. American ideas about democracy, self-government, and freedom of expression made the political domination of their homelands seem even more oppressive than when they were living there. Sometimes an ethnic American began to identify with the plight of the oppressed mother country because of discrimination in the United States. Patrick Ford embraced the Irish cause after months of futile searching for a job in anti-Irish Boston. He concluded that, as an Irish-American, he was the victim of "conditions of poverty and enslavement" in Ireland and that his situation and that of all Irish-Americans would improve only when Ireland was regenerated. Nor was Ford's view without foundation. The fortunes of the homeland affected the way ethnic Americans saw themselves as well as how others saw them. The independence of Poland after World War I raised the status and self-esteem of Polish-Americans, and the establishment of the State of Israel in 1948 affected American Jews similarly.

The outbreak of World War I and the United States' entry on the side of the Allies was the event that did most to spark ethnic American nationalism. The war was widely interpreted as a struggle between the "good" western democracies (including Russia after the revolution of 1917) and the "bad" German, Austrian, and Turkish Empires. Because of the principle of the "self determination" of nations, one of Wilson's war aims, ethnic Americans from the "subject nationalities" suddenly found the larger American community in sympathy with the political aspirations of their homelands.

In this atmosphere old nationalist societies were revitalized and new organizations with mass support were created. One of the most effective of these new organizations was the Polish National Defense Committee, which collected fifty million dollars worth of goods and services for the homeland and helped raise the volunteer Blue Army to fight for Polish independence. The world famous pianist Ignace Paderewski toured the United States to raise funds for the Committee. Polish-Americans lobbied continuously to keep Congress, President Wilson, and later the League of Nations aware of their desire for the restoration of Polish independence. Similar activities were undertaken by Ukrainians and South Slavs, who held massive conventions, bombarded the government with telegrams and resolutions, and, at Wilson's invitation, marched through the streets of Washington in national costumes on July 4, 1918.

Some nationalist societies saw their objectives achieved, although not necessarily because of their efforts. Polish independence, for example, was restored because it suited the purposes of the Great Powers. New, independent Balkan states were carved out of the defeated Austro-Hungarian and Turkish Empires. The existence of at least one of them, Yugoslavia, has been attributed to the activities of south Slavs in the United States. Jewish nationalism achieved its first step toward success with the Balfour Declaration—Britain's promise of a Jewish "national home" in Palestine. Although Zionism attracted increasing support from American Jews in the years after World War I, it did not become a mass movement until the Nazi murder of six million Jews during World War II. A trickle of dedicated Jewish nationalists, including Golda Meir, a Milwaukee housewife and schoolteacher who became Premier of Israel, emigrated from the United States to help rebuild the Promised Land. The establishment of the Irish Free State in southern Ireland shortly after World War I was a partial victory for Irish nationalists here and abroad, though the struggle for the independence of Northern Ireland continued.

Ukrainian Americans were bitterly disappointed with the results of World War I. They had hoped for Ukrainian independence, but once again the Ukraine was swallowed up by rapacious neighbor states. Like the Irish, the Ukrainians refused to give up. The leading Ukrainian-American newspapers sent an investigating committee to document political atrocities in the Ukraine. The Ukrainian community sent telegrams to Congress and to the League of Nations. So much money was raised by the far from prosperous Ukrainian-Americans for the benefit of the homeland that, according to one Ukrainian-American historian, their own needs went unmet. At the New York World's Fair of 1940, the then politically nonexistent Ukraine had an impressive pavilion, sponsored by the Ukrainian-American community.

The plight of the homeland was one of the few concerns shared by the diverse religious and socioeconomic elements in every sizable ethnic community. Not all ethnic Americans joined nationalistic societies, but most supported their activities, attending their benefits and contributing money to their appeals. As Mr. Dooley, the Irish-American humorist observed, "Be hivins, if Ireland cud be freed by a picnic, it'd not only be free today but an empire." For many immigrants, working for a nationalist society was a constructive way of assuaging the guilt they felt over having abandoned family, friends, and fatherland to come to America. For their children and grandchildren, nationalist activities were a socially acceptable—and not too demanding—way of affirming an ethnic identity which, though still valued, was slipping away with time and Americanization.

In order to obtain citizenship, ethnic Americans had learned to describe America's political machinery. During World War I, through the political activities of nationalist societies, they learned how to use that machinery. Nationalist societies developed ethnic lobbies which soon became as much a part of the scene in Washington as farm lobbies, labor lobbies, and corporation lobbies. Ethnic nationalists became increasingly American in their ideology as well as their tactics. They often linked the struggle of their homelands against foreign rule to the revolt of the thirteen American colonies. "What the United States fought for in 1776 is what Serbia is fighting for today," said a Serbian-American leader in 1914.

The failure of some nationalist causes resulted in an intensified commitment of its followers to the United States. Continued poverty and political oppression in the Ukraine ended the dream many Ukrainian Americans had of returning to the Ukraine. Paradoxically, the success of other nationalist movements had a similar effect. The restoration of Poland and the creation of independent Slavic states in the Balkans gave ethnic Americans from these backgrounds a real option for the first time. They could go home to what seemed to be improved conditions, or they could stay in the United States and become Americans. Thousands did return to their former homes in the 1920's. But most discovered that they were already "home," that they did not really want to live in the foreign nations they had helped to create. Sentimental ties remained, but now they were unambiguously committed to the United States.

Contributions of the Ethnic Community

An ethnic community was more than the sum of its institutional parts. Each had its own values and priorities, its own social and political atmosphere determined by the cultural baggage its members brought from the Old World and the circumstances of their lives in the new. Southern Italians, accustomed to relating mainly to their own extended families, were most successful at first in forming small, localized institutions. Jews, on the other hand, accustomed to ties far beyond their own family and village, soon established citywide, statewide, even national organizations. Twentieth century Germans, rich in professional leadership and financial resources, had many institutions. Ukrainians, lacking both, had relatively fewer.

Some immigrants never affiliated with their ethnic communities, either by choice or because none was available. The majority did affiliate and reaped many benefits. Through the institutions of the ethnic community, formal and informal, they received information in their own language to help them find jobs, become citizens, establish households, and rear children. Self-help societies and charities mitigated their poverty, and social events eased their loneliness. Religious services alleviated their spiritual hunger, and nationalist organizations enhanced their self-respect. It is not surprising that immigrants who participated most fully in the life of their ethnic communities adjusted most rapidly to their new environment.

There were other benefits, less tangible but equally important. The ethnic community offered status and recognition to people who otherwise might have attained neither. Outstanding ethnic entertainers, athletes, and artists were acclaimed by the general American public, but people with less spectacular abilities went unnoticed. Most immigrants, with their broken English and their menial jobs, had few opportunities to feel important. But within their ethnic communities, as officers of the church, or lodge, or special committee, these immigrants received the recognition they needed and deserved. Through their ethnic communities, thousands of talented men and women whose abilities might otherwise have been wasted were helped to make significant contributions to American life. Many who received their "basic training" in the ethnic community went on to positions of leadership in the outside world as well.

Finally, the ethnic community helped fill the moral vacuum in the lives of immigrants who had left behind established patterns of "proper" behavior, and the social pressures of extended families and close-knit communities that had enforced these patterns.

Ethnic institutions—schools, churches, lodges, athletic associations—affirmed traditional religious, social and family values, reserving their offices, their honors, and their approval for people whose behavior was morally acceptable. Because the only weapon the American ethnic community had to enforce its standards was disapproval, chronic violators were more likely to be ostracized than reformed. The ethnic community was a positive force in support of stable, responsible living. In a bewildering new environment, it gave immigrants solid ground to stand on in determining what their priorities should be and how they should behave toward one another.

But there were negative sides to the ethnic community as well. Group pride could spill over into destructive chauvinism. The desire to favor one's own, in employment for example, could lead to discrimination against outsiders. Ethnic communities, the victims of prejudice, harbored many prejudices themselves. An important Irish-American newspaper, the *Catholic World,* denounced Italians as "totally devoid of what may be termed the sense of respectability." Ethnic theater often presented derogatory stereotypes of other ethnic groups. Polish, Jewish, Irish, and Italian gangs engaged in bloody battles in defense of ethnic "turf," and ethnic Americans sometimes joined old stock Americans in violent attempts to keep blacks out of neighborhoods and institutions they regarded as their own.

Factionalism within an ethnic community, even within a single ethnic institution, was a serious problem. Quarrels within ethnic institutions and communities could be bitter, even degenerating on rare occasions into physical violence. But violence could be spiritual as well as physical. In their zeal to preserve traditional values and standards of behavior, ethnic communities could be cruel to the nonconformist. New ideas were sometimes sacrificed to tradition, or, worse still, to pettiness or narrow-mindedness. Community organizations created bureaucracies with their attendant dangers of corruption and lack of responsiveness to the people they were meant to serve. Leaders sometimes became less interested in leading than in maintaining their own positions and enhancing their own fortunes. It is not surprising that young people—and mavericks of any age—often found the organized ethnic community more stifling than stimulating.

Like all human institutions, ethnic communities reflected the faults and the weaknesses of the people who comprised them. Their problems were magnified by the fact that they struggled to survive in a majority society that was often indifferent or even hostile. Moreover, their self-appointed task—preserving a foreign tradition while helping their members become Americans—was fraught with ambiguities. Whatever policy an ethnic institution followed, the one thing it could count upon was criticism. Yet despite these difficulties, ethnic communities served their members so well that subsequent generations continued to maintain at least some affiliation with them.

In serving their members, ethnic communities also served America. They gave financial aid and insurance to a large percentage of the American poor at a time when our national life provided little economic protection for anyone. Ethnic communities educated millions of children and adults. They brought stability to urban neighborhoods and enriched the cultural and social life of the entire nation. Finally, they embodied and fostered many of the traditional virtues of which the United States appears most proud—voluntarism, self-help, neighborliness, democracy, and community spirit.

CHAPTER 9

Words and Feelings:
The Ethnic Press, Theater,
and Literature, 1820-1924

Ethnic Americans seemed possessed by an irresistible compulsion to record their experiences and their feelings. Poorly educated or even illiterate in the lands of their birth, immigrants in America produced a prodigious number of newspapers, plays, poems, songs, stories, memoirs, autobiographies, and novels. Why was there such an explosion of words within ethnic America? What feelings did those words convey?

A Torrent of Words

A new and pressing need for information helped cause the explosion of reading and writing in ethnic America. Traditional wisdom handed down by word of mouth was inadequate to deal successfully with life in urban, industrial America, where the only thing certain was constant change. Immigrants needed access to a constant stream of new information provided by the printed word if they were to succeed in their new environment. Realizing this, people who might have been content to remain illiterate in the peasant village made heroic efforts to learn to read in America, or even before they arrived. They insisted that their children learn to read not only the mother tongue but English as well.

The need for information was equalled by the need for self-expression. Immigration was a shattering emotional experience, the equivalent, according to one ethnic writer, of being "born again." People who had undergone this upheaval in their lives needed to put into ordered and permanent form the chaotic feelings and experiences that, unexamined, threatened to overwhelm them. This need to articulate, understand, and thereby transcend their own experience led to ethnic theater, poetry, memoirs, and other forms of literature.

Finally, there was a great outpouring of writing in the mother tongues in America because many of these languages had been suppressed in Europe. Poles, Bohemians, Slovenes, Ukrainians, and other "subject nationalities" had been living under the cultural as well as the political domination of outside powers. In the Russian-controlled Ukraine, for example, it was illegal to publish a book, produce a play, deliver a sermon, or give a lecture in the Ukrainian language. Education from the village school to the university was conducted in Russian. Similar situations existed in many other areas. A ban against teaching Polish in German-controlled areas of Poland led to a strike of over 150,000 Polish school children.

In such an atmosphere, the use of the suppressed language became the symbol of the national survival of the people that spoke it. Bohemian patriots had a saying, "As long as the language lives, the nation is not dead." Nationalism and literacy spread from a few intellectuals and patriots to a wider population, a process that moved much more quickly in the free atmosphere of the United States than in the homeland. In the United States, as in the homelands, use of the native tongue became a self-conscious political program. In the mid nineteenth century Lithuanian was no longer spoken by the literate classes in Lithuania; yet between 1834 and 1895 at least thirty-four Lithuanian language periodicals were published in the United States. The revival of the ancient Irish language, Gaelic, flourished in Boston before it did in Dublin. Slovakian peasants read newspapers in their native language in New York and Chicago, a patriotic exercise not permitted in the Austro-Hungarian Empire. When the United States offered opportunities for self-expression in their native language, immigrants seized these opportunities.

The Ethnic Press

In little Italy, little Poland, little Syria, the Irish shantytown, the Jewish ghetto, Chinatown, and the Japanese colony—the ethnic press was visible everywhere. Educated immigrants debated its editorials. The semiliterate spelled out headlines and advertisements. The illiterate listened while a friend or relative read. In the sweatshops immigrants pooled their pennies to pay one of their number to read aloud while they worked. By 1920 over a thousand foreign language periodicals and newspapers were being published in the United States with their circulation running into the millions. In urban centers such as New York, Chicago, and Detroit, large ethnic communities supported dozens of newspapers while no group—the Letts, the Estonians, the Wends, the Spanish Catalons—was too small to have at least one.

Foreign language publications were as varied as the communities that produced them. There were dailies, weeklies, monthlies—and papers that came out whenever their editors could assemble the material and the money to print an issue. The smallest had a few dozen subscribers; the largest had circulations of over a hundred thousand. The four leading Yiddish newspapers in New York City alone sold over a third of a million copies every day. Many ethnic publications were local, serving a particular town or village or even a particular neighborhood or parish. Others were national and even international. In *Al Hoda*, for example, Arab-Americans advertised to locate missing relatives in Cuba, Brazil, and Mexico.

Most foreign language papers began as "shoestring" operations, often the work of unemployed immigrant intellectuals. Frequently the original owner was bought out by a businessman, who put the paper on a sound financial basis. The *Desteaptate Romane*, a leading Rumanian newspaper, is a good example. It was begun by an educated but sickly Rumanian immigrant who faced deportation because he had no prospects for employment. On the advice of a helpful immigration official, he collected a few dollars from each of his friends and set up the *Desteaptate Romane*. He was reputed to write well, but could not manage the paper financially. Eventually he was bought out by the owner of a steamship ticket agency.

A successful Japanese born journalist, Shakuma Washizu, left a colorful account of the early days of the Japanese-American press. Washizu's background before immigration was typical of that of many ethnic journalists—"middle class family, published a newspaper or two, ran for a political office or two, went into business, but was never successful. . . ." His first job in the United States was with a newspaper where "the editorial sanctum was at the same time kitchen, dining room, printing shop, parlor, and bedroom, all in one. The editor . . . unshaved face . . . shabby dress . . . gave me the impression of a tramp."

Washizu tried working first for one small paper then another. Finally he issued his own comic magazine called *Agahazushi* (*Open the Jaws*). "The magazine continued up to twelve numbers, but the total income . . . was not more than fifteen dollars. I did not eat more than once a day for several months." Eventually he became the manager of a larger paper with brighter prospects. "We got together a number of those press men at a building which became gradually a resort for the homeless and poverty stricken fellows. As I was manager of the paper, everybody called me a great king. I was a sad king indeed—I had to do all the cooking." This venture, too, almost ended in disaster. An unfortunate caricature resulted in a lawsuit. "As we could not hire a lawyer to defend the case, we lost it." Washizu and a colleague went to jail for nine months, not an unmitigated disaster. "During that time both of us really lived, as we had plenty to eat. . . ."

Despite this inauspicious beginning, Washizu's paper, later called the *Japanese-American News*, became the largest and most influential Japanese daily in the United States. Most ethnic newspapers were not so fortunate. Nine out of ten did not survive their first year of publication. The successful ones, however, the *Jewish Daily Forward*, the Italian *Il Progresso Italo-Americano*, the Spanish *La Prensa*, the German *Staats-Zeitung*, and similar papers lived on decade after decade exerting an enormous influence in their respective communities.

Ethnic newspapers reflected a variety of ethnic interests. Many were the organs of mutual aid societies, churches, or lodges. Others were commercial ventures. There were literary papers, humorous papers, and papers for farmers, musicians, socialists, anarchists, trade unionists, religious factions, and freethinkers. Special journals were published for young people and for women. The nationally circulated Bohemian *Zenske Listy* of Chicago was a feminist journal, printed and edited by women and devoted not to "beauty lessons" and "household hints" but to efforts toward women's suffrage and "the uplifting of the attitude of working women."

The contents of ethnic newspapers varied widely, but certain things were characteristic of most. The front page was usually devoted to news of the mother country, so that the press, like other ethnic institutions, served as a link between the Old World and the New. Here the immigrant could find out what the harvest had been like at home, what was happening in the old church, and what political or economic reforms were in the offing. Nineteenth century Irish-American papers, for example (English in language, but ethnic in content), included news of the Great Famine, of the various reform factions in Ireland, and of the arrival of immigrant ships to the United States.

News of the United States was also reported, often summarized and translated from the American press. The better papers taught their readers about American life through skillful coverage and interpretation of national and local news. The socialist press, important among Jews, Finns, and Bohemians, organized the news within a radical ideological framework. Previously uneducated laboring people were stimulated to read and think by a radical press interested in the problems of "workers" and "bosses"—their problems. According to

Robert E. Parks' study of the immigrant press, "socialism gave the common man a point of view . . . from which he could think about actual life. It [the socialist ethnic press] made the sweatshop an intellectual problem."

Even after they were able to read the American press, immigrants and their children turned to the ethnic press for news of their own communities. In local ethnic papers they could learn the news of the neighborhood available nowhere else—who had been married, who had died, who had had a new baby, who had been baptized, confirmed, or become a *bar mitzvah*, who had been honored with the chairmanship of the church committee, the presidency of the lodge. Here they could follow the progress of the organized community—the success of the latest fundraising drive, the building of the new ethnic school, the arrival of the new minister from overseas, the creation of a new national agency or political lobby. And here they could read about, and rejoice in, the success of their own people, in business, politics, education, or whatever, both within the ethnic community and in the larger world outside.

The editorial columns of the ethnic press aired the controversies of the day. Anarchists, socialists, nationalists, members of religious factions, and secularists debated ideology and tactics, the editors often talking more to one another than to their subscribers. Most readers were more interested in practical subjects that affected everyday life. They welcomed features on child rearing, cooking, health care, how to obtain American citizenship, and how to vote.

Catering to these interests, feature writers were effective agents of Americanization and of education in general. Julian Chupka of the leading Ukrainian paper *Svoboda*, was typical of many such feature writers. He published articles entitled "Pictures of America," "the Constitution of the United States of North America," and "Something about the Laws and Courts of the United States, Especially in Pennsylvania." Abraham Cahan, Abner Tannenbaum, and other Jewish journalists introduced the Yiddish reading public to Darwinism and other scientific ideas, and to the science fiction of Jules Verne. A Lithuanian radical paper introduced its public to the philosophy of Nietzsche with a translation of *Thus Spake Zarathustra*.

The most widely read features were poetry, fiction, and the letters to the editor. Much of the poetry and fiction was sent in by readers with more sentimentality than literary talent. Pulp novels ground out by "hack" writers were published in installments, to keep their following eagerly awaiting the next edition. Not all of the literature published in the ethnic press was the product of amateurs or hacks, however. The foreign language press introduced its readers to the works of many talented professional writers from within the community and outside.

Ordinary readers as well as professional writers and journalists contributed to the ethnic press. Rural subscribers wrote in news of the weather, the passing seasons, and the harvests. Often they voiced their concerns about the decline of religion among the young and expressed their nostalgia for the scenes and the faces of the homeland. Elderly people exchanged information about old friends and relived old times, as in the following letter published in *Swenska Amerikanaren* (a Chicago based Swedish paper).

> Thanks Carl Jonason of Britain, South Dakota, for your letter in the paper. Indeed, I remember you, even though it was a long time ago. . . . I was surprised to see a letter from you, Nelson, the miller of Hjulsnasis. . . . In the large village of Skarap, we had many happy occasions, as the man of Skane said when he buried his dead wife; 'I can't keep from laughing, when I think of the happy hours I had with that wife of mine.' If any acquaintances who know me see this, let us hear from you sometime.

Editors served as priests, psychiatrists, social workers, and friends to readers who had nowhere else to turn. Many papers had "advice" columns, but none was as famous as the "Bintel Brief," ("Bundle of Letters") of the *Jewish Daily Forward*. Through the "Bintel Brief," poverty stricken people found jobs, husbands were united with their wives, and parents located children from whom they had been separated many years. Everyone found sensible advice for problems ranging from the most trivial to the most overwhelming:

> My father does not want me to use face powder. Is it a sin?
> The editor assures a young girl that it is not.

> Since I do not want my conscience to bother me, I ask you to decide whether a married woman has the right to go to school two evenings a week. My husband thinks I have no right to do this.
> The editor states unequivocally that the wife "absolutely has the right to go to school two evenings a week."

> A long, gloomy year, three hundred and sixty-five days, have gone by since I left my home and I am alone on the lonely road of life. . . . My heart is heavy for my parents whom I left behind. I want to run back. . . .
> The editor tells this young man that all immigrants suffer similar loneliness and advises him to remain where he is, work hard, and bring his parents to America.

> I am one of those unfortunates who for many years has suffered from the workers' disease (tuberculosis). I am the father of a three year old girl. . . . All who know my child hug her and kiss her. But I may not. I know this all too well, yet I can't help myself. Every time I kiss the child I

feel my wife's eyes on me as if she wanted to shout, 'Murderer'! but she doesn't utter a word. . . . What can I do?

The editor warns the man not to kiss his child and holds out the hope that with good medical treatment he may live to enjoy her for a long time.

My husband deserted me and our three small children. . . . I am able and willing to work . . . but unfortunately I am tied down because my baby is only six months old. The local Jewish Welfare Agencies are allowing me and my children to die of hunger . . . because my 'faithful' husband brought me over from Canada just four months ago and therefore I do not yet deserve to eat their bread. I will sell my beautiful children . . . for a secure home where they will have enough food and warm clothing for the winter.

The editor asks "What kind of society are we living in that forces a mother to such desperate straits." He urges help for the mother, help which his readers will undoubtedly provide. As for the delinquent husband, "Who knows what's wrong with him. Perhaps he, too, is unhappy."

Glancing through the advertisements in an ethnic newspaper is like peering into the tenement windows of the community. The papers of the newer communities—Poles, Italians, Greeks, Armenians— advertised boarding houses, cheap restaurants, and local dry good stores. The papers of longer established communities, Germans, for example, contained the advertisements of ethnic professionals and of "downtown" as well as local merchants.

As food preferences are among the most long-lived ethnic characteristics, all papers carried ads for groceries and delicatessens. Gold watches, the status symbols of the successful immigrant, were also widely advertised, as were electric belts, trusses, and other items dealing with health care. Often professionals of one ethnic group developed specialties which they advertised in other ethnic presses. Thus Chinese physicians advertised syphilis cures in the Greek press of San Francisco, and a Jewish lawyer, Fannie Horovitz, offered her services on "civil and criminal cases" in *Il Progresso Italo-Americano*.

Advertisements for books and music varied with the interests and educational levels of prospective customers. The Spanish, Rumanian, Italian, and Portuguese press advertised books on religion, love, and magic. The Portuguese *Alvaorado* of New Bedford offered its readers a 35ᶜ library featuring such titles as *The Virgin and the Sinner, Perpetual Adoration*, and the *Rose of Granada*, while *Il Progresso Italo-Americano* tempted its readers with *Meditations on the Sexual Problem, the First Night of Matrimony*, and *Telepathy and Dreams*. The more radical or intellectual journals of all ethnic communities advertised substantial volumes on science, history, economics, and on literature with a tinge of social criticism, such as the works of Émile Zola and Upton Sinclair.

"Wanted—girl or childless widow, 19-27 years old, freethinker, agreeing to a civil marriage, knowing how to read and write in Lithuanian, wanted by a man 29 years old, photographer, using no intoxicants or tobacco," read an advertisement in *Kelevis*, a Lithuanian paper in Boston. Similar ads appeared in many ethnic papers, a symptom of the loneliness of the immigrant cut off from the traditional village matchmaking machinery.

According to the Jewish Communal Register of 1917-1918, "the election of any candidate on the East Side (of New York) is impossible unless the Yiddish press favors him." The impact of the ethnic press on public opinion in all ethnic communities was enormous, a fact which did not go unnoticed by politicians and other special interest groups. Louis Hammerling, an immigrant from Galicia, organized the American Association of Foreign Language Newspapers to dispense Republican party advertising during the political campaign of 1914. Hammerling made a successful business of influencing the foreign language papers' policies in return for the advertising accounts he could throw their way. Questioned by a Senate committee, he replied "I am simply doing what I learned in this country from the American newspaper people. . . . There is hardly an advertiser who is not asked if he wants something in that paper when he advertises."

During World War I Hammerling was suspected of selling influence in the ethnic press to "disloyal" parties. His organization was taken over by Frances A. Keller and used by her Inter-Racial Council for "Americanization" and "better understanding between capital and labor." Despite the special pleading of groups such as Hammerling's and Keller's, the ethnic press remained largely independent, responsive to the needs and interests of the readers. The ethnic press played many roles. By preserving the traditional language and reporting news of the old country it cushioned the shock of immigration and helped preserve the traditional heritage of the ethnic American. At the same time, it was an important force for educating immigrants and helping them adjust successfully to the New World.

A questionnaire sent out by a Russian paper, the *Russkoye Slovo*, in 1919 suggests the educational impact of the ethnic press. Of 312 immigrant readers surveyed, only sixteen had read newspapers in Russia! In the United States, all 312 were regular readers of the Russian press, two thirds were regular theatergoers (almost none had attended theater in Russia) and over a fourth were also regular readers of the American press. Russian-American journalist Mark Villchur concluded that "An interest in the (Russian-American) press creates an interest in the book, in the theater, and the whole outlook of the Russian in America widens. Not only his own interests, the interests of his family and of his circle become near and dear to him, but also the problems of his country, of the republic in which he resides, and, gradually, of the whole wide world."

Ethnic newspapers performed other important functions. Through the ethnic press, communities exchanged ideas and information and were able to take on projects on a scale that would otherwise have been impossible, establishing colleges and universities, seminaries for their ministers, and national charities. The nationalist societies could never have conducted their activities in behalf of the homeland without the ethnic press. The ethnic press also stood as a guardian against unfair treatment of its constituency. One example typical of many was the action taken by *Svoboda* to help 365 Ukrainians tricked into becoming contract laborers in Hawaii. *Svoboda* led a campaign of demonstrations and letter writing to American Congressmen that resulted in the voiding of the harsh contracts and the freeing of the laborers.

People did not read the ethnic press because they wanted to be Americanized or educated or molded into a community. They read the ethnic press because it reflected their interests, their problems, and their feelings. The intimate relationship between loyal readers and their favorite paper is suggested by Ruth Levine, a longtime employee of the Yiddish *Der Tog (The Day)*. According to Levine, readers felt free to come to the editors, day or night, when they needed help with a job, with the police or immigration authorities, or with a medical or personal problem. Readers argued with the columnists, expected to be answered when they wrote, and carried yellowed clippings of their favorite articles in their pockets for years.

Not long ago, an agent for the now defunct Yiddish *Der Tog,* traveling through the Middle West, stopped to call on an old subscriber he had not seen for a long time. The woman who greeted him introduced herself as the subscriber's wife and told the agent that her husband had been dead for a year. "But you never stopped the subscription," said the agent. "I know," she replied simply. "I'm not Jewish, but I know how much the paper meant to him. I bring it to his grave."

The Theater

The ethnic theater was not an occasional Saturday night amusement; it was a vital part of life. The Chinese immigrant would work a fourteen hour day in a restaurant or laundry and then sit in rapt attention to watch a four or five hour theatrical production. German shopkeepers, craftsmen, and farmers spent many hours rehearsing their parts in amateur productions. Sweatshop workers went without meals to buy tickets for the Yiddish theater. Among people hard pressed for time and money, theater was not a luxury, but a necessity.

"To the Jews from uptown who had achieved social standing and wealth in the new country, a visit to the Yiddish theater was a nostalgic return to the land and traditions of their fathers," writes David Lifson, a historian of the Yiddish theater. "To the poor and hard working laborers and artisans, it meant glamour and exultation; it was as a service in the synagogue . . . (but) more rewarding." As Lifson suggests, ethnic theater, like the ethnic press, filled many needs. It linked the young and the old, the newcomer and the old-timer, the rich and the poor. It provided education, excitement, and entertainment. But its greatest significance was that, like the ethnic press, it was the creation of the people themselves. It mirrored their experiences and their emotions. Through theater, even the illiterate and the inarticulate expressed themselves. In the theater, one's innermost feelings were turned outward and examined at the safe distance of the footlights where they suddenly became less fearsome, less overwhelming.

The ethnic theater, like the ethnic press, was as varied as the communities that created it. Hundreds of amateur theaters throughout the land were sponsored by cultural or athletic societies such as the *Turnvereins* and *Sokols*, ethnic churches, settlement houses, and schools. The *Circulo Italiano* used theater to create better understanding between immigrants and their children, and immigrants and the larger community. Finnish, German, Hungarian, and Jewish workers used theater to educate their fellow workers about industrial problems and the need for a new socioeconomic order. Finally, many ethnic communities such as the Chinese, German, Italian, Hungarian, Irish, and Jewish, supported commercial theaters with professional actors and actresses, directors, and playwrights. They performed regularly in metropolitan centers and went "on the road" to reach outlying communities.

Ethnic theater was a theater of the people, transcending the usual lines of class and education. An amateur German theater active in Hermann, Missouri as early as 1843 was led by a tanner and an architect; its actors included craftsmen and day laborers as well as lawyers, a doctor, and a saloon keeper. Professional theater attracted audiences ranging from the intellectual elite to the illiterate. No group was more devoted to its theater than the East European Jews of New York City. Hutchins Hapgood's description of Yiddish theater on the East Side in the early 20th century suggests the meaning of ethnic theater as "theater of the people:"

> In the three Yiddish theaters on the Bowery is expressed the world of the ghetto—that New York City of Russian Jews, large, complex, with a full life and civilization. . . . Into these three buildings crowd the Jews of

all the ghetto classes—the sweatshop woman with her baby, the day laborer, the small Hester Street shopkeeper, the Russian-Jewish anarchist and socialist, the ghetto rabbi and scholar, the poet, the journalist. The poor and ignorant are the great majority. . . .

Great enthusiasm is manifested, sincere laughter and tears accompany the sincere acting on the stage. Pedlars of soda water, candy, and fantastic gewgaws of many kinds mix freely with the audience between the acts. Conversation during the play is received with strenuous hisses, but the falling of the curtain is the signal for groups of friends to get together and gossip about the play or the affairs of the week.

Like newspapers, ethnic theaters often began with little financial support. Many closed, reopened, and closed again only to reappear, perhaps in another location or another town, with the same actors and directors. Financial difficulties were not their only problems. Theaters frequently ran into trouble with the local police for giving performances on Sunday, the day most convenient for working class audiences. In 1897 the sheriff seized the properties of a Chinese theater in New York because the theater had violated the Sunday "blue laws." During World War I many German theaters were forced to close because of the boycotts and threats of superpatriots.

Every ethnic theater had its own distinctive flavor, its own history and development. Because theater could be enjoyed by everyone, even the less well educated immigrant groups could bring a theatrical tradition with them from the Old World. Thus while most ethnic newspapers developed in the United States and copied American models, such as banner headlines, sensationalism, sports pages, and cartoons, ethnic theaters kept their "foreign" characteristics and traditions much longer.

One of the oldest immigrant theaters was the Chinese, which held two distinct types of performances. For the Caucasian community, the Chinese presented variety acts, including juggling and dagger throwing. For their own audiences they gave long, highly stylized productions consisting of hundreds of acts, often taking many weeks for a completed performance. The actors were all males, some of whom impersonated women with well cultivated falsetto voices. Costumes were elaborate. Scenery, on the other hand, was sparse and impressionistic. Placards indicated where the action was taking place—a desert, or forest, or town. Servants in plain dress walked on stage to hand the actor whatever he needed—a pen, a sword, a cup, a fan. Simple stools, boxes, and tables were the only properties, and actors not needed for a particular scene sat at the back of the stage, in plain view of the audience, smoking or eating while waiting to go on again.

Chinese theater included special conventions familiar to the

Chinese audience but bewildering to the outside observer. There was much use of pantomime. "To represent his entering a house and slamming the door in the face of another character, an actor had only to take a chair from a servant, slam it down on its side at the feet of the other actor, and then stand on it," wrote an observer. "With equally clear and convincing pantomime he could ride a horse, whipping a stool smartly on the rump." In historical dramas a whirl represented the passing of a generation, a somersault the passing of a century. A dynasty famous for its orators was suggested by a gorgeously dressed warrior who "strutted up and down for ten minutes, saying not a word but gesticulating powerfully, leaping aloft, smiting, striking . . . keeping time in all his gestures to the deafening gong beats."

Italian theater evolved from the *societe filodrammatiche*, informal amateur groups who assembled to play the mandolin, sing, perform pantomime, and in general to enjoy themselves entertaining one another. Often these groups gave public performances, charging a small fee which was donated to a community charity. Eventually some of these groups became professional theater companies.

One of the liveliest and most successful professional Italian theaters in America was the *Circulo Famigliare Pisanelli*, a combination theater and café which opened in 1905 in the Italian North Beach section of San Francisco. This theater, and its larger successor, the Washington Square Theater, became the social and entertainment centers of the North Beach Italian community due to the energy, business acumen, and talent of their founder, actress and impresario Antonietta Pisanelli Alessandro.

Alessandro's theaters performed translations of Broadway plays and of classics by Shakespeare, Goethe, and Dumas, but her audience was most enthusiastic about presentations of traditional Italian entertainment that reminded them of home. Alessandro's own renditions of regional Italian folk songs were always well-received, as were the *zarzuellas*, short comedy acts featuring the regional stock characters and humor of the traditional Italian *Commedia dell'arte*. As in *Commedia dell'arte*, actors usually worked without scripts, relying upon spontaneous wit and skill at improvisation. The audience recognized the costumes, characters, and situations portrayed in the *zarzuellas* as characteristic of particular districts in Italy. If the district was their own, their pleasure was undoubtedly increased.

The most popular productions in Alessandro's theaters, and perhaps in most Italian theaters, were operas. Whatever else was on the program (which often included several plays of one or more acts, with folk songs between the acts), the *Circulo* featured a different opera every night. *La Traviata, Rigoletto, La Boheme,* and *Otello* were favorites. The simplicity of staging necessitated by the small stage and budget did not dampen the enthusiasm of the audience. According to a contemporary observer:

> Italians look upon opera as a necessity and also strictly as an amusement, and they want it strong and good, artistically and musically. They care little for scenery—they want the acting, and upon this and the music everything depends. . . . This unique Circulo makes little effort at scenic effects—the artists are expected to make their own scenes and pictures in dramatic acting. At times the little stage is well crowded with characters, but there seems to be enough room for the most striking situations and dramatic scenes, and the auditors are satisfied without the aid of scenery.

If each stage had its own distinctive flavor, there were common themes in the material they produced and common satisfactions for the audiences they attracted. Ethnic theaters kept alive the language and culture of the mother country by producing its national classics. Italian theater produced the great Italian operas, which many immigrant laborers could sing from memory. German theaters produced works by Schiller and Goethe. Historical dramas were popular in many ethnic theaters. Yiddish theaters often performed plays based on Biblical themes.

Ethnic theater exposed its patrons not only to the past greatness of their native land, but also to its contemporary cultural developments. Ukrainian, Japanese, Italian, and other theater groups from the Old World performed on tour in American ethnic theaters, and individual actors, dancers, musicians, and singers from overseas made guest appearances in the United States. German language theater produced the best works of such modern German dramatists as Gerhart Hauptmann and Frank Wedekind. In 1896 the Irving Place Theater produced Hauptmann's controversial *Die Weber* (*The Weavers*), a story of a strike among Silesian weavers hailed by the *New York Dramatic Mirror* as "probably the most graphic picture of human misery ever written." The play was not produced for English speaking audiences until 1915.

The Jewish stage played Yiddish drama from Eastern Europe as well as translations and adaptations of the works of Moliere, Schiller, Tolstoy, Shakespeare, Zola, Gorki, Ibsen, Strindberg, and Molnar. In the late nineteenth and early twentieth centuries Yiddish speaking theatergoers had a better chance than their native born counterparts to become familiar with the best literature and drama of many lands. Like the ethnic press, ethnic theater was, in the broadest sense, educational.

People did not go to the theater to be educated, however; they went to be entertained. Serious drama by the best playwrights was less popular with general audiences than comedy, romance, and melodrama. Despite the harsh realities of their lives—or perhaps because of these harsh realities—ethnic audiences loved laughter, farce, and burlesque. The spirit of fun in mid nineteenth century German theater is captured in a report in the Missouri Hannibal *Tri-Weekly Messenger*:

> The German theater opened with a very 'talon-ted' company . . . on Bird Street. . . . The piece enacted on the occasion, we are informed, was the beautiful Tragedy entitled *The Butcher's Dog,* or the *Last Link of Sausage!* This beautiful and affecting piece was received with a handful of pea-nuts and a [sic] boquet of cabages! Their next presentation will be *The Strangled Codfish*, or *the Death of the Mad Mackerel*.

Such fare was played with great enthusiasm, for the sheer fun of it. But comedy had a practical function also. It provided emotional release for the immigrant struggling with loneliness, homesickness, family problems, and the dreariness of a life of hard work and uncertainty. Often the stock character in ethnic comedy was an immigrant, "green," stupid, ignorant, taken advantage of by those around him, comic in his daily tragedies. Such tragedies were only too familiar to the audience. This kind of comedy allowed ethnic Americans to laugh at their own problems and to rejoice in how far they had come. They watched the misadventures of the "greenhorn" on the stage with sympathetic recognition, and with the satisfying knowledge that they would not make such foolish mistakes—anymore.

This was the secret of Farfariello, a stock comedy character in the Italian-American theater. As the various districts and provinces of Italy had produced characteristic stock comedy figures, the Italian community in America produced Farfariello. Farfariello was the brain child of Eduardo Migliaccio, an Italian immigrant who became an actor after being fired from a sweatshop for burning a hole in the pants he was pressing. Farfariello was the "wop" of New York's Lower East Side. He was the garbage collector, the ice man, the fruit vendor, the pick and shovel man, the uneducated "greenhorn" who murdered the English language as well as the Italian. Much of his humor was based upon puns, parodies of famous people (Enrico Caruso, for example), or easily recognized Italian-American types such as the fruit dealer, the grocer, the school girl, and the nurse. His routines included shrewd satirical comments upon the class structure both of Italy and of the Italian-American community. Farfariello was a hero as well as a clown, exposing the weaknesses of the wealthier, pretentious people around him, and somehow triumphing over them.

The Irish theater, like the Italian, exposed the foibles of its own community and did so with broad farce and rollicking song. Masters of this kind of theater in the late nineteenth century were Harrigan and Hart, whose irrepressible productions included on-stage fights, fires, and explosions. In *Squatters Sovereignty,* a play about "shanty" Irish who decide to set up housekeeping in Central Park, two brawling clans appear on the stage, accompanied at various times by a goat, a donkey, and a flock of geese. Audiences mourned when the goat died on stage after cutting his throat on the sharp edge of a tin can.

Harrigan and Hart poked fun at the second generation as well as the first and especially at the social climbing "lace curtain" Irish. They also enjoyed satirizing the Irish political machine. In one play the main character, Mulligan, invites the Irish city aldermen to his home. The aldermen drink themselves into a stupor.

"Whatever will I do?" Cordelia Mulligan asks her husband. "The aldermen are all sound asleep."

"Leave them be," said Dan. "While they sleep, the city's safe."

Much ethnic theater was what the Germans called "kitsch," sentimental stories about everyday life in the Old World and the New. A historian of the Yiddish theater describes these "formula" plays which were common to all ethnic theaters but especially popular on the Yiddish stage.

> Plot counts for nothing compared with idiom and gesture; what matters is that the stock types . . . be put through their paces. The poor man (has) . . . a beautiful unmarried daughter and the rich man is outwitted by the peddler . . . true love will frustrate the marriage broker . . . the typical policeman will stroke his mustache. . . . The tradition is melodramatic, sentimental, and unsophisticated. It is also moving, funny, and intensely human.

Aside from being good entertainment, ethnic melodramas served many of the same functions as television "soap operas" of today. They provided insight into the problems, though in exaggerated form, that the audience met in their own lives. The unwed mother, the wayward son, the ungrateful daughter, the cold husband, the cruel stepmother, the faithless wife—such were the stock characters of ethnic melodrama. The audience recognized the shadow of reality, wept, yet felt somehow comforted. At least their spouse was not as cruel as the one depicted on the stage, their children not as heartless, their poverty not as hopeless.

The themes of the different ethnic melodramas suggest the problems in the lives of their respective ethnic groups. The Chinese theater in San Francisco, for example, featured a play about a husband separated from his wife for many years by the fortunes of war, just as the typical Chinese immigrant was separated from his wife. Undoubtedly the audience was heartened by the fact that the wife of the play rejects all suitors and remains faithful to the end. The husband's situation is more ambiguous. A beautiful princess falls in love with him and forces him to marry her. Like the immigrant, he is torn between the old and the new. The play has a happy ending. After many years and many obstacles, the husband is reunited with his faithful wife. The real life drama of the Chinese immigrant separated from his family did not usually end so happily.

The plays of Jacob Gordin, master of Yiddish melodrama, reveal much about the Jewish community for whom he wrote. His Yiddish adaptation of *King Lear* transformed the English king into a pious Jewish father in America abused and neglected by his Americanized —and heartless—daughters, a theme sure to bring tears to the eyes of an audience to whom it often represented reality as well as theater. *Minna,* a play similar in theme to Ibsen's *A Doll's House,* explores the dilemma of a woman whose husband neither understands nor appreciates her. Minna wants to be free to lead a life of her own. Unlike Ibsen's Nora, however, Minna cannot break away from her child and from the role of "faithful wife" she has been brought up to play. In desperation, she commits suicide.

One of Gordin's best plays was *The Slaughter,* which Hapgood described as "the story of the symbolic murder of a fragile young girl by her parents who force her to marry a rich man who has all the vices and whom she hates." The wife stays with her cruel husband—and his cold, curt mistress and half-witted son—to prevent her parents from being sent to the poor house. Life is misery for her and her parents until she discovers that she is pregnant. But this happiness only leads to further tragedy.

> There is a superb scene of naive joy in the midst of all the sordid gloom. The scene is representative of the way the poor Jews welcome their offspring. There is the rapturous delight of the old people, the turbulent triumph of the husband, the satisfaction of the young wife. They make a holiday of it. Wine is brought. They all love one another for the time. . . . But indescribable violence and abuse follow, and the wife finally kills her husband, in a scene where realism riots into burlesque, as it frequently does on the Yiddish stage.

Tears, like laughter, filled a need in the immigrant's life. The theater gave people a socially acceptable opportunity to express the anguish that so many had bottled up inside them. Harry Golden understood this when he observed, "Many of the immigrants had families in the old country. The Yiddish theater helped them to remember and to cry." This is why a famous soprano, Lucy Gherman, made a career out of one song, "Ebiga Mama" ("Eternal Mother"), and thousands of shopgirls wept through performance after performance of Jennie Goldstein singing "Ich Bin Ein Mama" ("I Am a Mother"). Immigrants who had left home, family, a whole way of life, unpleasant as some aspects of that life had been, experienced a deep sense of bereavement. They had lost much and like all who are bereaved, they needed to mourn. The melodrama of ethnic theater helped them express their grief at the passing of the old. In so doing, it helped prepare them to accept the new.

Poetry, Autobiography, Satire

Newspapers and theaters were institutions through which entire communities expressed themselves. Within each community, individuals also found means of self-expression—through poetry, autobiography, and fiction. Although the works of a few ethnic writers appeared in English, or were translated, and received praise from "American" critics, most immigrant writing was published in the mother tongue by ethnic presses and was, and unfortunately still is, inaccessible to the general reader.

The product of many hours of painstaking work, much immigrant writing was never published at all. It may never even have been read by anyone but its author, who put it carefully away in a box in a corner of a bureau drawer. Sometimes such work was lost forever. Sometimes it emerged years later, rediscovered by a curious relative cleaning out an attic or a basement—perhaps a child or grandchild unable to read or understand the language in which the work was written.

Because their folk traditions were rich in verse and song, immigrants turned naturally to poetry as a vehicle for their deepest emotions. The ethnic press was filled with poems of nostalgia for the old landscapes, faces, and songs. The following two poems, translated from German and Ukrainian, respectively, are typical of this popular genre:

> O, if I could hear again
>   In German forests, green and cool,
> The birds in May, and dream beside
>   The black wood pool.
>
> O, to find and smell again
>   Wood violets meek,
> To fall asleep on woodlawn mosses,
>   The Rhineland's breezes on my cheek.

> O, my Ukrainian song,
>   You sweeten my days.
> For I learned you
>   From my dear mother.
> My mother rests in the grave
>   Of her native land,
> But her songs still re-echo
>   From my lips.

Many immigrant poems are documents of the author's reactions to the new life of the United States. Such poems are often sad. The following poem was written in English by a young Italian immigrant who had studied the language only a few months. As the poem suggests, the young man was unhappy with his job in a mill and eventually returned to his homeland.

> Nothing job, nothing job,
> I come back to Italy;
> Nothing job, nothing job,
> Adieu, land northerly. . . .
>
> Nothing job, nothing job,
> O! Sweet sky of my Italy;
> Nothing job, nothing job,
> How cold is this country. . . .
>
> Nothing job, nothing job,
> I return to Italy;
> Comrades, laborers, goodbye;
> Adieu, land of "Fourth of July."

More sophisticated was the Yiddish poetry of Morris Rosenfeld, whose verses were sung in workers' meetings. Rosenfeld wrote of the dehumanizing pace of the factory. He described the men and women whose health and family life were ruined by the long hours of tedious, spirit-breaking labor demanded by the early twentieth century American industrial system.

A TEAR ON THE IRON

> Oh, cold and dark is the shop! I hold the iron, stand, and press;—my heart is weak, I groan and cough,—my sick breast scarcely heaves.
>
> I groan and cough, and press and think;—my eye grows damp, a tear falls; the iron is hot,—my little tear, it seethes, and will not dry up.
>
> My head whirls, my heart breaks, I ask in woe; 'Oh, tell me, my friend in adversity and pain, O tear, why do you not dry up in seething?'
>
> I should have asked more of the unrest, the turbulent tear; but suddenly there began to flow more tears, tears without measure, and I at once understood that the river of tears is very deep. . . .

After a collection of his poetry was published in English in 1898 under the title "Songs from the Ghetto," Rosenfeld was acclaimed by critics and invited to read his works on tours of universities in the United States and Europe.

The author of the following poem, a Chinese immigrant, was not so "discovered." His poem, which appeared in an anthology of Chinese-American verse published in 1927, describes the isolation of the Chinese immigrant.

> He fought long years for life,
> For his daily bread,
> He, a Chinese, died in a strange land.
> In a little room where he lodged.
> No one knew, for a day, of his death,
> Then the landlady knocked at his door—
> She found him dead. . . .
> For seven years he worked throughout this land
> Doing good for others, not for self. . . .
> He knew so many persons,
> But he had none as friend.
> Buried in a lonely grave,
> He is gone! His work is finished! . . . .

While some immigrant poetry extolled the beauty and the excitement of the new land, most of it like the examples just given had at least a tinge of sadness. Like poetry, immigrant diaries and autobiographies told of loneliness and hardship, but they usually stressed the more positive aspects of the American experience—the fertility of the land, the kindness of friends and neighbors, the opportunities for education and advancement. In *Laughing in the Jungle,* Louis Adamic, a Yugoslav journalist and intellectual, describes the United States as an industrial jungle in which the strong young man can make his way only by defying adversities and laughing at hardships. In *The Promised Land,* on the other hand, Mary Antin finds the urban ghetto flowing with the milk and honey of teachers and social workers who offer encouragement and support to a talented immigrant child. Most immigrant autobiographies are more sanguine in their views of America than immigrant poems because their authors were often looking back from positions of security and success.

Typical in many ways is Constantine Panunzio's *The Soul of an Immigrant.* Panunzio traces his life story from his childhood in Southern Italy through his difficult early years in the United States to his later career as a minister involved in Americanization and social work in the Italian-American community. A valuable aspect of this autobiography is Panunzio's attempt to verbalize what he has gained in ideas rather than in material advancement from his immigration to America.

Panunzio begins by praising the American willingness to break with the past, to try something new—a new job, a new house, a new town, a new idea, in contrast to the Southern Italian way of staying with the familiar and the proven. "The mental outlook (in the United States) is one of free adventure and free movement," writes Panunzio. "I have adopted it as the first plank, I might call it, in my American philosophy of life." Other "planks" were to follow.

Panunzio remembered that his adult relatives in Italy had constantly worried about the children's overstepping the bounds of custom. He was glad to adopt the American system in which people paid attention "rather to the *right* or the *wrong* of an act, than to whether or not it is customary." He praised the American tendency to value a man not for his ancestors' achievements, as was often the case in Italy, but for his own achievements, or even for what he hoped to achieve in the future. One of the greatest things America did for him, Panunzio wrote, was to cure him of idle dreaming and make him a practical man. In America, according to Panunzio, even idealism was geared to action rather than to dreams.

Panunzio admired the native-born Americans for their pride, their self-reliance, and their refusal to ask favors as had been the custom in Italy. He resolved to adopt these virtues, too. Most important he learned "the power and value of optimism." Wars, poverty, uncertainty, "the morbidity of our religious teachings"—all had combined to create an atmosphere of "somber pessimism" in the home of his youth. In contrast, Panunzio found Americans indomitably cheerful.

> . . . the optimism of American life was first strikingly illustrated to me by the hilarious and exuberant cheering of men and women over a football game. What astounded me most was to see them cheer when their team was *losing* as well as when it was *winning*, as if to say, 'We will yet win' and thereby to overcome all obstacles to victory. . . . It may be that it is due in no small measure to the grandeur, the sunshine and the exuberance which God has showered in such abundance upon these vast and magnificent stretches! Whatever the reason . . . optimism grips the very soul of me. . . .

Ethnic Fiction

Every sizable ethnic community produced so large a group of short story writers and novelists that it is impossible to do more than suggest the scope of their work. Their subject matter was the entire range of ethnic life in the United States—the child growing up, the relationships between men and women, the sordidness of the ghetto, the world of work, satire, protest, success, and failure. Their style varied from stark realism to highly imaginative symbolism, from the matter-of-fact recording of outer actions to the psychological examination of inner feelings. To give examples of the range and flavor of ethnic fiction, the works of two writers will be considered in some detail—Anzia Yezierska, an East European Jew, and O. E. Rölvaag, a Norwegian. Both were immigrants and both wrote in the early decades of the twentieth century.

Anzia Yezierska was born in Russian Poland in 1885 and came to the United States as a girl of sixteen. She went to work immediately as a domestic in the kitchens of New York's Jewish quarter and then, for wages not much better, in the garment sweatshops. Meanwhile she struggled to get an education in the city's night schools. Her own experiences provided the material for many of her short stories, stories about immigrants "crazy to learn" and full of unarticulated hopes and ambitions. "I don't know what is with me the matter," says a girl in one of these stories, "I'm so choked. . . . My thoughts tear in me and I can't tell them to no one. I want to do something with my life and I don't know what."

By 1919, the publication date of *Hungry Hearts*, a collection of short stories about Jewish immigrants, Yezierska had decided what to do with her own life. She would record the experiences of her people, the East European immigrant Jews. This she did amazingly well. Though Yiddish was her native language, she wrote in English, skillfully capturing in this recently acquired tongue the rhythm and idiom of her community. Her writing lacks sophistication; but like the people it describes, it is full of color and emotion. Her short stories received favorable comment from American critics because of their undeniable "authenticity," and one of her novels, *Salome of the Tenements*, became a Paramount motion picture in 1925.

The theme of much of Yezierska's work is the inner beauty, the dignity, and the vitality of the immigrant Jews. Her characters live in the grim tenements of New York, haggle with the butcher and the grocer and do daily battle with the landlord, the truant officer, the social worker and the factory foreman. Despite the outward poverty of their environment, their inner lives are rich.

Typical of many of her stories is "The Lost Beautifulness." In this story an immigrant woman, Hannah, takes in extra washing at night and saves her pennies in order to paint her tenement kitchen shiny white. To her husband's ridicule, Hannah replies, "What do I get from living if I can't have a little beautifulness in my life?"

Hannah's yearning for beauty is misunderstood and abused by the outside world. Seeing the newly painted apartment so much improved, Hannah's landlord raises the rent beyond what she and her sick husband can pay. When Hannah's son comes home unexpectedly from the army, two wound stripes on his sleeve and a Distinguished Service

Medal on his chest, he finds the family evicted, the households goods piled on the sidewalk, and his mother mourning "so much lost beautifulness."

Like Hannah, many of Yezierska's characters are vicitimized by callous officials and landlords, by unfeeling teachers, social workers, and physicians. Their stories have great pathos. Yezierska does not want pity, nor even charity, either for her characters or for their real life counterparts. She wants the United States to live up to its stated ideals of fair treatment and equal opportunity for all. In "The Lost Beautifulness" Hannah takes her rapacious landlord to court; she puts America to the test. America fails; the court upholds the landlord in his eviction order. Hannah refuses an offer of money from the wealthy woman whose laundry she does, though this money would have enabled her to pay the higher rent. "You want to give me hush money to swallow down an unrightness that burns my flesh," she protests. "I want justice!"

Despite their troubles, Yezierska's characters are not defeated because, whatever their circumstances, they have a sense of their own worth. One of her best stories, "The Fat of the Land," tells of an impoverished widow whose four children escape the ghetto to become a fashionable hat designer, a factory owner, a football star, and a famous playwright. Completely acculturated, the children try to make their mother into a "proper" American lady or, all else failing, to keep her out of sight. But the mother will not be changed; nor will she be hidden. Into her daughter's elegant marble halled apartment house she stalks, her market basket giving off the familiar odors of herring and garlic, the scaly tail of a fresh carp protruding from its newspaper wrappings! Nor will she accept her children's negative evaluation of her:

> From where did they get the stuff to work themselves up in the world? Did they get it from the air. . . . Why don't the children of born American mothers write my Benny's plays? It is I, who never had a chance to be a person, who gave him the fire in his head. If I would have had a chance to go to school and learn the language, what couldn't I have been? It is I and my mother and my mother's mother and my father and my father's father who had such a black life in Poland; it is our choked up thoughts and feelings that are flashing up in my children and making them great in America.

While her work is deeply rooted in the life of the Jewish ghetto, much of what Yezierska writes is familiar to the immigrant of any background. In her partly autobiographical novel, *The Breadgivers*, she describes the bitter conflicts between immigrant parents and their American born children. Her work is filled with a sympathetic understanding of the plight of the poor. She recognizes, for example, that society has mechanisms for keeping the poor "in their place." One story tells of an immigrant girl who works her way through normal school in a commercial laundry and then finds herself unable to get any but the lowest paid, temporary positions because of her shabby appearance. "It was to the advantage of those who used me that my appearance should damn me," says the girl, "so as to get me to work for the low wages I was forced to accept."

Though many of Yezierska's characters are exploited and abused, they are not bitter. They believe in the United States as the place where miracles can and do happen. Their greatest wish is to be able to contribute. Yezierska's immigrants do a great deal of hard physical work; but they want to do other things too. "I got ideas how to make America better," says an immigrant girl in one of the stories to an uncomprehending trade school teacher. "Ain't thoughts useful? Does America want only the work from my body? . . . Us immigrants wants to be people—not 'hands'. . . . I came to help America make the new world." Yezierska's work is a plea for the native born Americans to recognize immigrants as fellow human beings and to allow them to make their contributions to their newly adopted homeland.

A Viking in America

Ole Edvart Rölvaag was born in Nordland, one of the most beautiful areas in Norway, in a fisherman's cottage on a rocky ledge forty feet above the sea. It was the same cottage that had been home to his great, great, great grandparents before him. Though he emigrated to South Dakota at the age of twenty, he never lost his love for the mountains and the sea of Norway. After attending Augustana Academy and St. Olaf College, Norwegian Lutheran schools, he returned to his homeland repeatedly to study Norwegian history and literature and to visit his family and friends. In the United States he became a professor of Norwegian literature, a novelist, and a lifelong activist in the struggle of Norwegian-Americans to preserve their language and culture.

Rölvaag was a literary artist with a highly developed and disciplined talent. His work is rich in symbols and images, much of which is lost in English translation, and reveals the inner as well as the outer life of its characters. While Yezierska excelled in the short story, Rölvaag needed a larger canvas. His most famous book, *Giants in the Earth,* is recognized as an epic of frontier life. This novel and its two sequels, *Pedor Victorious* and *Their Father's God* comprise a trilogy that explores the question central to all of Rölvaag's works: what were the costs of immigration?

Per Hansa, the hero of *Giants in the Earth* is a nineteenth century

Viking. He is bold, adventurous, ambitious. He navigates his covered wagon across the Dakota prairie as his ancestors had navigated their ships across the oceans. His motivation is the same; he will be the founder of a new kingdom. His labors are prodigious—and well rewarded. His grain ripens in the American sun, promising his children an even grander future than he had dreamed. There is a price to be paid, however—hardship, drought, locusts, fear of Indians. In the end the Viking kingdom in the New World, like its counterparts in the Old, must be purchased by blood. Per Hansa goes out into a blizzard to fetch a minister for his dying friend and becomes lost in the snow. His body is found the following spring, leaning against a haystack, facing west.

Rölvaag's novels explore the psychological as well as the physical costs of immigration. According to Rölvaag, there are some people who should never immigrate. Per Hansa's wife, Beret, is one of them. She cannot bear the loss of home; she misses the scenic beauty of Norway and the security of its traditions and institutions. Life without these things drives her to temporary insanity. When recognizable civilization arrives in the form of a Norwegian minister, she recovers. Like many frontier widows of every ethnic background, she successfully manages the farm and rears the children after the death of her husband. In Rölvaag's trilogy, Beret represents the strength of character, the almost intuitive wisdom of the person who is firmly rooted in tradition and in what Rölvaag meant by culture. His sympathies are with her, though he reveals her flaws—the pessimism and rigidity of her religious views, for example. In *Giants in the Earth,* Beret loses her home, her security, and finally her husband because of immigration. But there are other costs as well for Beret and immigrants like her, as Rölvaag reveals in *Pedor Victorious.*

> Hidden forces were taking the children away from her—Beret saw it clearly. And strangely enough, they were enticing the youngest first. Permand (Pedor) and Anna Marie would watch every opportunity to talk English to each other, surreptitiously; . . . . And never did she hear them so much as mention what pertained to them as Norwegians. . . . At times, as she listened to their talk, she would fall to wondering whether she actually was their mother—their language was not hers. Here, so it seemed, each did not bring forth after its own kind as the Lord ordained. Wheat did not yield wheat; nor cattle beget cattle. . . . Had nature's laws been annulled altogether in this land?

Pedor Victorious is a classic study of the gap between immigrants and their children. Unlike some immigrant parents who accepted the change in their children, even welcomed it, Beret marshals all her resources against it. Pedor, her youngest, is the focus of her efforts. She forces him to study nightly with her from a Norwegian primer, has him confirmed in the Norwegian church, and puts him in a "Norwegian" school—all to no avail. The rebellious Pedor rejects his mother's heritage. "When I am grown up I am going to go so far away that I'll never hear the word 'Norwegian' again," he says.

Rölvaag agonizes for Beret and the other Norwegian parents whose children, figuratively and often literally, no longer speak their language. "It is a tragedy for mother and child not to be able to converse intimately," writes Rölvaag. "Her songs he cannot understand. What her soul has found nourishment in, he cannot comprehend. She seems to him an anachronism, a senseless, unreasonable being. . . . Can you not feel the heartache of that mother . . .?"

The immigrant's American born children have the advantage of feeling at home in the new language and the New World; but, according to Rölvaag, they pay the price of being cut off from their roots. Rölvaag complained that the young Norwegian-Americans he taught were often shallow, lacking in character, ambition, ideals, and "resonance," because they had lost the Norwegian language and, through it, access to their ancestral culture. Mixed marriage is a frequent theme in ethnic literature, and Rölvaag handles it masterfully. In *Their Father's God,* the third volume of his trilogy, he shows the positive side of Pedor's marriage to Susie, a second generation Irish-Catholic, the real love and tenderness between the couple. But despite their apparently complete Americanization, the young people are not free of "their father's God." The centrifugal forces of different cultures, different religions, different family traditions, and different goals gradually pull them apart. The marriage does not last.

In *Their Father's God* Rölvaag speaks to his rapidly acculturating Norwegian-American readers through the character of Reverend Kahldahl. Reverend Kahldahl tells young Pedor about the adventurous deeds of his ancestors, pointing out that the achievements of the Vikings and of their American descendants, the immigrants, will live because "they are the visible token of a high creative courage, which has its roots in the cultural soil of their race."

Rölvaag believed that the United States needed the cultural richness of its immigrant cultures. He was a cultural pluralist who asked, "If richness of personal color is desirable in the individual, why should the monotonous gray be desirable as a national ideal?" While Yezierska was worried that prejudice on the part of the old stock Americans would prevent the newly arrived East European Jews from making their contribution to American life, Rölvaag was worried that too rapid assimilation would keep the Norwegian-Americans from making theirs.

Though Rölvaag wrote in Norwegian, his works were an attempt to show the native born Norwegian-Americans the beauty of their background in the United States. Convinced that young Norwegian-Americans needed an appreciation of their immigrant parents and grandparents if they were to feel "completely and wholeheartedly at home" in the United States, he advocated the study of Norwegian-American history as a means of inculcating American patriotism. "The homes that have been wrested from the prairies and forests of the Northwest have been bought with the sweat of their (the immigrants) brows and the agony of their souls, with many long years of toil and with their own warm blood," he told his students. "There is a strange glory over those homes. We desire that our own people shall be enabled to see that glory . . . the cultivation of love for home and history is the truest Americanization that any citizen may be taught." Like Yezierska, Rölvaag was deeply rooted in his own ethnic community. Also, like Yezierska, he was deeply American.

CHAPTER 10

Closing the Gates:
Nativism and Restrictionism,
1880-1924

While ethnic Americans were building their communities and settling down to life in America, old stock Americans were becoming increasingly uneasy about their presence. By 1924 even the most recent immigrant groups were learning English, becoming citizens and contributing to the economy. Indeed the foreign born were more likely to own their own homes and to have their children in school than the native born. Paradoxically, however, the more Americanized the newer immigrants became, the more hostility they seemed to arouse. In 1924 Congress passed broad restrictive legislation to preserve America from further intrusions of "dangerous" aliens.

Between 1880 and 1924 a rising tide of nativism engulfed first the Oriental-Americans and then those who had come from Southern and Eastern Europe. Distrust of foreigners, it will be remembered, had been common during the colonial era and had risen to a national political movement before the Civil War. This early nativism had always been offset, however, by a tradition of hospitality to the poor and the oppressed, by the conviction that America had room for everybody, and by the belief that the American environment would transform the most debased foreigner into a "new man." Unlike earlier nativism, however, the nativist crusade of the early twentieth century was able to realize its goal—the closing of the gates for immigrants from Asia and from Southern and Eastern Europe.

The new nativists attributed their victory to the fact that the

Oriental and East European immigrants barred in 1924 were inferior to the Irish, German, and Scandinavian immigrants who had arrived in earlier years. However, objective observers noted then what recent historians have documented—that immigrants from Southern and Eastern Europe were similar to those from Western Europe in skills and motivations and in the problems they encountered. Why, then, were they perceived as sinister, and why did not the traditional American hospitality and optimism come to their rescue? The answer is that twentieth century nativism, like its earlier counterpart, was not so much an objective response to the qualities of the immigrants as it was an expression of problems within the nation as a whole. Now, for the first time, these internal problems included a loss of the youthful self-confidence and optimism that had made the nation so hospitable to newcomers in earlier eras.

New Doubts and Fears

As the nineteenth century reached its close, many Americans were haunted by a vague pessimism about their own and the nation's future; and the reasons for this pessimism somehow involved the massive immigration of the time. The government's announcement in 1890 that the frontier no longer existed contributed to this pessimism. Most Americans agreed with the historian Frederick Jackson Turner that the frontier had provided opportunity for the poor and had helped absorb and assimilate foreigners. With the frontier gone, where was the "safety valve" for the impoverished urban worker, and how could the increasing numbers of immigrants become Americanized?

Middle class Americans felt threatened by the growing concentration of wealth in agriculture and industry. By the end of the nineteenth century the best farm lands were in the hands of the railroads or of large corporations (agribusiness) with which family farms were unable to compete. Bewildered and angry, many farmers vented their fury on the growing cities which lured their children and held their mortgages—and which teemed with immigrants!

Exclusion of the Chinese and Japanese

The decline in the supply of good and inexpensive land, fear of the giant corporations, frustration of ambitions to get ahead, fear of the future—these and other elements played a part in the campaign against the Chinese, the first people to be legally excluded from the United States. Songs and poems from San Francisco, like the following, "Twelve Hundred More" demonstrate the fears of the Caucasian working man:

O workingmen dear, and did you hear
The news that's going round?
Another China steamer
Has been landed here in town.

Today I read the papers
And it grieved my heart full sore
To see upon the title page,
O just 'Twelve Hundred More!'

O, California's coming down
As you can plainly see,
They are hiring all the Chinamen
And discharging you and me.

Twelve hundred honest laboring men
Thrown out of work today
By the landing of these Chinamen
In San Francisco Bay.

This state of things can never last
In this our golden land,
For soon you'll hear the avenging cry,
'Drive out the Chinaman!'

When the Chinese first arrived in California at the time of the
original Gold Rush, they were praised for their industriousness and
usefulness. By the late 1870's, however, when the above song was
popular, they were just as widely denounced for their servility and
deceitfulness. The Chinese were still living in their own communities,
running restaurants and laundries, working as agricultural laborers or
as factory hands, and generally entering occupations considered
undesirable by Caucasians. The Chinese had not changed. California
had changed, however. Formerly a land of boundless opportunity for
all, by the 1870's it was a state plagued by massive unemployment and
political corruption.

The entire nation suffered a serious economic depression in the
late 1870's, but its effects were particularly severe in California. A new
transcontinental railroad had recently been completed. The railroad
brought floods of immigrants from the east, refugees from the
depression, seeking opportunities that were not available. Newcomers
to California hoped to make their fortunes in agriculture or in
mining—but their hopes were frustrated. As the population rose, so
did the price of land, much of which was in the hands of the wealthy
few. Newcomers from the East were unable to buy good land and were
unwilling to work for others or reclaim waste areas, as Mexican-
Americans and Orientals did. As for mining, the days when all one
needed were a mule and a pan had vanished. Now mining was

monopolized by big corporations that could afford the heavy initial investment in equipment. The large agricultural, mining, and railroad interests that dominated the economy also dominated an increasingly corrupt state government. Thus ambitious newcomers to California found themselves blocked wherever they turned.

It was in this atmosphere that Dennis Kearney, an Irish born sailor who had lost his money in mining stocks, began the anti-Chinese agitation. Kearney denounced the land, mining, and railroad monopolies for denying the masses their rightful opportunities to rise. He blamed the Chinese, many of whom worked for these large corporations, for depressing wages and causing the widespread unemployment.

In an earlier day Kearney's speeches might have gone unnoticed, but this was the era of sensational or "yellow" journalism. Cheap newspapers were building mass circulation among the newly literate reading public by printing the most lurid and emotion provoking stories and pictures they could find. The San Francisco *Chronicle* published Kearney's speeches and found them an instant circulation booster. A rival paper, the *Morning Call* countered by also featuring Kearney's speeches. Thus a newspaper circulation war helped catapult the little known agitator into a position of prominence.

Kearney became a popular demagogue and leader of a new antibusiness, anti-Chinese political faction, the Workingmen's Party. Kearney's followers vented their wrath on corporate monopolies as well as on the Chinese. Because local politicians found it easier to join the campaign against the defenseless Chinese than take up the cause of serious economic reform, they encouraged the anti-Chinese campaign.

Propaganda led to actions as a rash of anti-Chinese riots spread throughout the West. In 1871 rioters killed twenty-one Chinese in San Francisco. In 1877 rioters burned twenty-five Chinese laundries, shooting many of the owners as they attempted to escape the flames. In 1880 rioters destroyed every Chinese home and business in Denver. In 1885 twenty-eight Chinese were killed and hundreds wounded in Rock Springs, Wyoming, as rioters drove the entire Chinese community from their homes. Laws forbade the Chinese to send their children to "white" schools, to own land, to offer bail, even to wear the traditional queues (pigtails). A new expression—"not a Chinaman's chance"— reflected what it was like to be a Chinese-American in the closing decades of the nineteenth century.

Kearney's Workingmen's Party controlled enough votes to make its support necessary to either of the major parties that hoped to govern in California. Similarly, on the national scene California's electoral votes were eagerly wooed by the evenly matched Republican and Democratic Parties. Therefore the anti-Chinese forces received a favorable hearing disproportionate to their actual numbers both locally and in Washington. The results were the local anti-Chinese laws already mentioned, and on the national level, the Chinese Exclusion Act of 1882, the first immigration restriction in our history.

The original Exclusion Act was to be in force for ten years and was aimed at excluding only unskilled workers. The Act was renewed again and again, however, and was used to exclude virtually everyone. Chinese immigration. Like Indians, blacks, and Mexicans, Chinese measure, the Scott Act, denied Chinese-Americans the right to visit their families in China and then return to the United States. The Chinese, almost all of whom had left their families overseas, were faced with dismal alternatives. They could return to China permanently, in which case their families would sink once again into poverty, or they could resign themselves to indefinite exile in the United States and continue to send home the remittances that supported their families in China. Reared in a cultural tradition that emphasized family responsibility above individual desires, most chose to stay. A Chinese-American historian Betty Lee Sung suggests the costs:

> They were denied the joys and cares of seeing their children grow up. They no longer knew the feast days, the holidays when faces dear and close swarmed about to lend gaiety and festivity to the air. They were deprived of performing the thousand and one small gestures of gratitude and love to their parents. . . . Yes, these men were condemned to a life . . . shorn of love and warmth, of home and family in a land where prejudice surrounded them and fate was benign if one did not suffer bodily attack.

Racial prejudice undoubtedly played a role in the move to restrict Chinese immigration. Like Indians, blacks, and Mexicans, Chinese were considered to be less human than the Caucasian majority. Once the Chinese were excluded, it was easy to exclude the Japanese later. When Japanese immigrants began to arrive on the West Coast in the late nineteenth and early twentieth century, their physical appearance caused them to be placed in the same "inferior" slot that had already been reserved for the Chinese. The Japanese community in America was numerically much smaller than the Chinese and, unlike the Chinese, Japanese immigrants were almost always literate and represented a broad socioeconomic spectrum of their native society. However, most Californians recognized no such distinctions. "The Japanese are starting the same tide of immigration we thought we had checked twenty years ago," said Mayor James D. Phelan of San Francisco. "The Chinese and Japanese are not the stuff of which American citizens are made."

"The Japanese Invasion, the Problem of the Hour," screamed banner headlines in the San Francisco *Chronicle* on February 23, 1905.

Once again the press found resistance to the presence of Orientals a circulation booster. Once again the working classes, especially the skilled trade unions, took up the cry, and once again the issue was economic as well as racial. *Meat vs. Rice, American Manhood vs. Asiatic Coolieism, Which Shall Survive?* read the title of an anti-Japanese pamphlet issued by the American Federation of Labor. Once again, local politicians found it advantageous to pick up the issue. California passed a special law denying Japanese immigrants the right to own land, and the San Francisco School Board ruled that all Japanese children must go to school in Chinatown. Agitation to restrict Japanese immigration swelled.

Better educated than the Chinese, the Japanese were better equipped to fight back. Unlike the Chinese, they were supported by the government of their native land, a recently westernized and industrialized naval power which had just won the Russo-Japanese War. President Theodore Roosevelt respected Japan as a Great Power and did not want to alienate her. When Japan protested the treatment of its subjects in the United States (in the eyes of Japan, immigrants remained Japanese subjects), Theodore Roosevelt sent his Secretary of Commerce and Labor, Victor Metcalf, to investigate. Metcalf reported that Japanese children caused no problem in the schools and that Japanese-Americans were subject to violence and other unjustified harassment.

Because of Metcalf's report and the protests of Japan and the Japanese-American community, Japanese children in California were spared the indignity of racial segregation. To assuage the concern of Caucasian Californians, Roosevelt negotiated a "Gentlemen's Agreement" with the Japanese government whereby Japan would limit the number of immigrants granted visas for the United States. Hereafter only a few skilled Japanese and the immediate families of immigrants already here would be admitted.

While European, African, or Latin American born immigrants could become citizens after living in the United States five years, Chinese and Japanese immigrants were denied this privilege. According to a law passed in 1790, citizenship was available to "any alien, being a free white person," a clause meant to exclude Indians and blacks. The Fourteenth Amendment, passed after the Civil War, opened American citizenship to blacks, but Orientals, as nonwhites, were still excluded. In 1914 Japanese born Takao Ozawa applied for naturalization. The Supreme Court denied his application on the basis of the law of 1790. Ironically, the court assured him that "there is not implied—either in the legislation or in our interpretation of it—any suggestion of individual unworthiness or racial inferiority. These considerations are in no manner involved."

The Depression of the 1890's

The agitation against Oriental-Americans had been a local affair, concentrated on the West Coast where the Chinese and Japanese had settled. Similar economic and psychological pressures would soon operate nationwide to cause hostility to the far more numerous European immigrants as well. In the 1890's stock market manipulation, overproduction, and speculation plunged the nation into the most serious economic crisis it had ever experienced. In 1894 one out of every five workers was unemployed, and millions roamed the countryside looking for jobs or, in despair, sinking into a life of vagrancy. No fewer than seventeen "industrial armies" marched on Washington in 1894 to demand government help, thereby frightening President Grover Cleveland, and much of the nation, into the mistaken idea that mob rule was abroad in the land. When employers cut wages, workers struck and were ruthlessly suppressed by the police or by private armies. Like industrial workers, farmers found their economic situation worsening. Their revolt, known as the Populist Movement, spread quickly through the South and the West.

Meanwhile the government provided no help and the very rich continued their display of what the economist Thorstein Veblen called "conspicuous consumption," buying everything from private opera houses for their own amusement to titled European husbands for their daughters. People brought up to believe that honest labor and good character guaranteed success, or at least adequate food for their families, were bewildered to find that the system no longer seemed to function. In this atmosphere of class conflict, disillusionment, and bitterness, a new nativism arose.

At first the new nativism revived the old themes of the 1850's, directing its attacks against all immigrants indiscriminantly. According to the popular press, immigrants were "the very scum and offal of Europe," dirty, ignorant, and prone to crime and pauperism. The American Protective Association revived old slanders about the immorality of Roman Catholics and impending Papal invasion of the United States. Its members, close to a million at its peak, pledged to vote against all Catholic candidates, to oppose aid to Catholic schools, and to avoid participation in strikes "whereby the Catholic employees may undermine and substitute their Protestant co-workers."

An old nativist theme that seemed to be especially appropriate to the new conditions was the denunciation of immigrants as radicals. Native born Americans as well as immigrants participated in the strikes that rocked the nation in the closing decades of the nineteenth century, but frightened property owners blamed these "un-American" activities on the influence of foreigners. In 1886 someone threw a bomb at a labor rally in Chicago, killing a policeman and several bystanders.

Though no one could be certain who threw the bomb, during what came to be called the Haymarket Riot, a group of alleged anarchists, mostly German born, were tried and four were hanged. Many Americans agreed with a newspaper statement that "there is no such thing as an American anarchist." They blamed the Chicago bombing and, indeed, all labor unrest, on "long-haired, wild-eyed, bad-smelling, atheistic, reckless foreign wretches, who never did an honest hour's work in their lives. . . ."

At first, stereotypes of immigrant poverty, immorality, and radicalism were applied to those of western as well as eastern European origin. Gradually, however, nativism focused upon the latter. New stereotypes involving Slavs, Italians, and Jews reflected the new worries of the American community. Working class native born Americans began to depict Slavic and Italian laborers as tools of the giant corporations—imported strike breakers, degraded people who stole jobs from Americans by accepting wages no decent human being could live on.

This "degraded labor" stereotype of Italians and Slavs in the East was strikingly similar to attacks on Chinese and Japanese workers in the West. Like the anti-Oriental stereotype, it was part of the deeply felt anger toward the big industrialists and monopolists. And like the anti-Oriental stereotype, it was a distortion of the facts. Big corporations favored the open immigration policy as a means of guaranteeing an ample supply of labor, but they did not cause immigration. The movement to America was largely spontaneous. Like everyone else, immigrants worked for as much as they could get. Their wages were lower than those of the native born, because they were concentrated in unskilled occupations.

During the years of heavy immigration, small craft industries were being replaced by assembly line machine production. This mechanization did allow management to replace expensive skilled labor with cheaper unskilled labor, much of which was foreign born. In the long run, these technological changes created many new jobs. As immigrants took the unskilled positions, native born workers moved up to supervisory, clerical, or highly skilled positions. But these trends were not apparent to unemployed American born workers caught in the throes of the depression of the 1890's. Organized labor took an anti-immigration stand which it maintained until the restrictionist victory of 1924. Manufacturers, on the other hand, eager to keep a large supply of cheap labor, fought restriction until after World War I.

While the stereotype of the degraded Italian or Slavic worker reflected the anxieties of the American worker, the stereotype of the unscrupulous Jewish financier expressed the anxieties of the American farmer. As the depression deepened populism spread and among some of its adherents took on ugly anti-Semitic imagery. To the beleaguered farmer, the Jew was Shylock, the usurer, or worse yet, a representative of the mythological international money trust that was keeping him in financial bondage. To discontented farmers, the Jew, a traditionally urban figure, also symbolized the hated city which increasingly dominated American life.

Many of the populists lived in the West or South and may never have met a Jew. Less understandably, Easterners shared their view. "The Russian Jews and the other Jews will completely control the finances and government of this country in ten years," warned a New York worker, "or they will all be dead. The people of this country won't be starved and driven to the wall by Jews." The fact that the overwhelming majority of Russian Jewish immigrants were themselves poor and often unemployed during the depression was ignored.

To the older, privileged classes—men such as Henry Adams, the New England aristocrat, and Prescott Hall, founder of the Immigration Restriction League—the Jewish immigrant symbolized the aggressiveness and rapacity of the new American business culture, the domination of the monied interests at the expense of the "best" people. Jews were stereotyped as pushy, aggressive, unethical in business, and ostentatious in the display of their wealth. While a few of the older German Jewish families had acquired wealth, the far more numerous Russian Jews were poor. No Jews could compare in fortune to the corporate giants of Protestant America, giants whose sharp business practices and vulgar life styles were notorious. The old aristocrats ultimately had to make their peace with the new multimillionaires, but the Jewish "upstarts" could be excluded from "society." Thus a materialistic and aggressive American culture attributed its own least attractive qualities to one segment of its population, its Jews.

Violence Against Southern and Eastern European Ethnics

In the case of Southern and Eastern Europeans, as in the case of Orientals, negative stereotypes led to violence. Ukrainian miners imported into Pennsylvania as strikebreakers in the 1870's met with continued violence from the Irish miners already there. Union membership was as dangerous for immigrants as scabbing. When Slavic and Hungarian miners protested Henry Clay Frick's lowering of their wage scale, the Pennsylvania state militia killed ten and wounded fifty. In a similar incident in Hazelton, Pennsylvania, sheriff's deputies killed twenty-one immigrant "animals" and wounded forty more. Slavic miners were given the lowest paid positions because "it goes against the grain in an English-speaking man to fetch and carry for a Slovak or a Pole."

Italian immigrants often received even harsher treatment than Slavs. Their darker appearance contributed to their problems. "You don't call an Italian a white man?" a construction boss was asked. "No sir, an Italian is a Dago." Like Slavs, Italians were attacked both as strikebreakers and as strikers, but much of the violence against them stemmed from the stereotype of the Italian criminal flashing his stiletto. In 1895 six Italians suspected of murdering a Colorado saloon keeper were lynched, and three suspects in Louisiana met the same fate the following year. The most serious incident took place in New Orleans in 1891, when members of the Sicilian colony were blamed for the murder of the chief of police. When a jury found the evidence insufficient for conviction, a mob, backed by some of the city's leading citizens, lynched eleven Italian suspects.

In Northern cities Jews were commonly taunted and even assaulted in the streets. More serious violence took place in the South. The few East European Jews who went South usually made their livings as shopkeepers or in other commercial activities, as did German Jews who had been in the South since the early part of the nineteenth century. Jews often were attacked by Southern Populists who found in them the most convenient representatives of the nonproductive, monied "oppressors." In the late 1800's, debt-ridden farmers in Louisiana wrecked Jewish stores and threatened the lives of their owners. In 1893, Mississippi vigilantes burned dozens of farmhouses belonging to Jewish landlords.

However, the worst anti-Semitic outbreak in the South took place long after the depression of the 1890's had ended. It was the Frank case in Atlanta in 1914. The son of a New York manufacturer, Leo Frank managed a plant in Atlanta in which a young woman worker was found murdered. Frank was convicted of the murder on the flimsiest of evidence, probably because the angry working class community saw him as a northern capitalist exploiting southern womanhood. When Jewish organizations in the North tried to help Frank, southerners resented this "outside interference". When the governor commuted Frank's death sentence, angry Georgians boycotted Jewish merchants throughout the state. Leo Frank was abducted from prison and murdered.

Like the lynching of blacks, which was even more common in this troubled period, violence against immigrants generally went unpunished, but unlike the lynching of blacks, it was at least verbally deplored. Despite the violence of extremists and the lobbying activities of groups like the American Protective Association and the Immigration Restriction League, no government action was taken in the last decade of the nineteenth century to restrict European immigration. The South still hoped to attract immigrants and to use them as a base for industrialization. Businessmen appreciated the value of an imported labor force. And despite their economic problems, many Americans retained at least some faith in the traditional melting pot—the ability of English America to absorb all comers, improving them and perhaps even itself in the process.

The New Century

The violent nativism of the 1890's subsided during the first decade and a half of the twentieth century. The Spanish-American War restored America's self-confidence—expansion was still taking place. The acquisition of Puerto Rico and the Philippines encouraged an optimistic "larger America" mentality. The depression ended, and the discovery of gold in Alaska eased the currency problems that had so obsessed the Populists. Renewed prosperity in the city and on the farm quieted the rumblings of class war. Progressive reformers cleaned out at least some of the political corruption so distressing to the "better" people. Meanwhile, institutional reforms such as the direct election of Senators, the direct primary, and, eventually, woman's suffrage, gave ordinary people a feeling, however unjustified, that they, rather than the millionaires, controlled the country.

The major efforts of the nativists during these years were directed toward the adoption of a literacy test as a prerequisite for the admission of every immigrant. The literacy test, as its advocate Henry Cabot Lodge pointed out, would screen out immigrants from Southern and Eastern Europe while admitting those from Western Europe. Critics countered by noting that the ability to read and write was a measure of past opportunity rather than of character or ability. Congress passed the literacy test three times between 1896 and 1915, but Presidents Cleveland and Wilson vetoed each bill—partly on principles and partly, in Wilson's case, to maintain the support of the ethnic American voters who had helped elect him.

The federal government did pass new legislation against the admission of prostitutes, criminals, lunatics, anarchists, the feeble-minded, those suffering from "loathsome" diseases, and those considered likely to become public charges. At the newly opened embarkation center on Ellis Island millions of immigrants streamed by the federal health inspectors, dreading the white chalk mark that would single them out for a closer look, perhaps even for deportation. Sometimes one member of a family was quarantined or deported, while others were admitted. Inspectors tried to be fair, but injustices undoubtedly occurred. A Greek immigrant was deported after months in the United States on the grounds that a physical defect would make him a public charge, though he had been totally self supporting since his arrival! The percentage of immigrants turned away reached a high of 6.9% in 1915, an insignificant number compared to the masses that continued to be admitted.

Uneasiness about the entrance of foreigners did not disappear, however, and the restrictionist organizations continued their activities. Their ultimate success was due to the introduction of two new factors—"scientific" racism espoused by large portions of the academic community and "one hundred per cent Americanism" engendered by the passions of World War I.

Racism

The idea that one group of people was intrinsically inferior to another was all too familiar to American blacks, Indians, and Orientals. But earlier racism, though instrumental in determining how Americans behaved toward one another, had never enjoyed the official backing of the scientific community. Now for the first time racism emerged as an academically respectable, experimentally "proven" doctrine espoused by eminent biologists, sociologists, anthropologists, and psychologists. Beginning several decades earlier in Europe than in the United States, the new racists measured skulls, calculated comparative cranial volumes, and administered the first IQ tests. On the basis of carefully quantified evidence, white Anglo-Saxon and Germanic investigators concluded that lighter skinned peoples were inherently superior to Negroes and Orientals and that even among whites, Anglo-Saxons and Teutons were superior to the Alpine and Mediterranean races.

Nineteenth century American writers had long praised the virtues of the Anglo-Saxon race, especially its supposed talent for pioneering and for self-government. These writers had defined "race" loosely, as a group of people sharing a common cultural tradition, shaped by a common environment or historical experience. The early popularity of Darwin's ideas on evolution encouraged Americans to stress the importance of environment over heredity and the idea of "the survival of the fittest" seemed to guarantee the victory of Anglo-Saxons over all other cultural elements in the great American melting pot.

Twentieth century racism was different, however. It dwelled less upon Darwinism than upon Mendel's laws of heredity. To the new racists, race was not a common culture which could be changed by a favorable environment. It was a common genetic pool which was immutable. Bad genes were not overcome by good; they survived to pollute the stock, human or animal, to the thousandth generation. No longer confident that Anglo-Saxonism could conquer all, the new American racists proposed restriction of immigration as a necessary safeguard for the vigor of the superior American stock.

American nativists found racism a useful justification for their previously acquired anti-immigration sentiments. Henry Cabot Lodge defended the literacy test with dire warnings that the superior qualities of American civilization would be "bred out" by masses of racially inferior newcomers. According to Francis Walker, a leading economist and president of the Massachusetts Institute of Technology, the immigrants from Southern and Eastern Europe were "beaten men from beaten races . . ." having "none of the ideas and aptitudes which belong to those who are descended from the tribes that met under the oak trees of old Germany to make laws and choose Chieftains." Pessimistic about the direction of American society, Walker shared a fashionable melancholy which a German writer, Max Nordau, called "vague qualms about the Dusk of Nations." According to Walker, American workers, unwilling to compete with cheap European labor, were limiting their family size, failing to reproduce themselves, and thus committing racial suicide. (Actually, the falling American birth rate was due to increased urbanization, better education, easier access to birth control information, and a wider range of options for women.) To Walker, and others like him, immigration was the biological death warrant of the nation.

Between 1914 and 1924 a flood of articles and books popularized the new racism. Edward Alsworth Ross, a widely read and respected sociologist, started the vogue in *Century* magazine with a series of articles evaluating every immigrant group in terms of supposedly inborn racial characteristics. Lothrop Stoddard, a Massachusetts lawyer with a degree in history and an obsession with race, wrote two books, *The Rising Tide of Color Against White World Supremacy* and *The Menace of the Under Man*, both warning that the inferior brown and yellow skinned peoples of the world would soon outnumber and vanquish the superior whites. The most influential of the new racist books was *The Passing of the Great Race* by Madison Grant, a member of an old, patrician New York family, who had acquired a smattering of information on genetics and anthropology, and who was vehemently anti-Semitic. Grant's book glorified the tall, blond Nordic as the "white man par excellence" on whom American culture rested and warned that the American stock would be ruined if we continued to admit swarms of inferior Europeans such as the Alpines, the Mediterraneans, and, worst of all, the Jews.

These American writers, as well as the European investigators whose works they used, made the mistake of linking genetically caused physical characteristics—hair, skin coloring, and height—with environmentally produced cultural characteristics such as poverty and illiteracy. They were superficially correct in observing that Southern and Eastern Europeans in early twentieth century America were more likely to live in slums than older "English stock," but this was due to circumstances, not genes.

White skinned Americans and Western Europeans exercised political domination over the rest of the globe in the early twentieth century because of their superior technology. White, Western social scientists concluded from this fact that their group was inherently superior. A similar study of the world one thousand or two thousand years earlier might have concluded on the same kind of evidence that the Chinese, or the Mediterranean peoples, or Africans were superior —especially if Chinese, Mediterranean, or African experts had been conducting the study! Moreover, the assumption that the society with the most efficient tools and the deadliest weapons is "superior" is certainly debatable.

The ideas of the racists were apparently confirmed by the reports of school authorities and army psychologists during World War I that young people of Southern and East European background scored lower on intelligence tests than those of West European or native American parentage. The early IQ tests, however, were based upon familiarity with middle class Anglo-Saxon language and culture. The longer an ethnic group had lived in the United States and the more completely assimilated it had become, the higher its members scored. Thus old stock Americans tested better than Irish and German Americans, who in turn tested better than most members of the Oriental or Southern and Eastern European immigration. Studies showing that Italians and Jews sent far fewer of their members to poorhouses than the Irish, that Polish immigrants learned English more quickly than German immigrants, and that the foreign born produced fewer criminals than the native born were ignored. They did not fit the stereotype.

The new scientific racism legitimized old prejudices throughout the country, encouraging the blaming of every problem from political corruption to poverty upon the presence of blacks, Orientals, Jews, Italians, or whatever "inferior" group seemed most readily available. The new racism gave the South scientific justification for depriving blacks of their vote and subjecting them to total segregation. The new racism also guaranteed the success of the movement to restrict new immigration. First, by linking the inferiority of the Eastern European immigration to that of blacks and Orientals, it mobilized the support of the South and the West. Secondly, by including Irish, Germans, and Scandinavians in the "desirable" category of superior peoples, it flattered them and neutralized their opposition. After all, they were not to be restricted.

World War I and "100% Americanism"

The impact of the new racism was not felt all at once. From an inner circle of intellectuals it spread like a virus, gradually infecting much of the nation. In contrast, a new nationalism, equally damaging to the cause of open immigration, burst like a bombshell upon everyone. When Germany's unrestricted submarine warfare brought the United States into World War I, the country plunged into a frenzy of shrill, uncompromising, "one hundred per cent Americanism." A wave of superpatriotic conformity inundated the country. The Espionage Act of 1918 established a penalty of twenty years imprisonment for criticism of the armed forces, the flag, or even the military uniform!

German-Americans, many of whom still took great pride in the culture and language of their fatherland, were hardest hit by the war because Germany was considered the main enemy. The American press portrayed Germany as a barbarous nation whose soldiers delighted in raping Belgian women and bayoneting their babies. Between the outbreak of the European war in 1914 and our entry in 1917, some German-Americans protested our general anti-German orientation, especially our supplying of arms to Britain and her allies. After the United States entered on Britain's side, the overwhelming majority of German-Americans and the German-American press supported the war.

To many American patriots, however, "Huns" could not be trusted at home or abroad. Everything German was suspect. The anti-German furor became so irrational and intense that the German language was purged from the curriculum of many high schools and colleges, German names of individuals, firms, and even towns were changed, and restaurants substituted "liberty cabbage" for sauerkraut. As late as 1919 the *New York Times* reported two veterans organizations ready to use machine guns to stop a performance at the German Irving Place Theater.

A special act of Congress repealed the charter of the Alliance, a national federation of German-American organizations, and a damper fell upon German-American communal life at every level. Individual German-Americans who did not support the war warmly enough or buy enough Liberty Bonds to satisfy their neighbors could find themselves harassed, whipped, tarred and feathered, and in at least one case, lynched. Despite little evidence of disloyal activity, many Americans believed members of the German-American community to be responsible for every wartime shortage—when they were not too busy poisoning the war supplies with influenza germs or putting ground glass in Red Cross bandages!

While never subjected to the hatred reserved for German-Americans, ethnic Americans from the Austro-Hungarian Empire and the Turkish Empire were also identified with enemy powers and thus were objects of suspicion. Patriots pointed out that Slavic labor controlled the production of coal and steel, and that Slavic-Americans were numerous enough to control local elections in certain areas. In an article in *Everybody's Magazine* in March 1918, Samuel Hopkins Adams warned America about Slavic aliens. "Reckon each as a pound of dynamite—surely a modest comparison. . . . Not all these enemy aliens are hostile. Not all dynamite explodes."

The experience of being at war while large portions of the civilian population were culturally or even politically identifiable with the enemy was intolerable to many. It led to a clamor for immediate "Americanization" as the only way to defuse once and for all the foreign "dynamite." Churches and settlements had been working in the area of Americanization for years, but now large numbers of schools, business firms, civic groups, local and state governments, and even the federal government became involved. A few of the old settlement house personnel tried to revive the idea that ethnic cultures could make worthwhile contributions to American life, but these contributions were usually defined as folk dances, exotic foods, and other "quaint" and superfluous frivolities. The major thrust of wartime Americanization programs was toward immediate American citizenship for all who were eligible and toward total cultural conformity to the mores of the majority community. Ethnic Americans were pressured to abandon their own languages, customs and traditions, their loyalties, even their memories, as quickly as possible to become "one hundred per cent" American. A wartime English class in one of Henry Ford's factories acted out the new spirit. Outlandishly dressed workers carrying banners with the names of their native lands walked across the stage, entered a huge melting pot, and emerged identically dressed in neat American business suits, carrying neat little American flags.

The tactics of the Americanization crusaders were not subtle. The Governor of Iowa tried to ban the use of languages other than English in all public conversations and over the telephone. Industries refused promotions, or even employment, to aliens who had not begun citizenship applications. Some firms made attendance at English classes a condition of employment. The state of California sent "foreign language speakers" among immigrant communities to convince them to buy Liberty Bonds and give to the Red Cross because "the time had come for every foreign-born to make his decision." The most important duty of these state agents was to avert labor unrest and strikes, and to convince immigrant workers to stay patriotically on the job or "they themselves would suffer in the end."

Always seen as an instrument of Americanization, schools were heavily involved in the wartime push for loyalty and conformity. Teachers pressured immigrant children to support the Red Cross and gave them loyalty pledges for their parents to sign. School personnel

were advised to use school plays, pageants and the like to instruct
children and their parents in patriotism. Blatant wartime propaganda
found its way into the classroom as in the following excerpt from
Lesson 46, a model English lesson for immigrants.

```
father—mother . . . . . . .I have a father and a mother.
sister—brother  . . . . . . .I have a sister and a brother.
relatives  . . . . . . . . . . . .I have other relatives.
babies  . . . . . . . . . . . . . .The Germans have killed many mothers and
                                   babies.
slaughter  . . . . . . . . . . .The Germans have slaughtered many children.
butcher . . . . . . . . . . . . .The Germans have butchered many old men
                                   and women.
fight . . . . . . . . . . . . . . . .I am going to fight the Germans.
protect  . . . . . . . . . . . . .I shall fight them to protect my family.
```

The war hastened the assimilation of German-Americans and of
many of the newer immigrants as well, though often this happened in
spite of the efforts of the Americanization crusaders. The point is
made in the following story that circulated in Washington during the
war years. When a committee of ardent Americanizers paid a call on a
Bohemian tenement family, the woman of the household suggested
they come back later. The visitors demanded indignantly if this meant
the family wanted to put off their entrance into American life. "No,
no!" the Bohemian woman replied hastily. "We're *perfectly* willing to be
Americanized. Why, we never turn *any* of them away. But there's
nobody home but me. The boys volunteered, my man's working on
munitions, and all the rest are out selling Liberty Bonds. I don't want
you to get mad, but *can't* you come back next week?"

Obviously members of ethnic communities were Americanized by
sharing a common patriotic effort with the larger American community. Though exempt from the draft, large numbers of noncitizens
volunteered for the armed forces, and ethnic Americans in general
furnished more than their numerical proportion of soldiers. Many
more worked in war industries and took part in voluntary home front
campaigns. Often ethnic Americans felt no affection for the Empires
which had held their nationalities as unwilling subjects. Wilson's
Fourteen Points, which included as American war aims self-
determination for all subject minorities in central Europe and the
restoration of an independent Poland, were greeted with great
enthusiasm by Slavic-Americans. In some cities the Polish community
bought more Liberty Bonds per capita than any other identifiable
group, though they were by no means the most affluent.

Paradoxically the overwhelming interest in the war displayed by the
ethnic communities hurt rather than helped them in their struggle

against restrictionism. During and after the war ethnic communities lobbied for settlements most advantageous to their homelands. Austrians, Hungarians, and Germans wanted their homelands to retain as many of their former possessions as possible. Bohemians, Lithuanians, Ukrainians, Slovenes, Poles, Syrians, and Lebanese wanted autonomy or independence for their homelands. Jews wanted the end of anti-Semitic oppression in Europe and the establishment of a Jewish state in Palestine. Confident that one of the American war aims, "self-determination for all nations," legitimized their causes, ethnic organizations made increasingly sophisticated use of lobbying and other American political institutions in their support. When the first consulate of the newly restored Poland opened in New York City, crowds of cheering and weeping Polish-Americans surrounded it, blocking traffic in every direction.

Americanization crusaders were appalled. They did not see the activities of ethnic communities in behalf of their homelands as the old American tradition that it was, nor as evidence that the ethnic groups were willing and able to use American political processes. Instead, they saw these activities as evidence of the failure of Americanization, which they had unrealistically defined as the disappearance of all Old World ties. They failed to distinguish between political allegiance, which immigrants now fully gave to the United States, and emotional loyalties, which included the old as well as the new. Convinced that their efforts had been in vain, many of the Americanizers were now receptive to the racist ideas that "the leopard cannot change its spots"—that ethnic communities presented a permanent menace to the national well-being.

The Red Scare

The hand of the restrictionists was strengthened still further by the fact that a vocal minority, American born and foreign born, objected to the war. Old stock American socialists, such as Eugene Debs were imprisoned for their opposition. More conspicuous, but not more numerous, were ethnic pacifists such as the Italian-American poet Arturo Giovannitti and the Russian-Jewish anarchist and feminist Emma Goldman. Accustomed to advocating unpopular causes, Goldman ignored the wartime laws against expression of dissent. "I defy the police, when the lives of millions are at stake," she said.

In the long run Bolshevism rather than pacifism was the most damaging ethnic stereotype. When the Russian Tsar was overthrown in the spring of 1917, Americans were virtually unanimous in their approval. But when the Bolsheviks took over the following fall, ruthlessly carrying out a Marxist program of the abolition of private property, Americans shuddered. American socialists, already divided over the issue of the war, split again over their attitude toward the Russian experiment. This, together with conflicts over leadership and a widespread conservative reaction in the United States in the postwar years, led to mass defections of native born Americans from the ranks of the Socialist Party. In the early 1920's ethnic Americans, for the first time, constituted the majority of the Socialist Party (though the overwhelming majority of ethnic Americans were not socialists). The stereotype of the immigrant as radical took on a new and fearful life.

In the immediate postwar years the changeover to peace time production led to unemployment and temporary economic dislocations. Serious strikes broke out in the steel and textile industries, and in 1919 the Boston police force went on strike, opening the city to looting and violence. A rash of bombings and bomb threats, the work of a handful of criminal, perhaps insane, radicals terrified the nation. All the postwar unrest and violence was laid at the doorstep of Bolshevism, foreign and domestic, and a Red Scare swept across the nation. "Like a prairie fire, the blaze of revolution was sweeping over every institution of law and order," wrote Attorney General A. Mitchell Palmer, " . . . eating its way into the homes of the American workman . . . licking the altars of the churches, leaping into the belfry of the school bell, crawling into the sacred corners of American homes, . . . burning up the foundations of society."

Panicked middle class Americans did not stop to distinguish between trade unionists and philosophical radicals on the one hand and criminal or violently revolutionary elements on the other. All were lumped together as "un-American" and identified with the foreign population. In this atmosphere the notorious "Palmer Raids" took place.

On the orders of the politically ambitious Attorney General Palmer, police burst into homes and meeting places all over the country, loading "suspicious" aliens onto trucks or marching them handcuffed through the streets. On the flimsiest of evidence—possession of radical literature or guilt by association—over three thousand aliens were deported, often leaving their wives and children destitute and ostracized. Only when Palmer attempted to get a peace time law enabling him to punish citizens as well as aliens for their associations and opinions did the public turn against him. In 1924 the *Saturday Evening Post* looked back at the anti-Red hysteria as "nothing but the last symptom of war fever." Meanwhile the nation had been engulfed in a wave of intolerance that blighted the lives of native born and foreign born alike.

The Palmer Raids were not an isolated incident but were part of a pattern of postwar bigotry that affected all racial, religious, and ethnic minorities. Whites rioted against blacks in such cities as Chicago and

Washington. Henry Ford launched a vicious anti-Semitic campaign in the *Dearborn Independent*. The state of Oregon outlawed parochial schools. Two Italian anarchists, Sacco and Vanzetti, were executed for robbery and murder in a trial where their political views weighed as heavily as the evidence.

Racism converged with wartime fears and postwar insecurities to cause the rapid rise of a newly organized Ku Klux Klan. Unlike its Reconstruction predecessor, the new Klan was national in scope and added to its traditional hatred of blacks, newer hatreds of Catholics, Jews, socialists, the foreign born, and any person or group that did not conform to its own narrow definitions of Americanism and Christian morality.

Claiming three million members and many more sympathizers, the new Klan was, among other things, an expression of the distrust Americans born and reared in rural and small town America felt toward the new urban life styles and values of the "roaring twenties." Many Klan members saw the cities as dens of radicalism and sexual immorality, where Jews and Bolsheviks plotted the overthrow of the nation while young girls (perhaps their own daughters) painted their lips, drank bootleg whiskey, and brazenly wore their skirts above their knees. The Klan was eventually ruined by revelations of corruption among its own leaders. For several years, however, it functioned as a perverted continuation of the crusading spirit of the Progressive Era and the Great War, mounting vigilante attacks against alcohol, freer sex morality, "obscene" movies, socialism, atheism, Darwinism, blacks, Jews, Catholics, and similar evils—including immigration.

The National Origins Quota

In this atmosphere the postwar Congress began to work once again on the issue of immigration restriction. During the war the literacy test had finally become law, but as a device to keep out the "undesirables" it was obviously ineffective. Between 1918 and 1921, 1,487,000 immigrants entered the country and only 6,142 were excluded as illiterate. Clearly, the restrictionists concluded, a different type of legislation was needed. Their experts pointed out that immigration was increasing and warned, once again, of the harmful effects of Southern and Eastern Europeans, especially of "abnormally twisted Jews . . . filthy, un-American, and often dangerous in their habits." Equally important, the business interests that had favored immigration as a source of cheap labor no longer did so. The increasing mechanization of business meant that large numbers of unskilled workers were no longer needed, especially if such workers were suspected of radical tendencies.

In 1920 Senator William P. Dillingham introduced a bill to limit annual immigration for each ethnic group to five per cent of the number of foreign born of that group in the 1910 census. The House cut the percentage from five to three per cent, and in 1921 President Harding signed the bill into law. American immigration policy had taken a new course. Exclusionists soon found fault with the 1921 law, however. Though it gave the highest quotas to Britain and Germany, its allotments for Italy, Poland, Greece, and similar "undesirable" areas were too large. A new system would have to be found.

Representative Albert Johnson of Washington, Chairman of the House Committee on Immigration and a long-time advocate of restrictionism, realized that the quotas for Southern and Eastern European countries were sizable because they were computed on the basis of the number of foreign born people from those countries in a year of heavy "new" immigration, 1910. He proposed going back to the census of 1890, when most of the foreign born were still from Western Europe. The House agreed, but reaching back to a thirty year old census to make the figures come out right was too blantantly discriminatory for the Senate. Senator David Reed of Pennsylvania solved the problem. He suggested that the number of immigrants allowed to come in from any given country be tied, not to the number of foreign born persons from that country in the United States in any given year, but to the percentage of that nationality group in the makeup of the entire American population. This system, too, would keep immigration safely western.

In 1924 the Reed proposal was passed, to be put into effect as soon as statisticians computed what the ethnic breakdown of the American population actually was. A committee of "experts" worked for five years trying to determine the ethnic composition of the American population, using census records and immigration statistics. Reliable information for the period before 1790, or indeed, before 1850 was virtually nonexistent. Even after that time records were fragmentary. The quota system ultimately put into effect was based mainly on guesswork.

The final law provided for the admission of a total of 150,000 immigrants annually. Its restrictionist provisions gave Great Britain a quota of 65,721 and Germany 25,957. Southern and Eastern Europe fared less well. Italy had a quota of 5,802, the Soviet Union, 2,784, and Greece only 307. Most Asians were denied entry on the grounds that they could not become naturalized citizens, and African immigration was excluded outright.

The American Jewish Committee, the Knights of Columbus, the National Liberal League, and similar organizations fought the new legislation. Ethnic leaders issued fact sheets to counteract the racist charges of the restrictionists. Cultural pluralists such as Horace Kallen argued that true Americanism lay in the coexistence of many ethnic cultures rather than in their homogenization. Ironically, by the time the legislation was passed its pseudoscientific basis was being undermined. Anthropologist Franz Boas, himself foreign born, demonstrated that such supposedly immutable physical traits as the height and build of immigrants from Eastern Europe had changed after only one generation in the United States. In his classic work *The Mind of Primitive Man*, Boas condemned "the tendency to view one's own civilization as higher than that of the whole rest of mankind." He identified this behavior with that of the primitive person "who considers every stranger as an enemy and who is not satisfied until the enemy is killed." Despite mounting opposition, even within the Congress, the bill was passed, apparently because of the momentum it had been gathering over the years. Ironically, by the time it passed the public had lost interest in immigration restriction. Even the press did not consider the passage of the new bill a major event.

After the National Origin Quota Bill became law, immigration dropped sharply. Western European countries did not fill their quotas, and Southern and Eastern European and Asian nations lacked significant, if any, quotas to fill. Only Western Hemisphere immigration from Canada, Mexico, and other Latin American countries continued. Congress wanted the good will of Latin America, and the ranchers, farmers, and businessmen of the Southwest needed cheap Mexican labor.

The Commissioner of Immigration at Ellis Island was soon able to report that virtually all immigrants now "looked like Americans." Nativism had triumphed. It had triumphed because racism, superpatriotism, and fear of social change had caused many Americans to blame whatever they did not like in American life upon the "aliens." It triumphed also because, for the first time in our history, Americans lacked the confidence that they could successfully assimilate all comers. The era of unrestricted immigration had ended. Massive European and Asian ethnic communities remained, however. With infusions of fresh blood from overseas cut off, what would be their future—if any—in American life?

CHAPTER 11

Continuity and Change:
The Second and Third Generations,
1924-1960

The National Origins Quota Act ushered in a new era, but people disagreed on what the new era would bring. Restrictionists and advocates of the melting pot theory anticipated the rapid disappearance of ethnic communities. With most European immigration ended, they expected foreign enclaves to assimilate, that is, to blend indistinguishably with the rest of the population, perhaps enriching the new "American" nationality with the best of their traits in the process. Cultural pluralists, on the other hand, hoped that a variety of distinctive ethnic cultures would perpetuate themselves. Ethnic leaders shared this hope; surely the institutions they had built with so much sacrifice of time, energy, and money would continue to flourish!

Assimilation vs. ethnic survival, the melting pot vs. cultural pluralism—sociologists, journalists, and community leaders aired their conflicting theories in the literature of the day. But it was the immigrants, their children, and their children's children who would decide. The final verdict is not yet in; but by mid century some things were clear. In many ways the second and third generations had acculturated, that is, they had adopted the language, dress, technology, and general life style of majority America. But they had not assimilated. Recognizable ethnic communities remained and ethnicity continued to play an important role in the lives of millions of individuals. By 1960 it was apparent that neither the advocates of the melting pot nor the cultural pluralists had presented an accurate picture of the future of ethnic America. Scholars began to work toward a new conceptual framework.

Some Things Changed—Language and Life style

"For a man to speak one language rather than another is a ritual act," wrote cultural anthropologist E. R. Leach in 1954. "... to speak the same language as one's neighbors expresses solidarity with these neighbors; to speak a different language from one's neighbors expresses social distance or even hostility." If Leach is correct, the attitude of most second generation ethnics toward Anglo-Saxon society is clear. They wanted to merge with it as soon as they could. The children of the immigrants abandoned their parents' languages with scarcely a backward glance; and their children, the third generation, rarely knew enough of the ancestral tongues even to abandon them.

Immigrants' children sensed very early that English was the only language valued by the world in which they lived. English was the language of the public school (and usually the parochial school as well). English was the language of comic books, movies, radio, and eventually television, the language of the dance hall, the marketplace, and the political arena, the key to getting a good job, winning the right spouse, and becoming a "real" American.

"The trouble is, they don't want to use the Greek language," complained an immigrant father. "If I ask my boys to read me something in Greek, they don't want to do it. If I want (them) to write a letter in Greek to the old country, they don't want to...." Many immigrants shared this father's complaint, as second generation children deliberately rejected the language of their parents. Adolescents "forgot" the language spoken in their homes since babyhood to avoid the embarrassment of being identified as "foreign", and, therefore, inferior. French-Canadian children reported making conscious efforts never to use French outside their own homes, even though it was the language they felt most comfortable with; they did not want to be labeled "ignorant Canucks."

Use of the traditional language survived in isolated pockets and in places where it was economically or socially necessary even to the second generation; in San Francisco's Chinatown, for example. The ethnic language also survived in areas adjacent to the native country, where constant travel could renew it—among Mexican-Americans in the Southwest, and among French-Canadians in New England. The state legislature of Iowa tried to maintain the old German speech of the nineteenth century town of Amana as a tourist attraction! More serious efforts at language maintenance were undertaken by ethnic churches, cultural organizations, and nationalist societies, but they made little headway against the prevailing conviction that English was the only acceptable speech for citizens of the United States. Elementary school teachers continued to erase children's knowledge of their parent's tongues, while university professors complained that American students had no language skills!

The second generation adopted a new life style as well as a new language. Symbolic of Americanization was the changing of many family names; Hershkowitz became Hersh, Bodinski became Boden, Rugero became Rogers. Edmund Sixtus Marciszewski became Ed Muskie.

Equally symbolic was the change in attitude toward money. Remembering the poverty of the old country, the insecurity of the early years in the United States, and the suffering of the Great Depression, the immigrant generation characteristically stressed the importance of saving. "I pay for the food, the coal, the rent, but other things, unless we need them, we don't buy them," said a Polish immigrant who had lived in the United States for many years. Among the immigrant Chinese, a person who spent freely on clothing, appliances, or cars was considered untrustworthy and immoral!

' The children and grandchildren of the immigrants were much less cautious in their attitude toward money. This was partly a reflection of their greater economic security. Also, adopting the spending habits of their fellow Americans, like adopting their language, was a way of establishing solidarity with the majority society. Thus the children of thrifty Slavic and south Italian peasants filled their modest homes with draperies, furniture, and the latest appliances. Foreign born parents who never took a vacation in their working lives watched American born children flock to mountain and seashore resorts or, more recently, go backpacking along wilderness trails. In the prosperous post World War II years, the descendants of Italian, Polish, and Irish immigrants returned to Italy, Poland, and Ireland as tourists.

Less pervasive, but also widespread, was the religious revolution. Many second generation ethnics turned away from the religious practices of their parents. Most Jews gave up the strict observance of the Sabbath and of the dietary laws because they found them inconvenient. A few representatives of every ethnic religion abandoned not only the practices of their parents, but the faith as well—a far more painful break for all concerned.

National as well as religious ties were neglected/by many second generation ethnics. Polish community leaders complained that the young were unmoved by any sense of Polish mission, and Irish old timers lamented the indifference of the young to the Irish heritage and national cause. "Stop calling me Chinese . . . I'm American, "insisted a typical Chinese-American college student of the 1950's. "My father happened to be born in China . . . but he's been here more than thirty years. . . . I have no interest in China."

Undoubtedly many aging immigrants looked at the new life styles of their Americanized children with dismay. "I feel like a chicken that has hatched a duck's egg," observed one. The differences between the first generation and their children should not be exaggerated, however. Immigrants, like their children, were moving toward the majority life style.

Although the rebellion of the young was a favorite theme in ethnic novels and autobiographies, it was neither universal nor irreversible. The religious life of the second and third generation illustrates this point. Second generation Catholics and Jews may have practiced their religion less meticulously than their parents, but they rarely converted to another faith. Their children, the third generation, experienced a widespread return to the traditional religion. Secure in their Americanism, the third generation did not need to avoid the church or synagogue as "foreign" or old-fashioned. During the 1950's, a religious revival swept the country. Church membership rose, especially among the middle class. For ethnics as for other Americans religious observance became a part of suburban conformity. Ethnic parents renewed old affiliations, revived half forgotten rituals, and created new rituals, believing that religion added warmth and color to family life and was "good for the children."

National loyalties were more submerged than religious loyalties, but given the proper circumstances they, too, could reappear. Thus when Germany invaded Poland in 1939 three generations of Polish-Americans huddled around their radios and wept. When Poland fell, a hundred thousand Polish-Americans of all ages marched mournfully through the streets of New York City. Similarly, American Jews of all ages and degrees of acculturation were swept into a new realization of their identity by the horrors of the Nazi slaughter of six million European Jews and by the drama of the reestablishment of a Jewish state, Israel.

Some Things Survived—Family Life, Neighborhoods, Jobs

"Men may change their clothes, their politics, their wives, their religions, their philosophies to a greater or lesser extent; they cannot change their grandfathers," observed Horace Kallen. In outward appearances, and in many of the routines of their daily lives, the children and grandchildren of the immigrants were indistinguishable from other Americans. Yet ethnicity survived as an ongoing set of attitudes and behaviors handed down, consciously and unconsciously, from generation to generation. Many immigrant parents could not pass on their ethnic language, literature, or even their folk songs and religious traditions. What they could and did pass on, however, were values and priorities, ways of expressing (or not expressing) emotion, subtle preferences, and unconscious practices that affected the texture of life in the home, on the job, and in the neighborhood. Ethnic patterns brought from the old country as "cultural baggage" survived in America if they were useful to the younger generations.

Distinctive patterns of family life were among the most lasting aspects of ethnicity. The continued survival of the close-knit Italian family is an excellent example. Second and third generation Italian-Americans, like their immigrant parents, invested an unusual amount of time and emergy in family life, sometimes limiting their social and even their business associations to members of their own extended families. This pattern originated in southern Italy, where life was hard, officials corrupt, and only family members could be trusted. It was reinforced in the United States by the hostility of the outside world toward Italian immigrants. Here, as in the old country, relatives were more reliable than outsiders, uncles hired young men when strangers would not, and aunts gave more reliable advice than social workers.

The Southern Italian pattern of unusually strong reliance on family survived in America because it was economically useful; and because it created a sense of warmth and belonging that was appreciated by both young and old. "I loathed Italian customs with all my heart," said a second generation Italian boy, "but I would never let anything stand between me and my family." When a correspondent complained to an Italian-American newspaper in the 1940's that he had few friends, the editor reminded him that friends were not important as long as he had his family.

Marriage continued to be affected by ethnic background. In many ethnic groups the relationship between the second generation husband and wife was less intense and less egalitarian than in the typical "American" marriage. Italian, Polish, and Greek women for example, were more likely to confide in their mothers, sisters, and women friends than in their husbands, who spent much of their leisure time in the company of other men. Among Greek and Italian Americans in particular the roles of the sexes remained more rigidly separated than in the general population. These women seldom worked outside the home after marriage (unless forced to do so by economic deprivation), took little part in community activities, and rarely challenged the authority of their husbands, at least not in public.

Traditional patterns tended to break down in the third generation in middle class families, which were more likely to adopt the American ideal of romantic love and companionship between husband and wife.

They survived longer, however, in working class families, where they were reinforced by religious traditions and economic realities. The jobs to which poorly educated working class ethnic women had access were so unrewarding, psychologically and financially, that there was little incentive to work outside the home and little opportunity in general to acquire a sense of independence.

Child rearing, like marriage, continued to be influenced by ethnic tradition. In many ethnic families, discipline was stricter than in the average "American" family and the authority of the parents more strongly maintained. "You don't see any joking or arguing in the Greek families as you do in others," remarked a Greek-American in the 1930's. Young people in Chinese and Japanese-American homes were less boisterous and more respectful of their elders than their nonethnic counterparts. In the mid 1950's a much larger proportion of young Japanese-American adults than the general population considered it shameful to send their parents to an old age home.

In Italian families children were expected to conform to the wishes and needs of the adults, while Jewish families were more likely to be "child centered." Adolescent boys in Italian families spent most of their time with their peers, whose influence upon them was very strong; Jewish children remained closer to their parents. Japanese-American mothers breast fed their infants longer than their American counterparts and were more protective of their young children, discouraging them from independent action at as early an age as their non-Japanese counterparts. Scandinavian and Oriental children were taught to control, even to hide their emotions, while Italian and Jewish children were taught to express theirs. Teaching of this kind was unconscious, by example rather than by precept, but effective nonetheless.

Research in comparative child rearing practices of the various ethnic groups has just begun, but it is clear already that significant differences did—and to a lesser degree still do—exist. Undoubtedly these differences contribute to the distinctiveness of adult ethnic communities.

Choices of neighborhoods, friends, and jobs are usually made at a more conscious level than choices about sex roles and the rearing of children. These areas, too, remained greatly influenced by ethnicity in the second and third generations and even beyond. Where people choose to live remains determined in part by their ethnicity. The ethnic map of the United States has changed very little in the past hundred years. The descendants of Scandinavian and German immigrants still cluster in the farms and small towns of the Midwest, and Irish, Polish, Italian, Jewish, and Arabic Americans remain heavily concentrated in the large cities of the Northeast and the Great Lakes states. French-Canadians remain primarily in New England, and Orientals primarily on the West Coast. Thus, despite the mobility of the American population, most ethnic Americans still live in the regions chosen by their immigrant predecessors.

Many ethnic individuals still live in ethnic neighborhoods, clearly identifiable by ethnic lodges, churches, and food stores and by the less visible but immensely important network of family relationships and lifelong friendships. In such neighborhoods, roots are deep and emotional attachments strong. When the residents of Boston's predominantly Italian West End were told that they would have to move because of an urban renewal project, their reaction was bitter. "The place you're born is where you want to die," said one young man. "I wish the world would end tonight. . . . I wish they'd tear the whole damn town down," said another. "I'm going to be lost without the West End. Where the hell can I go? . . . It pulls the heart out of a guy to lose all his friends."

When second or third generation ethnics moved out of their original neighborhoods to the suburbs, they often moved in identifiable groups. Major cities have newer neighborhoods and suburbs in which people of Irish, Italian, Polish, Jewish, and other distinctive backgrounds are heavily concentrated. The ethnic concentration in specific neighborhoods tends to decrease with succeeding generations, but it has not disappeared.

Ethnic neighborhoods have survived, not only because of the restrictive policies of real estate agents and the prejudice of the larger community, but also because many ethnic Americans enjoy living in them. Ethnic women in particular have often found the move to mixed suburbs a difficult one. Kept close to home by the needs of young children, they missed the tightly knit social group of family and friends in the old neighborhood and found it hard to adjust to the quick, and often shallow, friendships of suburbia.

Nostalgia for the city was common to second and third generation men and women of many ethnic groups. Suburban Chinese for example, continue to make regular Sunday pilgrimages to Chinatown because there "one can buy groceries, pick up the mail, visit Third Uncle, drop by the doctor's office, get some good food in the stomach and maybe catch the latest movie from Hong Kong, all in the same vicinity." When Jews moved to the suburbs after World War II, they passed over the more secluded country lanes for areas easily accessible to the cultural and educational facilities they had enjoyed in the city. When their children were grown, Jewish couples often moved back to the city again, though they were more likely to settle in newer apartment buildings than in their old neighborhoods. In many cities a hard core of Italians, Poles, Jews and other ethnics remained in their old neighborhoods as newer ethnics such as blacks, Puerto Ricans,

Mexican-Americans, or immigrants from Appalachia, moved in. Some did not want to move; others could not afford to move.

Ethnicity influenced the choice of jobs as well as neighborhoods. Like all Americans, the children and grandchildren of the immigrants wanted to "better" themselves, which meant a rejection of the occupation of their parents. Second generation women rarely worked as domestic servants, for example, an occupation common among their mothers; they were more likely to become sales clerks, factory operatives, teachers, or nurses.

Still, there was a surprising amount of continuity between the occupations of the first, second, and even the third generations of particular ethnic groups. The sons of German bakers, brewers, and cabinet makers took up similar but more highly skilled trades as upholsterers, metalsmiths, and bookbinders. The sons of unskilled Yugoslavian miners and industrial workers remained employed in these fields, moving up to skilled jobs as operatives, cranemen, and welders. Italians followed their parents into such trades as stone masonry, meat cutting, barbering, construction, and food distribution. Small private businesses continued to be popular among the second and third generation of Greeks, Jews, and Oriental Americans, as they had been among the first.

Some occupations, such as Italian skills in stone cutting, were brought from the old country. Others had been learned in the United States; there had been little heavy industry in the Balkan provinces from which Yugoslavian immigrants came. Sometimes young people chose their parents' occupations because they could be placed in a family business or sponsored for membership in a union dominated by their own ethnic community. The Irish capitalized on their early establishment of political power in the cities by remaining concentrated in civil service and other bureaucratic positions. Their favored profession was law. Individual career choices were undoubtedly influenced by the varying interests and abilities of the immigrant group. A recent study of ethnic school children indicated that Chinese-American children excelled in dealing with spatial relationships, a factor in their frequent choice of careers such as architecture and engineering.

In the third generation the upwardly mobile of every ethinc group began to break traditional occupational patterns. In the 1960's and 1970's the sons and daughters of Polish, Italian, and Irish laborers appeared in sharply increased numbers as scientists, physicians, university professors, and other professionals. For Jews, the move into academia and the professions took place a generation earlier. By the 1960's the children of second generation Jewish school teachers, social workers, and self-employed businessmen and professionals were entering more prestigious (though not necessarily more lucrative) fields, becoming college teachers, research scientists, lawyers in large firms, or entering occupations their parents had never been in, such as advertising and public relations. Since the hardest economic battles had been won by their parents, some members of the third generation could afford to be more concerned with prestige or leisure than with money. "My father's generation may have felt pressure to achieve success, but this generation is lazier," said one. "Sure I want money, but I don't want to work as hard for it as my father did," said another.

Still, prejudice and pragmatism led a surprising number of this successful, prestige and security oriented, third generation back to traditional ethnic occupations. In the mid 1970's Jewish organizations were still protesting the discriminatory practices that shut Jewish business school graduates out of top corporate positions. "Being Jewish doesn't help you when you want to advance as a metallurgist in industry," said a realistic university trained young man "so I gave up my salaried job to take over my father's scrap iron business." Chinese-American historian Betty Lee Sung writes of a young Chinese engineer who used his college training to renovate and mechanize a formerly despised family laundry business. Students and professionally employed Chinese, once eager to escape the family restaurant, found themselves returning there to work on weekends and holidays. "Now that they are no longer exclusively confined to restaurant work, they need no longer disdain it," wrote Sung. "Off hand I can name an architect, a vice president of a finance company, a welder in an aircraft factory, a medical student, and a dental student." Common occupations, like common neighborhoods and common family traditions, formed a social cement, helping to bind the second and third generations to one another and to the world of their parents and grandparents.

The Ethnic Community

The survival of ethnicity in the second and third generations was also encouraged by the continuing institutional life of the ethnic community. Despite increasing participation in the majority community life, most second and third generation ethnic Americans maintained at least some ties with their ethnic communities as well and many had deep commitments to particular institutions within that community. There were several reasons for this. Like the immigrants, they enjoyed the companionship and recognition they received in their own organizations and institutions. Like the immigrants, they had problems that could be understood and handled best by people with backgrounds similar to their own. Finally, like the immigrants, they were not welcomed in many of the activities of the Anglo-Saxon Protestant community.

Ethnic communities, as already described, consisted of a variety of institutions. Those that responded successfully to the changing needs of the second and third generations survived. Those that did not faded into insignificance. Ethnic churches were among the most successful in adjusting to the changes in language and life style that marked their more acculturated younger members. The churches continued the process begun even before 1924 of replacing the traditional language with English and supplementing worship with social and educational activities for all ages.

By midcentury ethnic churches were following their memberships to the suburbs, establishing impressive new buildings with gymnasiums and swimming pools for newly affluent congregations. Suburban churches and synagogues sponsored bowling leagues, chess tournaments, and classes in everything from Bible and ethics to child psychology and scuba diving. In the newer parishes Catholics of varying ethnic groups—German, Italian, Polish, Ukrainian, South Slav—worshipped together. In doing so they adopted a common "American" religious style—that of the Irish Catholics! By midcentury Italian Catholics were intermarrying with Irish Catholics and sending their children to Irish dominated parochial schools. Similarly, Russian Jews and German Jews were mixing in suburban synagogues and intermarrying with increasing frequency.

Changes in religious education reflected the changing needs and interests of the Americanized generations. Few parochial schools continued instruction in the traditional language, history and literature; parents no longer considered it important. In urban parishes the original ethnic children were gradually replaced by blacks and Puerto Ricans for whom the old ethnic curriculum was inappropriate. By midcentury Catholic parochial schools were teaching the ethnic tongues as foreign languages, where they were teaching them at all.

Though parochial schools no longer maintained the old languages, they kept their importance as centers of community loyalty and as repositories of ethnic values. Their tone, their discipline, and their constituency, if not their curriculum, remained distinct from that of the public schools. Though some Catholic intellectuals questioned their necessity, parochial schools were zealously maintained by second and third generation Catholic parents. Indeed, as urban public schools increasingly reflected the social problems of troubled cities, upwardly mobile families, including many blacks, sent their children to Catholic schools for educational rather than religious or even ethnic reasons. Enrollments in Catholic schools began to decline in the 1960's and 1970's because of a rise in cost, not because of a loss in confidence. By the 1970's, new efforts were underway to enlist public aid for parochial schools, many of which were on the edge of financial disaster.

Similarly, Greek, Jewish, and other supplementary, or "afternoon" ethnic schools did not disappear with the immigrant generation that had established them. They not only survived, they thrived, their enrollment even increasing with the emergence of the third generation. Like the Catholic parochial schools, these schools reflected the decline of the traditional language. Many chose to deemphasize language instruction because the parents thought it unnecessary and the children found it "too difficult." Increasingly, these schools taught a varied curriculum of ethnic history, religion, and customs in English. Many afternoon schools still tried to teach the traditional languages, but even their own teachers despaired of success.

In both the parochial schools and the afternoon and weekend schools, the ethnicity of the first generation was irretrievably gone by midcentury. Neither nostalgia, nor good intentions, nor the determination of "survivalist" educators appeared able to bring it back. For third generation children ethnic culture was a school subject to be self-consciously "studied," valued," "appreciated," and "believed in" rather than to be spontaneously experienced and lived.

Responding to this new situation, many ethnic schools tried to teach "identity," by offering courses in traditional ethnic dance, folk arts, music, and ethnic cooking. Another response was to turn from the teaching of religious or folk culture to the teaching of "high" culture, the classical literary and philosophical tradition of the mother country. The old language acquired new prestige, not as the everyday language of parents and grandparents, but as the language of Dante, or Sophocles, or Moliere. Using language skills acquired in ethnic or public schools, some third generation youth pursued the advanced study of the civilization of their ancestral country at an intellectual rather than an emotional level on the university campus. This abstract, intellectualized exploration of ethnic "high" culture indicated how far many members of the college educated third generation had moved from the spontaneous ethnic folkways of their grandparents.

Like the schools, other ethnic organizations changed to meet the needs of changing constitutencies, or gradually disappeared. Social lodges based upon their members' common birthplace in the old country declined both in number and importance. The original members grew old, and their children had no interest in joining. The depression of the 1930's depleted the resources of these lodges and of the mutual benefit societies associated with them, as did the increasingly heavy claims made by an aging membership.

Ethnic labor unions, on the other hand, often survived and enrolled the younger generation who, like their parents, found these organizations valuable aids in assuring adequate income and job security. Some ethnic unions changed over the years from one constituency to another. By 1960, for example, the formerly Jewish and Italian garment unions of New York were heavily Puerto Rican. Settlement houses, missions, and "Y's" also found their clients changing with the neighborhoods. Institutions that were unwilling or unable to make the adjustment necessary to be of service to the new populations did not survive.

Ethnic charities survived and even flourished as they changed to meet the needs of changing clientele. Many became recognized and highly respected components of their city's benevolent establishment. Syrian, Lebanese, and Jewish charity camps opened their doors to the poor of other groups when their own communities, now largely middle class, no longer sent enough needy children to fill them. Successful Y's and settlement houses phased out many of their welfare and "Americanization" activities, replacing them with social and cultural programs for constituencies who were no longer poor or "foreign." By the 1960's agencies such as the Jewish and Catholic Family Services were combating the ills of affluence as well as poverty, including the perplexing problem of drug abuse by the middle class young, and the effects of an increasing divorce rate. Chinese charities established "Golden Age" clubs for the growing number of foreign-born men who faced a lonely old age without relatives to care for them. Indeed, programs for the elderly occupied an increasing proportion of the attention of all ethnic charities.

Even when second and third generation ethnic Americans joined the organizations and institutions of the majority community, such affiliations often had an ethnic component. Many scout troops, for example, were sponsored by churches and synagogues or by public schools in strongly ethnic neighborhoods. Though nonsectarian and nonethnic in theory, such scout troops often functioned as ethnic institutions. Subtly or openly, second and third generation ethnics were frequently discouraged from joining clubs, charities, and other organizations which were in effect white, Anglo-Saxon preserves. In response, second and third generation ethnic Americans created an extensive network of parallel institutions for themselves—professional associations, lodges, resorts, summer camps, and even debutante balls for their daughters.

The most popular and broadly based second generation ethnic organizations were groups such as the Hellenic Progressive Association, the Chinese-American Citizens Alliance and the Japanese-American Citizens League. Like the old fraternal lodges which to some extent they replaced, these newer organizations fulfilled the need for "in-group" social life. Unlike many of the older lodges, however, they held their meetings completely in English, were totally secular, and focused on civic and political issues, especially on the fight against prejudice and discrimination. Still insecure in their Americanism, these second generation organizations were enthusiastic in asserting their devotion to the United States. In 1941, shortly before Pearl Harbor, members of the Japanese-American Citizens League recited the following creed:

> I am proud that I am an American citizen of Japanese ancestry, for my very background makes me appreciate more fully the wonderful advantages of this nation. Although some individuals may discriminate against me, I shall never become bitter. . . . I shall do all in my power to discourage such practices, but I shall do it in the American way . . . through courts of law, by education, by proving myself to be worthy of equal treatment and consideration.

In the 1960's, a more self-confident and militant third generation found much to criticize in what they regarded as the "Uncle Tom" organizations of their parents, organizations such as the Japanese-American Citizens League.

As the use of traditional non-English languages declined, so too did the foreign language press, theater, and literature. Foreign language newspapers decreased in number and in circulation. The number of German papers declined from 300 in 1920 to 60 in 1950, and by midcentury there were no Scandinavian language dailies left. Many of the foreign language papers that survived became increasingly conservative in their content. Catering to an aging clientele, and with few new subscribers, they took no chance of losing the readers they had.

Critics in every decade confidently predicted the imminent demise of the foreign language press. Nevertheless, it not only survived but in the 1950's and 1960's even began to grow again. Nonquota immigrants from Mexico, Puerto Rico, and Cuba revitalized the Spanish press and refugees from Eastern Europe had a similar effect on the Slavic presses. New weeklies, monthlies, and specialized journals were founded by well-educated ethnic refugees before and after World War II. In the 1960's there were eleven newspapers in Chinese alone. Every ethnic group continued to publish English language newspapers and magazines representing its ethnic churches, organizations, and political interests and recording its social and community news.

The foreign language theater declined after 1920, undermined by competition from the radio, movies, and television, as well as by the loss of the native language. The great ethnic theater traditions did not disappear, however. They merged with and enriched mainstream American entertainment. Actors such as Paul Muni and Jacob and Celia Adler of the famous Adler family moved from the Yiddish theater to Broadway, which added Yiddish expressions to its vocabulary and counted second and third generation Jews among its loyal audiences.

With the language barrier gone, theatrical figures of many ethnic backgrounds—Al Jolson, Eddie Cantor, Danny Kaye, Jack Benny, the Marx brothers, Bing Crosby, Gene Kelly, the Barrymores, Frank Sinatra, Perry Como, and Danny Thomas, to name only a few— became familiar to all Americans. Eventually, audiences no longer recognized the ethnicity of the performances they enjoyed—Jack Benny as the "cheap" Jew, or James Cagney as the tough little "fighting Irishman." "I'm a Yankee Doodle Dandy, Born on the Fourth of July," sang the very Irish George M. Cohan. Ethnic entertaining had taken out its citizenship papers.

In like manner, dozens of fine second generation ethnic authors became part of the American literary mainstream. Second generation novelists often wrote about their own ethnic communities. Writers representative of the "new ethnicity" of the 1960's and 1970's stressed the warmth, the vitality, and the emotional security to be found in ethnic life, but the "alienated" second generation writers of earlier decades presented a more negative view. James T. Farrell, for example, author of the controversial *Studs Lonigan* trilogy, described hard working but culturally impoverished Irish-American parents who bequeathed their children only "frustration, labor, and the bottle." Farrell's novels outraged many, not only because of their frankness in dealing with sex and violence, but also because of their unflattering portrayal of the Catholic Church, the family, and the Irish working class way of life. "I don't want to read any more of his books," an Irish-American said of Farrell. "He writes about the people I've spent all my life trying to get away from."

Like Farrell, many second generation intellectuals were alienated from their parent communities, yet not totally accepted by the general American society. Standing with one foot in each of two widely divergent cultures—and comfortable in neither—such people were referred to as "marginal men." Many of these "marginal" men and women became journalists, critics, sociologists, psychologists, historians, and economists. Taking advantage of the doubly rich perspectives of two cultural backgrounds, second generation ethnic intellectuals often became astute observers and commentators on the nature of American society.

Ethnicity and Social Mobility

American myth attributes economic and social success to the ability, or the luck, of the individual. But group identity—ethnicity—played an important role. Despite individual disclaimers, everyone assumes to some degree the status American society has assigned to his or her group. Thus the Italian physician shared the unfavorable status of the Italian gangster, while the lowliest white, Anglo-Saxon Protestant shared the favorable status of the WASP corporate executive. When a group considered "undesirable"—Italians, Jews, blacks, Orientals—moved into a neighborhood, previous residents considered the neighborhood to have gone "down," even though the value of its real estate may actually have risen.

According to another time-honored American myth, all immigrants arrived poor, worked hard, and were successful. While the myth contains elements of truth for some immigrants, it is oversimplified, even untrue, for many more. Between 1910 and 1950 foreign born males improved their economic status at a more rapid rate than the general American work force, but this does not mean that they got rich. Their rate of improvement was high because their starting positions had been so low! In most cases, success was modest. As late as the early 1970's, Polish, other Slavic Americans, Spanish-speaking Americans, and Irish Protestants were still heavily concentrated in low paying, low status occupations. Nor was economic mobility a steady rise when it did come. Gains made in the 1920's were wiped out in the depression of the 1930's. The World War II years were the first period of prosperity for most ethnic Americans. This taste of the "good life" was soon threatened, however, by a series of post war recessions and by an apparently unending inflationary spiral.

Ethnicity had an important impact upon a given individual's material success. Though individuals of every ethnic group achieved prominence in various fields, some ethnic groups were more successful, *as groups*, than others. Their members moved more rapidly and in greater numbers than others into the higher paid and higher status middle and upper middle class occupations, and into the more prestigious neighborhoods and community positions that accompanied these occupations. Using family income, education, and the relative prestige of occupations as criteria, the most successful groups by the mid 1960's were Jews, Orientals (especially Japanese), and Irish Catholics, all of whom were more successful than British Protestants. Germans and Scandinavians have done moderately well and Southern and Eastern Europeans generally less well (although Italians have average family incomes equaling those of British Protestants and appear to be rising rapidly). The least successful groups have been the Spanish-speaking minorities (many of whom are relatively recent arrivals), French-Canadians, and Irish Protestants.

While the newest immigrant groups were usually the poorest in the short run, economic status in the long run was not determined by length of residence in the United States. The Irish and the

French-Canadians arrived a generation or more before the majority of Jews who soon outdistanced them. Nor did language skills seem to matter for long. Jews, who came with no knowledge of English, moved ahead of the English-speaking Irish.

Discrimination and prejudice affected mobility, but the relationship was complex. Two of the most successful groups by midcentury were Jews and Japanese, yet discrimination against these groups was very strong. In the case of Jews, discrimination arose, at least in part, as an attempt to check their upward movement that began in the first and second generations. In the early twentieth century Jews were already enrolling heavily in the city colleges of New York and applying for positions in the more prestigious colleges and graduate schools in numbers greater than their proportion in the population. Anti-Semitic university administrators mouthed platitutes about maintaining "balanced" enrollments, while students complained that Jews were spoiling Harvard for "the native born Anglo Saxon young persons for whom it was really built." According to others, "in harmony with their policy of getting all they can for as little as possible," Jews were winning all the scholarships!

To keep Jews in what others considered "their place," academic institutions adopted quotas to limit the numbers admitted. In 1920, before the adoption of the quota system, about half the students at Cornell University School of Medicine were graduates of the heavily Jewish city colleges of New York. While the quota system was in operation, the number shrank to 1.4%. Nor was education the only area to adopt anti-Semitic policies. Hotels and resorts prided themselves on their "restricted" clientele, and major corporations hired Christians only. Half the advertisements for office help in the *Chicago Tribune* on July 6, 1941 specified "Gentiles only," or, more subtly, asked applicants to "state nationality or religion."

Prejudice and discrimination against Orientals was even more intense than against Jews. Popular literature such as Van Wyck Mason's Captain North stories and Sax Rohmer's tales of Dr. Fu Manchu portrayed all Orientals as vicious, depraved, and fiendishly cruel. In Mississippi, Chinese-American children, like Negro children, were segregated in separate and inferior schools. As for employment opportunities, in 1928 the Stanford University Placement Service reported that "it is almost impossible to place a Chinese or Japanese of either the first or the second generation in any kind of position, engineering, manufacturing, or business."

The most blatant act of discrimination against Orientals was the imprisonment of all Japanese-Americans, including American-born United States citizens, during World War II. Ordered by the military, approved by President Roosevelt, and later upheld by the Supreme

Court, this action was a response to widespread—but totally unfounded—fears of Japanese sabotage on the West Coast and reflected the long-standing anti-Japanese feeling of this area.

With virtually no advance notice, over 100,000 Japanese-American men, women, and children were evacuated from their homes, interned in "relocation centers" (race tracks, fairgrounds, stock exhibition halls), and then imprisoned in permanent camps, usually in the most desolate rural areas of the West and Midwest. Left-wing as well as right-wing commentators on American political life supported the internment of the Japanese. Carey McWilliams, then a member of the advisory board of the left-wing Japanese American Committee for Democracy, considered internment necessary for military and security reasons, and for the safety of the Japanese-Americans. In an article in *Harper's Magazine*, in September of 1942, he defended the policy with unintended irony.

> It would certainly not be accurate to characterize Santa Anita as a 'concentration camp.' To be sure, the camp is surrounded by barbed wire; it is guarded by a small detail of soldiers; searchlights play around the camp and up and down the streets at night; and the residents cannot leave the grounds. Their automobiles are all impounded; two roll calls are taken each day; . . . there is a military censorship on outgoing and incoming mail. . . . At Manzanar Camp, Hikaji Takeuchi, a twenty-two year old Nisei [second generation Japanese American] was shot by a guard, but the incident seems to have been the result of a misunderstanding. . . .

Family life was disrupted, old people and children were disoriented, and farms, shops, household property, and skills were lost. The Federal Reserve Bank estimated the financial losses at $400 million, less than ten per cent of which was ever repaid. By the time even this modest compensation was available, twenty years after the war, many of the original claimants were dead.

Length of residence in the United States, language barriers (or lack of them) and degrees of prejudice and discrimination then are not sufficient to explain why some groups were more successful in moving up the socioeconomic ladder than others. Other ethnic factors, such as educational and geographic background, skills, family and community structure, self image, and value system were important. As has already been discussed, immigrant groups from urban environments, groups who were accustomed to formal schooling and were aware of its value, and groups who were relatively less concerned that public schools would destroy cherished ethnic languages and cultures, were able to use the American public schools more effectively than others. The children of Japanese-Americans, and particularly of Jewish-

Americans, were often among the most highly motivated students, "overachievers" whose determination and hard work brought scholastic success.

As jobs for manual laborers declined in number and opportunities in service industries and professions expanded, "overeducated" Japanese and Jewish youth were able to move from the working class to the middle class. Mobility for Jews increased rapidly after World War II, when the revelation of Nazi atrocities made anti-Semitism less acceptable to American society. Ironically, the polarization of American society in the black-white confrontations of the 1960's helped Oriental Americans, who were able to successfully identify with the majority whites. Ironically, too, the World War II internment of the Japanese-Americans may have increased their mobility in the long run by producing a new generation of community leaders, and by breaking down old occupational and geographic patterns.

Skills as well as education gave some ethnic groups advantages over others. Groups with commercial experience—Lebanese, Armenians, Syrians, Jews, and West Indians, for example—were better able to function in the commercial society of twentieth century America than groups who came primarily with agrarian skills—South Italians, Irish, and Poles. Coming from cultures in which land was the major source of wealth and prestige, members of these ethnic groups often put their savings in a home and garden, or in elaborate church buildings, rather than in capital producing enterprises that paid dividends in future mobility. These culturally determined investment choices were often repeated by the second generation.

Other ethnic characteristics contributed toward socioeconomic mobility in the United States. Poor health and a high injury rate handicapped the Slavs, the Italians, and the Irish. Orientals and Jews appeared to be healthier. The Japanese, for reasons cultural, genetic, or both, were and still are the healthiest group in the United States, living on the average six or seven years longer than Caucasians. Certainly the fact that more breadwinners survived to assist their children into adulthood made upward mobility easier for these groups. Similarly, the fact that Protestant, Oriental, and especially Jewish immigrant groups limited their family size sharply as early as the second generation, while most Catholic groups did not do so until a generation later, enabled them to give each child a better economic start.

Ethnic family and community structures had an economic impact on comparative mobility. Strong families and tightly structured communities helped to increase economic mobility. While all immigrant families suffered some dislocations with immigration, Oriental, Jewish, and Italian families held together exceptionally well. Desertion and alcoholism, great handicaps to economic mobility, even survival, were relatively rare among these groups. Oriental children were brought up in a manner that encouraged close dependency upon family and community. Japanese children were taught that their misbehavior brought shame to their relatives and their entire ethnic group, while good performance reflected credit upon family and group. Family and group pride and community support for individual achievement served as powerful motivating factors.

Reflecting two thousand years of minority status, Jews often brought up their children to be unusually sensitive to the opinion of others about their behavior and their achievements. Jewish parents, like Japanese parents, were unusually protective. While the possessiveness of the Jewish mother has become an unpleasant cliché, her affectionate but manipulative behavior toward her children, especially her sons, contributed to their mobility. By keeping her children emotionally dependent upon her approval rather than upon the approval of peer groups, she was often successful in keeping them off the streets, in school, and thus on a track for socioeconomic advancement.

Of course every ethnic group had its "Jewish mothers"—and fathers—strong parents who dominated, protected, and directed their offspring and by doing so helped them escape the urban slums. John Pastore, the first Italian-American governor of Rhode Island, was such a child, and historian Samuel Lubell discovered that many of the more successful of Pastore's childhood acquaintances had similar upbringings.

> Those who have proven most successful—the doctors, lawyers, dentists, and the like—were all subject to the strictest discipline as children. To set them apart from the "tough" boys, the parents overdressed them to the point of having many considered sissies. As for the boy who had been the toughest kid on the block—he was now an iceman.

Obviously, "tough" kids did not always become icemen. Many school dropouts found very effective avenues to social mobility in the world of business. For some, the way to success was through illegitimate business, such as gambling, and bootlegging—the "rackets"—which American society generously patronized. In the 1920's and 1930's, ethnic bootleggers were aided by members of their own communities who considered Prohibition ridiculous and whose loyalties were with their friends and relatives rather than with the police.

Legitimate enterprises, too, found their own communities invaluable sources of support. One could—and still can—become financially successful by serving as shopkeeper, contractor, undertaker, doctor, or lawyer for the members of one's ethnic community. As sociologist Andrew Greeley pointed out,

> . . . in the large cities there are networks of intragroup client-professional relationships. The Italian doctor sees an Italian lawyer when he wants legal advice, both of them have their expensive suburban homes built by an Italian contractor, and all of them vote for an Italian political leader. . . . Thus an exchange of goods and services goes on within the religio-ethnic collectivity which may well have a multiplier effect in contributing to the economic well-being of this community as a whole.

The more tightly knit, or as critical outsiders saw it, the more "clannish" an ethnic community was, the more effectively this multiplier factor worked.

Unfortunately, however, business people and professionals serving their own communities usually had less prestige than those serving the total population. It was unusual for a businessman who attained wealth and prominence within his own community to be accorded comparable respect in the business world at large. Similarly, it was difficult for a professional person to move from a high position in an ethnic university, hospital, or other ethnic institution to a position of comparable status in a predominantly Anglo-Saxon institution.

Finally, socioeconomic mobility was influenced by the internal value systems of particular ethnic groups. Some groups brought with them, or quickly acquired, the so-called Protestant work ethic as they concentrated on moving up in American society. Other groups continued to place greater emphasis on noneconomic values such as family, leisure, friendship, and hospitality. For many first and second generation South Italians, for example, work was a means of survival; life's major satisfactions lay elsewhere. Among groups such as French Canadians and Mexican-Americans, individuals who advanced into the middle class sometimes did so at the risk of disapproval or, worse yet, isolation from their family and their community. To some extent these attitudes were a response to the realities of life—upward mobility was so illusive in the Mexican-American barrio that one avoided frustration by not pursuing it. On the other hand, these attitudes could also represent a conscious cultural choice, a rejection of the "rat race" and the materialism it represents, as well as an understanding that upward mobility often comes at a price. What Daniel Moynihan said of the Irish in *Beyond the Melting Pot* could apply equally well to members of other ethnic communities:

> Turning lower middle class is a painful process for a group such as the Irish who, as stevedores and truck drivers, made such a grand thing out of Saturday night. Most prize fighters and a good many saloon fighters

die in the gutter—but they have moments of glory unknown to accountants. Most Irish laborers died penniless, but they had been rich one night a week much of their lives, whereas their white collar children never know a moment of financial peace, much less affluence. A good deal of color goes out of life when a group begins to rise. A good deal of resentment enters.

The economic rise of ethnic Americans, whether it took place in one generation, two, or more, was not without its cost. Old-timers of every group complained that the children "nowadays" were spoiled by too many playthings and that the casual, noisy good times and human fellowship that once graced people's lives were gone. Still, as an elderly Jewish correspondent commented to the editor of the *Forward*, the people who longed for the "good old days" conveniently forgot the cold, the hunger, the sixteen hours of daily drudgery and all the other hardships of poverty in romantic nostalgia for their youth. There was no returning to the "good old days," and given the choice, few would really want to go back.

Ethnic America at Midcentury

European and Oriental ethnicity, then, did not disappear with the National Origins Quota Act. It survived in the private life of the individual and in the public life of the community. At midcentury millions of people, indistinguishable from the majority American society in all outward appearances, were living at least some parts of their lives in their own ethnic subcultures, separate from but parallel to the culture of the Anglo-Saxon majority. Ethnic subcultures of the second and third generations were not transplanted versions of overseas civilizations. They were "made in the U.S.A." by native born citizens who shared life styles, values, and interests based both on their common Old World heritage and their common New World experience.

People sharing an ethnic culture and community often shared common economic and political interests as well. Ethnic America never voted as a political bloc; it was neither sufficiently well organized nor sufficiently homogenous. On the other hand, common traditions from the Old World and common interests in the new gave particular ethnic communities distinctive political personalities. On some issues there were distinctive, even predictable, ethnic political positions. Legislation involving public school teachers in New York City evoked a Jewish political response because so many of the teachers were Jewish. Legislation involving the New York City police force, for the same reason, evoked an Irish response. Virtually every ethnic community had group responses to foreign policy issues involving their country of origin.

Sometimes a group of issues combined to evoke a broad ethnic response. During the presidential election of 1928, most Southern and Eastern European ethnics lived in northeastern urban centers, were Roman Catholics, and were opposed to Prohibition. Hence they voted *en masse* for the Democratic candidate, Al Smith, a Roman Catholic "wet" from the Lower East Side of New York City. Prohibition and Anglo-Saxon Protestantism, in the person of the "all-American" Herbert Hoover, defeated them.

Politicians of all parties tried to attract twentieth century ethnic voters as they had been doing since the days of Benjamin Franklin. But it was Franklin Roosevelt, president of the nation for four consecutive terms beginning in 1933, who cemented a long-term alliance between the Democratic party and ethnic America. Roosevelt's economic programs projected concern for the "little people," ethnics, blacks, and workers. His willingness to provide jobs and immediate relief during the depression, his support of the unionization of industrial workers, and his backing of measures such as Social Security won him the lasting gratitude of the largely working class ethnic population. Roosevelt's Democratic coalition, including the vast majority of the ethnic communities, ruled the country, with the exception of the Eisenhower years, from 1933 to 1968. The climax of that period for many ethnic Americans was the election of one of their own, Irish Catholic John F. Kennedy, to the highest office in the land in 1960. "Will you vote for Kennedy because he is a Catholic?" a campaign volunteer asked a working man in Buffalo, New York. "No," he replied. "Because I am."

Because ethnic Americans within each community had so much in common—jobs, neighborhoods, institutions, values, even political opinions, the second and, to a somewhat lesser extent even the third, generations continued to choose their friends and their spouses from within what sociologist Milton Gordon called their own "ethclass," people of their own ethnic group and social class. Among Orientals and South Italians, much socializing remained within the extended family and the immediate neighborhood. About eighty per cent of a sample of third generation Jews stated that their four closest friends were also Jewish. "I have no desire to avoid Gentiles, but I don't meet them." explained one.

The immigrant generation had been vehement in its disapproval of marriage outside the group. "He's better off dead," they said, or "She's no daughter of mine." While protesting against their parents' attitudes, the second generation usually conformed. Despite the shortage of Chinese women, three quarters of Chinese-American marriages from 1924 to 1935 were between members of the Chinese community. The intermarriage rate among second generation French-Canadians of Woonsocket, Rhode Island was only 8.8%. Young Japanese-Americans boldly asserted their right to choose their own marriage partners as they saw fit. In practice, however, they often used a mutual friend as a "go-between" to be sure that the prospective marriage, usually to another Japanese, was acceptable to their families.

The prevailing pattern of "in-group" marriages began to break down in the third generation. While only 8.8% of their parents had married outside the group, 35% of the third generation French-Canadians in the Woonsocket sample were doing so. Studies showed the Jewish intermarriage rate of the late 1960's was a third, or even higher. Ethnic leaders were almost unanimous in their alarm at this new trend. Yet if the "outsider" was successfully acculturated into the group, the group was strengthened, at least numerically, by the intermarriage. Long-term studies of the children and grandchildren of such marriages will be necessary before any conclusions can be drawn about their ultimate effect upon the survival of ethnic communities.

Ethnicity was not, of course, the only factor affecting the lives of the descendants of the European and Asian immigrants. Ethnic Americans were influenced by the variables affecting all Americans— geographic regionalism had a great impact. A Jewish family living for three generations in Savannah, Georgia, for example, acquired a southern life style that set them apart from the "Yankee" Jewish family of Brooklyn, New York. Similarly, the South Italian community of San Francisco developed differently than the South Italian community of Jersey City.

Social class, like geography, cut across ethnic lines, affecting the choices ethnic Americans made and how they lived. The experiences of the children of the wealthy Joe Kennedy, Ambassador to England, were hardly the same as those of the children of the Irish policeman from south Boston. Within each ethnic community individuals associated mainly with those of their own social class.

As acculturation increased, ethnic individuals found they had much in common with members of their own social class in other ethnic groups and in the majority Anglo-Saxon community. Undoubtedly this was one reason for the increase in ethnic intermarriage. Sociologist Will Herberg, writing about ethnic America in the 1950's, felt that religious cleavages were becoming more important than class lines or even traditional ethnic boundaries. According to Herberg, all of American society was moving toward organization into three supra-ethnic religious communities, Protestant, Catholic, and Jewish.

By the 1960's experts were going beyond the earlier melting pot vs. cultural pluralism dualism. They were beginning to describe ethnic communities as evolving cultural and religious units, as social networks, and as political and economic interest groups. Ethnic communities remained distinct from the majority society, yet in constant and increasing interaction with that society. The acculturation—and in some cases even the complete assimilation—of individuals gradually increased. Yet ethnicity, recognized or unrecognized, remained an important factor in the lives of both individuals and groups. Its importance was enhanced by the two developments that will be discussed in the next two chapters—first, the immigration that continued throughout the twentieth century despite the National Origins Quota Act and, second, the rise of the "New Ethnicity."

CHAPTER 12

Still They Come:
Immigration After 1924

If the National Origins Quota Act of 1924 hoped to save America from further alien ethnic incursions, it did not achieve its goal. While the children and grandchildren of the controversial European and Asian immigrants were growing up, an even newer immigration was on its way. Since 1924 hundreds of thousands of "nonquota" immigrants have arrived. The majority have come from Mexico and the Caribbean Islands, areas excluded from the provisions of the restrictive laws of 1924. A significant minority were Europeans and Asians admitted by special acts of Congress as refugees from political upheavals and wars. Three and a quarter million of these refugees entered the country between 1945 and 1963 alone.

In 1965 the National Origins Quota Act was replaced with a new immigration law. Under this new law, over 400,000 persons from all over the world have entered the country annually in the last ten years. According to Leslie Aldridge Westoff, in the *New York Times Magazine* (September 16, 1973), an equal number of illegal immigrants have been discovered each year by the Immigration and Naturalization Service. "And this is only the tip of the iceberg," suggests Westoff. The United States has not lost its magnetic attraction for the peoples of the world.

Legally and illegally, people continue to come. Like their predecessors, immigrants who arrived after 1924 were looking for a better life and, like their predecessors, they found both problems and opportunities. This chapter will describe the major ethnic groups who arrived after 1924—Mexican-Americans, Puerto Ricans, other

Caribbean groups, and the various refugee immigrants. It will also describe the abandonment of the national origins quotas in 1965 and the adoption of a new immigration policy.

Mexican-Americans—One of the Oldest and Newest Ethnic Communities

Rodolfo "Corky" Gonzales was born in Denver, Colorado in 1928. The son of migrant laborers, he put himself through high school by working in a slaughterhouse, won the featherweight national boxing championship, and then retired from the world of sports to help his people, the Mexican-Americans. His poem "Joachim" suggests the experience of this old, yet new immigrant group:

JOACHIM

I am still here!
I have endured in the rugged mountains of our country
I have survived in the toil and slavery of the fields
  I have existed
In the barrios of the city
In the suburbs of bigotry
In the mines of social snobbery
In the prisons of dejection
In the muck of exploitation
  and
In the fierce heat of racial hatred.

Mexican-Americans are the largest "foreign language" ethnic community in the United States, a minority group second in number only to blacks. One out of every three persons in New Mexico, one out of every six in Arizona and Texas, and one of every ten in California is a Mexican-American. More numerous and more clearly defined as an ethnic culture than most other immigrant communities today, Mexican-Americans are also the poorest, the least well educated, and the least socially mobile.

Long-established communities of Mexicans became part of the United States in 1848, against their will, with the annexation of Texas and the Southwest as a result of the Mexican-American War. They were joined by a trickle of Mexican immigrants throughout the nineteenth century. This immigration increased after 1910, as Mexicans fled the political turmoil of revolution and counterrevolution. The abolition of debt peonage made it easier for the peasants to leave, and the attraction of the more prosperous and more stable United States to the north was great.

As the twentieth century opened, a growing labor shortage in the

Southwestern United States stimulated the immigration of increasing numbers of Mexicans. The Reclamation Act of 1902 encouraged American farmers in the Southwest to replace the sparse population of sheepherders and cattlemen with agricultural laborers. Farmers were eager to hire low-paid Mexican agricultural workers. The need for Mexican labor was further intensified by the labor shortage created by World War I and by subsequent industrial expansion in the Southwest. Political pressure from this labor hungry region forced Congress to exempt Western Hemisphere immigrants from the provisions of the National Origins Quota legislation of 1924. Mexican immigration increased steadily. Between 1910 and 1930 one out of every eight Mexicans moved to the United States, "a hemorrhage from the Mexican nation."

Some of these immigrants found their way to cities such as Chicago and Detroit, where they worked side by side with East European immigrants and shared a parallel acculturation into American life. Most, however, remained in the rural Southwest, working as unskilled laborers, domestic servants, gardeners, and especially farm workers. Some settled permanently in small farming communities, known as "Mextowns"; others followed the crops, migrating with the seasons from planting to harvest. Families worked long hours in the fields to earn enough to survive the winter months until planting began again.

Migrant farm workers had no homes but the shacks erected for them by their employers and were often obliged to work without sanitary facilities or pure drinking water. The pace of life, the piecework systems, the callousness of foremen and employment agents, and the dehumanizing nature of the work itself created situations similar to those suffered by the European sweatshop worker decades earlier. In a short story, "The Plum Picker", Mexican-American Raymond Barrio describes the feelings of a fruit picker, Manuel, about his work, his life, and himself:

> It was the total immersion, the endless, ceaseless total use of all his energies and spirit and mind and being that tore him apart within. He didn't know what else he was good for or could do with his life. But there had to be something else. He had to be something more than a miserable plucking animal. Pluck, pluck, pluck. Feed, feed, feed, Glug, glug, glug. . . .
> Piecework. Fill the bucket, fill another, and still another. . . .
> The competition was not between pickers and growers.
> It was between pickers. . . .
> Between the poor and the hungry, the desperate and the hunted, the slave and the slave, slob against slob, the depraved and himself. You were your own terrible boss. That was the cleverest part of the whole thing. . . .
> You didn't even stop to take a drink, let alone a piss, for fear you'd get fined, fired. . . .

No matter which way he turned, he was trapped in an endless maze of apricot trees, as though forever, neat rows of them, neatly planted, row after row, just like the blackest bars on the jails of hell. . . .

Authorities discouraged Mexican immigration when jobs were scarce, resorting in times of stress to mass deportations. Mexican-Americans suffered greatly during the depression years of the 1930's. Faced with the prospect of paying relief funds to unemployed "greasers" when Anglo-Americans were also in need, authorities rounded up and deported at least a half million Mexican-Americans, many of whom were not aliens but American citizens. Families were divided, possessions lost. "They pushed most of my family into one van," remembers Jorge Acevedo. "We drove all day. The driver wouldn't stop for bathroom nor food nor water. Everybody knew by now we had been deported. Nobody knew why, but there was a lot of hatred and anger. . . . We had always known that we were hated. Now we had proof." In a similar operation in 1954, directed this time at illegal immigrants, 2.9 million Mexican-Americans were deported. Again, many local authorities paid little attention to the victims' citizenship or to the legality of their original entry into the country.

On the other hand, when cheap labor was needed, American authorities encouraged legal and illegal immigration from Mexico. The labor shortage of World War II and of the postwar boom years of economic development in the Southwest created a great demand for Mexican-American workers. In August 1942, the Mexican and United States governments instituted the "bracero" program which lasted, with the exception of a brief break in 1948, until December 1964. The Mexican word "bracero," from the Spanish *brazo* (arm), is a rough equivalent for the English "hired hand." The bracero program brought Mexicans to the United States under special immigration and contractual arrangements for temporary, seasonal employment. In addition to attracting many immigrants, both legal and illegal, the program brought millions of would-be participants to Mexican border towns where they created a formidable poverty problem for the Mexican government. The availability of a large pool of braceros and would-be braceros helped to keep wages low for Mexican-Americans already in the United States on a permanent basis.

In the 1950's and 1960's new industries, housing developments, shopping centers, and motels were springing up throughout the southwestern states. In these "boom" times, Mexican-Americans who would formerly have been farm workers found themselves changing tires at a Sears garage or sheets at a Holiday Inn, assembling automobiles at a Ford plant, or clerking at a J.C. Penney store. By 1960 over eighty per cent of the Mexican-American population was urban, whereas over half had been rural only a generation before. By 1970 the urban population was closer to ninety per cent and one third of all Mexican-Americans lived in Los Angeles, San Antonio, San Francisco, and El Paso. The attraction of the city can be summarized in one eloquent statistic; city dwellers had a per capita income double that of rural dwellers.

Every city in the Southwest has its Mexican-American quarter, or barrio. Some barrios were the original Spanish-speaking settlements around which the Anglo-Saxon city later grew. These barrios remained "downtown," in dilapidated inner city neighborhoods. Other barrios were originally rural farming or mining communities. Now they are located on the fringes of the Anglo-American city which has grown out to meet them. Where Mexican-Americans make up the majority of the population—in northern New Mexico, for example, or in the border towns of Texas—the barrio may be identical with the city.

Whatever their origin, today's barrios have certain things in common—substandard housing, littered streets, high unemployment rates, and frustrated residents. "When I came here, I wanted something better for my kids," said Ignacio Gonzales, a roofer's helper and relatively new resident of a Los Angeles barrio named, ironically "Maravilla," or Paradise. "But I don't know what to do. . . . Maybe we'll always live here. Who knows? It costs money to live like a gabacho (white-Anglo)."

Despite a small class of wealthy landowners, and a small, but growing group of white collar workers and professionals, most Mexican-Americans are poor. According to the University of California at Los Angeles Mexican-American Study Project, almost two thirds of rural Mexican-Americans live in poverty, as do one third of their urban counterparts. More than 1,700,000 Mexican-Americans live in substandard housing. In California they have an average per capita yearly income of $1380, which is $57 less than the black population and $700 less than the white population. Women, who head many barrio families, earn about half as much as men.

Nor does the situation appear greatly improved by time and acculturation. Whereas second generation European immigrants earned more than their parents and a mature third generation even more than the second, no such income progression is evident among Mexican-Americans. Exceptional individuals can and do advance their positions, but the statistical median income, according to the United States Census, remains about the same. Poverty is handed down from parents to children. The pathology of slum life—crime, gangs, prostitution, drugs, broken homes—infects every generation in the barrio.

The bitter side of barrio life was illustrated by the testimony of a nineteen year old Mexican-American girl at a recent national conference on poverty. The girl told how she had taken an overdose of sleeping pills at the age of thirteen because she was "tired of working and depressed." She was married at fifteen, her husband was sent to jail, and she was left to support their child alone:

> I got a car; the car broke down. I couldn't pay for it and they wanted to sue me, so I forged a check. . . . I started working the town. I got paid for it—they call it hustling—I needed the money . . . to go out and hustle, I had to be under the influence of narcotics.

A few weeks after the conference, the girl was dead of an overdose of narcotics.

The poverty and social problems of many Mexican-Americans have been rooted in at least three interrelated causes—prejudice on the part of Anglo-Americans, lack of education on the part of Mexican-Americans, and cultural differences between Mexican-American communities and the Anglo-American world in which they live and work. Most basic is the problem of prejudice. In the nineteenth century Mexican-Americans were considered inferior because they were a conquered people, dark-skinned, Catholic, and associated with a traditional American enemy, Spain. The twentieth century added new dimensions to this negative picture. American literature portrayed Mexicans as sly, cunning, and untrustworthy. Or, alternatively, as lazy, dozing in the sun and putting off worthwhile effort until "manana". As recently as 1970 a popular comic strip showed a fat, good-natured but sleepy Pancho, a sombrero over his space helmet, complaining to Flash Gordon that the space trip to Pluto was "Too short! Pancho never even slept!"

The darker-skinned Mexican-Americans have found themselves struggling against prejudices involving color as well as nationality and religion. California sociologist T. W. Parsons interviewed a group of Mexican-American teenagers in Castroville, California on this subject:

> The teenage boys said 'there wasn't much use of finishing high school if you are dark . . . you couldn't get a good job anyway.' Mexican girls who recently graduated from high school reported they had many difficulties in finding secretarial or clerical jobs. . . . They said that girls who looked 'almost white' got jobs first but that some of the Mexican-looking girls never did find the kind of employment they sought and finally had to go to work in the 'sheds' (local food packing companies).

After the removal of the Japanese-Americans to prison camps, Mexican-Americans became the scapegoats of a tense society during World War II. In a mass murder trial in California in January of 1943, seventeen Mexican-American youths were convicted and one served time in San Quentin prison before the District Court of Appeals dismissed the decision for lack of evidence. In the "Zoot Suit Riots" of June 1943, mobs of Anglo-American servicemen roamed the streets of Los Angeles assaulting young Mexican-Americans and blacks (who had taken to wearing the new "zoot suit" fashion). Civil and military authorities stood by for three days before intervening.

Professors as well as police showed the widespread prejudice against Mexican-Americans. "They are apparently of low mental caliber," wrote biologist L. L. Burlingame of Stanford University in 1940. In such an atmosphere of prejudice Mexican-Americans are often the last hired and the first fired. While working, they are subjected to discriminatory and degrading treatment, and they frequently receive "Mexican promotions"—more work, but no more money.

Educational disabilities have increased the difficulties of Mexican-Americans trying to succeed in Anglo-American society. According to an article by Philip Ortego in the *Center Magazine* (December 1970), Mexican-American children in the Southwest averaged only seven years of schooling (black children averaged nine, and Anglo children more than twelve). According to the National Advisory Committee on Mexican Education, "four out of five . . . fall two grades behind their Anglo classmates by the time they reach the fifth grade." In 1970, Mexican-American children were classified as retarded two and a half times as often as other children (on the basis of IQ tests geared to middle class, English-speaking children). In California, where Mexican-American students made up more than 14% of the public school enrollment, they constituted less than half of one per cent of the students at the University of California. Almost half the Mexican-Americans in Texas were functional illiterates.

Language problems were partially to blame for these shocking statistics. Spanish-speaking Mexican-American children were expected to learn English as a new language while mastering the regular first grade curriculum of reading and writing in English! In addition, many were handicapped by their family's poverty and by the cultural differences between home and school. Children of migrant workers usually did not stay in school in any one place long enough to learn.

While the goal of teaching English to Spanish-speaking children was certainly a valid one, the means used by many teachers to accomplish this did more educational harm than good. Young children were ridiculed, even punished, for using Spanish, the only language in which they could comfortably express themselves. The Anglo-American school scorned their mother tongue and belittled their cultural heritage. To succeed in such schools, children had to reject the things their families and communities held dear. Children who chose this course, who acceded to the demands and values of the Anglo-American school, still found themselves regarded as outsiders. Teachers ridiculed their Spanish accent, while peers shunned them as disloyal.

In the late 1960's school authorities began to experiment with bilingual and bicultural educational programs, hoping to improve the school experience of Mexican-American children, but progress was very slow. The dropout rate among Mexican-American children remained very high. Many Mexican-American children rejected the American school system because they felt it had rejected them. Stereotyped as stupid by teachers, they were shunted off into classes for the retarded or "tracked" into industrial education rather than college preparatory courses. One mother reported that a teacher actively discouraged her son from planning to be an engineer, suggesting that he take up carpentry instead because "he could start right away earning money." A California elementary school teacher made a practice of having "Johnny" lead five Mexican-American students in an orderly file out of the classroom. "His father owns one of the big farms in the area," she explained, "and one day he will have to know how to handle the Mexicans."

The problems of Mexican-Americans reflected not only the prejudice of teachers, employers, and other authorities, but also the cultural differences between the two communities. Recent studies indicated that Mexican-Americans have high aspirations, but that they often lack the knowledge of Anglo-American society to translate those aspirations into realities. Some sociologists have identified cultural patterns which they feel hinder Mexican-American upward mobility—large families, authoritarian rearing of children, a fatalistic acceptance of what life brings, and a dislike for aggressive, achievement oriented behavior.

Other scholars have pointed out that fatalism and similar traits are not characteristic of Mexican-American culture as such, but rather of all poverty cultures. The behavior patterns and values of middle class Mexican-Americans are close to those of their Anglo counterparts. The confusion about what is Mexican-American culture and what is "poverty" culture has created problems for contemporary Chicano (Mexican-American) leaders as well as for scholars. Some have warned their youth that in glorifying the life style of the barrio as being truly "Chicano" they are ignoring the rich heritage of upper class Mexican and Spanish culture. These leaders fear a false dichotomy will force young Mexican-Americans to choose between their Mexican ethnic identity on the one hand and social and economic mobility on the other.

Mexican-Americans in the Southwest have been able to preserve their distinctive language and life style (including ethnic preferences in music, food, family life, and recreation) longer than most other immigrant communities. Because some of their ancestors preceded the Anglo-Americans in settling the Southwest, many Mexican-Americans feel themselves a native rather than an immigrant population. Thus their motivation to become acculturated is less strong than that of European immigrants. Second, their relatively large numbers and high concentrations in the sparsely populated Southwest has helped them to preserve their own culture, as has the hostile attitude of the Anglo-American population. Finally, their proximity to the Mexican homeland, the constant flow of new immigrants, and the back and forth travel of residents of both nations have greatly strengthened Mexican-American ethnic identity.

Like all ethnic communities, however, Mexican-Americans have felt the pressures of change and have responded to those pressures. The younger generation have more formal education than their parents, are more likely to speak English, and are moving away from the unskilled jobs of their parents to higher status (if not higher paid) white collar positions. Social and occupational contacts between them and Anglo-Americans have resulted in an increasing rate of intermarriage.

Significant acculturation has taken place in family life. Like their European counterparts, Mexican peasants lived in closely knit villages in which the nuclear family received physical and emotional support from a network of relatives and friends. The first generation in the United States left this supportive network behind, as did their European counterparts. They suffered less from this, however, than comparable European groups, because as migrant workers they were able to maintain a strongly unified nuclear family. Husband, wife, and children traveled together and worked the fields together. At the end of the day, or week, or season, the husband collected and distributed the money earned by the entire family. The family stayed together, the children were closely supervised, and the authority of the father was maintained.

The urbanization of the Mexican-American family after World War II produced a radical alteration in these patterns. In the city the family no longer worked as a unit. Husband and wife were usually employed in separate factories and, according to writer and educator Ernesto Galarza, "the kids are out of sight and out of hand." Mechanization increased employment opportunities for women in low-paid factory work, while decreasing opportunities for men. According to Galarza, the result was disastrous for the traditional Mexican-American male. "The Mexican man today represents the bulk of the unemployment. He is no longer an economic or a moral factor in his family. Sometimes his kids can earn more pushing dope for an evening than he can in a month." Forty years ago young people addressed their fathers with respect as "el jefe" (the chief). Barrio youth today may refer to their fathers in deprecatory terms, such as "el viejo" (the old man).

In the traditional rural family, both in Mexico and the United States, women accepted a role of obedience, subservience, and sexual fidelity to their husbands, who protected and supported them. Men, on the other hand, were not supposed to assume any household responsibilities, but were expected to prove their virility by sexual exploits outside the marriage relationship. Recent studies of the better educated, English speaking third generation women show that they have adopted the dominant Anglo view of marriage as a more nearly egalitarian relationship. They expect their husband to assume some responsibility for home and children and consider sexual satisfaction within the marriage and not outside it as the ideal for both husband and wife.

Women have been increasingly active in the Mexican-American protest movements of the 1950's and 1960's, campaigning for school improvements and the unionization of farm and industrial workers. "These Mexican young women are taking very great advantage of their new opportunities," comments Galarza, "and they will not let any committee—whether it's to organize a confrontation or burn down a barn or talk back to the dean—they want to be there. This is a change and I think it's a change for the better. . . ."

A change has been taking place in the institutional as well as the family life of the Mexican-American. In rural Mexico there had been little role for the independent, voluntary associations so common in the United States. Whatever needs could not be met by the village community itself were referred to the Mexican government. Most Mexican immigrants, then, brought minimal organizational experience with them to the United States. Many were migrant workers who were rarely in one place long enough to establish the self-help institutions common to European immigrant groups. As a United States Government report of 1951 rather poetically put it,

> They pass through community after community, but they neither claim the community as home nor does the community claim them. . . . The migratory workers engage in a common occupation but their cohesion is scarcely greater than that of pebbles on the seashore. Each harvest collects and regroups them. They live under a common condition, but create no techniques for meeting common problems.

The Mexican-American community has not been completely destitute of organization, however. Nineteenth century New Mexico developed religious associations such as Our Lady of Light, the Poor Souls, and the secret religious order, Los Hermanos Penitentes. In the early twentieth century there were also small mutual aid and burial societies comparable to those developed by the early European immigrant communities. Unlike many European immigrant groups, however, Mexican-Americans did not convert these early societies into large-scale formal organizations. They preferred small, informal associations based upon family and kinship groups and held together by personal loyalties rather than by bureaucratic structures.

Between 1910 and 1941 the more acculturated middle class Mexican-Americans began to adopt the organizational style characteristic of second generation European and Asian ethnic Americans. In 1929 several local groups united to form the League of United Latin American Citizens, or LULAC. Similar in program to JACL (Japanese American Citizens League) and other second generation ethnic organizations, LULAC encouraged its members to conform to Anglo-American values, trained immigrants for citizenship, and defended as best it could the rights and the image of Mexican-Americans. Women's clubs such as the Pan American Round Table and the Good Neighbor Clubs shared LULAC's general aims of encouraging accommodation to the Anglo world.

Among working class Mexican-Americans short-lived local organizations sprang up to protest bad economic conditions. Field workers, pecan shellers, coal miners, and sheepherders organized local protests and strikes. The leaders often had more charisma than organizational ability, however, and the determined opposition of local authorities was hard to overcome. In the 1920's and early 1930's the American Federation of Labor tried to organize Mexican-American workers, but the unemployment of the depression years nullified their efforts.

After World War II, Mexican-American organizations began to move in new directions. A new generation began to question the goals of their parents. Young Mexican-Americans believed that accommodation with the Anglo world was neither possible nor desirable if it must be paid for with feelings of self-hate and neglect of one's own distinctive heritage. The new generation pursued their rights as Mexican-Americans more aggressively than had their parents. Under the leadership of Dr. Hector Garcia, veterans of World War II organized units throughout the Southwest. When a Mexican-American war hero, Félix Longoria, was denied burial in a Corpus Christi military cemetery, Dr. Garcia's veterans organizations took up the case. Longoria was eventually buried in Arlington National Cemetery. Ignacio Lopez, editor of a bilingual paper in California, organized the Unity Leagues. Unity League agitation resulted in the ending of school segregation for Mexican-American children in California in 1946 and in Texas in 1948.

By the end of the 1950's three new organizations represented the increasing political awareness of the community—MAPA (Mexican American Political Association) in California, PASO (Political Association of Spanish Speaking Organizations) in Texas, and ACCPE (American Coordinating Council on Political Education) in Arizona. The groups differed in matters of tactics—MAPA wanted only Mexican-American support, while PASO favored alliances with black civil rights groups, labor unions, and sympathetic Anglos. All agreed, however, on the importance of encouraging Mexican-Americans to register and to vote their own leaders into office.

Within the next few years candidates endorsed by MAPA and PASO were elected in California and in Texas. "After decades of political disenfranchisement and intimidation," wrote historian Ellwyn Stoddard, "at last there was evidence that a united Mexican American voting bloc could be victorious." Meanwhile, Cesar Chavez was beginning his activities among the farm workers of California. The Mexican American community was standing upon the threshhold of what Stoddard called "the period of ethnic autonomy and radicalism."

Other Nonquota Immigrants

Mexican-Americans constituted the largest group of nonquota immigrants, but they were by no means the only ones. A sprinkling of Spanish-speaking immigrants also arrived from South and Central America, from countries where extreme poverty was a powerful motivating push. A young immigrant from Guatemala recalls, "I remember that we only ate green bananas . . . green bananas, that's how poor our countries are . . . three out of five children die before they're five years old, back home. . . ."

Equally poor were the Filipino immigrants who entered free of any quota because the Philippine Islands were an American territory until 1946. Now that Chinese and Japanese immigration was forbidden, Filipinos joined Mexican-Americans to make up the agricultural and domestic servant supply of California. Like the Chinese and Japanese before them, the Filipinos who came were young, male—and enormously unpopular. Western Congressmen advocated independence for the Islands so that their population could be kept out of the United States!

Seeking better economic opportunities for themselves and their children, more than a hundred thousand immigrants from the Caribbean Islands entered the United States in each of the first three decades of the century. Until the post World War II period most were blacks from the British and French West Indies, Jamaica, Haiti, and Cuba. They settled in the Northeast, primarily in New York City, where they pursued a variety of occupations. Women utilized their needlecraft skills in the garment industry of New York. Highly trained cigar makers from Cuba and Jamaica practiced their craft in their new home. So many of these immigrants acquired professional training, either before immigrating to the United States or after their arrival, that by the 1930's a very high percentage of New York's black doctors, dentists, and lawyers were West Indians. Also, a high percentage of the city's black businessmen were West Indians, many of whom got their start through credit or loans extended to them by self-help societies within the West Indian community.

Salable skills, prior knowledge of English, and the ability to use community resources mitigated the rigors of economic adjustment for the most fortunate of the black immigrants, but social adjustment was difficult for all. West Indians had moved from islands where, as blacks, they constituted the majority of the population to a nation where they became identified with a historically despised minority. While darker color was often associated with lower social class in their homelands, West Indians were unprepared for the rigid and all encompassing color discrimination they encountered in the United States. Separated from American whites by an impenetrable color line, they were separated from American born blacks by significant cultural differences. Better educated and more self-confident than most American born blacks in the decades before World War II, their life styles had been influenced by the British and French traditions of their home islands. They were more likely to be Episcopalians or Catholics, than Baptists or Methodists, like most American born blacks, and their manners were more formal, their values more middle class. "Looking down upon American Negroes for their alleged ignorance and supineness," states immigration historian Maldwyn Jones, "the newcomers were cordially disliked in return for their supposed aloofness and aggressiveness."

One significant point of contact between American born blacks and West Indian immigrants was the career of Marcus Garvey. Born and educated in Jamaica, Garvey came to the United States in 1916. Struck by the deteriorated position of blacks in the United States and, indeed, all over the world (most of Africa was still under European control), Garvey asked himself: "Where is the Black man's government? Where is his King and kingdom? Where is his President, his country, and his ambassador, his army, his navy, his men of big affairs? I could not find them, and then I declared, I will help to make them."

Garvey founded the Universal Negro Improvement Association, which numbered its followers in the millions, and a variety of other black institutions, including a church, a newspaper, and a steamship line. He aroused the enthusiasm of millions of American born blacks, especially those of the lower socioeconomic strata, with his gospel of racial pride and black Zionism. "We are the descendants of a people determined to suffer no longer," he told an audience of 25,000, including delegates from Africa and Latin America. "We shall organize the 4,000,000,000 Negroes of the world into a vast organization to plant the banner of freedom on the great continent of Africa." While the post World War I Ku Klux Klan began its rapid rise, Garvey was among the first to proclaim that black was beautiful. His ideas aroused hostility among whites and among more conventional black leaders. In a proceeding that was political as well as judicial, Garvey was imprisoned for mail fraud and eventually deported.

The Puerto Ricans

Immigration from many islands in the French and British West Indies continued, but after 1945 the largest number of newcomers came from Puerto Rico. Like the Philippines, Puerto Rico had been an American territory since 1898, so its people could move freely between the island and the continental United States. American administration of the island aggravated the problems of poverty and overpopulation that led to immigration. One reason for poverty was the fact that the island's resources were controlled by absentee owners on the mainland. Public health improvements instituted by United States authorities cut the island's death rate, but not its birth rate, so a rapid population rise added to the poverty problem. Not even the American educational structure was an unmitigated blessing. The American government's vacillating policy as to whether to educate Puerto Ricans in English or in Spanish resulted in their being poorly educated in both.

In 1910 there were only about five hundred Puerto Ricans living in New York City; by 1940 there were 70,000. The great migration took place after 1945, however. In the early 1970's there were about a million and a half Puerto Ricans on the American mainland. Though still heavily concentrated in New York City, they also comprised sizable communities in New Jersey, Pennsylvania, Illinois, California, Ohio, and New England.

Under a new policy of self-government, Puerto Rico in the 1950's instituted "Operation Bootstrap," a massive attempt to solve the economic problems of the island through industrialization and education. The program was so successful that family income in Puerto Rico tripled in twenty years. Despite improving economic conditions on the island, Puerto Ricans continued to immigrate to the mainland. Improvement in Puerto Rico stimulated many to seek still further improvement in the United States. As early as 1948 over 85% of those who immigrated had been employed on the island. They did not come seeking *any* job; they came seeking a *better* job. They also came to join relatives already here and to enjoy the excitement they had heard was part of everyday life in New York City.

The earliest Puerto Rican immigrants were usually single males, farm workers who served as contract laborers in New Jersey and other agricultural areas. After 1945, however, immigrants usually came as family units and settled in New York and other urban centers. They took service jobs in hotels, restaurants, and laundries or became workers in urban industries such as steel, plastics, food processing, jewelry, and electronics. As Jews and Italians moved out of the garment industry, New York City's largest industry, Puerto Ricans took their places. According to a recent Harvard University study of the metropolitan region, Puerto Rican immigration has provided a supply of inexpensive labor that was instrumental in keeping this and other industries from leaving the city.

"Tidal Wave of Puerto Ricans Swamping the City," screamed a New York newspaper headline in 1946, when the net annual Puerto Rican immigration was only 40,000 people. As the last of the series of immigrant groups to enter New York City, the Puerto Ricans have aroused the same hatreds, fears, and suspicions as the Irish, Italians, Jews, and blacks who preceded them. Newspapers, even social workers, overestimated their numbers. Differences in language, skin coloring, and clothing gave Puerto Ricans high visibility and made them a natural target. Clarence Senior, author of a book friendly to Puerto Rican immigrants, received the following letter, quoted here with the original spelling and punctuation intact:

> So you are one of those—that are bring these monkey faced animals into this country. I consider a Puerto Rican lower than a pig. Those dirty black faced diseased dogs they are a menace to a decent people. I pray with all my might a violent death overtakes you. I am going to do everything in my power to fight them everybody I have spoken to hates there sight. Those knife carrying—. They loused up every neighborhood in New York.

The stereotypes of Puerto Ricans as neighborhood wreckers, criminals, and charges on the public purse evoke echoes of similar judgments about the ethnic groups that preceded them, and contain the same mixture of half truths and misconceptions. Puerto Ricans were undoubtedly associated with neighborhood decay. They had inherited the old brownstones and tenements that had housed Europeans and blacks before them and were now in a hopeless state of disrepair. Puerto Ricans were not surprised when the New York Health Commissioner announced that New York City had as many rats as it had people. Over half of the 565 people who reported rat bites in 1958 had Spanish surnames.

Nor were these rat infested quarters cheap. In 1960, according to

Senior, "the slum tenants on the west side of New York City, for instance, pay an average of $2.10 per square foot for their hovels while the inhabitants of the well-maintained elevator apartments within a block or two of Central Park West average $1.02." High rents and low salaries guaranteed that Puerto Ricans, like earlier immigrants, had to crowd many people into small spaces, resulting in still further deterioration of already poor housing.

Crime has risen rapidly throughout the United States in the past few decades and Puerto Ricans, like other "disadvantaged" citizens, have been part of this rise. Contrary to popular perceptions, their percentage of the crime rate in the 1950's, a time of heavy immigration, was only slightly above their percentage in the population. As in the case of earlier ethnic communities, delinquency is more often a problem among children born or reared on the mainland than among those born and reared in Puerto Rico. In recent years juvenile gangs have also become a problem in Puerto Rico. Puerto Ricans there blame them on the bad influence of young people returning from New York City!

More serious than crime (although crime is increasing among Puerto Ricans as among the rest of the American population) is the problem of drug addiction. Between 1964 and 1968, when Puerto Ricans constituted fifteen per cent of the population of New York, they accounted for almost a quarter of the heroin addicts. While Puerto Rican parents generally have the impression that the authorities could stop the drug traffic if they wanted to, the problem is not so simple. Puerto Rican youth turn to drugs to escape unpleasant life situations and because of powerful peer group pressures. "I used to see my friends doing it," reported a twelve year old Puerto Rican heroin addict, "and I didn't want to be left out. I started sniffing heroin, then skin-popping, and then mainlining." The youth supported his habit by stealing "anything I could find."

As late as the mid 1960's Puerto Rican adults had relatively little connection with organized crime, "the rackets," either because they were not interested or, more likely, because the tightly organized ethnic groups already in control would not let competitors in. As Dan Wakefield observed in his book on Puerto Ricans in New York, *Island in the City:*

> One of the few distinctions so far between the Puerto Ricans and the early immigrant groups to New York City is that the Puerto Ricans have developed no criminal gangs of adults as the Irish, Jews, and Italians did. This is perhaps a happy fact for the social workers but may in the long run be a sad one for the progress of the Puerto Ricans. Many old-time observers in the city believe this lack of an adult underworld is one of the reasons why Puerto Ricans have not yet achieved much power in politics.

Puerto Ricans arrived in New York in large numbers at about the same time—or shortly after—as the large influx of blacks from the rural South. Because many Puerto Ricans were more accustomed to urban life than rural blacks and because most Puerto Ricans were considered "white," a distinct advantage in American society, there was reason to believe that they would move ahead faster then the blacks and become adjusted to the city more rapidly. After surveying the census data of 1950, demographer Donald Bogue commented that " . . . Puerto Ricans may become assimilated as fast as the Italians, the Polish, and the Czechs have, and much faster than the Negroes and Mexicans." Reverend David Barry, director of a social agency long active in work with immigrants, said in 1957:

> No previous immigrant group so quickly numbered among its members so many policemen and welfare workers, teachers and social workers, office workers and independent businessmen, and eventually doctors and lawyers—after barely a dozen years in New York.

Indeed, in the 1950's there were many signs of Puerto Rican success. Puerto Rican bar, medical, and teacher associations attested to the growing numbers of Puerto Rican professionals. A Philadelphia report commented on the "entrepreneurial superiority" of Puerto Ricans, and by the mid 1960's there were an estimated seven thousand Puerto Rican owned stores, barber shops, and restaurants, including almost four thousand *bodegas*, Puerto Rican groceries. By 1960 second generation Puerto Ricans were earning considerably larger incomes than the immigrant generation, and the 1960's saw a doubling of the number of Puerto Ricans living in the suburbs.

This prosperity and upward mobility was limited, however, to an educated minority; the majority did not share in it. In New York City the community as a whole did not improve its position as rapidly during the 1960's as observers had anticpated. In fact, relative to the black population, the situation of Puerto Ricans deteriorated. In 1970 Puerto Ricans were educationally and occupationally the poorest segment of the New York City population, with a median income considerably below that of other New York groups, black and white. In 1960 Puerto Ricans constituted 18% of the families living under the poverty level; by 1968 they constituted almost 40%. In that year it was estimated that about one third of the Puerto Rican population of New York City was receiving welfare under the Aid to Families with Dependent Children program.

Many factors contributed to this unfortunate situation. Though the Puerto Rican government tried to help prospective immigrants learn English, language presented many difficulties. About half of the Puerto Rican children entering school for the first time in the continental United States knew little English. Like Mexican-American children, they found their school experience so frustrating that many became early dropouts. Adults and children who knew a little English sometimes hesitated to use it. Coming from a culture with a strong emphasis upon "dignidad" (dignity), they preferred not speaking English at all to speaking it badly. Meanwhile, school officials argued the relative merits of various approaches—total immersion in English, the teaching of English as a second language, or the continued use of both Spanish and English in a bilingual and, perhaps, a genuinely bicultural education. This debate resembled that over the education of Spanish-speaking, Mexican-American children in the West.

Other cultural factors presented special difficulties for Puerto Ricans. Hurrying, for example, was seen as loss of dignity in Puerto Rican culture; yet hurrying was necessary for survival in New York City! Puerto Rican culture stressed personal relationships. Puerto Ricans were accustomed to dealing with school, government, and other authorities on an individualized person-to-person basis. They found it difficult to deal with the formal bureaucracies of cities on the mainland and saw even the best officials as "cold" and "uncaring." American attitudes on skin color have also caused difficulties. Ranging from very light to very dark, Puerto Ricans have paid less attention to color than to other kinds of social distinctions. In the United States, however, dark Puerto Ricans found it expedient to speak Spanish very loudly to separate themselves from American blacks—and some light skinned Puerto Ricans have become suddenly embarassed about the presence of blacks within their community.

Family life in the United States presented new problems for Puerto Ricans as for previous immigrants. A traditional love of children combined with nonuse of contraception meant a relatively large number of dependents for each breadwinner in the family—a handicap to a group seeking upward mobility. The highly protective system of childrearing practiced in Puerto Rico caused difficulties, too. On the island, "good" girls were carefully watched, indeed, reared largely inside the home until they escaped into early marriage. On the mainland, Puerto Rican girls often demanded freedom which their parents considered it unwise and immoral to give them. The boys were given more freedom, but after a few days on the streets of New York they often behaved in ways that their parents found puzzling and unacceptable.

In Puerto Rico consensual unions—couples living together on a long-term basis without a formal marriage—were common, especially among the poor, and the children they produced were not stigmatized. In the United States such unions were considered immoral and their children illegitimate. When such unions, or indeed, any marriages, broke up on the island, a network of relatives—sisters, cousins, "aunties," and godparents—were available to care for the children. In the United States this network might not be on hand.

Puerto Rican immigrants had problems in the job market as well as in the home. Those who came to the United States were, on the whole, better educated than those who remained on the island, but a sixth grade level Spanish education was of little value in New York City's job market. Moreover, automation had eaten away at the supply of low skilled jobs, the "pick and shovel" jobs that had been available to the unskilled of earlier immigrant groups. Unemployment was not uncommon.

There was more organized help available to Puerto Ricans than to earlier immigrant groups, but this could be a mixed blessing. Welfare regulations helped to undermine the already weakened family; women and children were given money only if there was no man present in the household. With public relief available, there was less necessity to establish the network of self-help institutions that proved so important to the earlier ethnic communities. Open housing legislation and subsidized housing projects were helpful, but, like the welfare system, they also had negative effects. By scattering Puerto Ricans throughout the city, they hindered the establishment of the geographic concentrations that had given earlier ethnic communities internal cohesion and political "clout." The most recent immigrants to the city, Puerto Ricans have had difficulty competing with blacks and other larger, better organized, and more firmly entrenched ethnic communities for money, services, jobs, and perhaps most critical, for political representation. Although the Civil Rights Act of 1965 eliminated the English language literacy test for voter registration, Puerto Rican registration has remained low. As late as 1970 there were no elected Puerto Rican officials in the New York City government and only four in the state government.

One reason Puerto Ricans have had difficulties in building a cohesive community is that many of their institutions were inherited rather than created from scratch. Unlike many earlier immigrant groups, Puerto Ricans usually did not have to build their own churches, or unions, or press. About 85% Roman Catholic, they usually moved into pre-existing parishes led by the clergy of other ethnic backgrounds. Similarly, their unions had often been founded by, and continued to be led by, Italians, Jews, and Irish. The era of the mass media had arrived, making it less necessary for this newest ethnic community to create its own culture and entertainment. American magazines were available in Spanish, thirty movie houses in New York City showed the latest films from all over Latin America, and direct contact with the culture of Puerto Rico was only a brief airplane trip away.

The Puerto Rican community has, nonetheless, begun to establish powerful institutions of its own. Two older Spanish newspapers recently merged to create *El Diario de Nueva York*, a popular paper which reflects many of the interests of the community. Aside from the professional groups already mentioned, there have long been athletic leagues, cultural societies, and clubs in which immigrants from particular towns in Puerto Rico get together for socializing and mutual help, similar to the clubs established by earlier European and Asian immigrant groups.

As in the Mexican-American communities new organizations have arisen in recent years, organizations intended to meet the needs of the wider community. The Puerto Rican Forum was established in the mid 1950's as a community wide service organization. From it came Aspira, founded in 1961, to identify and motivate promising Puerto Rican young people, to direct them toward higher education, and to instill pride in their heritage as Puerto Ricans. Also from the Forum came the Puerto Rican Community Development Project, which aimed at promoting ethnic identity, social stability, and political strength within the Puerto Rican community. This organization assumed the role of visible representative of Puerto Ricans in New York City, involving itself in job training, tutoring, fighting drug addiction, and establishing neighborhood youth corps and block organizations. Another relatively recent organization is the Puerto Rican Family Institute. Using the Puerto Rican tradition of personalized rather than institutionalized relationships, the Institute matches newly arrived families with well-established "helper" families in their own neighborhoods.

Puerto Rican adjustments to America were hindered by changes in the mid twentieth century city itself—the relative shortage of unskilled jobs, and the difficulty of breaking into already well-established political and economic institutions. On the other hand, a wider variety of government programs and services existed to help the newcomers who remained optimistic, seeing themselves as following the upwardly mobile path of earlier immigrant groups. This was the first airborne community, an ethnic group that could fly to its homeland in a few hours. The effect this will have on the survival of the Puerto Rican culture remains to be seen. Meanwhile Puerto Ricans, like Mexican-Americans, entered the 1970's with a heightened sense of ethnic identity and a growing number of community leaders and community institutions.

The Refugees

The millions of immigrants from the Western Hemisphere who poured into the country after the passing of the National Origins Quota Act were joined by smaller numbers from the more familiar immigrant areas of Europe and Asia. During the 1930's, the United

States took in about a quarter of a million refugees from the Nazi regime. Between 1945 and 1959 the number rose to three quarters of a million, including war brides, "displaced persons," and refugees from communist countries, such as Cuba and Hungary. While most of these people were fleeing political upheavals, a few were the victims of natural disasters, Portuguese refugees from earthquakes in the Azores, for example. Most of the refugees were nonquota immigrants, admitted by special acts of Congress. During these same years, however, two and a half million immigrants entered under regular quota procedures. Nor has the flow of refugees stopped. In 1975 over one hundred thousand South Vietnamese refugees were admitted to the United States.

The first large group of refugees were the people fleeing Nazi regimes in the 1930's and early 1940's. Heavily, though not completely, Jewish, this group included distinguished men and women who made immense contributions to the intellectual and cultural life of the nation—Albert Einstein, Enrico Fermi, Paul Tillich, Bela Bartok, Marc Chagall, Sigrid Undset, and others.

Less distinguished would-be immigrants, people with no credentials but their desperation to escape impending genocide, found American hospitality during the 1930's very limited. Efforts to overturn the quota system and save more fugitives from Nazism failed. Public opinion reinforced the view already held by most Congressmen that a nation in the throes of economic depression could not afford to offer sanctuary to people who might compete with the native born for jobs. An ugly current of anti-Semitism also played its role in the United States government's refusal to pass emergency legislation opening our doors to more of the Jewish refugees who sought admittance.

In 1939 a bill was introduced into Congress to admit 20,000 German-Jewish refugee children under the age of fourteen outside of the regular quota structure. Within a day after the plan was announced thousands of families of all religions offered to adopt the children, and the Quakers offered to supervise the resettlement procedures. Congressmen raised a host of objections ranging from the scarcity of jobs (for children under fourteen!) to the "iniquity" of separating the children from their doomed parents. Secretary of State Cordell Hull complained to the Congressional committee that admitting the children would not only set a bad precedent, but would also necessitate "increased personnel . . . as well as additional office space." The bill was not passed. Presumably these twenty thousand children took their places among the six million exterminated in Hitler's "final solution" to the Jewish problem.

The post World War II period ushered in a more humanitarian, less racist approach to immigration policy. The depression was over, jobs were available, and the revelation of Nazi genocide made it increasingly unacceptable to label whole categories of people "undesirable." In the new atmosphere, special legislation began to erode the older racist immigration policies. During the war Congress established an immigration quota for the Chinese, who were our allies; and shortly after the war a similar quota was established for Japan. The quotas were minuscule, a hundred immigrants a year from each country; but for the first time in many decades it was possible for Orientals to enter the country legally.

Additional special legislation admitted war brides and "displaced persons" in the immediate postwar years—though this legislation, too, was formed to favor immigrants from Western rather than from Eastern Europe. Additional acts of Congress opened the doors to anti-Communist refugees fleeing Fidel Castro's Cuba and the unsuccessful anti-Communist revolution in Hungary in 1956. It can be argued that the American response even to these popular refugees was niggardly in proportion to the magnitude of our resources. For every one hundred thousand of its own population, the United States admitted only 22 Hungarian refugees, while Israel admitted 111, and Canada admitted 214.

Twentieth century immigrants had tales to tell as harrowing as those of immigrants of the past. Families walked hundreds of miles through woods and over mountains, hiding in fields and cellars, eating wild animals and roots to escape capture by the Nazis. Refugees left Cuba in small boats, making their way across open seas to Florida. A young Hungarian officer told how he escaped from a communist hospital, where he was being treated for wounds received in the 1956 uprising:

> We knew the doctor . . . and trusted him. As the [Communists] watched . . . the doctor gave us each an injection which put us to sleep. He then ordered our bodies sent to the morgue. At the morgue we were revived and placed in private homes on the outskirts of Budapest.

Too weak to walk, the officer was carried across the Raba River to safety in weather so severe that his clothing froze on his body.

The Vietnamese refugees of 1975 were unique insofar as the American government assumed the responsibility of transporting them to their new home. Nevertheless, for many the journey was not an easy one. In the confusion of the rapid collapse of the South Vietnamese regime, families were separated and some individuals who were fleeing the battlefields found themselves unexpectedly on planes or ships bound for the United States. Between fifteen and twenty-five thousand refugees spent four days without drinking water in ninety degree heat on barges awaiting transfer to American ships. According to an eyewitness, the deck of one of the barges was strewn with the abandoned possessions of the refugees and at least seventy-five dead bodies, mostly of women, children, and babies.

Once in the United States, refugees faced additional problems. During the depression of the 1930's, even the most skilled found it difficult to find employment. Hans Morgenthau, a well-known political scientist, worked as an elevator "boy". His wife was forced to stay home from her job clerking at Macy's department store because she was covered with bedbug bites. Jewish immigrants in the 1930's were plagued by anti-Semitism as well as by economic problems. An adviser to the State Department was convinced that the new Jewish immigrants "are never to become moderate, decent American citizens." The National Patriotic Council opposed the admission of Albert Einstein as a "German Bolshevik," whose theory of relativity was "of no scientific value or purpose, not understandable because there was nothing there to understand." Nor did the racist reaction to refugees end in the 1930's. In 1975 high school children in Florida talked of starting a "Gook Klux Klan" to oppose the settlement in their area of refugees from South Vietnam. Economic considerations as well as racial prejudice dictated that Vietnamese refugees be dispersed rather than be allowed to form geographically concentrated communities. It was felt that they would not become an employment or a welfare burden on any single state.

On the other hand, many people all over the country welcomed and helped the various waves of refugee immigrants. Religious and civic organizations "adopted" individuals and families, supplying them with everything from food, clothing, and toys to job offers. Public interest in the newcomers was usually genuine and well meaning, but there was also exploitation. A woman offered to present dolls to Hungarian refugee children if the *New York Times* would publish a picture of the presentation. The Eisenhower Administration actually hired a public relations firm to "sell" the Hungarian refugees to the American people, like laundry detergent or breakfast cereal! The advertising campaign was successful. The refugees were soon in such demand that someone cynically paraphrased the old saying, "brother, can you spare a Hungarian."

Special categories of ethnic newcomers had special kinds of problems. War brides from abroad had many adjustments to make when they rejoined their husbands, now out of uniform, after months or even years of separation. Sometimes reality did not live up to the glowing picture the soldier had painted of his civilian job and home town. Husbands, as well as wives, could be disappointed; girls who had seemed desirable in Germany or Japan might seem less so in New York or Kansas. Women who had been submissive and deferential in Europe and Asia sometimes became "Americanized" too quickly to suit their husbands!

Similar problems plagued elderly Chinese-American men who took advantage of new immigration regulations to import young Chinese brides from Hong Kong. Young women from postwar Hong Kong were quite different from their husbands' idealized memories of the traditional Chinese women of their youth. Historian Betty Lee Sung tells the story, far from unique, of a young Hong Kong bride who gave her startled Chinatown husband a most untraditional ultimatum: "Move out of this dilapidated apartment by Tuesday, or I get a divorce!"

New laws enabled Chinese born sons to join elderly Chinese-American fathers and this, too, created problems. Brought up in China, these young men were often disappointed in their father's economic situation in the United States. Lacking skills and unable to speak English, the Chinese youths often found themselves jobless and rejected by both the American born Chinese and the Caucasian communities. Juvenile delinquency, formerly rare, made its appearance in San Francisco's Chinatown, as did divorce and a suicide rate four times that of the rest of the city.

Some refugees made a quick and relatively painless adjustment to American life. Many of those who fled the Nazis and the Communists were well-educated middle class or upper middle class people, often with professional training. Such people had little trouble overcoming the language barrier. Their main problems were the regulations of American professional societies, regulations that required them to repeat years of training or pass special examinations before taking up their professions in their new homes.

Most of the German, Hungarian, and Cuban refugees were soon self-supporting and, indeed, made important contributions to their adopted country. The economic adjustment of the Vietnamese refugees appears to be more of a problem, at least in the short run, even though the majority of the Vietnamese refugees are better educated than most of their countrymen. Unlike the anti-Communist Hungarians and Cubans, who had been hailed as heroes, the South Vietnamese are an embarrassing reminder of a politically divisive and militarily frustrating American war. To complicate their situation further, the Vietnamese refugees lack the economic and psychological support of an older established Vietnamese community. Arriving during a serious economic recession, they were practically pushed out of government supported refugee camps into jobs that are often low paid and menial, regardless of their previous education or employment experience.

Results of Twentieth Century Immigration

Post 1924 immigration established the Spanish-speaking community as the nation's largest foreign language group. Moreover, as the growing Mexican-American, Puerto Rican, and Cuban communities remained close, psychologically and geographically, to their homelands and seemed determined to preserve their own language, they presented a new kind of challenge to American ethnicity. For the first time, the United States was forced to consider the impact of an institutionalized, relatively permanent, non-English-speaking subculture—the Spanish.

The new challenge was reflected in a new school situation. In the past, American public schools had taught immigrant languages as foreign languages; the school curriculum as a whole was in English. If parents wanted educational equality for a non-English language, they had to set up their own schools, as many of the Slavic immigrant communities had done. By the 1960's, however, public school systems began to experiment with bilingual education for Spanish-speaking children.

Bilingual teachers had been hired in New York as early as the 1950's with the hope that they could facilitate the children's acquisition of English and help them adjust more quickly to the demands of the public school. Even when they learned English, Puerto Rican and Mexican-American children fell behind other children in school achievement. Some attributed this learning gap to social class differences. If this was the case then "compensatory education," giving lower class Hispanic children in the schools the advantages middle class children had at home, appeared to be the answer. Another interpretation was that Puerto Rican and Mexican-American children were not "disadvantaged" or deprived, but were culturally different. According to this theory, their education should not concentrate upon making up supposed deficiencies, but should emphasize the strengths within the child's background and build upon creative elements in the distinctive Puerto Rican and Mexican heritages. If the latter theory is adopted, bilingual education will not be a temporary tool to help the child adjust to the majority culture. Rather, bilingual education will be a permanent feature of the education of Puerto Rican and Mexican-American children. Whether the majority American society can accept the latter idea—and indeed, whether Puerto Ricans and Mexican-Americans will choose this course—remains to be seen.

Post 1924 immigration has had still other effects. For the first time in American history, midcentury immigration has been predominantly female. This large influx of women has helped to balance and thus "normalize" life in the formerly predominantly male Asian communities. Politically, the immigration of refugees from communist countries has contributed to anti-Soviet and anti-Communist feeling in the United States. Refugees from East Germany, Hungary, Cuba, and Taiwan have continued to agitate the "captive nations" issue, though they have had little actual influence on foreign policy. An impressive number of professionals and other talented individuals among the refugee groups and, indeed, among all post 1924 immigrants, has enriched the nation's cultural, scientific, and educational life. Immigrant intellectuals also have brought new vitality to older American ethnic communities, stimulating the continued use of ethnic languages, and sparking a revival of ethnic newspapers, theaters, schools, and cultural and nationalist associations.

Finally, the admission of refugees, displaced persons, and war brides under special legislative acts, as well as the admission of millions of nonquota immigrants from Latin America, gradually eroded the impact of the National Origins Quota Act of 1924. By midcentury it was clear that the Act was not achieving its original purpose—the limitation of immigration to persons from the British Isles and from Northern and Western Europe.

Increasingly, this very purpose was called into question. After World War II neither the scientific nor the political community could comfortably defend notions of the superiority and inferiority of races and nationalities. In the 1950's and early 1960's, the Cold War helped to kill the National Origins quota system. With the United States competing with the Soviet Union and the Peoples Republic of China for the good will of the "third world," the uncommitted African and Asian nations, discriminatory immigration policies, like racially segregated schools, were not only morally wrong but politically embarrassing. With the Russians launching "sputniks" an immigration policy that admitted an Irish housemaid while keeping out a scientist from Thailand could no longer be justified as serving the national interest.

The first major revision of the National Origins Quota Act was the McCarran-Walter Act of 1952. The new act, passed over President Truman's veto, maintained the essential provisions of the quota system based upon the census of 1920. The main proponent of the new bill, Senator Patrick McCarran, warned that anyone who opposed it "would wittingly or unwittingly lend themselves to efforts which would poison the bloodstream of the country." The McCarran-Walter Act was blatantly discriminatory in many of its provisions, but it differed from the earlier National Origins Quota Act in two significant ways. First, it did include quotas for Asian nations—tiny quotas, compared to those for western Europeans, but at least Asians were included. Second, the McCarran-Walter Act introduced the principle of considering skills as a criterion for the admission of immigrants. The first half of all quotas were to be assigned to people with "high education, technical training, specialized experiences, or exceptional ability."

Efforts to abandon the national origins system altogether met with opposition from southerners worried about racial mixture and from conservatives afraid of "subversive" activity. "If we transfer the pattern of our immigration to countries and peoples who have historically maintained a totalitarian concept of government, it will be only a matter of time until our Republic will veer from its traditions of freedom and democracy," warned Senator James Eastland of Mississippi. Despite this opposition, criticism of the old system swelled. In 1963 President John F. Kennedy, strongly conscious of his own immigrant origins, took up the cause of immigration law reform. "The use of a national origin system is without basis in either logic or reason," he wrote. "It neither satisfies a national need nor accomplishes an international purpose . . . such a system is an anachronism, for it discriminates among applicants for admission into the United States on the accident of birth."

After Kennedy's death, President Johnson took up the cause. A series of Congressional hearings highlighted the inequities in the existing system. Witnesses pointed out that while an unskilled laborer from northern Europe could enter the country in a few weeks, skilled immigrants (including parents, children, and siblings of American citizens) from Japan or Turkey faced waiting periods of up to 322 years! Opposition faded. On October 3, 1965 President Johnson signed Public Law 89-236, abolishing altogether the use of the national origins quota system.

Public Law 89-236 did not open the gates to unlimited immigration. There was general agreement that the nation, no longer a frontier country and no longer in the early stages of industrialization, could not absorb the large numbers it had absorbed in the past. An annual limit was set—120,000 immigrants from the Western Hemisphere and 170,000 from the Eastern Hemisphere, with a 20,000 person limit on the number that could come annually from any one country. Within these numerical limits, preference went to spouses and immediate relatives of American citizens, professional persons, persons of "exceptional ability in the sciences or the arts," and "qualified immigrants who are capable of performing specified skilled or unskilled labor, not of a temporary or seasonal nature, for which a shortage of employable and willing persons exists in the United States."

The new law, like the old, raised troublesome questions. Few would quarrel with the preferential treatment of relatives of American citizens, but the preference given to scientists and other professionals was more controversial. In practice, such a preference established a "brain drain," drawing trained personnel away from underdeveloped nations that badly need their services. While the national immigration laws encouraged the coming of foreign professionals, virtually every state has laws making it difficult or impossible for aliens to practice their professions. In several states one must be an American citizen to be an accountant, architect, attorney, dentist, nurse, optometrist, physician, or engineer. Finally, one might quarrel with the morality of an immigration system that turns away the tired, the poor, the lone, uneducated immigrant so characteristic of earlier years, to admit only the educated, the talented, and the brilliant. It can be argued that education and talent, as much as nationality or race, are accidents of birth.

Nevertheless, most Americans agreed with President Johnson's assessment of the new immigration bill. Speaking at the base of the Statue of Liberty, Johnson told the nation:

> This bill is not a revolutionary bill. It does not affect the lives of millions. It will not reshape the structure of our daily lives, or add importantly to our wealth and power.
>
> Yet it is still one of the most important acts of this Congress and this Administration.
>
> For it repairs a deep and painful flaw in the fabric of American justice. . . . It will make us truer to ourselves as a country and as a people. It will strengthen us in a hundred unseen ways. . . .
>
> The days of unlimited immigration are past. But those who come will come because of what they are—not because of the land from which they spring.

CHAPTER 13

The New Ethnicity

"Irish Power!" "Kiss me, I'm Italian." "Thank God I'm Polish!" In the early 1970's ethnic slogans blossomed on lapel buttons, on posters, and on automobile bumpers. From coast to coast, they decorated power boats, motorcycles, bicycles, and skis. "Every group is bragging about its heritage now," said an Armenian dentist from Long Island. "Today it's glamorous to be different."

A quick look at American life in the late 1960's and early 1970's supports the Armenian dentist's opinion. Clothes with an ethnic motif were fashionable. Ethnic restaurants were crowded, with more opening every day. Ethnic schools, churches, theaters, and summer camps seemed to have a new lease on life. Books poured off the press dealing with the history and culture of Italians, Jews, Poles, Irish, Puerto Ricans, Mexicans, as well as blacks and Native Americans. In *The Unmeltable Ethnics*, Michael Novak asserted that the "melting pot" was inoperable and cultural pluralism here to stay. Peter Schrag's *Decline of the Wasp* suggested that white Anglo-Saxon Protestant America had lost its traditional dominance; the ethnics were inheriting the land!

Some commentators took issue with the sweeping historical generalizations of Novak and Schrag. They worried that the "new ethnicity" was a dangerous upsurge of tribalism that would destroy the unifying bonds of a common American culture. Some felt that the new emphasis on ethnic differences would obscure what to them seemed more important realities of cleavages based on economic class. Others, pointing out the nation's addiction to novelty of any kind, declared "bumper sticker" ethnicity one more fad among many. Still, no one could deny that a revival of interest in ethnicity was taking place, both among ethnic Americans themselves and within the general community. This chapter will explore the origins of the new ethnicity and the problems and opportunities it opened up for all Americans.

Why the Ethnic Revival?

A variety of factors came together in the post World War II United States to set the stage for the new ethnicity. Many ethnic communities were roused into heightened self-consciousness by events originating overseas. The arrival of thousands of displaced persons and refugees from communist Eastern Europe for example, stimulated ethnic institutions and consciousness among American Slavic communities. Immigrants from Poland, Latvia, Czechoslovakia, and the Ukraine allied themselves with third generation Americans to lobby for the "captive nations."

The Six Day War of 1967 and the Yom Kippur War of 1973, which threatened the very existence of Israel, galvanized many of the most assimilated Jews, professionals and academics, for example, into a new affiliation with the Jewish community. American physicians left their practices to treat the wounded in Israeli hospitals, American college students brought in the harvest to free Israeli civilians for combat, and children gave their nickels and dimes and old people their social security checks to the Israel Emergency Fund. As the Middle East moved from crisis to crisis, support for the state of Israel became the touchstone of American Jewish ethnic identity.

Arab communities in the United States also reacted to the situation in the Middle East. Initial Arab military successes in the Yom Kippur War aroused a new sense of ethnic pride among Americans of Arabic descent, especially among the young. Nor was the Arab ethnic revival limited to politics. Recent immigrants from the Middle East, many of them students or young professionals, led their communities toward a new interest in traditional Arabic culture and in the religion of Islam.

The Irish were among the oldest and most nearly assimilated of the ethnic communities. Yet, terrorism in Northern Ireland, where a Catholic minority still chafed under rule by a Protestant majority, had repercussions in Boston, New York, and Philadelphia. According to a report in *Philadelphia Magazine*, over one hundred Northern Aid Committees in the United States were formed to collect funds for the Provisional Wing of the Irish Republican Army. Irish-American Mike Mallowe described the impact of such committees in the Philadelphia area:

> Typically, a local Northern Aid Chapter is composed of about 50 hard core sympathizers whose members are evenly divided between newly arrived immigrants . . . and native born Irish-Americans who feel as

deeply committed as their counterparts from the Ould Sod. . . . The immigrants gain a sense of American sophistication and efficiency while the Americans gain a fresh infusion of new blood and idealism. . . .

The best part of the IRA's greening of Philadelphia is the effect it is having on the Irish generation gap. Many young Irish are embracing the cause wholeheartedly. Their parents are suddenly discovering better ways to spend Sunday evenings and Saturday afternoons than on the golf course or at the country club, and grandparents, once forgotten on their geriatric shelves, are finding themselves celebrities simply because they recall the old days. . . . Unexpectedly, the Northern Aid Committees are helping to foster a sense of Irish family unity that had been rapidly disappearing as bank accounts grew.

Not all the impetus for the new ethnicity came from overseas. Many forces within American life of the 1960's and 1970's also contributed to it. The 1960's saw a revolt, especially among the young, against the conformity and blandness of the previous decade. The colorless "organization man," and the monotonous suburban subdevelopments were suddenly in disfavor. Individuality became increasingly important, and in this context cultural differences could be openly cherished rather than hidden or abandoned. Among people suddenly awakened to the pleasures of handicrafts and homemade bread, ethnic foods, traditions, and life styles took on a new attractiveness. The counterculture of the 1960's legitimized ethnicity.

An increasing number of people in the troubled 1960's turned their attention to the "urban crisis." City planners such as Jane Jacobs pointed out that the most livable urban neighborhoods were the stable, strongly organized, old ethnic neighborhoods. Here family, friendship, and institutional ties bound people together in orderly patterns of interdependent existence. Sociologists and other academicians in the 1960's were discovering what immigrant communities could have told them from decades of experience—the value of a sense of community, both in creating personal and family stability and in promoting safe and satisfying neighborhoods. Ethnic neighborhoods were often run-down areas, with poor and aging facilities, but their inhabitants could now take renewed pride in living in them.

Ethnicity had never really disappeared. It had remained a large factor in many lives, though, like an iceberg, much of it was submerged or invisible. Perhaps the newest thing about the "new ethnicity" was the new freedom people now felt to acknowledge its presence. The third and fourth generations were finally secure enough in American life to acknowledge their ethnicity, both to themselves and to others. "Twenty years ago, the Rumanian who came here didn't speak English, had a low-paying job, and was not accepted. Today none of this is true, and he is proud to be a Rumanian," said a Rumanian-American clergyman.

An active member of an Armenian dance group agreed, "Now the Armenians have made it; we're part of American life. What it really boils down to is that people aren't ashamed to be foreign any more."

Finally, the descendants of immigrants identified themselves as ethnics in the 1960's and 1970's in increasing numbers because fewer acceptable alternatives were available. In the depression years of the 1930's many of the second generation had found a sense of personal identity through radical political and social groups and through the newly active labor movement. During the religious revival of the 1950's, it appeared likely that religious identity would replace ethnicity as the main personal focal point.

Events proved otherwise. By the 1960's the working class ideologies of the "Old Left" were considered hopelessly out of date, by the "New Left" as well as by the Right. The industrial worker, once a motion picture hero played by John Garfield, had degenerated into the slowwitted television bigot, Archie Bunker. In 1935 it had been more acceptable to identify as a worker than as an Irish, Italian, or Polish-American, but by 1970 the reverse was true. By the 1970's the religious revival, at least among large traditional churches, was over. Neither economic ideology nor religious affiliation appeared likely to displace ethnicity, at least in the foreseeable future.

New Leadership, New Activism

While many factors made it easier for ethnic Americans to return to their backgrounds with new pride and interest, the most important stimulus for the new ethnicity was the black civil rights revolution. The civil rights marches of the 1950's and the exposés of black ghetto poverty in the 1960's were beamed into American living rooms in "living color." Ethnic Americans watched as blacks demanded their fair share of the American dream—civil rights, jobs, housing, education, and political recognition. They heard about black history, black culture, black pride, and saw the black community organizing to achieve its goals.

If black is beautiful, reasoned some ethnic Americans, is it not also beautiful to be Mexican, Puerto Rican, Polish, Italian, or Jewish? If black studies are valid and desirable, why not academic programs in the heritage of other ethnic groups as well? If blacks could organize to protest discrimination and fight for better living conditions, why should not other ethnic communities do the same? By the late 1960's new activist leaders were directing their ethnic communities along the paths laid out by blacks—toward pride in their cultural heritage and toward social and political activism.

One of the first groups to develop this new type of ethnic leadership was the Mexican-American community. Angered by what they perceived as the neglect of their community's acute needs and influenced by the example of black militance, Mexican-American leaders became increasingly militant. On September 16, 1965, Cesar Chavez launched the grape pickers strike at Delano, California, to unionize impoverished Mexican-American farm workers. After nationwide publicity, the strike was settled in 1970 when the last major grape grower signed a union contract granting a minimum wage.

Like Martin Luther King, Cesar Chavez believed in nonviolent protest and sought alliances with sympathizers everywhere. But as the black movement of the 1960's tended to move from moderate to more militant leadership, so too did the Mexican-American movement. Other leaders moved left of Chavez. The mystical Reies Lòpez Tijerina of New Mexico for example, led a drive for the return of the old communal lands of the Southwest to the Mexican-American community. Ambivalent toward broad coalitions and alliances, Tijerina used "direct action", such as his attempt at armed take over of the Rio Arriba Courthouse in 1967.

In the barrios of Los Angeles, David Sanchez founded the Brown Berets, an organization of young men who, like the Black Panthers, felt it necessary to defend themselves against the white police. The Brown Berets tried to instill pride and group unity among the ghetto youth. "Gang fights are going out," said their minister of public relations. "We're getting kids from all the different gangs into the Brown Berets. It's going to be one big gang. We try to teach our people not to fight with each other. . . ."

One of the most important new leaders of the urban community was Rodolpho "Corky" Gonzales. Having participated in federal poverty programs and become disillusioned with them, Gonzales complained that the best leadership of the community was being "bought out" by what he considered tokenism. Like the more radical blacks, he rejected integration as unlikely and undesirable. "Integration is an empty bag," he stated. . . . "it's like getting up out of the small end of the funnel. One may make it, but the rest of the people stay at the bottom."

By the late 1960's young Mexican-Americans were calling themselves Chicanos, a term formerly applied only to the poor and ignorant among their community. Activism spread, especially among the better educated. High school students in California and in Denver staged strikes protesting the neglect of their heritage in the public school curriculum. College students and professionals formed a variety of new organizations. "Chicanos, do not believe that the gabacho's (Anglo) life, values, and culture are better," admonished a college newspaper in 1969. "Be proud of what you are and demand what you have coming." But by the early 1970's, "direct action" was declining among Chicanos as it had among blacks. A more sophisticated Mexican-American community turned increasingly to political activity and community organization, focusing its efforts on specific problems such as education, housing, jobs, drug abuse, and police brutality.

The story of Edward J. Piszak illustrates the arrival of the new ethnicity among European ethnic communities. A second generation Polish-American who made his fortune in the frozen seafood business, Piszak grew up in a mixed working class neighborhood in Philadelphia with little awareness of his ethnic background. Unconsciously, he had internalized the American stereotype of the "dumb Polak." A trip to Warsaw in 1964 changed that. Piszak describes the impression the Polish capital made upon him:

> I remember, as the plane came down over Warsaw, thinking, 'My God! Who built this beautiful city?' I didn't know Polaks could do things like this, build these fine buildings and do all the engineering and design and construction. That's not what they teach you in America.

Involved in an employment program for the "disadvantaged" in his factories, Piszak began to compare the situation of the Pole in America with that of the black. "The Polish-American had much in common with the black," he said. "He was uprooted, found himself in a strange land, forfeited his identity and usually was undereducated, from the bottom of society. He didn't even know he had a cultural heritage."

To remedy this situation, Piszak launched Project Pole, patterned after the many black history and culture programs of the late 1960's. He placed ads in newspapers in Detroit, Chicago, Washington, Philadelphia, and Buffalo telling about the great people Poland has produced—Nicolaus Copernicus, Frederic Chopin, Joseph Conrad, Marie Curie. He distributed posters, art books, and other literature on Polish culture, encouraged tourism to Poland, and got a half million dollar appropriation from Congress to make the Kosciuszko House in Philadelphia a national Polish-American shrine.

Polish-American leaders in other cities took up similar projects. A Polish-American cultural group in Detroit opened the Adam Mickiewicz Library, which by 1974 had 8000 books, 1000 records, and over a hundred periodicals dealing with Poland or with Polish-America. In 1973, the group lined up Polish, Italian, and Ukrainian clubs to visit Detroit booksellers and protest the sale of a derogatory Polish and Italian joke book. Their efforts were successful; the booksellers took the offensive work off their shelves. The attitude of some of the newly aroused European ethnics such as these Polish-Americans is summed up by Mike Krolewski, curator of the Adam Mickiewicz Library: "Without our backgrounds, whatever nationality it happens to be, we are nothing."

The Cultural Renaissance

Italians, Armenians, Greeks, Rumanians, Jews, Chinese, Japanese, Puerto Ricans, and other ethnic communities underwent their own ethnic renaissances. The smaller ethnic churches reported increases in membership in the early 1970's, while larger, nonethnic churches reported declines. In Jackson, Michigan, the Rumanian Orthodox church had a waiting list for its summer camp, which taught Rumanian religion and church music as well as table tennis and swimming. New York's St. Nicholas Greek Orthodox Church reported that its afternoon Greek language school doubled its enrollment from 200 to 400 in five years. Armenians opened elementary schools in Michigan and Massachusetts, began an annual Armenian track and field meet in California, and started an Armenian golf tournament in Manhasset, New York.

Ethnic culture spilled out of ethnic schools into institutions serving the general public. Public high schools in various cities introduced courses in Polish, Italian, Hebrew, and Armenian. In the early 1970's, the University of California at Los Angeles enrolled 150 students a year in Armenian language and civilization courses and granted masters degrees and doctorates in Armenian studies. Leading universities established chairs of Jewish studies, and in 1973 a summer program in Yiddish language, literature, and culture had a larger enrollment than any other summer program at Columbia University.

Oriental-Americans shared in the ethnic revival. Japanese parents took their children to visit the internment camps of World War II. Japanese-American youth enrolled in university courses in their ancestral history and culture and in traditional arts such as flower arranging. Chinese teenagers flocked to Chinese language films from Hong Kong (with English subtitles!) "I worked all my life to get out of Chinatown and I finally got to Walnut Creek," said a successful second generation Chinese-American, "and my children want to go back to Chinatown. I don't understand this." Doubtless these children considered this bewildered parent a "banana,"—yellow on the outside, white on the inside!

The ethnic revival aroused an interest in ethnic culture among the general public as well as within the ethnic communities. Folk festivals in major cities displayed ethnic songs, dances, foods, and handicrafts. Foreign language radio stations multiplied, and ethnic television programming was introduced. Plays, books, and films about ethnic life became immensely popular, *Fiddler on the Roof* and *The Godfather,* for example.

Revivals of old Yiddish plays were attended by nostalgic audiences in New York and Miami, but the most vital ethnic theatre in the 1960's and 1970's was that of blacks, Puerto Ricans, and Mexican-Americans.

One of the most successful Puerto Rican plays was *The Ox Cart,* by Rene Marques. It described the deterioration of a simple farm family that moved first to San Juan and then to New York to "improve" itself. The play ends shortly after the death of the oldest son. The grief-stricken mother sets out for the mountains of rural Puerto Rico, hoping to recapture the lost traditions and values that had held the family together in earlier, happier times. Such a play must have had a powerful impact on Puerto Rican immigrants working out their own balance sheets on the positive and negative effects of urbanization and immigration.

Mexican-American activists of the 1960's and early 1970's used theater not only for entertainment, but also for education and social propaganda, much as European immigrant workers had done decades before. El Teatro Campesino, a bilingual farmworker's theater, borrowed from contemporary European theater as well as from traditional Mexican folk drama to produce *actos,* short plays explaining the plight of the pickers and the need for unionization. Luis Valdez, one of the founders of El Teatro Campesino, described its actors and productions:

> All our actors are farmworkers. . . . Starting from scratch with a real life incident, character, or idea, everybody in the Teatro contributes to the development of an acto. . . . We use no scenery, no scripts, and no curtain. We use costumes and props only casually—an old pair of pants, a wine bottle, a pair of dark glasses, a mask. But mostly we like to show we are still strikers underneath. . . . To simplify things, we hang signs around our necks, sometimes in black and white, sometimes in lively colors, indicating the characters portrayed.

El Teatro Campesino was valuable because it explored a social movement without asking its poorly educated, often foreign born participants to read and write. The existence of the theater itself condemned the loss of human talent caused by the deadening life farm workers were forced to lead. "More than that," said Valdez, "it affords us the opportunity to laugh as free men."

The Puerto Rican and Mexican-American communities produced increasing numbers of poets, novelists, and authors of short stories, autobiographies, and nonfiction. The works of such authors were varied, but they were often colored by their ethnic origins. Durango Mendoza, whose mother was Native American and whose father was a Mexican-American, explained:

> . . . being brown in a white culture, or Chicano in an Indian culture, gives a certain flavor to being a man that is unique. Propaganda and race—or culture—selling is not my bag. But being brown and springing from

brown roots is my reality—a reality that has shaped my life and given me a great concern for all people, a concern that I might not otherwise have known as strongly.

The variety of writing done within the framework of the new ethnicity is enormous, ranging from John Figueroa's vivid descriptions of the Puerto Rican barrio of East Harlem, to Jerre Mangione's reconstruction of Sicilian immigrant life in Rochester, to the widely read works of Jewish writers such as Saul Bellow, Bernard Malamud, and Chaim Potok.

Achievements

The new, activist leaders have been increasingly successful in fighting negative ethnic stereotypes in the American media. Italian-American protests eliminated the use of "Mafia" as a synonym for organized crime in the movies and on television. Offensive advertisements such as the Mexican "bandito" stealing cornchips on a television commercial and a bucktoothed, pigtailed Chinese on a powdered drink mix package were dropped because of organized ethnic protest. Newspapers and magazines featured articles on ethnic traditions, ethnic neighborhoods, and ethnic problems. Prime time television celebrated the new ethnicity with shows featuring comedians, detectives, and other central figures with recognizable ethnic identities.

More significant gains were made in civil rights. MALDEF, the Mexican American Legal Defense and Educational Fund, brought successful class action suits on behalf of Mexican-Americans seeking equal rights in education, employment, and political participation. Bilingual schools were begun on an experimental basis for Mexican-American and Puerto Rican children. Spanish speaking voters in New York City and Philadelphia were provided with ballots in Spanish. Affirmative action programs were designed to help Spanish surnamed individuals, as well as blacks and women, enter universities and professional schools and obtain good jobs. Much remains to be done, but at least a beginning was made.

For the first time, ethnicity was recognized as an important factor in many areas of American life. In health care, for example, research began on diseases encountered primarily in particular ethnic groups. Psychologists, psychiatrists, and social workers considered the impact of ethnic cultures upon behavior patterns, mental health, and social problems. In 1972 the medical school of Stanford University used skillfully prepared ethnic materials—a cookbook, a horoscope calendar, bilingual phonograph records, and radio and television dramatizations—to motivate Mexican-Americans toward habits that would reduce heart disease. Such constructive uses of knowledge about ethnicity are, unfortunately, still rare, but here too, beginnings were made.

Problems

If the new ethnicity made ethnic Americans more aware of their cultural heritage, it also made them more aware of their contemporary problems. Ethnic leaders were concerned that the new interest in ethnic culture was an "elitist" movement. They complained that the vast majority of their constituency cared less about history and literature than about their favorite ethnic foods. Would the new ethnic studies programs attract serious academic students, they asked, or would these programs degenerate into consciousness-raising sessions or exercises in nostalgia?

There were many other problems. Despite the public acceptance of many aspects of the new ethnicity, ethnic Americans were subjected to subtle forms of economic and social discrimination that would not go away. Affirmative action programs helped some with Spanish surnames, but it could be argued that these same programs worked against people with Italian, Slavic, or Jewish surnames. Covertly and overtly, ethnic groups continued to battle one another in many areas of American life. Polish and Italian Catholics still complained that the Irish shut them out of positions of influence in the American Catholic Church. Southern and Eastern European groups fought the Irish on the one hand and blacks and Puerto Ricans on the other for control of unions, jobs, neighborhoods, and political machines. Ethnic communities battled one another, and nonethnics as well, for control of lucrative underworld activities such as gambling, prostitution, and drug distribution.

Ethnic leaders found much to worry about within their own communities. Despite the new ethnicity, intermarriage and assimilation took an increasing toll. So too did the pressures and dislocations common to all Americans. In the 1960's and 1970's, for the first time, divorce became as common among Catholics and Jews as among Protestants. Groups that had prided themselves upon the stability of their family life found their social service agencies overwhelmed with cases of broken families and disturbed children. Poverty remained a major problem among Puerto Rican and Mexican-Americans, but even the most successful ethnic communities were dismayed to discover surprisingly large amounts of poverty among their members. Many of the ethnic poor were old people, left behind in decaying parts of the inner city where they struggled to survive on inadequate pensions or social security.

"Middle America"

The new ethnicity focused the attention of scholars on the formerly little noticed problems of a large group variously titled "white ethnics," "the silent majority," or "middle America". By whatever name, this group consists of the forty million children and grandchildren of the Southern and Eastern European ethnic communities. Most of them live in the major cities of the Northeast and the Great Lakes area, are Roman Catholic, and make their livings as industrial workers, clerks, or small shopkeepers. And most of them had increasing difficulties coping with the economic and social problems of the 1960's and 1970's.

The largest single problem was inflation, which ate away at already barely adequate paychecks. In 1969 the average industrial worker with three dependents took home $87.00 a week—less than the sum defined as necessary by the United States government to maintain an "adequate" standard of living and, surprisingly, a dollar less than the same worker had taken home in 1965! In the early 1970's prices rose faster than wages, so the "middle American" saw the purchasing power of his or her paycheck decline sharply. An electrician described the feelings of workers like himself:

> He gets a dollar raise and seventy cents of it goes to inflation. His wife says, 'Hey John, look, what's going on around here? We need more money.' He is confused. On his TV screen he sees angry blacks and browns getting it for themselves, and he thinks society is giving it only to them. He feels that he is supporting the poor and that the welfare and city budgets come off of his back. . . .

As the above quotation suggests, there were problems other than inflation. By the early 1970's working class white ethnics were filled with resentment. They watched affluent WASPS and more fortunate ethnics move to the suburbs, leaving them and blacks to cope with the long neglected problems of the cities—a shrinking tax base, antiquated schools, poor housing, inadequate services, unsafe streets. Though their wages were often little higher than welfare payments, they were excluded from many of the new social programs directed at the very poor. Many were too proud—or too ashamed—to accept help from such programs even when they qualified. Like the very poor, working class ethnics saw the American dream on their television screens—the luxurious suburban homes, the glamorous vacations, prestigious colleges for their children—and like the very poor, they knew that this dream was beyond their reach.

Working class white ethnics had other causes for resentment. Despite recent efforts of ethnic spokesman to correct the situation, they received little positive attention from the nation as a whole. In circles too enlightened to tolerate anti-black jokes, jokes derogatory to

Poles and Italians remained common. A technological society involved in putting a man on the moon had little respect for the unskilled, or even the skilled, manual laborer. "Who wants to be an electrician nowadays? If you are not a computer expert, you are nothing."

But middle Americans could rarely afford the specialized training their society valued, and were often dissuaded even from trying to get such training. Shunted into vocational or "general" high school programs rather than college preparatory classes, their youth were stigmatized as "fender benders" or "greasers" by contemptuous teachers, counselors, and classmates. Often young men of this group, lacking self-confidence, accepted routine, dead end jobs because they expected nothing better.

Working class white ethnic women also suffered from a negative self-image. Poorly educated, they marked time as sales clerks or office workers until marriage, which they had been brought up to consider the appropriate and satisfying career for a woman. Marriage was not a panacea, however. A study of working class women by Lee Rainwater, Richard Coleman, and Gerald Handel revealed that many regarded themselves as "little people" whose lives were "just dull." They did not believe that anyone cared what they thought. According to a paper given by Dr. Pauling B. Bart at the Radcliffe Institute Conference on Women in 1972:

> The question characteristically asked women is 'Are you a housewife or do you work?' implying that the seventy to ninety hour week women outside the labor force endure when they have children and a house to care for is not work. It is not surprising that their self-image may suffer. . . . Housewifery is menial work, and we do not regard our menials highly.

Economically insecure, lacking higher education, and low in self-esteem, many working class white ethnics found the political and social changes of the 1960's and early 1970's difficult to understand and to accept. Campus rebellions, urban riots, civil disobedience, hippies, yippies, draft resisters, and the antiwar movement were astonishing to people brought up to believe in hard work, respect for authority, and unquestioning patriotism. Faced with the civil rights movement, changing urban neighborhoods, busing, birth control, abortion, drugs, pornography, rising crime rates and inflation, many felt that "our lives were changing faster than our own self-image or basic values."

For people who had little, rapid social change—even positive, long overdue social change—could be a frightening experience. To make matters worse, traditional sources of support were less readily available. Civil service and political reform had destroyed much of the power of the old ethnic ward politician, whose influence had been a port in time of storm. "Affirmative action" plans appeared to advance racial minorities over white ethnics, even those with seniority. Automation, recurrent recessions, and a stubbornly unyielding unemployment rate made it hard to find new jobs when old ones were lost. Unions, a traditional source of help, seemed unresponsive, if not corrupt. The average working man was rarely active in his union and six out of seven working women were not union members at all. Even the Roman Catholic Church could not be counted on to provide the comfort of familiarity. In the wake of Vatican II "folk" masses were accompanied by rock guitar, nuns shed their habits, and priests campaigned for the abolition of celibacy.

Many of the problems of white ethnics were linked to the problems of the cities. The nation's tax structure resulted in the concentration of public monies in Washington, so that the amount available for local needs was limited. As the affluent moved to the suburbs, the cities were left with fewer and fewer resources to meet ever increasing needs. Industry, too, moved to the suburbs, and public transportation was poor, making access to jobs more difficult for blacks and whites who remained in the old neighborhoods.

Politically, many cities were securely in the hands of an Anglo-Saxon Protestant elite or the well-organized, firmly entrenched Irish. Before World War II, Southern and Eastern European communities usually lacked the affluence and the organization to gain control of the nation's cities. In the 1960's, when they were ready to assume positions of power, it was much harder to do so because the cities were declining. When the cities had been expanding, entrenched groups could move upward into more desirable positions, leaving vacancies for the newcomers to fill. But now, with few new positions available, the old guard was reluctant to yield what it had.

Finally, now that Southern and Eastern Europeans had served their time in the lower ranks of the urban structure and considered themselves entitled to political leadership and the jobs and other advantages that went with it, they faced a determined new competitor—an increasingly numerous and well-organized black community. Black Americans, too, were immigrants to the cities. While small communities had lived there since colonial days, most arrived from rural South in the twentieth century. Blacks felt that they, too, had served their time—three hundred years—and were entitled to the benefits of urban America.

Whites and Blacks—The Urban Battlefield

The new ethnicity bore a complex love-hate relationship to black America. As already described, much of the new ethnicity was imitative of the black civil rights movement. Irish, Slavic, and Jewish votes in the cities had supplied much of the political muscle for the civil rights revolution and antipoverty programs of the 1960's. Most ethnics were ardent supporters of John and Robert Kennedy, both of whom were considered liberal on social issues. In the conservative landslide of 1972, when 68% of Protestant America voted for Richard Nixon, George McGovern won over half of the Slavic vote and two-thirds of the Jewish vote.

Yet by the late 1960's white ethnics found themselves in city after city facing blacks in ugly confrontations over neighborhoods, jobs, schools, and often over political control of the city itself. Liberals, hoping to hasten the long overdue progress of black Americans, began to characterize working class white ethnics as mindless bigots. Television news cameras showed white ethnics stoning a school bus carrying black children to a formerly white school or vandalizing a home into which a black family was moving. These ugly scenes supported the view of white ethnics as bigots. So did the voting patterns of those white ethnics who backed candidates like Louise Day Hicks, opponent of school integration in Boston, Frank Rizzo, the "law and order" mayor of Philadelphia, and George Wallace, segregationist governor of Alabama.

While white America as a whole was riddled with racism, there is no evidence that ethnics were more bigoted than others. Many studies suggest that certain groups, Jews and Irish Catholics in particular, are less bigoted than most. In recent years working class white ethnics have appeared more bigoted than other Americans because their interests have clashed with those of blacks more frequently than the interests of the affluent and highly educated. Ethnic Americans realized what sociologist Peter Rossi pointed out:

> . . . without changes in social policy, the costs of producing racial equality are going to be borne more heavily by the white working class than by any other group in the society. The working class will have to share jobs, schools, neighborhoods, political posts, influence in city hall, and so on with blacks—types of sharing that come close to where people really live . . .

White ethnics, many of whom had little, resented being asked to shoulder so much of the burden of correcting the centuries old injustice of racism, while people with more advantages pointed accusing fingers from the shelter of affluent suburbs, private schools, and well-guarded luxury apartments. Also, to economically marginal but rigidly "respectable" white working class ethnics, the black stereotype represented the poverty, the social problems, and the lower class way of life which they had only recently escaped—and into which they were terrified of falling once again.

Racism was undoubtedly one cause of conflict between white ethnics and blacks in the cities, but it was not the only cause, nor perhaps even the most crucial one. Conflicts between groups entrenched in a given area and newcomers seeking a place there had been commonplace throughout America's past. Confrontations between white ethnics and blacks in America's troubled cities can be viewed in the context of other intergroup conflicts involving ethnic succession in jobs, neighborhoods, and politics. Catholics and Protestants had shed blood over school controversies in the nineteenth century. The first Polish family to move into an Irish neighborhood in the nineteenth century was scarcely more welcome than the first black family to move into a Polish neighborhood a hundred years later.

To many white working class ethnics, the neighborhood was not just a geographic place; it was a way of life, a community in which every shop, tavern, and street corner was a beloved institution. The residents of such a neighborhood therefore feared the influx of newcomers who they felt, rightly or wrongly, would change the pattern of community life. Moreover, having invested virtually all they possessed in their homes, many white ethnics were especially vulnerable to the warnings of unscrupulous real estate agents that if blacks move in, "property values will go down." Rapidly changing neighborhoods, regardless of the ethnic groups involved, often experienced rising crime rates. Racially integrated neighborhoods were often punished by banks that refused to extend credit for the improvements that would have prevented deterioration.

Jobs, like neighborhoods, were not impersonal, interchangeable positions to ethnic Americans, but rather a way of life to be handed down to future generations. A skilled craftsman charged with racial discrimination in his union, expressed this in a letter to the *New York Times:*

> Some men leave their sons money, some large investments, some business connections, and some a profession. I have only one worthwhile thing to give; my trade. I hope to follow a centuries old tradition and sponsor my son for an apprenticeship. . . . It is said that I discriminate against Negroes. . . . Which of us when it comes to a choice will not choose a son over all others?

In many cities political battles raged as conservative, working class white ethnics fought coalitions of liberal upper class Anglo-Saxons and blacks for control of the cities. Sometimes one side won, sometimes another. The stakes were high, for they included the distribution of jobs, patronage, and government funds. No conflict aroused as much bitterness, however, as the battles within the schools.

By the 1960's, many of the teachers and administrators in urban school systems were Irish, Jewish, and Italian; by the 1960's, the majority of the students in many of these systems were black. Politicians, teachers' unions, administrators, ethnic leaders, and parents became locked in heated conflict. White teachers and administrators wanted to maintain the existing seniority system in the schools, while blacks wanted representation, even control, at all levels. White teachers and administrators complained that blacks wanted to be promoted out of turn, to "change the rules of the game," and that too much political and parental influence on the schools would destroy the quality of education. Blacks charged that racially prejudiced white teachers and administrators were failing to educate black children, that black children needed role models of their own race in the schools, and that community control could lead to the improvement rather than to the deterioration of education. A declining birth rate and economic recession meant fewer job opportunities for teachers and administrators—black and white—thus compounding the difficulties.

The most explosive issue of all was the issue of busing as a means of ending de facto racial segregation in urban public schools. The federal judiciary had ruled that racially segregated schools were inherently unequal in the North as well as in the South. Most blacks favored integration as morally right and educationally sound. Many white ethnics, on the other hand, had strongly possessive feelings about "their" public schools which, like their neighborhoods and jobs, were seen as an integral part of a cherished way of life, a way of life that was being threatened from all sides and must be defended at all costs. The conflict was exacerbated by the poor quality of education in many black and white urban schools, and the scarcity of funds and ideas for improvements.

White ethnic resistance to the integration of neighborhoods, jobs, and schools was in part an attempt to deny unpleasant realities. White ethnic neighborhoods, like black neighborhoods, were old and in need of repair. White schools, like black schools, were antiquated, badly financed, and often ineffective. Crime was a growing problem throughout the cities in "Whitetown" as well as the black ghetto. Hostility to blacks was an effort on the part of some white ethnics to deny their own ever increasing difficulties by blaming them on "outsiders." Crime, neighborhood deterioration, poor schools, and unemployment were seen as *black* problems which could be kept away if only blacks were kept away.

New Directions

Of course the pressing problems of the cities were not black problems or white problems, but were human problems affecting everyone. Racism and social insecurity on the part of urban whites and bitterness and exasperation on the part of blacks obscured the fact that the two groups had many common interests. The two groups, both "have-nots" in American society, constituted the bulk of the remaining urban population. As such, they had a common stake in the improvement of housing, job opportunities, education, health care, and other services in the deteriorating cities.

Because of these common interests, the new ethnicity did not need to be anti-black. "I want something positive," said ethnic leader Barbara Mikulski of Baltimore. "I want to see a national movement developed to help American ethnics, but not at the expense of any other minority groups." In 1970, at the National Center for Urban Ethnic Affairs, Mikulski urged blacks and white ethnics to stop fighting and start cooperating:

> Government is polarizing people by the creation of myths. . . . The ethnic worker is fooled into thinking that the blacks are getting everything. . . . The two groups end up fighting each other for the same jobs and competing so that the new schools and recreation centers will be in their respective communities. What results is an angry confrontation for tokens, where there should be an alliance for a whole new Agenda for America.

The "New Agenda" for blacks and whites would include full employment, a greater allocation of the nation's resources to meet human needs, black and white, and quality education for everyone.

Tentative beginnings have been made toward creating the alliance of which Mikulski spoke—blacks and white ethnics working together for a "new agenda for Americans." Ethnic leaders such as Steve Adubo of Newark and Kenneth Kovach of Cleveland, and ethnic organizations have shown concern for the problems of blacks as well as of their own groups. In Detroit and Cleveland issue oriented coalitions worked for change in areas that affected both groups—urban renewal, education, the quality of city services, consumer and environmental problems. Most of these coalitions were short-lived, falling apart when the issue on which they were built was resolved. Under their auspices, however, court cases have been won and city ordinances passed.

The late 1960's and early 1970's also saw the opening of new political directions for ethnic America. Realistic politicians have always paid attention to ethnicity, attending ethnic banquets, acknowledging ethnic holidays, appointing some (but not too many!) ethnics to office, and, when necessary, "balancing" a ticket with candidates from powerful ethnic groups. Such efforts intensified in response to the new ethnicity.

Common experiences with poverty and discrimination had produced solid ethnic support for the Democratic Party from Franklin

Roosevelt's New Deal to Lyndon Johnson's War on Poverty. By the mid 1960's, however, ethnic Americans were rethinking their political positions. The affluent were moving toward suburbia and Republicanism, while working class whites were no longer convinced that the Democrats, whose programs now were for the very poor, had their interests at heart.

In the Presidential campaigns of 1968 and 1972, Richard Nixon made a determined effort to capture the votes of the formerly Democratic white ethnics, a large component of his "silent majority." His strategy was to appeal to the white ethnics' economic insecurities and to their fear of social change, particularly their fear of blacks, "hippies," and the "New Left". Though this strategy was not completely successful (Slavs and Jews voted for McGovern, as did the heavily Catholic, heavily ethnic state of Massachusetts), sufficiently great inroads were made in the old Democratic coalition of labor and minorities to produce Nixon victories in both elections.

By 1975, however, the ethnic vote was still "up for grabs." The ethnic votes Nixon had attracted to the Republican Party through appeals to traditional moral values, "law and order," and patriotism could hardly be expected to remain there after the exposure of the hypocrisy and corruption of Watergate. Patriotism and the "cult of gratitude" to the United States remained strong among ethnic Americans, however, as did a concern with traditional ethical values. Perhaps it was more than coincidence that many of the people prominent in efforts to uncover the Watergate scandal and bring honor back to America's public life—Judge John Sirica, Congressman Peter Rodino, special prosecutor Leon Jaworski—were the children of immigrants.

In the long run, ethnic Americans, like all Americans, would give their political support to the candidates and parties that met their needs. In an article in *Commonwealth* (September 1970), Michael Novak enumerated these needs:

> more self-determination and pride on the job, more prestige in the nation, more dignity—as well as better housing, a sharp control on inflation, full employment, more scholarships and welfare (so that nonwhites and whites don't have to compete for the same small piece of pie), more beauty and peace and easy transport and security in the cities and boroughs in which they live.

In the 1976 national elections, Jimmy Carter was able to reestablish the old Roosevelt coalition by convincing almost all black voters, over 70% of the Jewish voters, and 54% of urban Catholic voters that the Democratic Party was more likely than the Republican Party to provide jobs and improve the quality of their lives. The national political experience of the 1960's and 1970's indicated that white ethnics, like other voters, will support candidates who represent their interests, regardless of traditional party loyalties and affiliations.

Social as well as political trends opened new directions for ethnic Americans. The great expansion of educational facilities in the 1960's, including the community college movement, enabled young white ethnics—and older people as well—to pursue higher education in unprecedented numbers. Though community colleges, like high schools, could become traps tracking working class students into "dead end" vocational, rather than academic programs, new employment possibilities as well as new ideas about values and life styles have opened up to many of the students who have attended them.

Finally, the growing feminist movement of the 1960's and 1970's has also opened up new directions for ethnic Americans. In the late 1960's, ethnic women tended to consider the new feminists "bra burners," and wanted nothing to do with them. Working class women had little stake in middle class feminist issues such as the exclusion of women from corporate, academic, and political life. Rhetoric that called for freedom from male oppression alienated women brought up to depend upon their husbands for a sense of security. Nor did working class women want job equality with their blue-collar husbands. "We know that when they come home from work every day they feel they've been treated like the machines they operate."

By the mid 1970's, however, several factors were operating to bring ethnic women into the feminist movement. The movement itself made greater efforts to meet their needs, stressing such issues as equal pay for equal work, unemployment compensation for pregnant women, better medical care, better child care facilities, and social security for housewives. Often college educated daughters introduced their middle-aged ethnic mothers to feminist ideas and organizations. Finally, the rising rates of inflation and the increasing frequency of separation and divorce forced increasing numbers of ethnic women into the labor force, giving them firsthand experience with the kinds of discrimination the feminists were attacking.

Like their immigrant grandmothers, many poor and working class ethnic women have been drawn into the wider community and to the women's movement by efforts to improve their children's schools and to fight violence, drugs, and other problems in their neighborhoods. The recent activism of Puerto Rican and Mexican-American women raised serious questions about the "machismo" tradition of male superiority in their ethnic backgrounds. "The doctrine of Machismo has been used by our men to take out their frustrations on their wives and sisters," said a radical Mexican-American newspaper in Albuquerque, New Mexico. "We must support our women in their struggle for economic and social equality and recognize that our women are equals within our struggle for Liberation."

Asian and European ethnic women moved in the same direction. Labor union women, many of them ethnics, organized on a national basis to demand equality on the job. Radical caucuses of Catholic and Jewish women demanded sexual equality within these traditional ethnic religions. A study of white working class women in Chicago in 1972 stated that women who considered feminists "kooks" nevertheless agreed with them that women should have an equal voice in household decisions, that women were as capable as men of being leaders in science, education, and politics, and perhaps most surprising, that "a woman who does not marry can be a normal and adequate woman."

Like Mexican-American and Puerto Rican women, some European ethnics became involved in community improvement activities during the 1960's. Though these women might express no conscious interest in women's liberation, their activism had an impact upon the old life styles. "When a wife comes home after testifying at a city council hearing, she is fundamentally changing the balance of power in her marriage," said Nancy Seifer, author of a recent study of working class women. By the early 1970's, many working class women, the middle aged as well as the young, were convinced that they could "build a future different from the traditional path laid out by their mothers and grandmothers." The women's movement, like the black civil rights movement, and like the new educational opportunities, was opening new directions for ethnic America.

"To Seek America"

Accustomed to equating universalism with "good" and to identifying Americanism with the Anglo-Saxon heritage, many Americans in the mid 1970's were still uncomfortable with the concept of ethnicity. Critics of the "new ethnicity" worried that it would lead to a destructive fragmentation of American life, that it would cause difficulties for the individual who chose not to identify with an ethnic group, and that it would increase prejudice and intergroup conflict, particularly between blacks and whites. Swedish sociologist Gunnar Myrdal characterized the new ethnicity as "upperclass intellectual romanticism." According to Myrdal, emphasis upon unimportant cultural differences would divert attention from the real economic and social cleavages that threaten American society. Others were afraid that the traditional American ideology of individual rights would be replaced by one in which groups, rather than individuals, have rights and privileges—a "quota-ization" of American life.

Defenders of the new ethnicity countered that they were not

creating cleavages in American society, only recognizing diversities that already existed and had been ignored too long. They maintained that teaching young people about their ethnic heritages would confirm their own sense of self-worth, making them more, rather than less, tolerant of those who were different. "As I discover my own identity, I become more free and I want the same thing for all human beings," wrote an ethnic leader.

Though there were suggestions that the American political structure should be revamped to give ethnic and other groups institutionalized voting power *as groups,* most advocates of the new ethnicity did not support this. "All boundaries are understood to be permeable," suggested historian John Higham, describing his model for an ethnically diverse American society. "Ethnic nuclei, on the other hand, are respected as enduring centers of social action. If self-preservation requires, they may claim exemption from certain universal rules, as the Amish now do from the school laws in some states. Both integration and ethnic cohesion are recognized as worthy goals, which different individuals will accept in different degrees."

Advocates of the new ethnicity differed among themselves whether its emphasis should be the exploration of cultural uniqueness or the development of political and social action programs. If the latter, toward what goals should the program be directed and with what allies? Should the new ethnicity stress the real needs and problems of ethnic Americans so as to improve the material lot of its constituents? Or should it stress their equally real progress and achievements to combat destructive stereotypes and build group pride?

One thing that everyone interested in the new ethnicity agreed upon was the need for further investigation, both of the role ethnicity plays in the life of the individual and of the role ethnic communities play in the life of the nation. Scholars have just begun to describe the cultural characteristics of ethnic communities, communities which, like everything else in the United States, are constantly changing. They have also just begun to explore the dynamics of ethnic communities as economic and political interest groups competing for the rewards of American society and as nuclei for social relationships, emotional loyalties, and value systems.

Ethnicity is one of the oldest factors in American life; yet it has just begun to be explored. As the linguist Joshua Fishman pointed out in a study of foreign language loyalty in the United States, ethnicity in mid twentieth century America is not an all-or-nothing affair, nor is it logical, nor is it uniform from individual to individual or group to group:

> For some it is composed of half-forgotten memories, unexplored longings, and intermittent preferences; for others it is active, structured,

elaborated, and constant. . . . For some it is a badge of shame to ignore, fight, and eradicate; for others, it is a source of pride, a focus of initial loyalties and integration from which wider loyalties and wider integration can proceed . . . the varieties and variabilities of ethnicity in America are largely unknown. . . .

As Fishman points out, ignorance of ethnicity is self ignorance—for *all* Americans. All Americans are rooted in particular cultural backgrounds that affect how we see ourselves and others and how we behave, as individuals and as groups. All Americans have faced, and will continue to face, the problems most clearly seen in the lives of immigrants. They will have to work out their own relationships between the present and the past, between the individual and the group, between continuity and change. Like immigrants, all Americans enter every day into a society in the process of growth and change. Words written by Waldo Frank in 1919 during a great wave of foreign immigration remain pertinent today: "We go forth all to seek America. And in the seeking we create her. And in the quality of our search shall be the nature of the America we create."

Bibliographic Essay

The literature on immigrant groups and ethnic life in the United States is voluminous. The following essay will introduce some of the most important works, old and new; suggest the kinds of materials that have been used in the preparation of this book; and provide a starting point for the reader who wishes to investigate further.

Titles preceded by an asterisk (*) have appeared in a paperback edition.

I. General Works on the History of Immigration

The best single history is Maldwyn Allen Jones, *American Immigration* (1960), a comprehensive survey with a good bibliography. For a more recent, briefer treatment, see Leonard Dinnerstein and David Reimer, *Ethnic Americans: A History of Immigration and Assimilation* (1975), which concentrates on the late nineteenth and twentieth centuries and includes useful demographic statistics. The classic introduction to the more personal aspects of immigration is Oscar Handlin, *The Uprooted* (1951, 2nd edition 1973) which stresses the psychological and cultural alienation felt by the immigrants abruptly separated from familiar persons, places, and ways of living. Handlin's thesis has been challenged by Rudolph Vecoli, whose article "Contadini in Chicago: A Critique of *The Uprooted*," *Journal of American History*, LI (December 1964), 407-417, argues that Italian immigrants were able to bring their Old World traditions and institutions with them and thus did not suffer the psychologically devastating "uprootedness" described by Handlin.

Louis Hartz examines immigration to the United States in a comparative framework in *The Founding of New Societies: Studies in the History of the United States, Latin America, South Africa, Canada, and*

Australia (1964). Two excellent works on the "push" from Europe and the "pull" of the New World are Marcus Lee Hansen, *The Atlantic Migration 1607-1860: A History of the Continuing Settlement of the United States* (1940) and Philip Taylor, **The Distant Magnet: European Emigration to the U.S.A.* (1971), which covers the century from 1830 to 1930. See also Harry V. Jerome's older work, *Migration and Business Cycles* (1926). For details of the immigrant's journey to America, consult Maldwyn Allen Jones' anecdotal *Destination America: 1815-1914* (1976) and William Tefft and Thomas Dunne, *Ellis Island* (1971), both of which include photographs, and Terry Coleman, **Going To America* (1972). Thomas Monroe Pitkin's recent account, *Keepers of the Gate: A History of Ellis Island* (1975) chronicles the administration of Ellis Island and includes information on the controversy over immigration restriction.

There are a number of useful documentary collections on European immigration, including both primary and secondary materials. Two of the earliest and best, compiled by social worker and staunch opponent of restrictionism Edith Abbott, are *Historical Aspects of the Immigration Problem: Select Documents* (1926, reprinted 1969), which covers the period before 1882, and *Immigration: Select Documents and Case Records* (1924, reprinted 1969), which includes early twentieth century immigration as well. Both contain immigrant letters, diaries, government documents, and other primary historical, sociological, and legal sources. More recent compilations are Oscar Handlin, **Immigration as a Factor in American History* (1959) and the more comprehensive collection edited by Stanley Feldstein and Lawrence Costello, **The Ordeal of Assimilation: A Documentary History of the White Working Class* (1974), which includes documents on the "new ethnicity" of the 1960's and early 1970's. An attractive collection of essays on the Southern and Eastern European immigration of the early twentieth century is John J. Appel, **The New Immigration* (1971) with material on immigrant housing, community institutions, education, the exploitation of women, and the restrictionist controversy.

II. Ethnicity and Assimilation: Sociological Perspectives

Sociologist Andrew Greeley's lively **Why Can't They Be More Like Us?* (1971) is the best introduction to the concept of ethnicity and its importance in the behavior of ethnic Americans today. For a more sophisticated analysis of the impact of ethnicity on politics, family life, economic and educational mobility, and relations between white ethnics and blacks, see Greeley's later volume, *Ethnicity in the United States: A Preliminary Reconnaissance* (1974), which includes a bibliography and a list of provocative questions for further investigation.

Three early but still rewarding works introducing the theory of cultural pluralism are Horace M. Kallen's article "Democracy Versus the Melting Pot," in *The Nation,* February 18 and 25, 1915, reprinted in Horace M. Kallen, *Culture and Democracy in the United States,* (1924, reprinted 1970); Isaac B. Berkson, *Theories of Americanization: A Critical Study* (1920, reprinted 1969); and Julius Drachsler, *Democracy and Assimilation, The Blending of Immigrant Heritages in America* (1920).

Among the post World War II writers on the role of ethnic groups in American society, Will Herberg, **Protestant, Catholic, Jew: An Essay in American Religious Sociology* (1955), suggests that the United States was a "triple melting pot," where ethnic groups fused into three permanent and distinctive religious groupings. For a development of the theory of ethnic communities as political and economic interest groups, see Nathan Glazer and Daniel P. Moynihan, **Beyond the Melting Pot: The Negroes, Puerto Ricans, Jews, Italians, and Irish of New York City* (1963, 2nd edition 1970). Milton Gordon, **Assimilation in American Life: The Role of Race, Religion, and National Origins* (1964) explores the process of assimilation, pointing out that ethnic communities may adopt the life style of the majority society (cultural assimilation) while maintaining their own quite separate institutional and social structures. Other useful discussions of the nature of assimilation may be found in William Newman, **American Pluralism: A Study of Minority Groups and Social Theory* (1973) and John Higham, **Send These to Me: Jews and Other Immigrants in Urban America* (1975).

III. Works on Particular Ethnic Communities

A. BLACKS, NATIVE AMERICANS, ANGLO-AMERICANS

The most comprehensive text on blacks in the United States, with an excellent bibliography, is John Hope Franklin, **From Slavery to Freedom. A History of Negro Americans* (3rd edition 1967). For shorter accounts, see Lerone Bennett, **Before the Mayflower: A History of the Negro in America, 1619-1966* (1966) and Rayford Logan, **The Negro in the United States: A Brief History* (1966). Among the many useful documentary collections are **The Afro-Americans: Readings* (1970), edited by Ross Baker; **The Negro in America: A Documentary History* (1967), edited by Leslie Fischel and Benjamin Quarles; **A Documentary History of the Negro People in the United States* (1951), edited by Herbert Aptheker; and **Black Women in White America: A Documentary History* (1973), edited by Gerda Lerner. For listings of works on particular topics, individuals, or periods, consult Dorothy Porter, *The Negro in the*

United States: A Selected Bibliography (1970) and James McPherson, et. al., *Blacks in America: Bibliographical Essays* (1971).

For material on the Native Americans before the coming of the Europeans, see William T. Sanders and Joseph P. Marino, **New World Prehistory: Archaeology of the American Indian* (1970). Useful surveys are Edward Spicer, **A Short History of the Indians of the United States* (1969) and, by the same author, **Cycles of Conquest: The Impact of Spain, Mexico, and the United States on the Indians of the Southwest 1533-1960* (1962); William T. Hagan, **American Indians* (1961), which stresses the impact of Anglo-American governmental policies; and Murray L. Wax, *American Indians: Unity and Diversity* (1971), a sociological study with considerable historical background. Two interesting documentary collections are Francis Prucha, **The Indian in American History* (1971), selections from classic works on Indian history; and Joseph H. Cash and Herbert T. Hoover, **To Be An Indian* (1971), interviews with contemporary Indian spokesmen. For additional materials, see William T. Hagan's bibliography, **The Indian in American History* (1963, revised edition 1972).

The English "core culture" is treated as an ethnic group in E. Digby Baltzell, **The Protestant Establishment: Aristocracy and Caste in America* (1964), and Charles H. Anderson, **White Protestant Americans: From National Origins to Religious Group* (1970). For a negative assessment of this group compared to other European ethnic groups, see Peter Schrag's controversial *The Decline of the Wasp* (1973). Materials on specific English-speaking immigrant communities and their integration into American society include Rowland T. Berthoff, *British Immigrants in Industrial America, 1790-1950* (1953, reprinted 1968); Charlotte Erickson, *Invisible Immigrants: The Adaptation of the English and Scottish Immigrants in Nineteenth Century America* (1972); Alan Conway, *The Welsh in America* (1961); and John Rowe, *The Hard Rock Men: Cornish Immigrants and the North American Mining Frontier* (1974). Henry J. Ford's older work, *The Scotch-Irish in America* (1915, reprinted 1969), is especially valuable on Scotch-Irish religion and education in colonial America, while James Leyburn's newer and more comprehensive *The Scotch-Irish: A Social History* (1962) is excellent on the relationships between the Scotch-Irish and other ethnic groups, including the Indians, and on Scotch-Irish participation in colonial political life and in the Revolution.

B. EUROPEAN ETHNIC COMMUNITIES

For material on French-speaking immigrants in the seventeenth and eighteenth centuries, see Arthur Henry Hirsch, *The Huguenots of*

Colonial South Carolina (1928), and Elizabeth Huntington Avery, *The Influence of French Immigration on the Political History of the United States* (1890, reprinted 1972). The story of the French-speaking immigrants from Canada is told in Jacques Ducharme, *The Shadows of the Trees: The Story of the French Canadians in New England* (1943). For material on the colonial Dutch, see Maud W. Goodwin, *The Dutch and English on the Hudson* (1919). For a general survey, see Henry S. Lucas' exhaustive *Dutch Immigration to the United States and Canada, 1789-1950* (1955) and the briefer recent account by Gerald F. de Jong, *The Dutch in America, 1609-1974* (1975).

One of the first books to examine the social and political impact of immigrants upon American cities was Oscar Handlin's excellent **Boston's Immigrants* (1968) which deals primarily with the Irish. Other useful treatments of this ethnic group are George Potter, *To the Golden Door: The Story of the Irish in Ireland and America* (1960, reprinted 1974); William Shannon, *The American Irish* (1966); and Andrew Greeley, **That Most Distressful Nation* (1973). Two of the many specialized studies deserving attention are Edwin Levine's examination of the Irish in politics, *The Irish and Irish Politicians* (1966), and Thomas N. Brown's excellent study of Irish-American efforts on behalf of the homeland, **Irish-American Nationalism* (1966).

Albert Faust's monumental two-volume work, *The German Element in the United States with Special Reference to Its Political, Moral, Social, and Educational Influence* (1927, reprinted 1969) is short on interpretation but contains a wealth of information. More interpretive is John Hawgood's account of the attempts to create German states in the United States and of the German reaction to American nativism, *The Tragedy of German-America: The Germans in the United States of America During the Nineteenth Century* (1940, reprinted 1970). A particularly interesting specialized study is Frederick C. Luebke, *Bonds of Loyalty: German-Americans and World War I* (1974), which suggests that the wartime anti-German hysteria was the surfacing of long-standing hostility of English-Americans to German-Americans, a hostility engendered by cultural conflicts over such issues as public education, Sabbatarianism, and suffrage. See also William Parsons, *The Pennsylvania Dutch: A Persistent Minority* (1976).

Theodore C. Blegen's scholarly, *Norwegian Migration to America* (1931, reprinted 1969), and Carlton Qualey's, *Norwegian Settlement in the United States* (1938, reprinted 1970), provide an excellent introduction to Norwegian-American history. The comprehensive study of the Swedes in colonial America is Amandus Johnson, *The Swedish Settlement on the Delaware* (2 volumes, 1911, reprinted 1970). For the later periods, see Florence Edith Janson, *The Background of Swedish Immigration, 1840-1930* (1931, reprinted 1969), a superb study of the complex motivation in emigration, and Sture Lindmark, *Swedish-America 1914-1932* (1971), which emphasizes Swedish-American efforts to maintain ethnic life and institutions in twentieth-century America. For material on the Danes, see Kristian Hvidt's scholarly, *Flight to America: The Social Background of 300,000 Danish Emigrants* (1975), and Noel J. Choresman, **Ethnic Influence on Urban Groups: The Danish Americans* (1966, reprinted 1975), with information on family life, community structure, and economic activity in America. On the Finns, see William A. Hoglund, *Finnish Immigrants in America* (1960), and John Wargelin, *The Americanization of the Finns* (1924, reprinted 1972).

A brief statistical study by Francis M. Rogers, *Americans of Portuguese Descent: A Lesson in Differentiation* (1974), analyzes the impact of factors such as region of origin, time of immigration, and political affiliation on different waves of Portuguese immigrants. Also of interest on this little studied group is an older study of the problems of assimilation, Donald Taft, *Two Portuguese Communities in New England* (1923, reprinted 1969). Two older works on Greek-Americans, Henry P. Fairchild, *Greek Immigration to the United States* (1911), and J. P. Xenides, *The Greeks in America* (1922) contain useful information, but the definitive history of Greek America is Theodore Saloutos, *The Greeks in the United States* (1963). For the Armenians, see Malcolm H. Vartan, *The Armenians in America* (1919), and Aram Yeretzian, *A History of Armenian Immigration to America with Special Reference to Los Angeles* (1923, reprinted 1974).

For the story of Arabic speaking communities, see Philip K. Hitti *The Syrians in America* (1924); Habeeb Katibah, *Arabic-speaking Americans* (1946) and *The Story of Lebanon and Its Emigrants* (1968). The past decade has seen a surge of new writing on the Arab-American communities. See the two very useful collections, **Arabic Speaking Communities in American Cities* (1974), edited by Barbara C. Aswad, which includes studies of Christian and Moslem communities in Michigan, bilingual Arabic children, and occupational patterns, as well as a good bibliography; and *Arab Americans: Studies in Assimilation* (1969), edited by Elaine Hagopian and Ann Padan, which includes studies on Arab nationalism, community institutions, and the changing roles of women.

Two useful older works on Polish-Americans are Paul Fox, *The Poles in America* (1922, reprinted 1970) and W. I. Thomas and F. Znaniecki, *The Polish Peasant in Europe and America* (2 volumes, 1927; other editions available). The latter is a classic sociological study based mainly upon letters written by Poles and Polish-Americans during the peak immigration years of the early twentieth century. The study emphasizes the disorganization of personal and community life that sometimes resulted from immigration. For more recent histories see two books by Joseph Wytrwal, *America's Polish Heritage: A Social History of the Poles in America* (1961), especially good on institutions such as the Polish National Alliance and the Polish Roman Catholic Union of America, and *The Poles in America* (1969). The most recent general survey is the excellent **Polish Americans: Status and Competition in an Ethnic Community* (1976), by Helen Znaniecki Lopata. Many special studies have been written by the father of Polish-American historiography, Miecislaus Haiman, including *The Polish Past in America 1608-1895* (1975) and *Poles in New York in the 17th and 18th Centuries* (1938).

For information on other Central and Eastern European immigrant communities, see Wasyl Halich, *Ukrainians in the United States* (1937, reprinted 1970); Thomas Capek, *The Czechs in America* (1928, reprinted 1969); Emil Lengyel, *Americans from Hungary* (1948, reprinted 1975); Gerald G. Govorchin, *Americans from Yugoslavia* (1961); George J. Prpic, *Croatian Immigrants in America* (1971); Jerome Davis, *The Russian Immigrant* (1929, reprinted 1969); Maruta Karklis, Liga Streips, and Laimonis Streips, *The Latvians in America, 1640-1973* (1974); and Emily Balch, *Our Slavic Fellow Citizens* (1910, reprinted 1969).

The most useful recent synthesis of American Jewish history is Henry Feingold, **Zion in America: The Jewish Experience from Colonial Times to the Present* (1974). Among the earlier histories of value are Oscar Handlin, *Adventure in Freedom: Three Hundred Years of Jewish Life in America* (1954, reprinted 1971), and Nathan Glazer, **American Judaism* (1957, revised edition 1972), which stresses the impact of successive waves of immigration on religious life and thought. For an introductory sociology of the contemporary Jewish community, including material on education, family structure, institutional life, and ethnic identity, see Marshall Sklare, **America's Jews* (1971). Special characteristics of Jewish assimilation and acculturation are explored with insight and sophistication in C. Bezalel Sherman, **The Jew Within American Society: A Study in Ethnic Individuality* (1965), and Joseph Blau, *Judaism in America: from Curiosity to Third Faith* (1976). Among the excellent studies of particular periods and topics are Jacob R. Marcus' three-volume, *The Colonial American Jew: 1492-1776* (1970); Bertram Korn, *American Jewry and the Civil War* (1951); Irving Howe,* *World of Our Fathers* (1976), on the early twentieth century Eastern European immigration; and Melvin Urofsky, **American Zionism from Herzl to the Holocaust* (1975).

The classic introduction to Italian immigration throughout the Western Hemisphere is Robert Foerster, *Italian Emigration of Our Times* (1919, reprinted 1969). For a wealth of information on population, occupation, housing, health, education, and social welfare among

Italian immigrants in the United States in the early twentieth century, see John Horace Mariano, *The Italian Contribution to American Democracy* (1922, reprinted 1975), an early antirestrictionist study. Among the most useful of the many recent works on the Italian-American experience are Joseph Lopreato, **Italian Americans* (1970), which includes material on the Old World background, acculturation, education, and economic mobility, and Alexander DeConde, *Half Bitter, Half Sweet: An Excursion into Italian-American History* (1971). Two useful collections are Wayne Moquin, *Documentary History of Italian-Americans* (1974) and the volume of scholarly essays edited by S. M. Tomasi and M. H. Engel, **The Italian Experience in the United States* (1971). For a lively account of three generations of South Italian mores, see Richard Gambino, **Blood of My Blood* (1974).

C. ASIAN AND WESTERN HEMISPHERE IMMIGRANT COMMUNITIES

An early account of Chinese immigration which still has much valuable information is Mary R. Coolidge, *Chinese Immigration* (1909, reprinted 1969). For a lively, recent historical survey, see Betty Lee Sung, *Mountain of Gold* (1967), reprinted in a paperback edition as *The Story of the Chinese in America* (1971). For a sociological treatment of the contemporary Chinese community, see Rose Hum Lee, *The Chinese in the United States of America* (1960). In *Longtime Californ': A Documentary Study of an American Chinatown* (1975) edited by Victor G. and Brett de Barry Nee, a cross section of Chinese-Americans describe their hardships and achievements. The myth that Chinese-Americans have been universally successful in America is examined and shattered in Dean Lan's provocative study, *Prestige with Limitations: Realities of the Chinese-American Elite* (1976).

Yamato Ichihashi's early defense of Japanese immigrants, *Japanese in the United States,* (1932, reprinted 1969) is still valuable. For more recent treatments of the history and sociology of the Japanese-American community, see Harry Kitano, **Japanese Americans: The Evolution of a Subculture* (1969), and William Petersen, **Japanese Americans: Oppression and Success* (1971). Hilary Conroy and T. Scott Miyakawa have assembled an excellent collection of original scholarly essays, including material on education, Americanization, and economic life, in **East Across the Pacific: Historical and Sociological Studies of Japanese Assimilation and Immigration* (1972). Bill Hosokawa's study of second generation Japanese Americans, **Nisei: The Quiet Americans* (1969) emphasizes the impact of the relocation camp experience of World War II on the American born generation.

Literature on other Asian immigrant groups in the United States is scant. On the Filipinos, see Bruno Lasker, *Filipino Immigration to Continental United States and to Hawaii* (1931, reprinted 1969), and B. T. Catapusan, *The Filipino Social Adjustment in the United States* (1940, reprinted 1972). On the Koreans, see Hyung-Chan Kim, *The Koreans in America* (1974). Gail Kelly, *From Vietnam to America: Chronicle of the Vietnamese Immigration to the United States* (1977) is an excellent account of the immigration and resettlement of refugees from Vietnam. Based on government documents and extensive interviews with camp officials and refugees, Kelly's work highlights the contrast between Vietnamese needs and objectives and the American resettlement program, which was based on American political and economic imperatives.

For a general account of Canadian immigration, see Marcus Lee Hansen, *The Mingling of the Canadian and American Peoples* (1940, reprinted 1970). Twentieth century West Indian immigration is described by Ira de A. Reid in *The Negro Immigrant: His Background Characteristics and Social Adjustment, 1899-1937* (1939, reprinted 1969). For another aspect of black immigration from the Caribbean, see Glenn Hendricks, *The Dominican Diaspora: From the Dominican Republic to New York City, Villagers in Transition* (1974). The extensive literature on the midtwentieth century Puerto Rican migration includes Elena Padilla's anthropological study, *Up From Puerto Rico* (1958); Dan Wakefield's journalistic portrait of East Harlem, *Island in the City* (1959, reprinted 1975); Clarence Senior's plea for understanding, *The Puerto Ricans: Strangers—Then Neighbors* (1961, new edition 1965), which stresses the economic and educational progress being made by Puerto Rican immigrants; and Joseph P. Fitzpatrick's excellent sociological survey *Puerto Rican Americans: The Meaning of Migration to the Mainland* (1971), which covers education, family life, religion, health, and recent social and political movements within the community.

The first major survey of Mexican American history, the journalistic work of Carey McWilliams, *North from Mexico: The Spanish Speaking People in the United States* (1948) is a useful introduction. Two older works by Manuel Gamio, *Mexican Immigration to the United States* (1930, reprinted 1969) and *The Mexican Immigrant, His Life Story* (1931, reprinted 1969) provide information about Mexican immigration in the early decades of the twentieth century, including valuable first person accounts of the experiences of Mexican-American immigrants. An excellent historical survey incorporating recent scholarship is Rodolfo Acuna, *Occupied America: The Chicano Struggle for Liberation* (1972). For a contemporary sociological overview, especially good on the impact of urbanization and the problems of economic mobility, see Ellwyn Stoddard *Mexican Americans* (1973). Donald Meinig, *Southwest:*

Three Peoples in Geographical Change, 1600-1970 (1971) is a unique study of the interaction between peoples and an environment.

IV. Special Studies

A. IMMIGRATION AND IMMIGRANT GROUPS

For information on world migration patterns, consult Ragnar Numelin, *The Wandering Spirit: A Study of Human Migration* (1937) and Franklin D. Scott's anthology **World Migration in Modern Times* (1968). Two important works on immigrants who left the United States to return to their homelands are Theodore Saloutos' groundbreaking *They Remember America: The Story of Greek-American Repatriates* (1956) and Betty Boyd Caroli, *Italian Repatriation from the United States, 1900-1914* (1974). Caroli demonstrates that life in America profoundly changed those who experienced it even for a short period and suggests the importance of the American "safety valve" for Italy's excess population. For communication between immigrants who remained in America and those they left behind, see H. Arnold Barton, editor, *Letters From the Promised Land: Swedes in America, 1840-1914* (1975) and Theodore Blegen, *Land of Their Choice: The Immigrants Write Home* (1955).

The historical and sociological studies of ethnic communities at particular times or locations are too numerous to list. Among these, are such excellent works as Moses Rischin, **The Promised City: New York's Jews, 1870-1914* (1962); Selig Adler and Thomas Connelly, *From Ararat to Suburbia: The History of the Jewish Community of Buffalo* (1960); Frederick Bohme, *A History of the Italians in New Mexico* (1975); Humbert Nelli, **The Italians in Chicago, 1880-1930: A Study in Ethnic Mobility* (1973); Thomas Kessner, **The Golden Door: Italian and Jewish Immigrant Mobility in New York City, 1880-1915* (1977); Evans Wood, *Hamtramck, Then and Now* (1955), and Dennis Clark, *The Irish in Philadelphia: Ten Generations of Urban Experience* (1974). Of particular interest are a number of recent studies comparing the experiences of two or more ethnic groups. Among these are H. Brett Melendy, **The Oriental Americans* (1972); Josef J. Barton, *Peasants and Strangers: Italians, Rumanians, and Slovaks in an American City, 1890-1950* (1975), an example of the new quantitative social history dealing with Cleveland; Thomas Archdeacon, *New York City, 1664-1710: Conquest and Change* (1976), an analysis of how the English and the French Huguenots took social and political control of the city away from the Dutch; Eleanor C. Nordyke, *The Peopling of Hawaii* (1977); Elizabeth

A. H. John, *Storms Brewed in Other Men's Worlds: The Confrontation of Indians, Spanish, and French in the Southwest 1540-1795* (1975); and the collection edited by Allen F. Davis and Mark H. Haller, **The Peoples of Philadelphia: A History of Ethnic Groups and Lower Class Life, 1790-1940* (1973).

B. IMMIGRANT WOMEN, YOUTH, AND THE FAMILY

A rising interest in the history of women, youth, and the family is only beginning to be reflected in the literature on ethnic America. Many of the best materials on immigrant women are older works, usually written by women, such as Bessie Pebotsky, *The Slavic Immigrant Woman* (1925, reprinted 1971); Louise C. Odencrantz, *Italian Women in Industry* (1919); Caroline Manning, *The Immigrant Woman and Her Job* (1930, reprinted 1970); Elizabeth Beadsley Butler, *Woman and the Trades: Pittsburgh, 1907-1908* (1909, reprinted 1969); Grace Abbott, *The Immigrant and the Community* (1917, reprinted 1971), which includes material on health care, work, and the immigrant journey; and Sophonisba Breckinridge, *New Homes for Old* (1920, reprinted 1971), excellent on housework, child care, and family relations in the early part of the twentieth century. For studies of mid-twentieth century white, working class women, many of them second and third generation ethnics, see Lee Rainwater, Richard Coleman, and Gerald Handel, *Workingman's Wife* (1959); Mirra Komarovsky, **Blue-Collar Marriage* (1964); and Nancy Seifer, **Absent From the Majority: Working Class Women in America* (1973), which discusses the impact of the women's movement, the "new ethnicity," and other social and political changes of the late 1960's and early 1970's.

There is no single definitive history of immigrant women, but valuable material, which includes accounts of physicians, labor leaders, and other outstanding women of the past, can be found in Cecyle Neidle, **America's Immigrant Women* (1975); Linda Grant de Pauw, **Four Traditions: Women of New York During the American Revolution* (1974), about Iroquois, Afro-American, Dutch, and English women in the eighteenth century; Rosalyn Baxandall, Linda Gordon, and Susan Reverby, **America's Working Women: A Documentary History* (1976), a collection of excerpts from diaries, songs, and other documents; Charlotte Baum, et. al., *The Jewish Woman in America* (1976); and Barbara M. Wertheimer, **We Were There: The Story of Working Women* (1977).

Two particularly valuable works on the relationship between the feminist movement and contemporary ethnic women are Barbara Peters and Victoria Samuels, *Dialogue on Diversity: A New Agenda for*

Women (1976) and Elizabeth Koltun, editor, **The Jewish Woman: New Perspectives* (1976).

For a moving volume of oral history in which immigrant women describe the circumstances of their coming to America, their family lives, their work, and their feelings about themselves, see Sydelle Kramer and Jenny Masur, *Jewish Grandmothers* (1976). Another worthwhile oral history is Nancy Seifer, *Nobody Speaks for Me* (1976), in which black, Hispanic, and European ethnic women activists of the 1970's describe their personal and community lives. For information on new research directions and materials, see Maxine Seller, "Beyond the Stereotype: A New Look at the Immigrant Woman, 1880-1924," *Journal of Ethnic Studies,* Vol. 3 (Spring 1975) and Betty Boyd Caroli, "Italian Women in America: Sources for Study," *Italian Americana,* Vol. 2, #2 (Spring 1976).

Materials on immigrant and ethnic children can be culled from the recent three-volume work edited by Robert Bremner, *Children and Youth in America: A Documentary History* (1970, 1971, 1974); from the writings of Jane Addams, especially **The Spirit of Youth and the City Streets* (1909, reprinted 1972); and Grace Abbott's two-volume documentary collection, *The Child and the State* (1938, reprinted 1968), which contains valuable materials on child labor. For more recent material, see Francesco Cordasco and Eugene Bucchioni, *The Puerto Rican Community and Its Children* (1972), and Michael Novak's collection of essays, **Growing Up Slavic* (1975).

Arthur Calhoun's classic study, *A Social History of the American Family from Colonial Times to the Present* (3 volumes, 1917-1919, reprinted 1945) contains older relevant information on ethnic families. The best collection of recent scholarship on this topic is Charles H. Mindel and Robert W. Habenstein, **Ethnic Families in America: Patterns and Variations* (1976), with articles on the changing family structures of fifteen groups, including blacks and Native Americans as well as European and Hispanic peoples. For a useful overview of inter-marriage, see Milton L. Barron, **The Blending Americans* (1972).

C. EDUCATION AND AMERICANIZATION

For ethnic education in colonial America, see William Kilpatrick, *The Dutch Schools of New Netherland and Colonial New York* (1912, reprinted 1969) and James Pyle Wickersham, *A History of Education in Pennsylvania* (1885, reprinted 1969), which contains information on the education of the Germans. The quarrel between the Catholic Church and the Public School Society in mid-nineteenth century New York, as well as controversies surrounding the education of twentieth century ethnic communities, are ably described in Diane Ravitch, **The*

Great School Wars: New York City, 1805-1973: A History of the Public Schools as Battlefields of Social Change (1974). Revisionist interpretations that challenge the traditional view of public schools as promoters of immigrants' socioeconomic mobility are Michael Katz, *The Irony of Early School Reform: Educational Innovation in Mid-Nineteenth Century Massachusetts* (1968), and Colin Greer's provocative *The Great School Legend: A Revisionist Interpretation of American Public Education* (1973).

Among the many valuable studies of the educational experiences and problems of particular immigrant communities are Leonard Covello's classic study, *The Social Background of the Italo-American School Child* (1967), which includes material on South Italian family structure, and suggestions for an American school curriculum more responsive to ethnic communities; *Puerto Ricans and Educational Opportunity* (1972), an original Arno Pess anthology of reports and other documents on the educational problems of Puerto Rican children in the public schools; Alfred Castaneda, Manuel Ramirez III, Carlos E. Cortes, and Mario Barrera, editors, *Mexican Americans and Educational Change* (1974), a collection of papers focusing on the politics of educational change and on bicultural and bilingual education for Mexican-American children. See also Thomas P. Carter, *Mexican Americans in School: A History of Educational Neglect* (1970).

The literature on the education and Americanization of Europeans in the early twentieth century is extensive. For viewpoints of experts of the period, see Leonard Ayres, *Laggards in Our Schools* (1907), a national survey of immigrant "retardation" in public schools; Frank Thompson, *The Schooling of the Immigrant* (1920, reprinted 1971); and William Sharlip and Albert Owens, *Adult Immigrant Education* (1928), with a special chapter on the education of immigrant women. Recent accounts of immigrant education in the late nineteenth and early twentieth century can be found in Lawrence A. Cremin, *The Transformation of the School: Progressivism in American Education, 1876-1957* (1961); David Tyack, *The One Best System: A History of American Urban Education* (1974); Edward Hartmann, *The Movement to Americanize the Immigrant* (1948); John Bodnar, "Materialism and Morality: Slavic-American Immigrants and Education, 1890-1940," *Journal of Ethnic Studies,* Vol. 3 (Winter 1976); and Mark Krug, *The Melting of the Ethnics: Education of the Immigrants, 1880-1914* (1976). Two relevant recent studies are Gerd Korman, *Industrialization, Immigrants, and Americanizers: The View from Milwaukee, 1866-1921* (1967), which examines the role of business interests in Americanization and Robert Carlson, *The Quest for Conformity: Americanization Through Education* (1975), a concise survey of Americanization theory and practice from the colonial period through the 1960's with a good bibliographical essay.

The most stimulating work on education, broadly defined, within ethnic communities themselves is Joshua Fishman and Vladimir Nahirny, *Language Loyalty in the United States* (1966), a groundbreaking work which examines ethnic schools, newspapers, magazines, radio, and television as means of perpetuating ethnic languages and cultural traditions. For additional material on ethnic schools, see James A. Burns, *The Growth and Development of the Catholic School System in the United States* (1912, reprinted 1969); Andrew Greeley, William McCready and Kathleen McCourt, *Catholic Schools in a Declining Church* (1976), which emphasizes continuing Catholic commitment to the parochial school system; James W. Sanders, *The Education of an Urban Minority: Catholics in Chicago, 1833-1965* (1977); and Lloyd Gartner, **Jewish Education in the United States* (1970). For a view of a public school system with strong ethnic components, see Peter Schrag, *Village School Downtown: Boston's Schools, Boston's Politics* (1967).

D. THE IMMIGRANT IN THE CITY: LIVING CONDITIONS, SOCIAL PROBLEMS, ECONOMIC MOBILITY

The recent interest in urban history has produced many studies of immigrant life in the city, such as Robert Ernst, *Immigrant Life in New York City, 1825-1863* (1965); Stanley Lieberson, *Ethnic Patterns in American Cities* (1962), on immigrant neighborhoods; and David Ward's brief but important *Cities and Immigrants* (1971), which analyzes the relationships between ethnic neighborhoods, and changing economic conditions and transportation networks. For sociological studies of lower class and working class Italian neighborhoods, see William Whyte, **Street Corner Society: The Social Structure of an Italian Slum* (1943, revised edition 1955) and Herbert Gans, **The Urban Villagers: Group and Class Life of Italian Americans* (1962). See also Gerald D. Suttles' stimulating study, **The Social Order of the Slum: Ethnicity and Territory in the Inner City* (1968).

For glimpses into the social pathology of urban ethnic life, see Herbert Asbury, **The Gangs of New York* (1927, revised edition 1971), a social history of New York City's underworld in the nineteenth century and Joseph L. Albini, **The American Mafia: Genesis of a Legend* (1971). For sympathetic accounts of immigrants' difficulties in trying to find justice within the American legal system, see Kate Claghorn, *The Immigrant's Day in Court* (1923, reprinted 1969), and *The Mexican American and the Law* (1974), edited by Carlos E. Cortes, an anthology which includes case histories, petitions, and other documents. On health and safety problems, see Michael Davis, *Immigrant Health and the Community* (1921, reprinted 1971); Crystal Eastman, *Work Accidents and the Law* (1910, reprinted 1969); and Beatrice Bishop Berle, *Eighty*

Puerto Rican Families in New York City: Health and Disease Studied in Context (1958, reprinted 1975), a study suggesting that illness was related to the anxiety and frustration caused by "the discrepancy between an individual's aspirations and the limited employment opportunities open to him." *Italians in the City: Health and Related Social Problems* (1975), edited by Francesco Cordasco, contains special reports on the health of Italian women and the growth rates of Italian children in New York City in the early twentieth century. For a stimulating feminist perspective linking nativism with the response to immigrant health problems in the early twentieth century, see Barbara Ehrenreich and Deirdre English, *Complaints and Disorders: The Sexual Politics of Sickness* (1973). The authors attribute the success of the movement for the dissemination of birth control information in urban slums to nativist fear of immigrant fertility and point out that public health measures were adopted because the middle class feared "contamination" from the ethnic ghettos. On mental health and ethnicity, see Rita Stein, *Disturbed Youth and Ethnic Family Patterns* (1972).

Some of the best sources on social welfare are the works of the Progressive reformers, such as Jacob Riis, **How the Other Half Lives* (1890 and numerous reprints) and *The Battle With the Slums* (1902, reprinted 1969); John Spargo, **The Bitter Cry of the Children* (1908, reprinted 1969); Lillian Wald, **The House on Henry Street* (1915, reprinted 1969); and Jane Addams, **Twenty Years at Hull-House* (1910, reprinted 1966). For recent interpretations of the motives and achievements of Progressive reformers, see Paul McBride, *Culture Clash: Immigrants and Reformers, 1880-1920* (1975) and Allen F. Davis, **Spearheads for Reform: The Social Settlements and the Progressive Movement, 1890-1914* (1967). The most useful general history of nineteenth and twentieth century social welfare policy and attitudes is Robert Bremner, **From the Depths: the Discovery of Poverty in the United States* (1956).

Using census data, tax records, and other quantitative sources, recent historians have explored problems of socioeconomic mobility. Richard Hutchinson, *Immigrants and Their Children, 1850-1950* (1956, new edition 1976) analyzes the geographic and occupational patterns and distribution of major European ethnic populations throughout the nation over several generations. For mobility studies of particular cities, see Stephan Thernstrom, **Poverty and Progress: Social Mobility in a Nineteenth Century City* (1964), on the economic mobility of Irish laborers and their sons in Newberryport, Massachusetts, and **The Other Bostonians: Poverty and Progress in the American Metropolis, 1880-1970* (1973), comparing the mobility of major European communities in Boston. For similar studies of other cities, see

Nineteenth Century Cities: Essays in the New Urban History (1969), edited by Stephan Thernstrom and Richard Sennett.

E. INSIDE ETHNIC AMERICA: COMMUNITY LIFE, POLITICS, THE NEW ETHNICITY

One of the best descriptions of the various organizations and institutions in the immigrant communities, stressing their importance as agents of education and Americanization, is John Daniels, *America Via the Neighborhood* (1920, reprinted 1971), which includes a listing of many of the major ethnic organizations of the early twentieth century. Also useful are W. Lloyd Warner and Leo Srole, *The Social Systems of American Ethnic Groups* (1945, reprinted 1976) and Gerald Suttles, *The Social Construction of Communities* (1972). There are a number of useful studies of specific institutions, such as Odd Sverre Lovoll's study of Norwegian fraternal orders, *A Folk Epic: the Bygdelag in America* (1975); Borris Bogen, *Jewish Philanthropy: An Exposition of the Principles and Methods in Jewish Social Service in the United States* (1917, reprinted 1969); and Philip Gleason's history of the Central-Verein, a national federation of German-American Catholic Societies, *The Conservative Reformers: German-American Catholics and the Social Order* (1968). Victor Greene's *For God and Country: The Rise of Polish and Lithuanian Ethnic Consciousness in America, 1861-1910* (1975) explores the role of factionalism among the parish leadership in stimulating awareness of ethnic identity in the Polish and Lithuanian communities.

Among the many studies dealing with the role of religion in ethnic communities are William Mulder's account of the Norwegian, Swedish, and Danish Mormon immigrants, *Homeward to Zion: The Mormon Migration from Scandinavia* (1957) and George Stephenson, *The Religious Aspects of Swedish Immigration* (1932, reprinted 1969). The effort of Protestant missions to "uplift" the nineteenth century urban poor, many of whom were Catholic immigrants, is examined in Caroll Smith Rosenberg, *Religion and the Rise of the American City: The New York City Mission Movement, 1812-1870* (1971). The religious history of the same period from the Catholic immigrant point of view is described by Jay P. Dolan in *The Immigrant Church: New York's Irish and German Catholics, 1815-1865* (1975), stressing the rise of the Church as a tightly organized socially conservative bastion against Protestant America. Aaron Abell, *American Catholicism and Social Action: A Search for Social Justice, 1865-1950* (1960) emphasizes the material and educational assistance the Church offered the immigrant poor, while Richard M. Linkh, *American Catholicism and European Immigrants, 1900-1924* (1975) argues that the Church offered little aid to Southeastern

European immigrants before World War I and was halfhearted in its efforts to promote Americanization.

While studies of individual ethnic presses, such as Mordecai Soltes, *The Yiddish Press: An Americanizing Agency* (1925, reprinted 1969) and Carl Wittke, *The German-Language Press in America* (1953, reprinted 1972), can be located through specialized bibliographies, the best single comprehensive source on foreign language newspapers is Robert E. Park, *The Immigrant Press and Its Control* (1922, reprinted 1971). The author's concern about the loyalty of the ethnic press during World War I is less interesting than the valuable information he provides about the origins and circulation of ethnic newspapers and his extensive quotations of news, editorials, poetry, humor, and advertisements from ethnic papers. There is no general work on ethnic theatre, but information on this subject can be found in David Lifson, *The Yiddish Theater in America* (1965), which includes photographs; Henriette Naeseth, *The Swedish Theatre of Chicago 1868-1950* (1951), which covers other aspects of Swedish cultural life as well; and Maxine Seller, "Antonietta Pisanelli Alessandro and the Italian Theatre of San Francisco," *Educational Theatre Journal*, Vol. 28, #2 (May 1976); and J. Rosenberg, "The Emerging Chicano Drama," *Bulletin of the Cross Cultural Southwest Ethnic Study Center*, Vol. 3, #3 (September 1976).

Serious critical studies of immigrant and ethnic literature are still scarce, but the following works provide an introduction to this literature: Dorothy Burton Skardal, *The Divided Heart* (1974), a social history of Scandinavian-American life as reflected in its immigrant literature; Nona Balakian, *The Armenian-American Writer: A New Accent in American Fiction* (1958); Rose Basile Green, *The Italian-American Novel: A Document of the Interaction of Two Cultures* (1974); and Allen Guttman, *The Jewish Writer in America: Assimilation and the Crisis of Identity* (1971). For a vivid contemporary account of Yiddish literature and theatre, see Hutchins Hapgood, **The Spirit of the Ghetto* (1902, reprinted 1966 and 1976).

Ivan Light's **Ethnic Enterprise in America* (1972) compares the business activities of Chinese, Japanese, and blacks. Since the overwhelming majority of immigrants were members of the working class, there is a rich literature on labor activities and immigrant radicalism. See Wayne G. Broehl, Jr., *The Molly Maguires* (1964) on Irish labor violence in the coal mines of Pennsylvania; Victor Greene, *The Slavic Community on Strike: Immigrant Labor in Pennsylvania Anthracite* (1968); Malech Epstein's two-volume, *Jewish Labor in the United States: 1882-1952* (1950, revised edition 1969); and Edwin Fenton, *Immigrants and Unions, A Case Study: Italians and American Labor* (1975), a richly documented study demonstrating that when they were welcomed by the leadership, and when economic conditions were particularly favorable, Italians participated enthusiastically in unions and found this participation an important means of Americanization.

F. ETHNICS AND AMERICANS: THE POLITICS OF INTER-GROUP RELATIONS

In recent years historians have acknowledged that ethnicity as well as class affects voter allegiance. The political behavior of ethnic Americans has been explored in studies such as Samuel Lubell's pioneering *The Future of American Politics* (1952); John Allswang, *A House for all People: Chicago's Ethnic Groups and Their Politics, 1890-1936* (1971); and Thomas Pavlak, *Ethnic Identification and Political Behavior* (1976). Alex Gottfried's *Boss Cermak of Chicago: A Study of Political Leadership* (1962) examines the rise of an immigrant political boss who capitalized on his ethnic power base. In *Senator Robert F. Wagner and the Rise of Urban Liberalism* (1968), J. Joseph Huthmacher shows ethnic communities as agents of reform. The impact of ethnic communities on foreign policy in the twentieth century is traced in Louis Gerson, *The Hyphenate in Recent American Politics and Diplomacy* (1964) and in Joseph P. O'Grady, *The Immigrants' Influence on Wilson's Peace Policies* (1967), which suggests that on this issue the impact of immigrant lobbies was not a decisive one.

In *The White Ethnic Movement and Ethnic Politics* (1973), Perry Weed explores the effort of the major political parties to gain the white ethnic vote in the decades following World War II. Other works on the politics and other aspects of the "new ethnicity" of the 1960's and 1970's are Peter Schrag, *The Forgotten Americans* (1969); Michael Novak's controversial and stimulating *The Rise of the Unmeltable Ethnics* (1971); and Richard Krickus, *Pursuing the American Dream: White Ethnics and the New Populism* (1976), which explores neighborhood and school conflicts between white ethnics and blacks. Two excellent collections dealing with issues such as education, discrimination, urban renewal, affirmative action, employment, and the complex relationships between white ethnics, blacks, and WASPS are Murray Friedman, *Overcoming Middle Class Rage* (1971) and Michael Wenk, S. M. Tomasi, and Geno Baroni, *Pieces of a Dream: The Ethnic Worker's Crisis with America* (1972).

There are many studies of discrimination against individual ethnic communities, such as Chang-Tsu Wu's edited volume, *Chink! Anti-Chinese Prejudice in America* (1972) and Roger Daniels, *Concentration Camps USA: Japanese Americans and World War II* (1971). The best general histories of nativism, its intellectual and emotional origins, and its political consequences, are Ray Billington, *The Protestant Crusade,*

1800-1860 (1964) and John Higham, **Strangers in the Land: Patterns of American Nativism, 1860-1925* (1955), which has an excellent and comprehensive treatment of the background of the immigration restriction of the 1920's. For further insight into anti-immigrant feeling, see Robert K. Murray, **Red Scare: A Study in National Hysteria, 1919-1920* (1955) and Thomas Corran, *Xenophobia and Immigration, 1820-1952* (1975), which emphasizes Anglo-Saxon fear of being overwhelmed by other cultures.

For material on American immigration policy since the National Origins Quota Act of 1924, see Robert A. Divine, *American Immigration Policy, 1924-1952* (1957, reprinted 1972) and Marion T. Bennett, *American Immigration Policies, a History* (1963). America's failure to save significant numbers of European Jews from Nazi extermination by admitting them into the country has been chronicled and linked to anti-Semitism, indifference, and the economic depression of the 1930's in Henry Feingold, *The Politics of Rescue: The Roosevelt Administration and the Holocaust, 1938-1945* (1970) and Arthur Morse, **While Six Million Died* (1968). For the impact of post World War II changes in immigration laws, see D. S. North and W. G. Weissert, *Immigrants and the American Labor Market* (1973), which includes a discussion of the "brain drain," and S. M. Tomasi and C. B. Keely, **Whom Have We Welcomed?* (1975), which summarizes current policy, examines the question of illegal aliens, and considers proposed legislative and administrative changes.

V. Literary Sources

Though some immigrant writers undoubtedly exaggerated their hardships, their successes, or both, ethnic autobiographies, novels, short stories, poems, and plays provide valuable source material for the student of ethnic life. The following are a representative sampling of this vast literature.

A. IMMIGRANT AUTOBIOGRAPHIES

Short selections from autobiographies and memoirs can be found in collections such as Thomas C. Wheeler, **The Immigrant Experience: the Anguish of Becoming American* (1971); Cecyle S. Neidle, *The New Americans* (1967); and Oscar Handlin, *Children of the Uprooted* (1966), which deals with the second, or "marginal," generation. The National Council of Jewish Women in Pittsburgh has assembled a collective memoir based on oral histories of immigrant Jews in that city, *By Myself I'm a Book* (1972).

Among the many fascinating individual memoirs are the following: *Woman at Work* (1951, reprinted 1973), by Mary Anderson; *The Open Door* (1968), by Laurenda Andrade, a high school teacher of Portuguese who immigrated from the Azores; *Laughing in the Jungle* (1932, reprinted 1969), by Louis Adamic, who immigrated from Yugoslavia at the age of fourteen and found that survival in the United States depended upon brute strength and a sense of humor; *The Promised Land* (1912), by Mary Antin, a Russian Jew whose public school experience launched her career as a writer; *Son of Italy* (1924, reprinted 1975), by the poet Pascal D'Angelo; *The Americanization of Edward Bok: the Autobiography of a Dutch Boy Fifty Years After* (1921, reprinted 1972), by Edward Bok; *Living My Life* (1931, reprinted 1970), a two-volume memoir by the Russian-Jewish anarchist and feminist Emma Goldman; *Rosa: The Life of an Italian Immigrant* (1970) as told to Marie Hall Ets; *The Autobiography of Mother Jones* (1925, reprinted 1969), by Mary Harris Jones, Irish born labor organizer; *Mount Allegro* (1942, reprinted 1972) humorously written boyhood memories of Italian-American author Jerre Mangione; *The Soul of an Immigrant* (1928, reprinted 1969), by Italian born minister and social worker Constantine Panunzio; *The Woman Warrior* (1976), Americanization and intergeneration conflict as seen by second generation Chinese-American Maxine Hong Kingston; *Upstream* (1922) by Jewish journalist Ludwig Lewisohn; *Down These Mean Streets* (1967), growing up Puerto Rican, by Thomas Piri; *From Immigrant to Inventor* (1924), by Serbian physicist Michael Pupin; *Bread Upon the Waters* (1945) by Rose Pesotta, Russian Jewish immigrant elected four times to the vice presidency of the International Ladies Garment Workers Union; *Caste and Outcast* (1923) by Dhan Gopal Mukerji; and *A Far Journey* (1914) by Syrian minister Abraham M. Ribhany.

B. ETHNIC NOVELS

The following ethnic novels, a small sampling of the genre, present insights into first, second, and sometimes third generation ethnic life. For portraits of Greek-American life, see Harry Mark Petrakis, *Lion at My Heart* (1959), *The Odyssey of Kostas Volakis* (1963), and *A Dream of Kings* (1966); Peter Sourian, *Miri* (1957), and Mary Vardoulakis, *Gold in the Streets* (1945), about migration from Crete to a Massachusetts mill town. For Polish-American life see John Alexander Abucewicz, *Fool's White* (1969), about an immigrant's daughter who decides to become a nun and Richard Bankowsky's tetrology on the rise and fall of an immigrant family in New Jersey, *The Glass Rose* (1958), *After Pentecost* (1961), *On a Dark Night* (1964), and *The Pale Criminal* (1967). For other

East European groups see Thomas Bell, *Out of This Furnace* (1941), about the sufferings of Slovakian immigrant workers in the steel mills of Pennsylvania; Michael Novak, *Naked I Leave* (1970), the story of an upwardly mobile third generation Slavic immigrant's encounter with majority America, and Louis Adamic, *Grandsons: A Story of American Lives* (1935), *Two Way Passage* (1941), and *What's Your Name* (1942).

Pedro Juan Soto's **Hot Land, Cold Season* (1961) is a novel about a Puerto Rican immigrant who returns to the island in search of his identity. Hazel Lin, *The Physician* (1951) is a Chinese-American novel, and Jose Yglesias, *A Wake in Ybor City* (1963) tells of Cubans in Florida. For Armenian life, see Richard Hagopian, *Faraway the Spring* (1952) and Marjorie Housepian *A Houseful of Love* (1957). For the German experience, see Hermann Hagedorn, *The Hyphenated Family* (1960) and Elsie Singmaster, *The Magic Mirror* (1934). Working class Irish Catholic life is depicted by James Farrell in *Studs Lonigan* (1935) and *Danny O'Neill* (1936), each the first of a series. On Irish-American life, see also Tom McHale, *Farragan's Retreat* (1971) and Flannery O'Connor, **Wise Blood* (1962). For Norwegian immigration there is an outstanding trilogy by O. E. Rölvaag, **Giants in the Earth* (1927), *Peder Victorious* (1929), and *Our Father's God* (1931).

The Italian and the Jewish experiences are captured in many excellent novels. Among the best of the Italian are Pietro Di Donato, **Christ in Concrete* (1939) and *Three Circles of Light* (1960); Mario Puzo, *The Fortunate Pilgrim* (1964); Garibaldi Lapolla, *The Grand Gennaro* (1935); John Fante, *Wait Until Spring, Bandini* (1938); and Rocco Fumento, *Tree of Dark Reflections* (1962). For Jewish life see Abraham Cahan, **The Rise of David Levinsky* (1917) and *Yekl, A Tale of the New York Ghetto* (1896); Michael Gold, **Jews Without Money* (1930); Henry Roth, **Call It Sleep* (1934); Charles Angoff's series of novels beginning with *In the Morning Light* (1952); and Anzia Yezierska's *Bread Givers* (1925). For views of the contemporary Jewish community, see the works of Saul Bellow, Bernard Malamud, Chaim Potok, and Meyer Levin.

C. POETRY, SHORT STORIES, PLAYS

For Jewish immigrant poetry, see the anthologies by Irving Howe and Eliezer Greenberg, *A Treasury of Yiddish Poetry* (1969) and Jehiel and Sarah Cooperman, *America in Yiddish Poetry* (1967); and Morris Rosenfeld's moving poems on life in the Jewish ghettos of Europe and America, *Songs from the Ghetto* (1898). For Italian-American proletarian immigrant poetry, see Vincent Ferrini, *No Smoke* (1941), *Blood of the Tenement* (1944), and *Injunction* (1943) and Arturo Giovanitti, *The Collected Poems of Arturo Giovanitti* (1962). The Americanization of the

Italian immigrant is described in Joseph Tuccio's volume of poems, *My Own People* (1943). For traditional Polish poems and folklore see *The Wayside Willow* (1945) and *The Polish Land* (1943), collected by Klub Polski. For Hungarian-American poetry see Leslie Konnyu, *Collected Poems* (1968).

Short stories portraying ethnic life, most of them by ethnic writers, can be found in anthologies such as Myron Simon, *Ethnic Writers in America* (1972) and Abe C. Ravitz, *The American Disinherited: A Profile in Fiction*. (1970). Stories about particular groups include Anzia Yezierska, *Hungry Hearts* (1920) and *Children of Loneliness: Stories of Immigrant Life in America* (1923), and Max Rosenfeld's collection *A Union for Shabbos: Stories of Jewish Life in America* (1967), on the East European Jewish experience; James T. Farrell, *Short Stories* (1946) and Leo Rich Ward, *Holding Up the Hills* (1941) on the Irish; Harry Mark Petrakis, *Pericles on Thirty-First Street* (1965) and *Waves of Night and Other Stories* (1969) on the Greeks; Susie Hoogasian-Villa, *One Hundred Armenian Tales and Their Folkloristic Relevance* (1966) and Richard Hagopian, *The Dove Brings Peace* (1944) on the Armenians; and Monica Krawcyzk, *If the Branch Blossoms and Other Stories* (1950) and Nelson Algren, *The Neon Wilderness* (1947) on the Poles. *The Chicanos: Mexican American Voices* (1971), edited by Ed Ludwig and James Santibanez, contains stories, poetry, and essays. See also *AIIIEEEEE! An Anthology of Asian-American Writers* (1974), edited by Frank Chin, J. P. Chan, L. F. Inada, and S. Wong.

Examples of Yiddish drama in English translation can be found in *Three Plays by David Pinski* (1918) and David Lifson, *Epic and Folk Plays of the Yiddish Theater* (1975). Many of the works of Eugene O'Neill, such as *Anna Christie* (1973) and *Long Day's Journey Into Night* (1956) reflect aspects of Irish-American life. Recent plays about American ethnic life are collected in Francis Griffith and Joseph Mersand, *Eight American Ethnic Plays* (1974).

VI. For Further Investigation

For further information on specific topics or groups, consult bibliographies such as Richard Kolin, *Bibliography of Ethnicity and Ethnic Groups* (1973); Franklin Scott, *The Peopling of America: Perspectives on Immigration* (1972); Wayne Miller, *A Comprehensive Bibliography for the Study of American Minorities* (1977), a comprehensive two-volume reference work, and by the same author, the more concise guide, *A Handbook for the Study of American Minorities* (1977); and the bibliographical volume published by the National Council for the Social Studies, William H. Cartwright and Richard L. Watson, Jr., *The Reinterpretation of American History and Culture* (1973), with separately authored chapters on sources for the study of Native Americans, blacks, Mexican-Americans, Asian-Americans, and European ethnic groups.

Among the many useful bibliographies on individual ethnic groups are J. W. Zurawski, *Polish-American History and Culture: A Classified Bibliography* (1975); William Wong Lum, *Asians in America: A Bibliography* (1969); Francesco Cordasco and Salvatore J. LaGumina, *Italians in the United States: A Bibliography of Reports, Texts, Critical Studies and Related Materials* (1972); Paul McBride, *The Italians in America: An Interdisciplinary Bibliography* (1976); Luis Nogales, *The Mexican American: A Selected and Annotated Bibliography* (1971); Leo Pap, *The Portuguese in the United States: A Bibliography* (1976); D. H. Tolzmann, *German Americana: A Bibliography* (1975); and Irene P. Norell, *Literature of the Filipino-American in the United States: A Selective and Annotated Bibliography* (1976). Materials on the education of immigrant children are listed in Francesco Cordasco, *Immigrant Children in American Schools: A Classified and Annotated Bibliography, with Selected Source Documents* (1976). For listings of literary works on ethnic life, consult Louis Kaplan and James T. Coole, *A Bibliography of American Autobiographies* (1961); Otis Coan and Richard G. Lillard, *America in Fiction* (1967); Babett F. Inglehart and Anthony Mangione, *The Image of Pluralism in American Literature: The American Experience of European Ethnic Groups* (1974); and Daniel Weinberg, "Viewing the Immigrant Experience in America Through Fiction and Autobiography—With a Select Bibliography," *The History Teacher*, Vol. IX, #3, (May 1976), pp. 409-432.

Scholarly articles about various aspects of ethnicity and the experience of ethnic groups can be found in the academic journals of such disciplines as history, sociology, anthropology, and education as well as in various interdisciplinary periodicals. Some of the most useful specialized publications are *International Migration Review, Journal of Ethnic Studies, Ethnicity, American Jewish Historical Quarterly, Jewish Social Studies, Norwegian-American Studies, Polish-American Studies, Italian Americana, American-Hungarian Review, Amerasia Journal, Swedish Pioneer Historical Quarterly,* and the *Journal of Irish Studies.* For a listing of ethnic publications, popular and scholarly, see Lubomyr R. Wynar, *Encyclopedic Directory of Ethnic Newspapers and Periodicals in the United States* (revised edition 1976).

Primary source materials are limited only by the imagination and resourcefulness of the researcher. Among the varieties commonly used are census data, the reports of local, state, and national commissions on health, education, housing, employment, crime, and similar specific topics, the records of private and public welfare organizations, union, and political groups, and the documents of ethnic institutions such as churches, lodges, and cultural or nationalist societies. These and similar materials can often be located in large university or public libraries, and in specialized archival and resource centers such as the Balch Institute in Philadelphia; the Center for Migration Studies on Staten Island, New York; and the Center for Immigration Studies in St. Paul, Minnesota. Primary sources can also be found in local and state historical societies and in the archives of ethnic organizations and historical societies. For a listing of these ethnic societies, including their publications, see Lubomyr R. Wynar, *Encyclopedic Directory of Ethnic Organizations in the United States* (1975).

Index

Polish National Defense Committee, 167
Polish University of Chicago, 164
Political Association of Spanish Speaking Organizations (PASO), 255
Politics, 52, 85-88
Populist movement, 204, 205
Portuguese, 105, 264
Post, Christian Ferdinand, 21
Potato, importance of, 60-61
Potato famine (Ireland), 6
Presbyterian Church, 27, 28
Press, 35, 52, 173-180, 232
  see also Newspapers
Princeton University, 37
Printz, Johan, 30
Progress and Poverty (George), 89
Progressive education, 139-140
Progressive Movement, 134-135, 144-145
  see also Reform
Progresso Italo-Americano, II, 175, 178
Project Pole, 277
Promised Land, The (Antin), 108, 190
Prostitution, 79, 80
Provoost, Maria, 16
Public Law 89-236, 270
Puerto Rican Community Development Project, 263
Puerto Rican Family Institute, 263
Puerto Rican Forum, 263
Puerto Ricans, 9, 226, 229, 231, 244, 257-263, 268, 278, 279

Quakers, 46, 60
Queens College (Rutgers), 26

Race, 3-4
Racism, 209-211
Railroads
  role in emigration, 64-65

role of immigrants in construction of, 72-73
Rapp, George, 90-91
Rauschenbusch, Walter, 135
Ravage, Marcus, 107
Ravitch, Diane, 139-140
Raza, la, 4
Reclamation Act of 1902, 246
Red Scare, 215-217
Reed, David, 218
Reform, 5, 88-90, 139
Reform Judaism, 160
Refugees, 263-267
Regulators, 47, 49
Religion, 24, 44-45, 51, 105, 118, 156-161, 223
Revere, Paul, 37
Revolution of 1848, 60
Reynold, James B., 136
Richter, Mrs. Fernande, 150
Riis, Jacob, 114
Rise of David Levinsky, The (Cahan), 118-119
Rising, Johan, 30
Rising Tide of Color Against White World Supremacy, The (Stoddard), 210
Rölvaag, Ole Edvart, 70, 158-159, 192, 194-197
Roman Catholic Church, 3, 157, 160, 284
Roosevelt, Franklin D., 235-236, 241
Roosevelt, Theodore, 203
Rose, Ernestine, 92
Rosenfeld, Morris, 189-190
Ross, Edward Alsworth, 210
Rossi, Peter, 285
Royko, Mike, 112
Rush, Benjamin, 33, 53
Russkoye Slovo, 179

Sabbatarianism, 94
Sacco and Vanzetti, 217